D1555652

The Catholic Tradition

REV. CHARLES J. DOLLEN
DR. JAMES K. McGOWAN
DR. JAMES J. MEGIVERN
EDITORS

The Catholic Tradition

Spirituality

Volume 2

A Consortium Book

Library of Congress Card Catalog Number: 79-1977
ISBN: 0-8434-0737-9
ISBN: 0-8434-0725-5 series

The publisher gratefully acknowledges permission to quote from the following copyrighted sources. In cases where those properties contain scholarly apparatus such as footnotes, such footnotes have been omitted in the interest of the general reader.

AVE MARIA PRESS

Chapters excerpted from *Poustinia*, by Catherine de Hueck Doherty. Copyright © 1975, Ave Maria Press. Reprinted with permission of the publisher.

BRUCE PUBLISHING COMPANY

Selection from *The Whole Christ* by Émile Mersch, S.J., translated by John R. Kelly, copyright 1938.

COLLINS PUBLISHERS

Selections from *Autobiography of a Saint* by Thérèse of Lisieux, translated by Ronald Knox, The Harvill Press. Copyright © 1958 Translation: Executors of Ronald Knox. Reprinted by permission of Collins Publishers.

J. M. DENT & SONS LTD.

Selections from *Apologia Pro Vita Sua* by John Henry Cardinal Newman, 1864. From 1949 reprint.

FARRAR, STRAUS & GIROUX, INC.

"The Power and Meaning of Love" from *Disputed Questions* by Thomas Merton. Copyright © 1953, 1959, 1960 by The Abbey of Our Lady of Gethsemani. Reprinted with permission of Farrar, Straus & Giroux, Inc.

FIDES/CLARETIAN

Chapters 3 and 5 from *Seeds of the Desert* by René Voillaume, translated by Willard Hill, copyright © 1964. Reprinted by permission of the publisher.

Table of Contents

THE CATHOLIC TRADITION: Spirituality

Louis of Granada
1504-1588

Louis of Granada has a sense of the universe that seems strange and distant to contemporary men. For him, the universe is sacred. The human and the universe are woven into a unity. The universe naturally evoked wonder and admiration; it manifests and reflects God's glory and love; it supports the human and makes the human, as the child of God, possible. The step from reflection on the universe to prayer and adoration is a simple one for him. He invites the reader to take that step with him.

Popular preacher and writer, Louis of Granada lived in sixteenth century Spain. He was immersed in the excitement and vitality of his country's greatest century and, in the spiritual domain, made a significant contribution to that greatness. In an empire enjoying incredible wealth, Louis was born poor by circumstance and died poor by choice. When invitations to assume positions of power in the church hierarchy were extended to him, Louis preferred to decline. Given his vision of the universe, true wealth and power lay elsewhere.

As a youth he had the good fortune to receive an excellent education. In 1524 he entered the Order of Preachers and undertook studies in philosophy and theology. His unusual talents both for preaching and for administrative positions were quickly noticed. His preaching took him across most of Spain and eventually Portugal. The members of his preaching order in Portugal chose him to be their provincial. Aware of the importance of the written word for communicating ideas, he added a writing career to his preaching and administrative work. His books were well received. During the Inquisition some of them were suspect and even put on a list of forbidden books, but he was cleared of all suspicion during the Council of Trent.

The writings of Louis are a blend of the theological tradition of Thomas Aquinas, ideas arising from sixteenth century humanism, a deep knowledge and love of the peasant people of Spain and Portugal, and a life anchored in prayer. Because of his beautiful and simple style which leaves ample room for expressing emotion, he has been described as a theologian of the people.

Louis challenges each individual to work toward perfection by using the means best suited to his or her temperament, background, and vocation. Each person is free to choose the most suitable path; but choose, one must. He sees seven basic paths to perfection: prayer, a life of virtue, contempt of the world, contemplation of God in nature, the life of the cross, the commandments and the sacraments, the imitation of the saints. Actually the seven ways are interrelated; some mixture of the various ways is necessary. Louis accepted sin and weakness as an obvious fact. He was convinced that the human was called to a life of perfection in God through Christ and wanted to make the spiritual journey through life attractive to everyone. This is what got him into trouble during his lifetime. Theologians with elitist tendencies judged as heretical his efforts to make Christian perfection available to ordinary people.

The following selection is taken from Louis' Summa of the Christian Life on creation. Here we meet a man who sees beauty everywhere. Whoever does not see beauty, whoever is not filled with wonder and admiration simply does not understand nature. Louis reveals unusual sensitivity to the elements—air, wind, earth, rain, sea, sun. All are at the service of mankind, all must be read in relation to God. The tragedy of the greedy, the wealthy and the powerful is that they forget and become capable of destroying the harmony between God, man and universe. He who sees nature for what it truly is becomes the grateful being in harmony with God and universe.

2

SUMMA OF THE CHRISTIAN LIFE

CHAPTER XIV

CREATION OF THE WORLD

What has been said up to this point is based on that which Sacred Scripture tells us of the immensity and greatness of our Creator. We shall now continue the same subject by considering the works which He has made in the universe, because they also give clear testimony of the greatness of God.

Before we consider the visible works of God, we should point out one of the many differences between the Creator and His creatures. All created things have limits and boundaries to which their natures and powers extend. Consequently, they have a limited or finite being and limited powers, knowledge, and faculties which flow from that being. This limitation is according to the measure that the Creator willed to impart to His creatures, giving more to some and less to others.

But since God Himself was not created by any superior being, neither is there any being that can put limits or boundaries to His essence, power, knowledge, goodness, happiness, or any of His other perfections and attributes. And since there are no limits or restrictions of any kind in God, He is infinite in every respect. Therefore, His being is infinite as also are His beauty, His glory, His riches, His mercy, His justice, and all His attributes. He is on that account incomprehensible and ineffable and no creature that has been made or could be made will ever comprehend Him; God alone can perfectly know and comprehend Himself.

We have an appropriate example of this in the kings of this world. They distribute the duties and offices in their kingdom to various persons, as it pleases them, limiting the jurisdiction and power given to each one lest it be prejudicial to others. But the king who thus restricts this delegated power, possesses in himself the supreme and universal authority throughout his entire kingdom, so that he acknowledges no one superior to himself. Consequently, there is in the kingdom no jurisdiction or power, however great, that is not surpassed by that of the king. Such jurisdiction and power is called infinite or absolute, in the sense that it is not restricted to any limit or boundary within its own area of jurisdiction.

Comparing the relationship between the Creator and His creatures with that of a king and his subalternates, we can readily grasp the notion of God's infinity. True, the example fails in this respect, that the authority of the king is infinite only in a relative sense, while that of the Creator is absolute and infinite in everyone.

The same truth can be demonstrated in another way. According to philosophers and theologians, God is so great a being that it is not only impossible that there actually exist a being greater than He, but one could not even imagine a greater being. Since a being that possesses infinite perfections is much greater than one that possesses finite and limited perfections, if the perfections of God were in any way limited, we would be able to imagine other perfections greater than His. But this is impossible, for we have already stated that our concept of God is that of a being so great that we could not even imagine one that is greater.

Before we enter in this sanctuary wherein we are to consider such great things, let us take as our theme and starting point the words of the angel who represented the person of God. When asked his name by the father of Samson, he replied: "Why askest thou my name, which is wonderful?" This is a word well suited to the greatness of God and all His works, for there is nothing however small which, if well considered, will not cause hearts to marvel at the Creator, saying to us in His name: "Why askest thou my name, which is wonderful?"

That cannot be considered true eloquence, says Cicero, which does not arouse wonder and admiration in the listeners. But if merely human genius, aided by study and diligence, is able to construct so perfect and polished an oration that it causes admiration in all who hear it, how should one react to the works fashioned by infinite Wisdom, in comparison with which the wisdom of the cherubim is pure ignorance? Surely, if one is not filled with admiration and wonder in the contemplation of the works of the Creator, it is because one does not understand them, for their majesty and brilliance are sufficient to dazzle the human mind.

Before commencing our consideration of the works of creation, we must observe that although it is true, as St. Augustine says and as we read in Ecclesiasticus, that God created the entire universe and all things in it simultaneously, nevertheless Moses prudently divides the works of creation into six days. God created all things out of love of Himself, that is to say, as a manifestation of the greatness of His perfections, but our intellects cannot easily encompass so immense a world and all the things that are in it. Rather, we would be overwhelmed if we tried to consider all these marvelous things at the same time. For that reason, the inspired writer divided this work into many parts. Even then, each work of the six days is of itself so great and significant that it must again be divided into many parts in order to be considered perfectly and adequately.

We must also note that creation in its proper sense does not mean to make one thing from another (this is called generation), but to make something from nothing. Such a power is so proper to God that it cannot be communicated to any creature, however perfect. Observing the changes that are effected in natural things, we see that the greater the distance from one extreme to the other, the greater the power required to cause such a change. But the distance between non-being and being is infinite; consequently, an infinite power is required for the work of creation. This power is found in God alone, who "calleth those things that are not, as those that are."

We shall first treat of the world and its principal parts, namely, the heavens and the elements. Then we shall treat in particular of all living bodies: plants, animals, and man, who was created on the sixth and last day. And since the Christian reader will derive greater profit from this doctrine, if he knows the full purpose to which it is directed, let him know that my intention is not only to declare that there is a God who is Creator and Lord of all things, but much more to demonstrate the divine providence that shines forth through all creatures, as well as the other perfections that accompany it, especially the divine goodness, wisdom, and omnipotence, for these are, as Isaias says, the three fingers on which God has poised the bulk of the earth.

Of the three last-named perfections, which in God are all one, divine goodness desires to do well to His creatures, divine wisdom plans and ordains how this is to be done, and divine omnipotence executes and effects what His goodness desires and His wisdom ordains. These three perfections are, so to speak, the component parts of divine providence, by which God, with a pious and fatherly concern, furnishes a wide variety of things that are necessary for His creatures. It is my intention to demonstrate how these four divine perfections and countless others shine forth in all the things of this world, the great as well as the small.

The fruitfulness and value of such a consideration can be understood from the words of David: "Blessed are they that search His testimonies; that seek Him with their whole heart." And they will be no less blessed who search God's works; not only those of grace, but also those of nature, because they all spring from the same source. Uncreated Wisdom promises: "They that explain Me shall have life everlasting." That is what we are seeking to do here: to reveal the plan of divine Wisdom as it is manifested in all created things.

A great aid in acquiring oratorical skill is to observe the plan and technique that a great orator employs in his speeches. St. Augustine considered it extremely helpful that he himself had done so in regard to certain passages in St. Paul. How much better a study it is to observe the admirable plan of divine wisdom in the structure and government of the created universe. And if it is written of the Queen of Saba that "she had no longer any spirit in her" when she saw all the wisdom of Solomon and the house that he had built, how much more will the devout soul be humbled when, gazing upon the works of incomprehensible wisdom, he seeks to comprehend the art and prudence with which they have been made?

CHAPTER XV

THE SPLENDOR OF THE FIRMAMENT

The purpose of the following considerations is to see how the divine perfections are reflected in the created works of God, so that our hearts may be moved to love the goodness of God and our minds may be aroused to a holy fear and reverence for such great majesty. May we likewise be inspired with hope in His paternal care and providence and with greater admiration for the mighty power and wisdom that shine forth through the works of His hands.

We accept as a fundamental proposition that when, through His infinite goodness, the most gracious and sovereign Lord determined to create man and place him in this world, so that by knowing and loving and obeying his Creator he might merit the happiness of the world to come, He likewise determined to provide man with all the things necessary for his sustenance and preservation. Consequently, God created the visible world and all things in it for the use and necessities of human life.

In any workshop two things are required: the material from which things are made and the worker who makes the things. In the great workshop of the universe these two requirements have been amply provided for by the Creator. The material from which new things are made is the variety of elements, and the agents that generate new things from the elements are the heavenly bodies, such as the planets and stars. Granted that God is the First Cause and moves every other cause, these heavenly bodies are among the principal instruments that God uses for the government of the world. So dependent is the world on these planets that the ancient philosophers used to teach that if their movement were to stop, all other motion would cease.

Since the heavenly bodies are among the principal agents of the First Mover, God has ennobled them and made them excel over all other bodies. They are seemingly incorruptible, so that even after the thousands of years since they were created, they appear to continue in the same entirety and beauty that they possessed from the beginning. Time, the destroyer of all things, seems not to have impaired any of them.

God also endowed them with brilliant light, not only for the ornament of the universe, but also for the benefit of human life, as the Psalmist says: "Praise ye the Lord of lords ... who made the great light, ... the sun to rule the day ... the moon and the stars to rule the night." He gave them such constancy in their movements that they seem never to have varied from the orderly motion that He placed in them from the beginning. As a result, all those whose function it is to rule and govern others, either in the Church or in nations, can learn from the planets how well regulated and constant they must be in their lives so that there will be no disorder in the lives of those under their care. But if the light that is supposed to illumine the darkness of others is obscured, then how great will be the darkness! And if one blind man leads another, what is to be expected but that both shall fall?

The magnificence of the heavenly bodies is such that it causes admiration in anyone who considers it. Indeed, it would seem incredible, were it not that we know that nothing is impossible to Him who created them. And the beauty of the firmament, who can describe it? How pleasant it is, in the serenity of a midsummer's night, to see the full moon in all its brightness, surpassing in clarity the light of all the stars! And when there is no moon, what is more enchanting and more indicative of the omnipotence and beauty of God than the vast heavens sprinkled with a variety of stars, so numerous that no one can count them except Him who made them? But the custom of seeing these things so often robs us of admiration for their beauty and of the incentive to praise the divine Artist who has thus beautified the mighty vault of the heavens.

If a child were born in a prison and lived there until he reached the age of manhood, without ever seeing anything outside the prison walls; if, in addition, he had become a man of intelligence and learning, then the first time he left the prison and saw the starry sky on a tranquil night, certainly he could not help but be astonished at such great beauty. Nor could he help but exclaim: "Who could have adorned such great heavens with so many precious jewels and with diamonds so brilliant? Who could have created such a great number of lamps to give light to the world? Who could have filled the meadow of the skies with such a variety of flowers? Who, but some most beautiful and omnipotent Creator?

A pagan philosopher once said: "To look at the heavens is to become a philosopher." In other words, when one contemplates the great variety and beauty of the firmament, he recognizes the wisdom and power of its Author. So the Psalmist exclaims: "O Lord our Lord, how admirable is Thy name in the whole earth! For Thy magnificence is elevated above the heavens. . . . For I will behold Thy heavens, the works of Thy fingers; the moon and the stars which Thou hast founded."

If the beauty of the planets is admirable, no less remarkable is the influence they exert on the things of the earth. This is especially true of the sun. For example, when it is farthest removed from the earth, as during the autumn and winter, the trees and bushes lose their foliage and become sterile and almost dead. Then in the spring, when it is closer to the earth, the fields are again dressed in green, the trees are covered with buds and leaves, and the vines and bushes bring forth new shoots, as if impatient to manifest the beauty that they contain hidden within themselves. So many marvelous qualities are to be found in the sun that when the ancient philosopher Anaxagoras was asked why he was born, he answered that it was to see the sun.

But although the sun is so remarkable a planet, few persons marvel at the powers and virtues which the Creator has given it, because, as Seneca says, the custom of seeing things that always operate in the same manner makes them cease to appear admirable, however great they may be. No one marvels at things as long as they follow their regular course, but when they depart from it, all are amazed and asked what the change could signify. Men marvel at new things rather than at great things. However, St. Augustine says that wise men marvel more at great things than at new and unusual things, because they have eyes to see the dignity and excellence of the former and to evaluate them properly.

One of the greatest and most universal effects of the sun is that it gives light and brilliance to all the other planets and stars that are scattered throughout the firmament. And since these lesser planets exert their influence on the world by means of the light that they receive from the sun, it follows that, after God, the sun is the first cause of all generation, corruption, change, and alteration which take place in the world. The sun also draws the vapors of the oceans on high and when they reach the regions where the air is very cool, they condense and are turned into rain which irrigates the land, thus producing the fruits and grains by which men and animals are nourished. In this sense we can say that the sun gives us bread, wine, meat, fruits, and almost everything else that is necessary for life.

It is also the sun that causes the four seasons of the year, as its distance from the earth is lessened and increased. Divine providence regulates these seasons both for the health of our bodies and for the production of the fruits of the earth by which we are sustained, and so equally is the time divided among them that none of them prevails over the other. Just as masters who have servants and families are accustomed to allot a certain sum each year for their maintenance, so also the Lord, whose family is the entire world, provides for the maintenance of each of the members of His great house and family by means of the four seasons. Thus the divine Ruler sustains and governs this world, increasing His family each year and providing food and nourishment for it. Who, then, seeing the order of divine providence, would not exclaim with the Psalmist: "How great are Thy works, O Lord; Thou hast made all things in wisdom; the earth is filled with Thy riches."

By its presence or absence the sun also divides time into day and night, to the happiness and welfare of the earth's inhabitants. The day is of greater benefit for the duties and tasks of human life, while the night is more beneficial to the plants of the earth, for after the long warm days, plants are refreshed by the coolness and dew of the night hours. At night also men and animals, fatigued with the labors of the day, take their rest. The night is likewise the time most suitable for man to refresh his soul with spiritual things, for then he is freed from the cares and business of the day. Then he can meditate in silence on the goodness of God, singing His praises, as David says: "In the daytime the Lord hath commanded His mercy and a canticle to Him in the night. With me is prayer to the God of my life. I will say to God: Thou art my support." To this practice of prayer David especially invites those who live in the house of the Lord, all ye servants of the Lord who stand in the house of the Lord, in the courts of the house of our God. In the night lift up your hands to the holy places, and bless ye the Lord." Jeremias calls men to the same duty with these words: "Rise up at midnight, and pour forth your heart as water before God," and the prophet Isaias lifted up his soul to God and exclaimed: "My soul hath desired Thee in the night; yea, and with my spirit within me, in the morning early I will watch to Thee."

Therefore, in the calm, silent night, arouse your heart to humble devotion, fixing your eyes on the beauty of the moon or the splendor of the stars which proclaim the beauty and glory of their Creator. Indeed, the brightness of the stars presages the beauty of the glorified bodies which will be ours on the day of resurrection. "There are bodies celestial, and bodies terrestrial, but one is the glory of the celestial and another of the terrestrial. One is the glory of the sun, another the glory of the moon, and another the glory of the stars. For star differeth from star in glory. So also is the resurrection of the dead. It is sown in corruption, it shall rise in incorruption. It is sown in dishonor, it shall rise in glory. It is sown in weakness, it shall rise in power."

In addition to all these things, the sun enlightens everything that God has created in the heavens and on the earth, so that nothing is hidden from it. And as the sun is the most visible of all corporeal things and the one least able to be gazed upon because of its great brilliance and the weakness of our vision, so also God is the most intelligible of all beings and yet He is the one least comprehended because of the loftiness of His essence and the lowliness of our understanding. Likewise, of all bodily creatures, the sun is the most communicative of light and heat, so that if one closes the door to keep out the sun, it enters through the chinks of the door. What better symbol of the infinite goodness of God, who liberally communicates His riches to all creatures, making them, as St. Dionysius says, as much like unto Himself as their natures permit and even seeking those who flee from Him!

From the resplendent brilliance of the sun the stars receive their brightness and efficacy, just as from the plenitude and abundance of the grace of Christ, the Savior, all just souls receive light and power to perform good works. Moreover, as the presence of the sun is the cause of light and its absence results in darkness, so also the presence of Christ in souls enlightens and teaches them, shows them the way to heaven, and points out the obstacles that must be avoided. But when He is absent from souls, they remain in darkness and obscurity; as a result, they stumble and fall into a thousand occasions of sin, without knowing what they do or realizing what a great danger it is to their salvation when they live thus.

In so many ways does the sun manifest the perfections of God. What sight more delightful and beautiful could be offered to our eyes than that of the sun in its morning rising? With the clarity of its splendor it dispels the darkness and sheds it light on all things, gladdening the heavens, the earth, and the sea. We can compare its beauty to that of a bridegroom and its strength to that of a giant.

But now let us leave the consideration of the sun to speak briefly of its vicar, the moon. To this planet the Creator has committed the task of providing light in the absence of the sun, otherwise the world would be left in total darkness. In addition to many other characteristics, the moon has great power over the waters of the ocean. As the magnet draws iron filings to itself, so the Creator gave to the moon the power of attracting to itself the waters of the ocean, thus causing the ebb and flow of the tides. The moon holds the reins, so to speak, whereby it controls the ocean.

In addition to its power over the ocean, the moon also influences the bodies of men and animals. Thus, we notice the alterations that the moon causes in the human body, especially in the sick, according as the moon is full or in crescent. What we should especially notice is the remarkable power that the Creator has given to this planet, in spite of the fact that it is so distant from the earth and has no light of itself, but receives it from the sun.

Lastly, consider the stars. The number and power and effects of the stars, who can describe them except the Lord, of whom David said that He alone can number the stars and call each one by name? Thus does the Psalmist reveal the complete dependence of the stars on their Creator, who caused the things which are not as if they were, giving existence to those things which have it not.

Of this dependence and obedience the prophet Baruch says: "And the stars have given light in their watches, and rejoiced; they were called, and they said: Here we are. And with cheerfulness they have shined forth to Him that made them." In saying that God calls each one by name, the prophet means that He alone knows the properties and nature of the stars and that He has given them their names accordingly. No human tongue can speak of these things, for they are reserved to divine wisdom. Among the many uses and benefits of the stars, they serve as guides for those who traverse the seas. Since there are no markings, in the waters by which the sailor can direct his navigation, he raises his eyes to the heavens and finds his guidance in the stars, especially in the north star, which never changes but serves as a stable and certain guide of the seaways.

CHAPTER XVI

BENEFITS OF AIR AND RAIN

In treating of each of the elements, we shall begin with a consideration of the air, the benefits of which are numerous. First of all, it is because of the air that men and animals are able to breathe. Moreover, the coolness of the air refreshes them and tempers the heat of their bodies. It is also the medium through which the light of the sun reaches them, at the same time that it diffuses the light rays so that the heat of the sun is beneficial rather than harmful.

The air also performs an important function in the production of rain. The heat of the sun causes vapors to rise from the waters of the earth and when these vapors reach the upper regions where the air is cold, they condense into drops of water and fall from the skies as rain. We witness a similar phenomenon in distilleries or perfumeries, where the intense heat of the fire drives the moisture from the herbs or flowers and the vapor ascends to a cooler area, condenses into liquid, and then drips into the vessel prepared for it. This is another example of the manner in which art imitates nature.

It is likewise a cause of admiration to see how the Creator has ordained that the rains should fall from above. If all the wise men of the world were to discuss in what way the earth should be irrigated, they could not discover any method more convenient and efficacious than this one. The water falls from the heavens as if it were run through the small holes of a sieve, and thus it is equally distributed in all parts of the ground. It penetrates into the earth itself to give nourishment to plants at their roots, while externally it refreshes the leaves and fruits of the trees.

This is one of God's marvels to which Job refers when he says: "He bindeth up the waters in His clouds, so that they break not out and fall down together." So also Moses writes in praise of the Promised Land: "For the land which thou goest to possess, is not like the land of Egypt, from whence thou camest out, where, when the seed is sown, waters are brought in to water it, after the manner of gardens. But it is a land of hills and plains, expecting rain from heaven. And the Lord thy God dost always visit it, and His eyes are on it from the beginning of the year unto the end thereof. If then you obey my commandments, which I command you this day, that you love the Lord your God, and serve Him with all your heart, and with all your soul, He will give to your land the early rain and the latter rain, that you may gather in your corn, and your wine, and your oil, and your day out of the fields to feed your cattle, and that you may eat and be filled." The Psalmist likewise sings the praise of this blessing when he says: "Who covereth the heaven with clouds, and prepareth rain for the earth." Again, Job says that God not only irrigates the seeded and tilled lands but even the deserted places and the uncharted paths, so that they produce green and fresh foliage.

But who could ever explain and sufficiently extol the many blessings that come to us because of rain? Whoever considers it attentively will see that everything necessary for human life is somehow provided by the Creator through this medium. It is because of the rain that we have bread, wine, oil, fruits, vegetables, medicinal herbs, and pasture for the animals that provide our meat as well as the wool and leather for our clothing and shoes. The Psalmist was aware of this when he said that God "maketh grass to grow on the mountains, and herbs for the service of men." He also states that man gives food to animals because the animals, in turn, perform many services for man. So numerous are the benefits that we receive from the rain that one of the ancient Greek philosophers, Thales by name, maintained that water is the material from which all things are made.

So great and universal are the blessings of rain that the Creator Himself holds the keys to it and reserves to Himself its distribution. He uses it to give sustenance to His faithful servants and chastisement to the rebellious, by depriving them of this benefit. Thus it is written in the book of Job that God so judges and punishes His people and in the Book of Leviticus we read how God will provide for His faithful ones: "If you walk in My precepts, and keep My commandments, and do them, I will give you rain in due seasons. And the ground shall bring forth its increase, and the trees shall be filled with fruit." But for those who despise His laws and condemn His judgments, God promises that He will visit them with poverty and a burning heat that will destroy their lives. They shall sow their seed in vain; the ground will not bring forth its increase nor the trees yield their fruit.

Not only sins but also ingratitude for such great blessings can be the cause of losing them, as we learn through the words of Jeremias: "They have not said in their heart: Let us fear the Lord our God, who giveth us the early and the latter rain in due season; who preserveth for us the fullness of the yearly harvest." Surely it is a great cause of sorrow that there are so few who acknowledge this great blessing from the Creator and who give thanks to Him and serve Him because of it, especially since He gives us so many other things through the bountiful rain that we would not subsist without it. We should think of these things when we see the rain falling from the heavens and understand that the Lord sends us these things. Otherwise we imitate the irrational animals, who receive pasture and sustenance from God but neither acknowledge the Giver nor give thanks to Him, for they lack reason.

The wind is another blessing from divine providence and the Psalmist acknowledged it as such when he stated: "He bringeth forth winds out of His stores." First of all, the winds carry the clouds and the waters that are in them wherever the Creator

15

wishes those rains to be sent. So we see that it rains in Spain when the wind is from the southwest, coming in from the sea and bringing the rain clouds from that direction. On the other hand, in Africa the rains come with the north wind, which likewise passes over the sea and brings that continent the rain-filled clouds which are the waterbuckets of God.

And what would happen to navigation and ocean commerce between islands and nations if there were no winds and the air were always calm? The winds enable the navigators to travel to the very ends of the earth, so that they can collect the products that are plentiful in one place but scarce in another and bring back the things that others have in abundance but which we lack. Thus all things are made common and all nations receive a sufficiency. The whole world becomes a common market place. What is more, these same winds have carried the missionaries to all parts of the world and the gospel message that they brought is the best kind of merchandise that could be transported from one place to another.

The winds also serve another purpose, as Seneca points out, for they purify the air and remove from it any corruption or harmful substance with which it may be contaminated. We need but recall the great pestilence in the city of Lisbon in 1570, which was ended when an unusually cold and strong wind carried away the germ-laden air and caused the sea water to overflow into the wells and fountains along the coastline.

The winds also help the farmer to winnow the corn and to remove dust and straw from the grain. And when he is oppressed by the withering heat of summer, a fresh breeze lessens the force of the heat and refreshes him. From these examples Christian souls can learn how to refer all things to God and how to be edified by God's works. Let them also consider how great must be the torments of the eternal flames where the damned are burning in the never-ending fire and can never hope for any kind of alleviation or refreshment.

CHAPTER XVII

THE GRANDEUR OF THE SEA

We now come to a consideration of the second element, water, which at the beginning of creation covered the entire earth, as the air covered all the water. But since no one could have inhabited the earth under such conditions, the Creator, who made the earth for the service of man and made man for Himself, commanded that the waters be gathered together to form seas and oceans and thus uncover the earth as our dwelling place.

There are many aspects of the oceans that are worthy of consideration, such as their grandeur, fruitfulness, and depths, their shores and ports, their risings and fallings, and, finally, the great benefits that they bring us. All these qualities preach a silent sermon of praise to Him who created them. So the Psalmist praised God for the grandeur of the oceans when he said: "How great are Thy works, O Lord! Thou hast made all things in wisdom; the earth is filled with Thy riches. So is this great sea, which stretcheth wide its arms."

The Creator ordained these things so that all nations might enjoy the benefits of the various bodies of water which serve to bring nations closer together by means of navigation and serve also as a source of nourishment for men by supplying a great variety of fish and other sea food. Consequently, the Creator willed that the ocean should have many bays and gulfs so that the fish would seek shelter there and thus be more easily caught. Moreover, in all the seas and oceans there are ports and harbors where ships can rest secure from tempests and storms and the violence of the winds.

The omnipotence and providence of the Creator are likewise manifested in the multitude of islands that are distributed throughout the oceans and seas. St. Ambrose compares them to little jewels that adorn the great bodies of water. God in His providence has fashioned them as a stopping-place where sailors can renew their strength, find refreshment, and take refuge in time of storm. The omnipotence of God shines forth in the conservation of these little islands, especially when the towering waves would almost seem to cover them over or the angry seas would threaten to wash them away. It is a marvel of which God spoke through the mouth of Job: "Who shut up the sea with doors, when it broke forth as issuing out of the womb; when I made a cloud the garment thereof, and wrapped it in a mist as in swaddling bands? I set My bounds around it, and made it bars and doors; and I said: Hitherto thou shalt come, and shalt go no further, and here thou shalt break thy swelling waves."

All the elements have a tendency to seek their natural positions or places and the natural place for water, as we have seen, is to cover the entire earth. But God, by His word alone, has removed it from its natural place and has gathered it together into oceans and seas. Thus it has remained for many thousands of years and the waters have not surpassed the limits which He assigned to them. God uses this obedience of insensate creation as an argument to confound the disobedience and irreverence of men. So He says through Jeremias: "Will not you then fear Me . . . and will you not repent at My presence? I have set the sand a bound for the sea, an everlasting ordinance, which it shall not pass over; and the waves thereof shall toss themselves, and shall not prevail; they shall swell, and shall not pass over it."

Who would not be moved to adore the omnipotence and providence of the Creator who is able to establish and maintain what He wishes? He has placed a limitation and restraint on the waters of the world so that they will not cover the entire earth. Although the waves of the ocean beat furiously against the sand and shore, they never dare to pass beyond the assigned limits. Beating against the shores and boundaries of the earth, the waters of the ocean see the law of the Creator written there and they turn back, much like a runaway horse feels the pull of the reins and bridle and stops and turns around, although he does not want to do so.

The sea both divides the lands and nations and promotes friendship and concord among those same nations. The Creator desires that nations should be friendly with each other. Consequently, He did not give each nation all that is necessary for life, because the dependence of one nation on another prompts them to be friendly to each other. But the highways and roads that cross the continents are often difficult to travel and it is

18

impossible to transport every kind of merchandise over the roads of the earth. Therefore, the Creator provided this new path on which ships both great and small could navigate and one ship can carry a cargo that would require the use of many beasts of burden. Thus the ocean is like a great fair or market place where all the nations of the world exchange goods and each receives the things necessary to itself.

We should note also that the ocean serves as a symbol of the meekness of God as well as His anger and indignation. What is more meek and tranquil than the ocean when it is calm and no winds blow, or when a soft and gentle breeze sends the rippling waves to the shore, where with regular succession they break silently and return to the ocean? This is a symbol of the meekness and gentleness of God toward the good and the just. But when the sea is buffetted by violent winds and lifts its terrifying waves high into the sky, revealing the dark chasms of depth; when it lashes with fierce strength against the sides of ships, raising them on high and suddenly dropping them with a jolt, so that the men who are at the mercy of the sea are placed in mortal fear and trembling for their lives, we have a symbol of the divine wrath and of the magnitude of divine power that is able to stir up such tempests and appease them when He wills.

The Psalmist speaks to us of this when he says: "O Lord God of hosts, who is like to Thee? Thou art mighty, O Lord, and Thy truth is round about Thee. Thou rulest the power of the sea, and appeasest the motion of the waves thereof. . . . Thine are the heavens, and thine is the earth; the world and the fullness thereof Thou hast founded; the north and the sea Thou has created."

There is yet another benefit of the ocean which is so great that the pen hesitates to treat of it. For what words could describe the wide variety of fish that are found in the sea? What great wisdom has fashioned them, not only in such a multitude of species, but in so many different shapes and sizes? Some are small and others are of incredible size, and between the two extremes is infinite variety. The same God created the whale and the frog but He did not labor more in the making of one or the other.

With a pair of scissors a child can cut many different figures or designs out of cloth or paper because the cloth or paper are perfectly submissive to the designs and wishes of the child. Yet, the child does no more than fashion a figure or shape, without adding anything further to the cloth or paper. But the Creator not only gives form and figure to the things He fashions, He gives them life and sense and movement. He gives them the power to seek nourishment, defensive measures for their preservation, and a fruitful means for the conservation of the species.

Who can count the eggs of the shad or the codfish or any other fish? Yet each egg is capable of producing another fish as large as the one from which the egg originally came. Like a tender mother, the ocean receives these eggs and protects and nurtures them until they evolve into fish. And since divine providence has created fish for the sustenance of men, but the fisherman cannot see the fish in the waters as the hunter sees the game on the land or in the air, God disposed that the number of fish should be so great that some could usually be caught wherever the net would be let down. The number and variety of animals and birds is almost countless, but greater still is the number of fish in the sea.

How pleasing are the works of the Lord, and all are made with consummate wisdom. Consider, finally, the sweetness and taste of the various kinds of fish and sea foods. St. Ambrose exclaims that these delicacies were created before man himself and that man's temptation already existed before man was created. But the Creator did not intend these things as temptations for man; they were created for his sustenance. God treats us as His beloved children and He intends the tastiness of these foods to lead us to love and praise the Lord who provided them. But many men are so slothful and self-centered that although all the creatures of the world invite us to praise the Giver of all gifts, these men are so occupied with pampering their appetites that it never occurs to them to give thanks to God or to acknowledge that these things have been given to us without any merits on our part.

CHAPTER XVIII

THE BEAUTY AND FERTILITY OF THE EARTH

We now come to the consideration of the earth, our common mother, from which man's body originally came and by which we are nourished. Of all the elements, the earth is the lowest and least active, yet it is more serviceable and profitable to us than any other. So the Psalmist states: "The heaven of heaven is the Lord's, but the earth He has given to the children of men." In obedience to the command of God, the earth receives us as a benign mother when we are born, sustains us after we are born, and at the end of our life again receives us into her lap and faithfully guards our bodies until the day of resurrection.

The earth is also more gentle and favorable to us than the other elements. The oceans and rivers sometimes cause tidal waves and floods that do considerable damage to men and their property. The air is sometimes whipped into tornadoes, hurricanes, or windstorms that damage the crops and destroy the work of the poor laborers. But the earth is the faithful servant of man. What fruits it produces! What beautiful colors it presents! And who could describe the riches of the earth, especially when we consider the variety of metals that were taken from it for five thousand years before the coming of Christ and have been mined since that time and will be extracted until the end of time. As the poet Ovid says, men will ultimately arrived at the very gates of hell in their pursuit of the gold and silver and precious stones that are hidden in the bowels of the earth.

Still more noteworthy are the fountains and rivers that irrigate and refresh the earth. As the Creator has placed veins and arteries throughout the human body to sustain and refresh it, so also He has provided a network of rivers to refresh and irrigate the great body of the earth. But in many parts of the earth there is a deficiency of springs and rivers, and for that reason divine providence has ordained that the whole earth should be saturated wtih water, so that by digging wells men can supply for the lack of springs or rivers.

Again, who will not be filled with wonder when considering the origin and source from which these rivers and springs proceed? In many lands far removed from the sea we discover wide ribbons of water cutting across the plains or gushing springs racing down the mountain sides. What is the source of this water? How is it that the water flows at all times of the year, both in winter and summer, and never runs dry even after thousands of years? The Psalmists praises God because He brings forth winds out of His stores, but how much more He should be praised for having deposited in the earth such great supplies of water.

This should prompt us to give glory to God for so great a benefit and to marvel at His providence and power. One would have to be very stupid indeed not to see this. A story is told about an uneducated negro who was crossing the river between Córdoba and Castro del Rio. After gazing at the rushing water, he turned to his master and said: "Flowing, flowing, and never filled up; flowing, flowing, and never ending; a great thing is God." This illiterate negro confounds us and reminds us to praise God for this blessing. Even more pointedly did the angel of the Apocalypse invite men to praise God when he flew down from heaven, crying out to the people of the earth: "Fear the Lord, and give Him honor, because the hour of His judgment is come, and adore ye Him, that made heaven and earth, the sea, and the fountains of waters."

Since we are treating of the earth, it is fitting that we should say something of its fertility and the fruits it produces. This brings us to a consideration of living things, for the heavens, the stars, and the other elements which we have previously discussed do not have life. Since things that possess life are more perfect than those which do not, they are a greater manifestation of the wisdom and providence of the Creator, and the more perfect the life, the more clearly do they reflect their Maker. God, as they say, is not penny-wise and pound-foolish. The more perfect a thing is, the greater is His care and providence over it and the more clearly does He manifest His wisdom through it.

To God alone we owe the great blessings of the fruits of the earth. By His word alone He created the plants and trees of the earth, as we read: "Let the earth bring forth the green herb, and such as may seed, and the fruit tree yielding fruit after its kind, which may have seed in itself upon the earth." Once spoken, the command was effected and the earth was clothed in verdure and adorned with many flowers and plants and trees.

Who can describe the beauty of the fields? What can our words convey of such splendor? But we have the testimony of Scripture, where the holy patriarch compares the blessing and grace of the saints with the sweet aroma of a fertile field: "Behold the smell of my son is as the smell of a plentiful field, which the Lord hath blessed."

Who can portray the beauty of the purple violets, the white lilies, the blood-red rose? What artist could reproduce on his canvas a summer's meadow with its flowers of various hues, some yellow, some red, and others a mixture of many colors? Indeed, one cannot say what pleases him most, the color of the flower, the delicacy of its shape, or the sweet odor that comes from it. The eyes feast on the beautiful spectacle while the perfume of the flowers delights the sense of smell. Such is the grace and beauty which the Creator applies to Himself when He says: "The beauty of the fields is in Me."

Gaze upon the lily and note its dazzling whiteness. See how the slender stem rises gracefully and terminates in a chalice of lovely petals that protect and enclose grains of gold so that no harm may come to them. What human artist could ever make anything like it? The Savior Himself praised the lilies of the field when He said that not even Solomon in all his glory was dressed as richly as one of these flowers.

Even more amazing is the fact that the seeds scattered on the earth do not bring forth fruit unless they first die. St. Ambrose waxed eloquent on this point when he described the way in which a grain of wheat grows, using this as an example of how one can seek and find God in all things. He describes how the earth receives the grain of wheat and, like a mother, gathers the seed to her womb. Gradually the seed is changed into a sprout and ultimately becomes full-grown. When it reaches maturity, it produces a sheath or head that contains little pods wherein new seeds are formed. Thus, the cold cannot damage the seeds nor can the sun burn them with its intense heat; the wind will not blow them away nor will water damage them. The sheath also protects the grains of wheat from the birds, not only by reason of the pods that contain the seeds, but also by means of little pointed whiskers or strands that protrude from the sheath. And because the slender stem could not of itself bear the weight of the sheath of wheat, it is strengthened by a covering of leaves with which it is adorned and by the knots or knuckles that are distributed at intervals along the stem. This is not true of oats, however, for this grain does not need such protection. We see from this that the divine Creator does not fail us in those things that are necessary but neither does He make things that are useless.

The earth also produces many kinds of vegetables for our sustenance. Some are kept dry and can be used at any time during the entire year; others we eat as soon as they are ripe. Some grow under the ground and others above it, and of those that grow above the ground, some reproduce seeds within themselves, to be used for future planting. We read that the children of Israel yearned for such vegetables while crossing the desert. Here again we have evidence of divine providence, which not only provides fresh fruit in the summertime for the refreshment of the body, but also made vegetables that are to be eaten in due season. Not content with providing us with the flesh of so many animals, fish, and birds, and with a variety of fruits and abundant grains, He also gave us many kinds of vegetables so that no type of nourishment would be lacking to us. But how badly man uses these gifts! Even while he enjoys them, he does not think to raise his eyes to see the hand from which these gifts and benefits flow, not only to the good, but even to sinners.

From what has been said, it will be understood that the naked pagans of Africa are not the only barbarians, but there are many civilized barbarians dressed in the costliest garments. If a traveler were to stop at the home of a wealthy citizen and if the rich man, without any obligation, were to receive the stranger as a guest and treat him with every possible kindness; if he were to seat his guest at a table laden with the choicest foods that he had in the house; if, after eating, the traveler should depart without bidding his host farewell or thanking him for his hospitality and generosity, what would we think of such a person? We would say that he was more of a barbarian than the most inhuman savage.

What, then, is the status of so many wealthy and powerful men who sit every day at a table laden with the countless gifts that God has provided, not for Himself nor for the angels, but for the sustenance and well-being of man, and yet they neither thank Him who, without any obligation on His part, has so generously provided for man, nor do they even advert to the liberality of God? Every day they see the proof of God's blessings but they never give a thought to His generous and magnificent providence. Who will deny that men such as these, who live in complete forgetfulness of God, are worse than barbarians? They are like the rich man in the Gospel who dined every day in great splendor, but gave not a thought to God or to the poor beggar who sat at his gate.

The provision and abundance of the things on this earth are a clear manifestation of the providence of God, who is a Father to His family. But what shall we say of the variety of beautiful flowers, which do not serve for man's sustenance but for his delight? What other reason is there for the carnations, marigolds, lilies, irises, violets, and numerous other flowers that fill the gardens and cover the hills and fields and meadows? Consider their various colors, the beauty and artistry with which they are fashioned, the order and harmony of the leaves with which they are embellished, and the delightful scents which many of them emit. Of what service are all these things, except to give man something on which he can feast his eyes? Even more, they give joy to the soul when, in contemplating the flowers, a man can recognize the beauty of God and the great care that He has shown for us in showering us with gifts.

God is not content merely with providing us with the necessities of life; He has created things for our recreation and delight. Not only did He desire that we should gaze upon the splendor of the stars on a serene night, but He desired also that we should enjoy the sight of the multicolored flowers against the fertile valleys and green plains, like another heaven splashed with flowery stars. Such beauty serves a double purpose: on the one hand, it delights us with its loveliness and splendor; on the other hand, it arouses us to the praise of the Creator who made all these things, not for Himself or for the angels or for brute animals, but for the honest pleasure of men.

Let us take any one flower from among the great variety and ask: Since God does nothing without a purpose, why did He create this most beautiful and sweet-smelling flower? It is not, surely, for the sustenance of man nor for medicinal use or any other utility. Then, what other purpose can this flower have but to delight our vision with its beauty and our sense of smell with its sweet aroma? Consider also how many different kinds of flowers God created for the same purpose and how many other things He has made for the delight of the other senses. Consider the brilliance of jewels and precious stones which dazzle the eye, the music of the birds which pleases the ear, the various perfumes and herbs which captivate our sense of smell, and the infinity of savors which satisfy our sense of taste.

All these things declare to us the sweetness and benignity of the sovereign Lord who had such a regard for men that He not only created a variety of foods and other things necessary for man's sustenance, but He took special care to create many different things for man's honest recreation. So liberally did God provide for man that none of the bodily senses lacks its proper object in which it can find delight. What greater proof of our Father's love for us than the gratuitous blessings He has bestowed on us?

Not content with this, God also created a variety of trees, such as the laurel, the myrtle, the cypress, the cedars, the poplar, and the ivy which adorns the walls of gardens and serves them as cover of protection. Some trees bear fruit and others are sterile; some give nourishment to men, others to beasts; some never lose their leaves, others change each year; some serve only for shade and adornment; others serve various purposes. Among the fruit-bearing trees, some give fruit for consumption in the summer; others give fruit that can be kept for the wintertime. Here again we see a manifestation of God's liberality and providence in creating trees of various kinds so that there would be both a sufficiency and a variety of fruits.

Consider the variety of plums and apples and grapes. Not only that, but consider how even on the one tree, the fruit does not ripen all at once, but gradually. Thus, we see that on the fig tree some fruit ripens while the rest is yet green and in this way the one tree provides a supply of fruit over a longer period. But

26

the wisdom of divine providence is still more evident in the summer fruits. In the heat and dryness of the summer, men naturally seek the refreshment of cool and juicy fruits which the Creator has provided at that season. Nor does the fact that many men get sick on fruit militate against God's providence, for this is not the fault of the fruit but of the intemperate man who uses God's gifts badly. In like manner, it is not the fault of the wine that many use it immoderately, but it is the fault of the one who partakes of it.

No less does divine wisdom manifest itself in the structure of the trees themselves. If a man wishes to build a house, he first prepares the foundations on which the house will be supported. So also in fashioning trees, God has decreed that before the tree raises its branches into the air, it should be firmly rooted in the earth, and these roots will be in proportion to the height and breadth of the tree. The higher the tree, the deeper its roots. Once the young tree is firmly rooted, the trunk gradually thickens until it resembles a column or pillar of a building and can support the canopy of the branches with their leaves and blossoms and, later, the mature fruit. Seneca observes that in spite of the great diversity of trees and shrubs and plants, no one leaf is exactly like any other but there is always a difference in size, shape, color, or some other detail. He made the same observation in regard to the diversity of human faces, noting that there is scarcely one man who looks like another.

No less remarkable is the manner in which trees are nourished and maintained. The little hairlike strands that protrude from the roots absorb moisture from the earth and then the heat of the sun draws this moisture upward through the trunk of the tree and through all its branches. The bark of the tree serves as a protective covering over the pores of the tree through which the moisture passes. The leaves are equipped with veins similar to those in the human body. A large vein divides the leaf into two equal parts and the smaller subsidiary veins which branch off from it carry nourishment to all parts of the leaf. I once observed this in the leaves of a pear tree which had been so eaten by worms that the whole network of minute veins was exposed.

Not only is the tree sustained and nourished, but it also grows to a great size because of its vegetative soul. Animals pos-

27

sess the powers of the vegetative soul as well as those of a sensitive soul; consequently they are not only occupied with the sustenance and growth of the body, but even more so with functions of the external senses. Plants, however, lack a sensitive soul and therefore their powers are concentrated on nourishment and growth. So also we see that men who are more given to study or contemplation have more flaccid bodies because they exercise their intellectual faculties rather than their bodily members.

And who could fail to observe the beauty of the trees when they are laden with ripe fruit? What, for example, is more pleasing to the sight than an apple tree when its branches are weighted down with apples of different shades of color that send forth a delightful odor? Again, how beautiful is the grapevine with its copious green leaves, among which are half-concealed the large clusters of grapes of various shapes and colors? They are like so many jewels suspended from the branches of the vine.

Nor did providence fail to take precautions to safeguard the ripe fruits. The trees have leaves not only for beauty and shade but also to protect the fruit from the heat of the sun, which would wither the fruit. And if the fruit is especially tender, as are figs or grapes, the leaves are larger, in order to afford greater protection. However, the leaves do not cover the trees and vines like a solid blanket, but little openings are provided here and there so that the warm winds and snatches of sunlight can touch the ripening fruits.

God's providence is even more evident when we consider the manner in which the fruits of the tree are protected from greater dangers. The fruit of the tall pines, which grow in windy places or on mountain sides, would never ripen had God not fashioned the pine comb wherein each seed is placed in its own compartment and so well protected that all the fury of the winds cannot dislodge it. So also the chestnut trees, the fruit of which becomes the food of the poor when they have no bread, are found in mountainous places and subject to the violence and coldness of the winds. Therefore, the chestnut is covered with a prickly husk and with two inner tunics, one very hard and the other soft. Thus the chestnuts are protected against damage from the heat of the sun and the force of the winds. Moreover, since some trees bear a fruit that is large and heavy, such as the citrus fruits, the Creator provided that the branches of such trees should be strong and thick so that they could more easily support the weight of the fruit. And thus we see that in no created thing has divine providence been wanting or wasteful.

Let us, finally, consider the beauty of the pomegranate. How well it manifests the artistry of the Creator! First, the Creator has covered this fruit on the outside with a tunic that is made to its measure and completely encircles it to protect it from the violence of the sun and wind. The outside of this tunic or skin is hard and durable, but its inside is soft and downy so that it will not injure the tender fruit contained within. The seeds of the fruit are distributed into sections and each section is divided by a membrane more delicate than silk. Further, if any one of these quarters or sections should become spoiled, the membrane preserves the neighboring sections so that they are not contaminated. In much the same way, God divided the lobes of our brain and surrounded each with a membrane so that harm done to one section would not affect the others. Each seed of the pomegranate contains within itself a white bony substance so that its soft exterior will be better preserved and at its base it has a little stem, as thin as a thread, through which the seed receives its nourishment, in much the same way as the embryo in the womb of its mother is nourished through the umbilical cord. The seeds rest upon a white, soft substance similar to that of the inside of the skin that covers the entire fruit. Lastly, a royal crown adorns the top of the pomegranate, as if the Creator wished to designate it as the queen of all fruits. From the color of its seeds, which are as beautiful as coral, to its delicious taste and health-giving qualities, there is no fruit to compare with the pomegranate.

But why is it that men, who are so astute at philosophizing about human affairs, do not see the wise and loving providence that has created so beneficial and beautiful a fruit? The bride in the Canticle of Canticles understands this much better, for she invites the bridegroom to go forth to the vineyards to see if the flowers be ready to bring forth fruits and if the pomegranates flourish. And since we have mentioned the vineyard, let us consider that although the vine is a small tree, its fruit is not at all insignificant. It supplies grapes for the whole year and the wine that strengthens and gladdens the heart of man. It also provides vinegar, must, and raisins. Therefore it is fitting that the Savior should compare Himself to the vine when He says: "I am the vine; you, the branches. . . . As the branch cannot bear fruit of itself, unless it abide in the vine, so neither can you, unless you abide in Me."

Since the vine is small and cannot grow to great heights, it has been provided with tendrils that attach themselves to the branches of trees and climb to the height of the tree itself. Here we have a symbol of our redemption, for in the same way we, who are so base and lowly in comparison with the angels, ascend on high by clinging to that cedar of Lebanon which is Christ, our Redeemer. By uniting ourselves to Him with the bonds of love we shall rise with Him and ascend to heaven with Him. St. Gregory says that since we were unable to grasp the divine greatness, God abased Himself in coming down to earth in order to lift us up and carry us on His shoulders. For by the mystery of the Incarnation human nature was ennobled and exalted above the angels.

We have mentioned that some trees are sterile and purely forest trees, and yet God has created them out of regard for our needs. For men need not only sustenance by way of food, but they also need houses and dwellings as a protection against the inclemency of the weather, and God has created trees suitable for this purpose. He ordained that fruit trees should usually be low and that their branches should extend outward like long arms so that the fruit could be more easily gathered. But the pine, the oak, the poplar, and other trees that were made to supply wood for building are tall and straight. Lastly, many different kinds of trees provide food for the animals that eat of their leaves and bark, supply fuel for the fire that is so necessary to men, and serve as a source of medicinal elements that are beneficial to human health.

In closing our consideration of this matter, we must not neglect to recognize the great care that divine providence has shown for the conservation of the various species of plants. First, He provided that an abundance of seeds should be produced by each plant so that seeds would never be lacking from which a plant could be reproduced; and secondly, He endowed each seed with such power that from the smallest seed a shrub or tree is reproduced. We see proof of both of these things in the mustard seed to which the Savior referred in the Gospel parable. Each tree produces millions of seeds and each seed is capable of producing another tree that will again produce millions of seeds. A melon seed produces a vine of melons and each new melon contains numerous seeds that can again produce new melons. Or think of the seeds of an orange and how many other oranges and seeds they can produce.

How, then, can there ever be lacking a sufficiency of fruits and plants, when there is so much material from which they can be reproduced? How well God has provided for us! And when you have considered God's generosity in these things, consider also how copious was the redemption that He sent to us through the incarnation of His Son. If He was liberal in providing for the preservation of plants, how much more liberal and merciful has He been in restoring and sanctifying the human race? The Apostle realized this when he said that the riches of grace which the Son of God brought down to earth are incomprehensible. And Christ Himself said: "I am come that they may have life, and may have it more abundantly."

St. John of the Cross
1542-1591

In 1926, Pope Pius XI declared St. John of the Cross a Doctor of the Church, one of the greatest honors that the Church can bestow on one of its members. This action was based on the conviction that the soundness of his spiritual theology can make a lasting contribution to the search of mankind for reunion with his own origins and can serve as a guide for anyone striving to live a more perfect life.

John's life was a highly dramatic one. As a child he knew poverty. His father came from a wealthy family but was totally disowned because he married a poor woman. John was the third son. The father died shortly after his birth; the mother struggled to raise the three children well. Gifted with a keen mind, John progressed through elementary studies, while also undertaking apprenticeships in various crafts. He continued through college, entered the Carmelite Order in 1563, completed philosophical and theological studies and was ordained in 1567. A year later he met Teresa of Avila, who was in the process of reforming the Carmelite Order. He professed the Carmelite Primitive Rule in 1568 and worked with Teresa in founding the Discalced Carmelites. Frequently in his efforts, he met opposition and rejection. In 1577 he was kidnapped by some Carmelites and imprisoned for nine months. After an escape, he continued his work of administering, counseling, preaching, and serving. He fell sick with leg ulcers in September 1591, went to monastery where he was unknown, there experienced more rejection and, in December of the same year, quietly and peacefully died.

A person with as much hardship, suffering, rejection and mistreatment as John experienced, could understandably be bitter. John of the Cross turned it all into an incredibly rich spiritual life. He saw God everywhere and in everyone, in nature, in animals, in his fellowman. He had an incredible capacity both to give and to receive love. His interior peace and calm were unshakeable. A profound life of prayer nourished his thirst for union with God. And he was unusually gifted with a poetic sense of existence.

The writings of John of the Cross are an overflow of this wonderful personality. He wrote three major treatises, some poems, letters and counsels. All deal with the spiritual life. The Ascent of Mount Carmel — The Dark Night *is the treatise from which we have taken a selection. According to John himself, the purpose of the treatise is to explain how to reach divine union quickly. It offers guidance both for beginners and for experienced persons. It will enable them to unburden themselves of earthly things and to live in the nakedness and freedom of spirit that is necessary for divine union. The entire work is summarized at the beginning in a poem, the stanzas of which serve as a basis for all that John has to say.*

The Ascent, comprising three books, discusses the mortification of the appetites and the soul's journey in faith. He explains why the term night is used for these stages in the process of perfection. All that in any way would be an obstacle to union with God must be purged from the soul. The Dark Night, which has two books, describes the process by which God purifies the soul. This also is described as a night, for it is a purgative contemplation that is both dark and painful. The soul that journeys through the entire process arrives at union with God as a way of life.

The doctrine of St. John of the Cross is rich. The reader who engages John's writings will find them challenging and rewarding. He offers insights on the Christian mystery that could possibly enable contemporary man to find his way back to the original harmony of the universe.

THE ASCENT OF MT. CARMEL—
THE DARK NIGHT OF THE SOUL

A SONG OF THE SOUL'S HAPPINESS IN HAVING PASSED THROUGH THE DARK NIGHT OF FAITH, IN NAKEDNESS AND PURGATION, TO UNION WITH ITS BELOVED.

1. One dark night,
   Fired with love's urgent longings
   —Ah, the sheer grace!—
   I went out unseen,
   My house being now all stilled;

2. In darkness, and secure,
   By the secret ladder, disguised,
   —Ah, the sheer grace!—
   In darkness and concealment,
   My house being now all stilled;

3. On that glad night,
   In secret, for no one saw me,
   Nor did I look at anything,
   With no other light or guide
   Than the one that burned in my heart;

4. This guided me
   More surely than the light of noon
   To where He waited for me
   —Him I knew so well—
   In a place where no one else appeared.

5. O guiding night!
   O night more lovely than the dawn!
   O night that has united
   The Lover with His beloved,
   Transforming the beloved in her Lover.

6. Upon my flowering breast
   Which I kept wholly for Him alone,
   There He lay sleeping,

And I caressing Him
There in a breeze from the fanning cedars.

7. When the breeze blew from the turret
Parting His hair,
He wounded my neck
With His gentle hand,
Suspending all my senses.

8. I abandoned and forgot myself,
Laying my face on my Beloved;
All things ceased; I went out from myself,
Leaving my cares
Forgotten among the lilies.

PROLOGUE

A deeper enlightenment and wider experience than mine is necessary to explain the dark night through which a soul journeys toward that divine light of perfect union with God which is achieved, insofar as possible in this life, through love. The darknesses and trials, spiritual and temporal, that fortunate souls ordinarily encounter on their way to the high state of perfection are so numerous and profound that human science cannot understand them adequately; nor does experience of them equip one to explain them. He who suffers them will know what this experience is like, but he will find himself unable to describe it.

In discussing this dark night, therefore, I shall not rely on experience or knowledge, for these can fail and deceive us. Although I shall not neglect whatever possible use I can make of them, my help in all that, with God's favor, I shall say, will be Sacred Scripture, at least in the most important matters, or those which are difficult to understand. Taking Scripture as our guide we do not err, since the Holy Ghost speaks to us through it. If I should misunderstand or be mistaken on some point, whether I deduce it from Scripture or not, my intention will not be to deviate from the true meaning of Sacred Scripture or from the doctrine of our Holy Mother the Catholic Church. If this should happen, I submit entirely to the Church, or even to anyone who judges more competently about the matter than I.

I am not undertaking this arduous task because of any particular confidence in my own abilities. Rather, I am confident that the Lord will help me explain this matter, because it is extremely necessary to so many souls. Even though these souls have begun to walk along the road of virtue, and our Lord desires to place them in the dark night so they may move on to the divine union, they do not advance. Sometimes, the reason is, they do not want to enter the dark night or allow themselves to be placed in it, and sometimes they misunderstand themselves and are without suitable and alert directors who will show them the way to the summit. God gives many souls the talent and grace for advancing, and should they desire to make the effort they would arrive at this high state. And so it is sad to see them continue in their lowly method of communion with God because they do not want or know how to advance, or because they receive no direction on breaking away from the methods of beginners. Even if our Lord finally comes to their aid to the extent of making them advance without these helps, they reach the summit much later, expend more effort, and gain less merit, because they do not willingly adapt themselves to God's work of placing them on the pure and reliable road leading to union. Although God does lead them—since He can do so without their cooperation—they do not accept His guidance. In resisting God who is conducting them, they make little progress, and their merit is lessened, because they do not apply their wills, and as a result they must endure greater suffering. Some souls, instead of abandoning themselves to God and cooperating with Him, hamper him by their indiscreet activity or resistance. They resemble children who kick and cry, and struggle to walk by themselves when their mothers want to carry them; in walking by themselves they make no headway, or if they do, it is at a child's pace.

With God's help, then, we shall propose doctrine and counsel for beginners and proficients that they may understand or at least know how to practice abandonment to God's guidance when He wants them to advance.

For some spiritual directors are likely to be a hindrance and harm rather than a help to these souls that journey on this road. Such directors have neither enlightenment nor experience of these ways. They are like the builders of the tower of Babel. [Gn. 11:1-9] When these builders were supposed to provide the proper materials for the project, they brought entirely different supplies, because they failed to understand the language. And thus nothing was accomplished. Hence, it is arduous and difficult for a soul in these periods of the spiritual life when it cannot understand itself nor find anyone else who understands it.

It will happen that while an individual is being conducted by God along a sublime path of dark contemplation and aridity, in which he feels lost, he will encounter in the midst of the fullness of his darknesses, trials, conflicts, and temptations someone who, in the style of Job's comforters [Jb. 4:8-11], will proclaim that all of this is due to melancholia, or depression, or temperament, or to some hidden wickedness, and that as a result God has forsaken him. Therefore the usual verdict is that, since such trials afflict this person, he must have lived an evil life.

Others will tell him that he is falling back, since he finds no satisfaction or consolation as he previously did in the things of God. Such talk only doubles the trial of the poor soul, because its greatest suffering is caused by the knowledge of its own miseries; that it is full of evil and sin is as clear as day, and even clearer, for, as we shall say presently, God is the author of this enlightenment in the night of contemplation. And when this soul finds someone who agrees with what it feels (that these trials are all its own fault), its suffering and distress grow without bounds. And this suffering usually becomes worse than death. Such a confessor is not satisfied with this but, in judging these trials to be the result of sin, he urges souls who endure them to go over their past and make many general confessions— which is another crucifixion. The director does not understand that now perhaps is not the time for such activity. Indeed, it is a period for leaving these persons alone in the purgation God is working in them, a time to give comfort and encouragement that they may desire to endure this suffering as long as God wills, for until then, no remedy—whatever the soul does, or the confessor says—is adequate.

We shall discuss all this with the divine help: how the individual should behave; what method the confessor should use in dealing with him; the signs for the recognition of this purification of the soul (which we call the *dark night*), whether it is the purification of the sense or of the spirit; how we can determine if this affliction is caused by melancholia or any other deficiency of sense or spirit.

Some souls—or their confessors—may think that God is leading them along this road of the dark night of spiritual purgation, but perhaps this is not the case. What they suffer will owe its origin to one of these deficiencies. Likewise, many individuals think they are not praying, when, indeed their prayer is intense. Others place high value on their prayer, while it is little more than nonexistent.

Some people—and it is sad to see them—work and tire themselves greatly, and yet go backwards; they look for perfection in exercises that are of no profit to them, but rather a hindrance. Others continue to make fine progress in peace and tranquillity.

Some individuals encounter an encumbrance in the very consolations and favors God bestows on them for the sake of their advancement, and they advance not at all.

We will also discuss many other experiences of those who walk along this road: joys, afflictions, hopes, and sorrows—some of these originating from the spirit of perfection, others from the spirit of imperfection.

Our goal will be, with God's help, to explain all these points, so that everyone who reads this book will in some way discover the road that he is walking along, and the one he ought to follow if he wants to reach the summit of this mount.

The reader should not be surprised if this doctrine on the dark night (through which a soul advances toward God) appears somewhat obscure. This, I believe, will be the case as he begins to read, but as he reads on he will understand it better, since the latter parts will explain the former. Then, if he reads this work a second time, the matter will seem clearer and the doctrine sounder.

But if some people still find difficulty in understanding this doctrine, it will be due to my deficient knowledge and awkward style, for the doctrine itself is good and very necessary. But I am inclined to believe that even if it were presented with greater accuracy and polish, only a few would find profit in it, because we are not writing on pleasing and delightful themes addressed to the kind of spiritual people who like to approach God along sweet and satisfying paths. We are presenting a substantial and solid doctrine for all those who desire to reach this nakedness of spirit.

My main intention is not to address everyone, but only some of the persons of our holy Order of the Primitive Observance of Mount Carmel, both friars and nuns, whom God favors by putting them on the path leading up this mount, since they are the ones who asked me to write this work. Because they are already detached to a great extent from the temporal things of this world, they will more easily grasp this doctrine on the nakedness of spirit.

BOOK TWO

CHAPTER 1

The beginning of the treatise on the dark night of the spirit. Explains when this night commences.

If God intends to lead the soul on, He does not put it in this dark night of spirit immediately after its going out from the aridities and trials of the first purgation and night of sense. Instead, after having emerged from the state of beginners, it usually spends many years exercising itself in the state of proficients. In this new state, as one liberated from a cramped prison cell, the soul goes about the things of God with much more freedom and satisfaction of spirit and with more abundant interior delight than it did in the beginning before entering the night of sense. Its imagination and faculties are no longer bound to discursive meditation and spiritual solicitude, as was their custom. The soul readily finds in its spirit, without the work of meditation, a very serene, loving contemplation and spiritual delight. Nonetheless, since the purgation of the soul is not complete (the purgation of the principal part, that of the spirit, is lacking, and without it the sensory purgation, however strong it may have been, is incomplete because of a communication existing between the two parts of the soul which form only one *suppositum*), certain needs, aridities, darknesses, and conflicts are felt. These are sometimes far more intense than those of the past and are like omens or messengers of the coming night of the spirit.

But they are not lasting, as they will be in the night that is to come. For after enduring the short period or periods of time, or even days, in this night and tempest, the soul immediately returns to its customary serenity. Thus God purges some individuals who are not destined to ascend to so lofty a degree of love as are others. He brings them into this night of contemplation and spiritual purgation at intervals, frequently causing the night to come and then the dawn so that David's affirmation might be fulfilled: *He sends His crystal* (contemplation) *like morsels.* [Ps. 147:17] These morsels of dark contemplation, though, are never as intense as is that frightful night of contemplation we are about to describe, in which God places the soul purposely in order to bring it to the divine union.

The delight and interior gratification which these proficients enjoy abundantly and readily is communicated more copiously to them than previously and consequently overflows into the senses more than was usual before the sensory purgation. Since the sensory part of the soul is now purer, it can, after its own mode, experience the delights of the spirit more easily.

But since, after all, the sensory part of the soul is weak and incapable of vigorous spiritual communications, these proficients, because of such communications experienced in the sensitive part, suffer many infirmities, injuries, and weaknesses of stomach, and as a result fatigue of spirit. As the Wise Man says: *The corruptible body is a load upon the soul.* [Wis. 9:15] Consequently the communications imparted to proficients cannot be very strong, nor very intense, nor very spiritual— which is a requirement of the divine union—because of the weakness and corruption of the senses which have their share in them.

Thus we have raptures and transports and the dislocation of bones, which always occur when the communications are not purely spiritual (communicated to the spirit alone) as are those of the perfect, who are already purified by the night of spirit. For in the perfect, these raptures and bodily torments cease, and they enjoy freedom of spirit without a detriment to or transport of their senses.

To point out why these proficients must enter this night of spirit, we shall note some of their imperfections and some of the dangers they confront.

CHAPTER 2

Other imperfections of these proficients.

The imperfections in these proficients are of two kinds: habitual and actual.

The habitual are the imperfect affections and habits still remaining like roots in the spirit, for the sensory purgation could not reach the spirit. The difference between the two purgations is like the difference between pulling up roots and cutting off a branch, or rubbing out a fresh stain and an old, deeply embedded one. As we said, the purgation of the senses is only the gate to and beginning of the contemplation which leads to the purgation of spirit. This sensitive purgation, as we also explained, serves more for the accommodation of the senses to the spirit than for the union of the spirit with God. The stains of the old man still linger in the spirit, although this may not be apparent or perceptible. If these are not wiped away by the use of the soap and strong lye of this purgative night, the spirit will be unable to reach the purity of divine union.

These proficients also have the so-called *hebetudo mentis,* the natural dullness everyone contracts through sin, and a distracted and inattentive spirit. The spirit must be illumined, clarified, and recollected by means of the hardships and conflicts of this night.

All those who have not passed beyond the state of proficients possess these habitual imperfections which cannot, as we said, coexist with the perfect state of the union of love.

Not all of these proficients fall into actual imperfections in the same way. Some encounter greater difficulties and dangers than those we mentioned, for their experience of these goods in the senses is so exterior and easily come by. Since they receive such abundance of spiritual communications and apprehensions in the sensory and spiritual parts of their souls and frequently behold imaginative and spiritual visions (for all of this plus other delightful feelings are the lot of those who are in this state, and a soul is often tricked through them by its own phantasy as well as by the devil), and since the devil is so pleased to suggest to souls and impress upon them apprehensions and feelings, these proficients are easily charmed and beguiled, if they are not careful to renounce such apprehensions and feelings and energetically defend themselves through faith.

This is the stage in which the devil induces many into believing vain visions and false prophecies. He strives to make them presume that God and the saints speak with them; and frequently they believe their phantasy. It is here that the devil customarily fills them with presumption and pride. Drawn by vanity and arrogance, they will allow themselves to be seen in exterior acts of apparent holiness, such as raptures and other exhibitions. They become audacious with God and lose holy fear which is the key to and guardian of all the virtues. Illusions and deceptions so multiply in some, and they become so inveterate in them, that it is very doubtful whether they will return to the pure road of virtue and authentic spirituality. They fall into these miseries by being too secure in their surrender to these apprehensions and spiritual feelings; and this, just when they were beginning to make progress along the way.

So much could be said about the imperfections of these proficients and of how irremediable they are—since proficients think their blessings are more spiritual than formerly—that I desire to pass over the matter. I only assert, in order to establish the necessity of the spiritual night (the purgation) for anyone who is to advance, that no proficient, however strenuous his efforts, will avoid many of these natural affections and imperfect habits; and these must be purified before he passes on to the divine union.

Furthermore, to repeat what was said above, these spiritual communications cannot be so intense, so pure, and so vigorous as is requisite for this union, because the lower part of the soul still shares in them. Thus, to reach union, the soul must enter the second night of the spirit. In this night both the sensory and spiritual parts are despoiled of all these apprehensions and delights, and the soul is made to walk in dark and pure faith, which is the proper and adequate means to divine union, as God says through Osee: *I will espouse you* (unite you) *to me through faith.* [Os. 2:20]

CHAPTER 3

An explanation for what is to follow.

These souls, then, are now proficients. Their senses have been fed with sweet communications so that, allured by the gratification flowing from the spirit, they could be accommodated and united to the spirit. Each part of the soul can now in its own way receive nourishment from the same spiritual food and from the same dish of only one *suppositum* and subject. These two parts thus united and conformed are jointly prepared to suffer the rough and arduous purgation of the spirit which awaits them. In this purgation, these two portions of the soul will undergo complete purification, for one part is never adequately purged without the other. The real purgation of the senses begins with the spirit. Hence the night of the senses we explained should be called a certain reformation and bridling of the appetite rather than a purgation. The reason is that all the imperfections and disorders of the sensory part are rooted in the spirit and from it receive their strength. All good and evil habits reside in the spirit and until these habits are purged, the senses cannot be completely purified of their rebellions and vices.

In this night that follows both parts are jointly purified. This was the purpose of the reformation of the first night and the calm that resulted from it: that the sensory part, united in a certain way with the spirit, might undergo the purgation and suffering with greater fortitude. Such is the fortitude necessary for so strong and arduous a purgation that if the lower part in its weakness is not reformed first and afterwards strengthened in God through the experience of sweet and delightful communion with Him, it has neither the fortitude nor the preparedness to endure it.

These proficients are still very lowly and natural in their communion with God and in their activity directed toward Him because the gold of the spirit is not purified and illumined. They still think of God and speak of Him as little children, and their knowledge and experience of Him is like that of little children, as St. Paul asserts. [1 Cor. 13:11] The reason is that they have not reached perfection, which is union of the soul with God. Through this union, as full-grown men, they do mighty works in their spirit, since their faculties and works are more divine than human, as we shall point out. Wishing to strip them in fact of this old man and clothe them with the new which is created according to God in the newness of sense, as the Apostle says [Col. 3:9-10; Eph. 4:22-24; Rom. 12:2], God divests the faculties, affections, and senses, both spiritual and sensory, interior and exterior. He leaves the intellect in darkness, the will in aridity, the memory in emptiness, and the affections in supreme affliction, bitterness, and anguish, by depriving the soul of the feeling and satisfaction it previously obtained from spiritual blessings. For this privation is one of the conditions required that the spiritual form, which is the union of love, may be introduced in the spirit and united with it. The Lord works all of this in the soul by means of a pure and dark contemplation, as is indicated in the first stanza. Although we explained this stanza in reference to the first night of the senses, the soul understands it mainly in relation to this second night of the spirit, since this night is the principal purification of the soul. With this in mind, we shall quote it and explain it again.

CHAPTER 4

First Stanza

One dark night,
Fired with love's urgent longings
—Ah, the sheer grace!—
I went out unseen,
My house being now all stilled;

EXPLANATION

Understanding this stanza now to refer to contemplative purgation or nakedness and poverty of spirit (which are all about the same), we can thus explain it, as though the soul says:

Poor, abandoned, and unsupported by any of the apprehensions of my soul (in the darkness of my intellect, the distress of my will, and in the affliction and anguish of my memory), left to darkness in pure faith, which is a dark night for these natural faculties, and with only my will touched by the sorrows, afflictions, and longings of love of God, I went out from myself. That is, I departed from my low manner of understanding, and my feeble way of loving, and my poor and limited method of finding satisfaction in God. I did this unhindered by either the flesh or the devil.

This was great happiness and a sheer grace for me, because through the annihilation and calming of my faculties, passions, appetites, and affections, by which my experience and satisfaction in God was base, I went out from my human operation and way of acting to God's operation and way of acting. That is:

My intellect departed from itself, changing from human and natural to divine. For, united with God through this purgation, it no longer understands by means of its natural vigor and light, but by means of the divine wisdom to which it was united.

And my will departed from itself and became divine. United with the divine love, it no longer loves in a lowly manner, with its natural strength, but with the strength and purity of the Holy Spirit; and thus the will does not operate humanly in relation to God.

And the memory, too, was changed into presentiments of eternal glory.

And finally, all the strength and affections of the soul, by means of this night and purgation of the old man, are renewed with divine qualities and delight.

An explanation of the first verse follows:

One dark night,

CHAPTER 5

Begins to explain how this dark contemplation is not only night for the soul but also affliction and torment.

This dark night is an inflow of God into the soul, which purges it of its habitual ignorances and imperfections, natural and spiritual, and which the contemplatives call infused contemplation or mystical theology. Through this contemplation, God teaches the soul secretly and instructs it in perfection of love without its doing anything nor understanding how this happens.

Insofar as infused contemplation is loving wisdom of God, it produces two principal effects in the soul: it prepares the soul for the union with God through love by both purging and illumining it. Hence the same loving wisdom that purges and illumines the blessed spirits, purges and illumines the soul here on earth.

Yet a doubt arises: Why, if it is a divine light (for it illumines and purges a person of his ignorances), does the soul call it a dark night?

In answer to this, there are two reasons why this divine wisdom is not only night and darkness for the soul, but also affliction and torment. First, because of the height of the divine wisdom which exceeds the capacity of the soul. Second, because of the soul's baseness and impurity; and on this account it is painful, afflictive, and also dark for the soul.

To prove the first reason, we must presuppose a certain principle of the Philosopher: that the clearer and more obvious divine things are in themselves, the darker and more hidden they are to the soul naturally. [Aristotle, *Metaphys.*, lib. brevior, c. 1, ed. Didot, 486] The brighter the light, the more the owl is blinded; and the more one looks at the brilliant sun, the more the sun darkens the faculty of sight, deprives it and overwhelms it in its weakness.

Hence when the divine light of contemplation strikes a soul not yet entirely illumined, it causes spiritual darkness, for it not only surpasses the act of natural understanding but it also deprives the soul of this act and darkens it. This is why St. Dionysius and other mystical theologians call this infused contemplation a "ray of darkness"—that is, for the soul not yet illumined and purged. [Pseudo-Dionysius Areopagita, *De Mystica Theologia*, c. 1: PG 3, 999] For this great supernatural light overwhelms the intellect and deprives it of its natural vigor.

David also said that clouds and darkness are near God and surround Him [Ps. 17:12], not because this is true in itself, but because it appears thus to our weak intellects, which in being unable to attain so bright a light are blinded and darkened.

Hence he immediately added: *clouds passed before the great splendor of His presence* [Ps. 17:13], that is, between God and our intellect. As a result, when God communicates this bright ray of His secret wisdom to the soul not yet transformed, He causes thick darkness in its intellect.

It is also evident that this dark contemplation is painful to the soul in these beginnings. Since this divine infused contemplation has many extremely good properties, and the still unpurged soul that receives it has many extreme miseries, and because two contraries cannot coexist in one subject, the soul must necessarily undergo affliction and suffering. Because of the purgation of its imperfections caused by this contemplation, the soul becomes a battlefield in which these two contraries combat one another. We shall prove this by induction in the following way.

In regard to the first cause of one's affliction: because the light and wisdom of this contemplation is very bright and pure, and the soul in which it shines is dark and impure, a person will be deeply afflicted in receiving it within himself. When eyes are sickly, impure, and weak, they suffer pain if a bright light shines on them.

The soul, because of its impurity, suffers immensely at the time this divine light truly assails it. When this pure light strikes in order to expel all impurity, a person feels so unclean and wretched that it seems God is against him and that he is against God.

Because it seems that God has rejected it, the soul suffers such pain and grief that when God tried Job in this way it proved one of the worst of Job's trials, as he says: *Why have You set me against You, and I am heavy and burdensome to myself?* [Jb. 7:20] Clearly beholding its impurity by means of this pure light, although in darkness, the soul understands distinctly that it is worthy neither of God nor of any creature. And what most grieves it is that it thinks it will never be worthy, and that there are no more blessings for it. This divine and dark light causes deep immersion of the mind in the knowledge and feeling of one's own miseries and evils; it brings all these miseries into relief so that the soul sees clearly that of itself it will never possess anything else. We can interpret that passage from

David in this sense: *You have corrected man because of his iniquity and have undone and consumed his soul, as a spider is eviscerated in its work.* [Ps. 38:12]

A person suffers affliction in the second manner because of his natural, moral, and spiritual weakness. Since this divine contemplation assails him somewhat forcibly in order to subdue and strengthen his soul, he suffers so much in his weakness that he almost dies, particularly at times when the light is more powerful. Both the sense and the spirit, and though under an immense and dark load, undergo such agony and pain that the soul would consider death a relief. The prophet Job, having experienced this, declared: *I do not desire that He commune with me with much strength that He might not overwhelm me with the weight of His greatness.* [Jb. 23:6]

Under the stress of this oppression and weight, a man feels so much a stranger to being favored that he thinks, and so it is, that even that which previously upheld him has ended along with everything else, and that there is no one who will take pity on him. It is in this sense that Job also cried out: *Have pity on me, at least you my friends, for the hand of the Lord has touched me.* [Jb. 19:21]

How amazing and pitiful it is that the soul be so utterly weak and impure that the hand of God, though light and gentle, should feel so heavy and contrary. For the hand of God does not press down or weigh upon the soul, but only touches it; and this mercifully, for God's aim is to grant it favors and not chastise it.

CHAPTER 6

Other kinds of affliction suffered in this night.

The two extremes, divine and human, which are joined here, produce the third kind of pain and affliction the soul suffers here. The divine extreme is the purgative contemplation and the human extreme is the soul, the receiver of this contemplation. Since the divine extreme strikes in order to renew the soul and divinize it (by stripping it of the habitual affections and properties of the old man to which it is strongly united, attached, and conformed), it so disentangles and dissolves the spiritual substance—absorbing it in a profound darkness—that the soul at the sight of its miseries feels that it is melting away and being undone by a cruel spiritual death; it feels as if it were swallowed by a beast and being digested in the dark belly, and it suffers an anguish comparable to Jonas's when in the belly of the whale. [Jon. 2:1-3] It is fitting that the soul be in this sepulcher of dark death in order that it attain the spiritual resurrection for which it hopes.

David describes this suffering and affliction—although it is truly beyond all description—when he says: *The sighs of death encircled me, the sorrows of hell surrounded me, in my tribulation I cried out.* [Ps. 17:5-7]

But what the sorrowing soul feels most is the conviction that God has rejected it, and with an abhorrence of it cast it into darkness. The thought that God has abandoned it is a piteous and heavy affliction for the soul. When David also felt this affliction he cried: *In the manner of the wounded, dead in the sepulchers, abandoned now by Your hand so that You remember them no longer, so have You placed me in the deepest and lowest lake, in the darkness and shadow of death, and Your wrath weighs upon me, and all Your waves You have let loose upon me.* [Ps. 87:6-8]

When this purgative contemplation oppresses a man, he feels very vividly indeed the shadow of death, the sighs of death, and the sorrows of hell, all of which reflect the feeling of God's absence, of being chastised and rejected by Him, and of being unworthy of Him, as well as the object of His anger. The soul experiences all this and even more, for now it seems that this affliction will last forever.

A person also feels forsaken and despised by creatures, particularly by his friends. David immediately adds: *You have withdrawn my friends and acquaintances far from me; they have considered me an abomination.* [Ps. 87:9] Jonas, as one who also underwent this experience, both physically and spiritually in the belly of the whale, testifies: *You have cast me out into the deep, into the heart of the sea, and the current surrounded me; all its whirlpools and waves passed over me and I said: I am cast from the sight of Your eyes; yet I shall see Your holy temple again* (he says this because God purifies the soul

50

that it might see His temple); *the waters encircled me even to the soul, the abyss went round about me, the open sea covered my head, I descended to the lowest parts of the mountains, the locks of the earth closed me up forever.* [Jon. 2:4-7] The "locks" refer to the soul's imperfections which hinder it from enjoying the delights of this contemplation.

Another excellence of dark contemplation, its majesty and grandeur, causes a fourth kind of affliction to the soul. This property makes the soul feel within itself the other extreme—its own intimate poverty and misery. Such awareness is one of the chief afflictions it suffers in the purgation.

The soul experience an emptiness and poverty in regard to three classes of goods (temporal, natural, and spiritual) which are directed toward pleasing it, and is conscious of being in the midst of the contrary evils (the miseries of imperfections, aridities and voids in the apprehensions of the faculties, and an abandonment of the spirit in darkness).

Since God purges both the sensory and spiritual substance of the soul, and its interior and exterior faculties, it is fitting that it be brought into emptiness and poverty and abandonment in these parts, and left in dryness and darkness. For the sensory part is purified by aridity, the faculties by the void of their apprehensions, and the spirit by thick darkness.

God does all this by means of dark contemplation. And the soul not only suffers the void and suspension of these natural supports and apprehensions, which is a terrible anguish (like hanging in midair, unable to breathe), but it is also purged by this contemplation. As fire consumes the tarnish and rust of metal, this contemplation annihilates, empties, and consumes all the affections and imperfect habits the soul contracted throughout its life. Since these imperfections are deeply rooted in the substance of the soul, it usually suffers besides this poverty and this natural and spiritual emptiness an oppressive undoing and an inner torment. Thus the passage of Ezechiel may be verified: *Heap together the bones, and I shall burn them in the fire, the flesh shall be consumed, and the whole composition burned, and the bones destroyed.* [Ex. 24:10] He refers here to the affliction suffered in the emptiness and poverty of both the sensory and the spiritual substance of the soul. And he then adds: *Place it also thus empty on the embers that its metal may become hot and melt and its uncleanness be taken away from it and its rust consumed.* [Ez. 24:11] This passage points out the heavy affliction the soul suffers from the purgation caused by the fire of this contemplation. For the prophet asserts that in order to burn away the rust of the affections the soul must, as it were, be annihilated and undone in the measure that these passions and imperfections are connatural to it.

Because the soul is purified in this forge like gold in the crucible, as the Wise Man says [Wis. 3:6], it feels terrible annihilation in its very substance and extreme poverty as though it were approaching its end. This experience is expressed in David's cry: *Save me, Lord, for the waters have come in even unto my soul; I am stuck in the mire of the deep, and there is nowhere to stand; I have come unto the depth of the sea, and the tempest has overwhelmed me. I have labored in crying out, my throat has become hoarse, my eyes have failed while I hope in my God.* [Ps. 68:2-4]

God humbles the soul greatly in order to exalt it greatly afterwards. And if He did not ordain that these feelings, when quickened in the soul, be soon put to sleep again, a person would die in a few days. Only at intervals is one aware of these feelings in all their intensity. Sometimes this experience is so vivid that it seems to the soul that it sees hell and perdition open before it. These are the ones who go down into hell alive [Ps. 54:16], since their purgation on earth is similar to that of purgatory. For this purgation is that which would have to be undergone there. The soul that endures it here on earth either does not enter purgatory, or is detained there for only a short while. It gains more in one hour here on earth by this purgation than it would in many there.

CHAPTER 7

A continuation of the same subject; other afflictions and straits of the will.

The affliction and straits of the will are also immense. Sometimes these afflictions pierce the soul when it suddenly remembers the evils in which it sees itself immersed, and it becomes uncertain of any remedy. To this pain is added the remembrance of past prosperity, because usually persons who enter this night have previously had many consolations in God and rendered Him many services. They are now sorrowful in knowing that they are far from such good and can no longer enjoy it. Job tells also of his affliction: *I who was wont to be wealthy and rich am suddenly undone and broken; he has taken me by the neck, He has broken me and set me up as His mark so as to wound me. He has surrounded me with His lances, He wounded all my loins, He has not pardoned, He has scattered my bowels on the ground, He has torn me with wound upon wound, He has attacked me like a strong giant. I sewed sackcloth upon my skin and covered my flesh with ashes. My face is swollen with weeping, and my eyes blinded.* [Jb. 16: 13-17]

So numerous and burdensome are the pains of this night, and so many are the scriptural passages we could cite that we would have neither the time nor the energy to put it all in writing; and, doubtless, all that we can possibly say would fall short of expressing what this night really is. Through the texts already quoted we have some idea of it.

To conclude my commentary on this verse and further explain what this night causes in the soul, I shall refer to what Jeremias felt in it. Because his tribulations were so terrible, he speaks of them and weeps over them profusely: *I am the man who sees my poverty in the rod of His indignation. He has led me and brought me into darkness and not into light. He has turned and turned again His hand against me all the day. He has made my skin and my flesh old; He has broken my bones. He has built a fence round about me; and He has surrounded me with gall and labor. He has set me in darkness, as those who are dead forever. He has made a fence around me and against me that I might not go out; He has made my fetters heavy. And also when I might have cried out and entreated, He has shut out my prayer. He has closed up my exits and ways with square stones: He has destroyed my paths. He is become to me like a bear lying in wait, as a lion in hiding. He has turned aside my paths, and broken me in pieces; He has made me desolate.*

He has bent His bow and set me as a mark for His arrow. He has shot into my reins the daughters of His quiver. I have become a derision to all the people and laughter and scorn for them all the day. He has filled me with bitterness, He has inebriated me with absinthe. One by one He has broken my teeth; He has fed me with ashes. My soul is far removed from peace. I have forgotten good things. And I said: My end, my aim and my hope from the Lord is frustrated and finished. Remember my poverty and my distress, the absinthe and the gall. I shall be mindful and remember, and my soul will languish within me in afflictions. [Lam. 3:1-20]

Jeremias gives vent to all these lamentations about his afflictions and trials and depicts very vividly the sufferings of a soul in this purgation and spiritual night.

One ought to have deep compassion for the soul God puts in this tempestuous and frightful night. It may be true that the soul is fortunate because of what is being accomplished within it, for the great blessings will proceed from this night. Job affirms that out of darkness God will raise up in the soul profound blessings and change the shadow of death into light. [Jb. 12:22] He will do this in such a way that, as David says, the light will become what the darkness was. [Ps. 138:12] Nevertheless the soul is deserving of great pity because of the immense tribulation it suffers and its extreme uncertainty about a remedy. It believes, as Jeremias says [Lam. 3:18], that its evil will never end. And it feels as David that God has placed it in darkness like the dead of old, and that its spirit as a result is in anguish with it and its heart troubled. [Ps. 142:3-4]

Added to this, because of the solitude and desolation this night causes, is the fact that a person in this state finds neither consolation nor support in any doctrine or spiritual director. Although his spiritual director may point out many reasons for being comforted on account of the blessings contained in these afflictions, he cannot believe this. Because he is engulfed and immersed in that sentiment of evils by which he so clearly sees his own miseries, he believes his directors say these things because they do not understand him and do not see what he sees and feels. Instead of consolation he experiences greater sorrow thinking that the director's doctrine is no remedy for his evil. Indeed, it is not a remedy, for until the Lord finishes purging him in the way He desires, no remedy is a help to him in his sorrow. His helplessness is even greater because of the little he can do in this situation. He resembles one who is imprisoned in a dark dungeon, bound hands and feet, and able neither to move, nor see, nor feel any favor from heaven or earth. He remains in this condition until his spirit is humbled, softened, and purified, until it becomes so delicate, simple, and refined that it can be one with the Spirit of God, according to the degree of union of love that God, in His mercy, desires to grant. In conformity with this degree, the purgation is of greater or lesser force and endures for a longer or shorter time.

But if it is to be truly efficacious, it will last for some years, no matter how intense it may be; although there are intervals in which this dark contemplation ceases to assail the soul in a purgative mode and shines upon it illuminatively and lovingly. Then the soul, like one who has been unshackled and released from a dungeon and who can enjoy the benefit of spaciousness and freedom, experiences great sweetness of peace and loving friendship with God in a ready abundance of spiritual communication.

This illumination is for the soul a sign of the health the purgation is producing within it and a foretaste of the abundance for which it hopes. Sometimes the experience is so intense that it seems to the soul that its trials are over. For when the graces imparted are more purely spiritual they have this trait: When they are trials, it seems to a soul that it will never be liberated from them and that no more blessings await it, as was mentioned in the passages previously cited; when they are spiritual goods, the soul believes its evils have passed and that it will no longer lack blessings, as David confessed on being aware of these goods: *I said in my abundance: I shall never move.* [Ps. 29:7]

The soul experiences this because in the spirit the possession of one contrary removes of itself the actual possession and sentiment of the other contrary. This does not occur in the sensory part because of the weakness of its apprehensive power. But since the spirit is not yet completely purged and cleansed of affections contracted from the lower part, it can, insofar as it is affected by them, be changed and suffer affliction; although insofar as it is a spirit it does not change. We note that David changed [Ps. 29:8] and that he experienced many afflictions and evils, although in the time of his abundance he had thought and said that he would never be moved. Since the soul beholds itself actuated with that abundance of spiritual goods, and is unable to see the imperfection and impurity still rooted within it, it thinks its trials have ended.

But this thought is rare, for until the spiritual purification is completed, the tranquil communication is seldom so abundant as to conceal the roots which still remain. The soul does not cease to feel that something is lacking or remaining to be done and this feeling keeps it from fully enjoying the alleviation. It feels as though an enemy is within it who, although pacified and put to sleep, will awaken and cause trouble.

And this is true, for when a person feels safest, and least expects it, the purgation returns to engulf him in another degree more severe, dark, and piteous than the former and which lasts for another period of time, perhaps longer than the first. He thereby believes that his blessings are gone forever. That enjoyment of blessing that was his after the first trial, in which he thought he no longer had anything more to suffer, is not sufficient to prevent him from thinking in this second degree of anguish that now all is over and that the blessings formerly experienced will never more return. As I say, this strong conviction is caused by the actual apprehension of the spirit which annihilates within itself everything contrary to this conviction.

This is the reason the souls in purgatory suffer great doubts about whether they will ever leave and whether their afflictions will end. Although they habitually possess the three theological virtues (faith, hope, and charity), the actual feeling of the privation of God and of the afflictions does not permit them to enjoy the actual blessing and comfort of these virtues. Although they are aware that they love God, this gives them no consolation, because they think that God does not love them and that they are unworthy of His love. Because they see themselves deprived of Him and established in their own miseries, they feel that they truly bear within themselves every reason for being rejected and abhorred by God.

Thus, although a person suffering this purgation knows that he loves God and that he would give a thousand lives for Him (he would indeed, for souls undergoing these trials love God very earnestly), he finds no relief. This knowledge rather causes him deeper affliction. For in loving God so intensely that nothing else gives him concern, and aware of his own misery, he is unable to believe that God loves him. He believes that he neither has nor ever will have within himself anything deserving of God's love, but rather every reason for being abhorred not only by God but by every creature forever. He grieves to see within himself reasons for meriting rejection by Him Whom he so loves and longs for.

CHAPTER 8

Other afflictions that trouble the soul in this state.

Yet something else grieves and troubles a man in this state, and it is that, since this dark night impedes his faculties and affections, he cannot beseech God nor raise his mind and affection to Him. It seems as it did to Jeremias that God has placed a cloud in front of the soul so that its prayer might not pass through. [Lam. 3:44] That passage we already cited refers to this difficulty also: *He closed and locked my ways with square stones.* [Lam. 3:9] And if sometimes the soul does beseech God, it does this with so little strength and fervor that it thinks God does not hear or pay any attention to it, as the prophet Jeremias also lamented: *when I cried out and entreated, He excluded my prayer.* [Lam 3:8]

Indeed, this is not the time to speak with God, but the time to put one's mouth in the dust, as Jeremias says, that perhaps there might come some actual hope [Lam. 3:29], and the time to suffer this purgation patiently. God it is who is working now in the soul, and for this reason the soul can do nothing. Consequently, a person can neither pray vocally nor be attentive to spiritual matters, nor still less attend to temporal affairs and business. Furthermore, he frequently experiences such absorption and profound forgetfulness in the memory that long periods pass without his knowing what he did or thought about, and he knows not what he is doing or about to do, nor can he concentrate on the task at hand, even though he desires to.

Since this night not only purges the intellect of its light and the will of its affections, but also the memory of its discursive knowledge, it is fitting that the memory be annihilated in all things to fulfill what David said of this purgation: *I was annihilated and knew not.* [Ps. 72:22] David's unknowing refers to forgetfulness and a lack of knowledge in the memory. This abstraction and oblivion is caused by the interior recollection in which this contemplation absorbs the soul.

That the soul with its faculties be divinely tempered and prepared for the divine union of love, it must first be engulfed in this divine and dark spiritual light of contemplation, and thereby be withdrawn from all creature affections and apprehensions. The duration of this absorption is proportionate to the intensity of the contemplation. The more simply and purely the divine light strikes the soul, the more it darkens and empties and annihilates it in its particular apprehensions and affections concerning both earthly and heavenly things; and, also, the less simply and purely it shines, the less it deprives and darkens the soul.

It seems incredible that the brighter and purer the supernatural, divine light is, the darker it is for the soul; and that the less bright it is, the less dark it is to the soul. We can understand this truth clearly if we consider what we proved above from the teaching of the Philosopher: that the clearer and more evident supernatural things are in themselves, the darker they are to our intellects.

A comparison with natural light will illustrate this. We observe that the more a ray of sunlight shining through a window is void of dust particles, the less clearly it is seen, and that it is perceived more clearly when there are more dust particles in the air. The reason is that the light in itself is invisible and is rather the means by which the objects it strikes are seen; but it is also seen when it reflects on them. Were the light not to strike these objects, it would not be seen and neither would they. As a result, if a ray of sunlight should enter through one window, traverse the room, and go out through another window without coming in contact with any object or dust particles on which it could reflect, the room would have no more light than previously, neither would the ray be visible. Instead, upon close observation one notes that there is more darkness where the ray is present, because it takes away and darkens some of the other light; and this ray is invisible as we said because there are no objects on which it can reflect.

This precisely then, is what the divine ray of contemplation does. In striking the soul with its divine light, it surpasses the natural light and thereby darkens and deprives a man of all the natural affections and apprehensions he perceives by means of his natural light. It leaves an individual's spiritual and natural faculties not only in darkness, but in emptiness too. Leaving the soul thus empty and dark, the ray purges and illumines it with divine spiritual light, while the soul thinks it has no light and that it is in darkness, as illustrated in the case of the ray of sunlight which is invisible even in the middle of a room if the room is pure and void of any object on which the light may reflect. Yet when this spiritual light finds an object on which to shine, that is, when something is to be understood spiritually concerning perfection or imperfection, no matter how slight, or about a judgment on the truth or falsity of some matter, a man will understand more clearly than he did before he was in this darkness. And easily recognizing the imperfection which presents itself, a man grows conscious of the spiritual light he possesses; for the ray of light is dark and invisible until a hand or some other thing passes through it, and then both the object and the ray are recognized.

Since this light is so simple, so pure, and so general and is unaffected and unrestricted by any particular intelligible object, natural or divine, and since the faculties are empty and annihilated of all these apprehensions, the soul with universality and great facility perceives and penetrates anything earthly or heavenly presented to it. Hence the Apostle says that the spiritual man penetrates all things, even the deep things of God. [1 Cor. 2:10] What the Holy Spirit says through the Wise Man applies to this general and simple wisdom, that is, that it touches everywhere because of its purity [Wis. 7:24], because it is not particularized by any distinct object or affection.

And this is characteristic of the spirit purged and annihilated of all particular knowledge and affection: not finding satisfaction in anything, nor understanding anything in particular, and remaining in its emptiness and darkness, it embraces all things with great preparedness. And St. Paul's words are verified: *Nihil habentes, et omnia possidentes.* [2 Cor. 6:10] Such poverty of spirit deserves this blessedness.

CHAPTER 9

Although this night darkens the spirit, it does so to give light.

It remains to be said, then, that even though this happy night darkens the spirit, it does so only to impart light concerning all things; and even though it humbles a person and reveals his miseries, it does so only to exalt him; and even though it impoverishes and empties him of all possessions and natural affection, it does so only that he may reach out divinely to the enjoyment of all earthly and heavenly things, with a general freedom of spirit in them all.

That elements be commingled with all natural compounds, they must be unaffected by any particular color, odor, or taste, and thus they can concur with all tastes, odors, and colors. Similarly, the spirit must be simple, pure, and naked as to all natural affections, actual and habitual, in order to be able to freely communicate in fullness of spirit with the divine wisdom, in which, on account of the soul's purity, the delights of all things are tasted in a certain eminent degree. Without this purgation the soul would be wholly unable to experience the satisfaction of all this abundance of spiritual delight. Only one attachment or one particular object to which the spirit is actually or habitually bound is enough to hinder the experience or reception of the delicate and intimate delight of the spirit of love which contains eminently in itself all delights.

Because of their one attachment to the food and fleshmeat they had tasted in Egypt [Ex. 16:3], the children of Israel were unable to get any taste out of the delicate bread of angels—the manna of the desert, which, as Scripture says, contained all savors and was changed to the taste each one desired. [Wis. 16:20-21] Similarly the spirit, still affected by some actual

60

or habitual attachment or some particular knowledge or any other apprehension, is unable to taste the delight of the spirit of freedom.

The reason is that the affections, sentiments, and apprehensions of the perfect spirit, because they are divine, are of another sort and are so eminent and so different from the natural that their actual and habitual possession demands the annihilation and expulsion of the natural affections and apprehensions; for two contraries cannot coexist in one subject.

Hence, that the soul pass on to these grandeurs, this dark night of contemplation must necessarily annihilate it first and undo it in its lowly ways by putting it in darkness, dryness, conflict, and emptiness. For the light imparted to the soul is a most lofty divine light which transcends all natural light and which does not belong naturally to the intellect.

That the intellect reach union with the divine light and become divine in the state of perfection, this dark contemplation must first purge and annihilate it of its natural light and bring it actually into obscurity. It is fitting that this darkness last as long as is necessary for the expulsion and annihilation of the intellect's habitual way of understanding which was a long time in use, and that the divine light and illumination take its place. Since that strength of understanding was natural to the intellect, the darkness it here suffers is profound, frightful, and extremely painful. This darkness seems to be substantial darkness, since it is felt in the deep substance of the spirit.

The affection of love which is bestowed in the divine union of love is also divine, and, consequently, very spiritual, subtle, delicate, and interior, exceeding every affection and feeling of the will and every appetite. The will, as a result, must be first purged and annihilated of all its affections and feelings in order to experience and taste through union of love this divine affection and delight, which is so sublime and which does not naturally belong to the will. The soul is left in a dryness and distress proportionate with its habitual natural affections (whether for divine or human things), so that every kind of demon may be debilitated, dried up, and tried in the fire of this divine contemplation, as when Tobias placed the fish heart in the fire [Tb. 6:8], and the soul may become pure and simple, with a palate purged and healthy and ready to experience the sublime and marvelous touches of divine love. After the expulsion of all actual and habitual obstacles, it will behold itself transformed in these divine touches.

Furthermore, in this union for which the dark night is a preparation, the soul in its communion with God must be endowed and filled with a certain glorious splendor embodying innumerable delights. These delights surpass all the abundance the soul can possess naturally, for nature, so weak and impure, cannot receive these delights, as Isaias says: *Eye has not seen, nor ear heard, nor has it entered the heart of man what He has prepared,* etc. [Is. 64:4] As a result the soul must first be set in emptiness and poverty of spirit and purged of every natural support, consolation, and apprehension, earthly and heavenly. Thus empty, it is truly poor in spirit and stripped of the old man, and thereby able to live that new and blessed life which is the state of union with God, attained by means of this night.

Extraneous to its common experience and natural knowledge, the soul will have a very abundant and delightful divine sentiment and knowledge of all divine and human things. It must then be refined and inured, as far as its common and natural experience goes (for the eyes by which it now views these things will be as different from those of the past as is spirit from sense and divine from human), and placed in terrible anguish and distress by means of this purgative contemplation. And the memory must be abstracted from all agreeable and peaceful knowledge and feel interiorly alien to all things, in which it will seem that all things are different than before.

This night withdraws the spirit from its customary manner of experience to bring it to the divine experience which is foreign to every human way. It seems to the soul in this night that it is being carried out of itself by afflictions. At other times a man wonders if he is not being charmed, and he goes about with wonderment over what he sees and hears. Everything seems so very strange even though he is the same as always. The reason is that he is being made a stranger to his usual knowledge and experience of things so that annihilated in this respect he may be informed with the divine, which belongs more to the next life than to this.

A man suffers all these afflictive purgations of spirit that he may be reborn in the life of the spirit by means of this divine inflow, and through these sufferings the spirit of salvation is brought forth in fulfillment of the words of Isaias: *In your presence, O Lord, we have conceived and been in the pains of labor and have brought forth the spirit of salvation.* [Is. 26: 17-18]

Moreover, the soul should leave aside all its former peace, because it is prepared by means of this contemplative night to attain inner peace, which is of such a quality and so delightful that, as the Church says, it surpasses all understanding. [3rd Sun. of Advent, Epis. Phil. 4:7] That peace was not truly peace, because it was clothed with many imperfections; although to the soul walking in delight it seemed to be peace. It seemed to be a twofold peace, sensory and spiritual, since the soul beheld within itself a spiritual abundance. This sensory and spiritual peace, since it is still imperfect, must first be purged; the soul's peace must be disturbed and taken away. In the passage we quoted to demonstrate the distress of this night, Jeremias felt disturbed and wept over his loss of peace: *My soul is withdrawn and removed from peace.* [Lam. 3:17]

This night is a painful disturbance involving many fears, imaginings, and struggles within a man. Due to the apprehension and feeling of his miseries, he suspects that he is lost and that his blessings are gone forever. The sorrow and moaning of his spirit is so deep that it turns into vehement spiritual roars and clamoring, and sometimes he pronounces them vocally and dissolves in tears (if he has the strength and power to do so); although such relief is less frequent.

David, one who also had experience of this trial, refers to it very clearly in one of the psalms: *I was very afflicted and humbled; I roared with the groaning of my heart.* [Ps. 37:9] This roaring embodies great suffering. Sometimes due to the sudden and piercing remembrance of his wretchedness, a man's roaring becomes so loud and his affections so surrounded by suffering and pain that I know not how to describe it save by the simile holy Job used while undergoing this very trial: *as the overflowing waters so is my roaring.* [Jb. 3:24] As the waters sometimes overflow in such a way that they inundate everything, this roaring and feeling so increases that in seeping through and flooding everything, it fills all one's deep affections and energies with indescribable spiritual anguish and suffering.

These are the effects produced in the soul by this night which enshrouds the hopes one has for the light of day. The prophet Job also proclaims: *In the night my mouth is pierced with sufferings, and they that feed upon me do not sleep.* [Jb. 30:17] The mouth refers to the will pierced through by these sufferings which neither sleep nor cease to tear the soul to shreds. For these doubts and fears that penetrate the soul are never at rest.

This war or combat is profound because the peace awaiting the soul must be exceedingly profound; and the spiritual suffering is intimate and penetrating because the love to be possessed by the soul will also be intimate and refined. The more intimate and highly finished the work must be, so the more intimate, careful, and pure must the labor be; and commensurate with the solidity of the edifice is the energy involved in the work. As Job says, the soul is withering within itself and its inmost parts boiling without any hope. [Jb. 30:16, 27]

Because in the state of perfection toward which it journeys by means of this purgative night, the soul must reach the possession and enjoyment of innumerable blessings of gifts and virtues in both its substance and its faculties, it must first in a general way feel a withdrawal, deprivation, emptiness, and poverty regarding these blessings. And a person must be brought to think that he is far removed from them, and become so convinced that no one can persuade him otherwise or make him believe anything but that his blessings have come to an end. Jeremias points this out when he says in the passage already cited: *I have forgotten good things.* [Lam 3:17]

Let us examine now why this light of contemplation, which is so gentle and agreeable and which is the same light to which the soul must be united and in which it will find all its blessings in the desired state of perfection, produces such painful and disagreeable effects when in these initial stages it shines upon the soul.

We can answer this question easily by repeating what we already explained in part; that is, there is nothing in contemplation or the divine inflow which of itself can give pain, contemplation rather bestows sweetness and delight. The cause for not experiencing these agreeable effects is the soul's weakness and imperfection at the time, its inadequate preparation, and the qualities it possesses which are contrary to this light. Because of these the soul has to suffer when the divine light shines upon it.

CHAPTER 10

Explains this purgation thoroughly by means of a comparison.

For the sake of further clarity in this matter, we ought to note that this purgative and loving knowledge or divine light we are speaking of, has the same effect on a soul that fire has on a log of wood. The soul is purged and prepared for union with the divine light just as the wood is prepared for transformation into the fire. Fire, when applied to wood, first dehumidifies it, dispelling all moisture and making it give off any water it contains. Then it gradually turns the wood black, makes it dark and ugly, and even causes it to emit a bad odor. By drying out the wood, the fire brings to light and expels all those ugly and dark accidents which are contrary to fire. Finally, by heating and enkindling it from without, the fire transforms the wood into itself and makes it as beautiful as it is itself. Once transformed, the wood no longer has any activity or passivity of its own, except for its weight and its quantity which is denser than the fire. For it possesses the properties and performs the actions of fire: it is dry and it dries; it is hot and it gives off heat; it is brilliant and it illumines; and it is also light, much lighter than before. It is the fire that produces all these properties in the wood.

Similarly, we should philosophize about this divine, loving fire of contemplation. Before transforming the soul, it purges it of all contrary qualities. It produces blackness and darkness and brings to the fore the soul's ugliness; thus the soul seems worse than before and unsightly and abominable. This divine purge stirs up all the foul and vicious humors of which the soul was never before aware; never did it realize there was so much evil in itself, since these humors were so deeply rooted. And now that they may be expelled and annihilated they are brought to light and seen clearly through the illumination of this dark light of divine contemplation. Although the soul is no worse than before, neither in itself nor in its relationship with God, it feels undoubtedly so bad as to be not only unworthy that God should see it but deserving of His abhorrence; in fact, it feels that God now does abhor it.

This comparison illustrates many of the things we have been saying and shall say.

First, we can understand that the very loving light and wisdom into which the soul will be transformed is that which in the beginning purges and prepares it, just as the fire which transforms the wood by incorporating it into itself is that which was first preparing it for this transformation.

Second, we discern that the experience of these sufferings does not derive from this wisdom—for as the Wise Man says: *All good things come to the soul together with her* [Wis. 7:11]— but from the soul's own weakness and imperfection. Without this purgation it cannot receive the divine light, sweetness, and delight of wisdom, just as the log of wood until prepared cannot be transformed by the fire that is applied to it. And this is why the soul suffers so intensely. Ecclesiasticus confirms our assertion by telling what he suffered in order to be united with wisdom and enjoy it: *My soul wrestled for her, and my entrails were disturbed in acquiring her; therefore shall I possess a good possession.* [Ecclus. 51:25, 29]

Third, we can infer the manner in which souls suffer in purgatory. The fire, when applied, would be powerless over them if they did not have imperfections from which to suffer. These imperfections are the fuel which catches on fire, and once they are gone there is nothing left to burn. So it is here on earth; when the imperfections are gone, the soul's suffering terminates, and joy remains.

66

Fourth, we deduce that as the soul is purged and purified by this fire of love, it is further enkindled in love, just as the wood becomes hotter as the fire prepares it. A person, however, does not always feel this enkindling of love. But sometimes the contemplation shines less forcibly that he may have the opportunity to observe and even rejoice over the work being achieved, for then these good effects are revealed. It is as though one were to stop work and take the iron out of the forge to observe what is being accomplished. Thus the soul is able to perceive the good of which it was unaware while the work was proceeding. So too, when the flame stops acting upon the wood, there is a chance to see how much it has enkindled it.

Fifth, we can also gather from this comparison why, as we previously mentioned, the soul after this alleviation suffers again, more intensely and inwardly than before. After that manifestation and after a more exterior purification of imperfections, the fire of love returns to act more interiorly on the consumable matter of which the soul must be purified. The suffering of the soul becomes more intimate, subtle, spirituality, and deep-rootedness of the imperfections which are removed. This more interior purgation resembles the action of fire upon wood: As the fire penetrates more deeply into the wood its action becomes stronger and more vehement, preparing the innermost part in order to gain possession of it.

Sixth, we discover the reason it seems to the soul that all blessings are past and that it is full of evil. For at this time it is conscious of nothing but its own bitterness; just as in the example of the wood, for neither the air nor anything else gives it more than a consuming fire. Yet, when other manifestations like the previous are made, the soul's joy will be more interior because of the more intimate purification.

Seventh, we deduce that when the purification is soon to return, even though the soul's joy is ample during these intervals (so much so that it sometimes seems, as we pointed out, that the bitterness will never recur), there is a feeling, if it adverts (and sometimes it cannot help adverting), that some root remains. And this advertence does not allow complete joy, for it seems that the purification is threatening to assail it again. And when the soul does have this feeling, the purification soon returns. Finally, that more inward part still to be purged and illumined cannot be completely concealed by the portion already purified, just as there is a very perceptible difference between that inmost part of the wood still to be illumined and that which is already purged. When this purification returns to attack more interiorly, it is no wonder that once again the soul thinks all its good has come to an end and that its blessings are over. Placed in these more interior sufferings, it is blinded as to all exterior good.

With this example in mind as well as the explanation of verse 1 of the first stanza concerning this dark night and its terrible properties, it will be a good thing to leave these sad experiences and begin now to discuss the fruit of the soul's tears and the happy traits about which it begins to sing in this second verse:

Fired with love's urgent longings

CHAPTER 11

The beginning of an explanation of verse 2 of the first stanza. Tells how the fruit of these dark straits is a vehement passion of divine love.

In this second verse the soul refers to the fire of love which, like material fire acting on wood, penetrates it in this night of painful contemplation. Although this enkindling of love we are now discussing is in some way similar to that which occurs in the sensory part of the soul, it is as different from it in another way as is the soul from the body or the spiritual part from the sensory part. For this enkindling of love occurs in the spirit and through it the soul in the midst of these dark conflicts feels vividly and keenly that it is being wounded by a strong divine love, and it has a certain feeling and foretaste of God. Yet it understands nothing in particular, for as we said the intellect is in darkness.

The spirit herein experiences an impassioned and intense love, because this spiritual inflaming engenders the passion of love. Since this love is infused, it is more passive than active and thus generates in the soul a strong passion of love. This

68

love is now beginning to possess something of union with God and thereby shares to a certain extent in its properties. These properties are actions of God more than of the soul and they reside in it passively, although the soul does give its consent. But only the love of God which is being united to the soul imparts the heat, strength, temper, and passion of love, or fire, as the soul terms it here. This love finds that the soul is equipped to receive the wound and union in the measure that all its appetites are brought into subjection, alienated, incapacitated, and unable to be satisfied by any heavenly or earthly thing.

This happens very particularly in this dark purgation, as was said, since God so weans and recollects the appetites that they cannot find satisfaction in any of their objects. God proceeds thus so that by withdrawing the appetites from other objects and recollecting them in Himself, He strengthens the soul and gives it the capacity for this strong union of love, which He begins to accord by means of this purgation. In this union the soul will love God intensely with all its strength and all its sensory and spiritual appetites. Such love is impossible if these appetites are scattered by their satisfaction in other things. In order to receive the strength of this union of love, David proclaimed to God: *I will keep my strength for You* [Ps. 58:10], that is, all the ability, appetites, and strength of my faculties, by not desiring to make use of them or find satisfaction in anything outside of You.

One might, then, in a certain way ponder how remarkable and how strong this enkindling of love in the spirit can be. God gathers together all the strength, faculties, and appetites of the soul, spiritual and sensory alike, that the energy and power of this whole harmonious composite may be employed in this love. The soul consequently arrives at the true fulfillment of the first commandment which, neither disdaining anything human nor excluding it from this love, states: *You shall love your God with your whole heart and with your whole mind and with your whole soul and with all your strength.* [Dt. 6:5]

When the soul is wounded, touched, and impassioned, all its strength and its appetites are recollected in this burning of love. How will we be able to understand the movements and impulses of all this strength and these appetites? They are

69

aroused when the soul becomes aware of the fire and wound of this forceful love and still neither possesses it nor gets satisfaction from it, but remains in darkness and doubt. Doubtless, suffering hunger like dogs, as David says, these souls wander about the city and howl and sigh because they are not filled with this love. [Ps. 58:7, 15-16]

The touch of this divine love and fire so dries up the spirit and so enkindles the soul's longings to slake its thirst for this love that a person will go over these longings in his mind a thousand times and pine for God in a thousand ways. David expresses this state very well in a psalm: *My soul thirsts for You; in how many ways does my flesh long for You* [Ps. 62:2], that is, in its desires. And another translation puts it this way: *My soul thirsts for You, my soul loses itself or dies for You.*

As a result the soul proclaims in this verse: fired "with love's urgent longings," and not, "with an urgent longing of love." In all its thought and in all its business and in all events, it loves in many ways and desires and also suffers in its desire in many ways, and at all times and in many places. It finds rest in nothing, for it feels this anxiety in the burning wound, as the prophet Job explains: *As the hart desires the shade and as the hireling desires the end of his work, so have I had empty months and numbered to myself long and wearisome nights. If I lie down to sleep I shall say: When will I arise? And then I will await the evening and will be filled with sorrows until the darkness of the night.* [Jb. 7:2-4]

Everything becomes narrow for this soul: there is no room for it within itself, neither is there any room for it in heaven or on earth; and it is filled with sorrows unto darkness, as Job says speaking spiritually and from our point of view. This affliction the soul undergoes here is a suffering unaccompanied by the comfort of certain hope for some spiritual light and good.

A man's anxiety and affliction in this burning of love is more intense because it is doubly increased: first, through the spiritual darknesses in which he is engulfed and which afflict him with doubts and fears; second, through the love of God which inflames and stimulates and wondrously stirs him with a loving wound. Isaias clearly explains these two ways of suffering

70

in this state when he says: *My soul desired You in the night* [Is. 26:9], that is, in the midst of misery. This is the one way of suffering in this dark night. *Yet within my spirit,* he says, *until the morning I will watch to You.* [Is. 26:9] And this is the second way of suffering: with desire and anxiety of love in the innermost parts of the spirit. Nonetheless, in the midst of these dark and loving afflictions, the soul feels the presence of someone and an interior strength which so fortifies and accompanies it that when this weight of anxious darkness passes, it often feels alone, empty, and weak. The reason is that since the strength and efficacy of the dark fire of love which assails it is communicated and impressed upon it passively, the darkness, strength, and warmth of love ceases when the assault terminates.

CHAPTER 12

The resemblance of this frightful night to purgatory. How the divine wisdom illumines men who suffer this night on earth by the same illumination with which He illumines and purges the angels in heaven.

We can therefore understand that just as this dark night of loving fire purges in darkness it also inflames the soul in darkness. We can also note that as the spirits in the other life are purged with a dark material fire, so in this life souls are purged and cleansed with a dark, loving spiritual fire. For such is the difference: Souls are cleansed in the other life by fire, but here on earth they are cleansed and illumined by love. David asked for this love when he said: *Cor mundum crea in me Deus,* etc. [Ps. 50:12] Purity of heart is nothing less than the love and grace of God. The clean of heart are called blessed by our Saviour [Mt. 5:8], and to call them blessed is equivalent to saying they are taken with love, for blessedness is derived from nothing else but love.

Jeremias shows clearly that the soul is purged by the illumination of this fire of loving wisdom (for God never bestows mystical wisdom without love, since love itself infuses it) where he says: *He sent fire into my bones and instructed me.* [Lam. 1:13] And David says that *God's wisdom is silver tried in the fire* [Ps. 11:7], that is, in the purgative fire of love.

71

This contemplation infuses both love and wisdom in each soul according to its capacity and necessity. It illumines the soul and purges it of its ignorances, as the Wise Man declares it did to him.

Another deduction is that this very wisdom of God, which purges and illumines these souls, purges the angels of their ignorances and gives them understanding by illumining them on matters they are ignorant of. This wisdom descends from God through the first hierarchies unto the last, and from these last unto men. It is rightly and truly said in Scripture that all the works of the angels and the inspirations they impart are also accomplished or granted by God. For ordinarily these works and inspirations are derived from God by means of the angels, and the angels also in turn give them one to another without delay. This communication is like that of a ray of sunlight shining through many windows placed one after the other. Although it is true that of itself the ray of light passes through them all, nevertheless each window communicates this light to the other with a certain modification according to its own quality. The communication is more or less intense insofar as the window is closer to or farther from the sun.

Consequently, the nearer the higher spirits (and those that follow) are to God, the more purged and clarified they are by a more general purification; the last spirits will receive a fainter and more remote illumination. Man, the last one to whom this loving contemplation of God is communicated, when God so desires, must receive it according to his own mode, which is limited and painful.

God's light, which illumines the angels by clarifying and giving them the savor of love—for they are pure spirits prepared for this inflow—illumines man, as we said, by darkening him and giving him pain and anguish, since naturally he is impure and feeble. This communication affects him as sunlight affects the sick and bleared eye. This very fire of love enamors a man impassionedly and afflictively until it spiritualizes and refines him through purification, and he becomes capable of the tranquil reception of this loving inflow, as are the angels and those already purified. With the Lord's help we will explain this state later. In the meanwhile, however, the soul receives this contemplation and loving knowledge in distress and longing of love.

The soul does not always feel this inflaming and urgent longing of love. In the beginning of the spiritual purgation, the divine fire spends itself in drying out and preparing the wood—that is, the soul—rather than in heating it. Yet as time passes and the fire begins to give off heat, the soul usually experiences the burning and warmth of love.

As the intellect becomes more purged by means of this darkness, it happens sometimes that this mystical and loving theology besides inflaming the will also wounds the intellect, by illumining it with some knowledge and light, so delightfully and delicately that the will is thereby marvelously enkindled in fervor. This divine fire burns in the will—while the will remains passive—like a living flame and in such a way that this love now seems to be a live fire because of the living knowledge communicated. David says in the psalm: *My heart grew hot within me and a certain fire was enkindled while I was knowing.* [Ps. 38:4]

This enkindling of love and the union of these two faculties, the intellect and the will, is something immensely rich and delightful for the soul, because it is a certain touch of the divinity and already the beginning of the perfection of the union of love for which the soul hopes. Thus one does not receive this touch of so sublime and experience and love of God without having suffered many trials and a great part of purgation. But so extensive a purgation is not required for other inferior and more common touches.

You may deduce from our explanation that when God infuses these spiritual goods the will can very easily love without the intellect understanding, just as the intellect can know without the will loving. Since this dark night of contemplation consists of divine light and love—just as fire gives off both light and heat—it is not incongruous that this loving light, when communicated, sometimes acts more upon the will through the fire of love and leaves the intellect in darkness by not wounding it with light, or that at other times it illumines the intellect with understanding and leaves the will in dryness. All of this is similar to feeling the warmth of fire without seeing its light or seeing the light without feeling the fire's heat. The Lord works in this way because He infuses contemplation as He wills.

CHAPTER 13

Other delightful effects of this dark night of contemplation in the soul.

Through this inflaming of love we can understand some of the delightful effects this dark night of contemplation now gradually produces in the soul. Sometimes, as we said, it illumines in the midst of these darknesses, and the light shines in the darkness [Jn. 1:5], serenely communicating this mystical knowledge to the intellect and leaving the will in dryness, that is, without the actual union of love. The serenity is so delicate and delightful to the feeling of the soul that it is ineffable. This experience of God is felt now in one way and now in another.

Sometimes, as we said, this contemplation acts upon the intellect and will together and sublimely, tenderly, and forcibly enkindles love. We already pointed out that once the intellect is more purged these two faculties are sometimes united; and in the measure that they are both purged, this union becomes so much more perfect and deeper in quality. Yet before reaching this degree, it is more common to experience the touch of burning in the will than the touch of understanding in the intellect.

A question arises here: Why does one in the beginning more commonly experience in the purgative contemplation an inflaming of love in the will rather than understanding in the intellect, since these two faculties are equally being purged?

We may answer that this passive love does not act upon the will directly because the will is free, and that this burning of love is more the passion of love than a free act of the will. The warmth of love wounds the substance of the soul and thus moves the affections passively. As a result the enkindling of love is called the passion of love rather than a free act of the will. An act of the will is such only insofar as it is free. Yet, since these passions and affections bear a relation to the will, it is said that if the soul is impassioned with some affection, the will is. This is true, because the will thus becomes captive and loses its freedom, carried away by the impetus and force of the passion. As a result we say that this enkindling of love takes place in the will, that is, the appetites of the will are enkindled. This enkindling is called the passion of love rather than the free exercise of the will. Since only the receptive capacity of the intellect can take in the naked and passive knowledge and since the intellect, unless purged, cannot receive this knowledge, the soul, prior to the purgation of the intellect, experiences the touch of knowledge less frequently than the passion of love. For to feel the passion of love, it is unnecessary that the will be so purged in relation to the passions; the passions even help it experience impassioned love.

Since this fire and thirst of love is spiritual, it is far different from the other enkindling of love we discussed in the night of the senses. Although the senses share in this love, because they do not fail to participate in the work of the spirit, the root and keenness of the thirst is felt in the higher part of the soul. The spirit so feels and understands what it experiences and the lack which this desire causes in it that all the suffering of sense— even though incomparably greater than that of the night of senses—is nothing in comparison to this spiritual suffering. For the soul is conscious deeply within itself of the lack of an immense and incomparable good.

We ought to point out that the burning of love is not felt at the beginning of this spiritual night because the fire of love has not begun to catch. Nevertheless, God gives from the outset an esteeming love of Himself, so intense that, as we said, the soul's greatest suffering in the trials of this night is the anguish of thinking it has lost God and been abandoned by Him. We can always assert, then, that from the commencement of this night the soul is touched with urgent longings of love; of esteeming love, sometimes, at other times also of burning love.

Seemingly the greatest suffering the soul experiences in these trials is this fear. If a man could be assured that all is not over and lost but that what he suffers is for the better—as indeed it is—and that God is not angry with him, he would be unconcerned about all these sufferings, rather he would rejoice in the knowledge that God is pleased with them. His love of esteem for God is so intense, even though obscure and imperceptible, that he would be happy not only to suffer these things but even die many times in order to please Him. When the fire now inflames the soul together with the esteem of God already possessed, an individual usually acquires such strength, courage, and longing relative to God, through the warmth of the love which is being communicated, that with singular boldness he would do strange things, in whatever way necessary, in order to encounter Him Whom he loves. Because of the strength and inebriation of his love and desire, he would perform these actions without any considerations or concerns.

Mary Magdalen, in spite of her past, paid no heed to the crowds of men, prominent as well as unknown, at the banquet. She did not consider the opportuneness of weeping and shedding tears in the presence of our Lord's guests. Her only concern was to reach Him, for Whom her soul was already wounded and on fire, without any delay and without waiting for another more appropriate time. [Lk. 7:37-38] And such is the inebriation and courage of love: knowing that her Beloved was shut up in the tomb by a huge sealed rock and surrounded by guards so that the disciples could not steal His body, she did not permit this to keep her from going out with ointments before daybreak to anoint Him. [Mt. 27:64-66; Mk. 16:1-2]

Finally, this inebriation and urgent longing of love prompted her to ask the man she thought was gardener if he had stolen Him and, that if he had, to tell her where he put Him so that she could take Him away. [Jn. 20:15] She did not stop to realize that her question in the light of sound judgment was foolish, for obviously if he had stolen the Lord he would not have told her, and still less would he have allowed her to take Him away.

The strength and vehemence of love has this trait: Everything seems possible to it and it believes everyone is occupied as it is; it does not believe anyone could be employed in any other way or seek anyone other than Him Whom it seeks and loves; it believes there is nothing else to desire or to occupy it and that everyone is engaged in seeking and loving Him. When the bride went searching for her Beloved in the plazas and suburbs, she thought that others were doing the same and told them that if they found Him they should inform Him that she was suffering for love of Him. [Ct. 3:2; 5:8] Mary's love was so ardent that she thought she would go and take Him away, however great the impediments, if the gardener would tell where He was hidden.

Such are the traits of these longings of love which the soul experiences when it is advanced in this spiritual purgation. The wounded soul rises up at night, in this purgative darkness, according to the affections of the will; as the lioness or she-bear that goes in search of her cubs when they are taken away and cannot be found, it anxiously and forcibly goes out in search of its God. Since it is immersed in darkness, it feels His absence and that it is dying with love of Him. Such is impatient love, which one cannot long endure without either receiving its object or dying. Rachel bore this love for children when she said: *Give me children, otherwise I will die.* [Gn. 30:1]

It should be explained here why, even though the soul feels as miserable and unworthy of God as it does in these purgative darknesses, it possesses an energy bold enough to go out to be joined with God.

The reason is that since love now imparts a force by which the soul loves authentically, and since it is the nature of love to seek to be united, joined, equaled, and assimilated to the loved object in order to be perfected in the good of love, the soul hungers and thirsts for this union or perfection of love still unattained. And the strength love has now bestowed, and by which the will has become impassioned, makes this inflamed will daring. Since the intellect is not illumined but in darkness, the soul feels unworthy and knows that it is miserable.

I do not want to fail to explain why this divine light, even though it is always light for the soul, does not illumine immediately upon striking as it will afterwards, but instead causes trials and darknesses.

We already said something on this matter. Yet, we may reply particularly that the darknesses and evils the soul experiences when this light strikes are not darknesses and evils of the light but of the soul itself. And it is this light which illumines it so it may see these evils. From the beginning the divine light illumines the soul; yet at the outset it can only see through this light what is nearest—or rather within—itself, namely, its own darknesses and miseries. It sees these by the mercy of God, and it did not see them before because this supernatural light did not shine in it. Accordingly, it only feels darknesses and evils at the outset. After being purged through the knowledge and feeling of these darknesses and evils, it will have eyes capable of the vision of the goods of the divine light. Once all these darknesses and imperfections are expelled, it seems that the immense benefits and goods the soul is acquiring in this happy night of contemplation begin to appear.

It is clear, consequently, how God grants the soul a favor by cleansing and curing it. He cleanses it with a strong lye and a bitter purge in its sensory and spiritual parts of all imperfect affections and habits relative to temporal, natural, sensory, and spiritual things, by darkening the interior faculties and emptying them of all these objects, and by restraining and drying up the sensory and spiritual affections and weakening and refining the natural forces of the soul with respect to these things. A man would never have been able to accomplish this work himself, as we shall soon explain. Accordingly, God makes the soul die to all that He is not, so that when it is stripped and flayed of its old skin, He may clothe it anew. Its youth is renewed like the eagle's [Ps. 102:5], clothed in the new man which is created, as the Apostle says, according to God. [Eph. 4:24] This renovation is: an illumination of the human intellect with supernatural light so that it becomes divine, united with the divine; an informing of the will with love of God so that it is no longer less than divine and loves in no other way than divinely, united and made one with the divine will and love; and also a divine conversion and change of the memory, the affections, and the appetites according to God. And thus this soul will be a soul of heaven, heavenly and more divine than human.

As we have gradually seen, God accomplishes all this work in the soul by illumining it and firing it divinely with love's urgent longing for God alone. Rightly and reasonably does the soul add the third verse of the canticle:

—Ah, the sheer grace!—

CHAPTER 14

An explanation of the three last verses of the first stanza.

This sheer grace resulted from what is expressed in the following verses:

> I went out unseen,
> My house being now all stilled;

We have the metaphor of one who in order to execute his plan better, and without hindrance, goes out at night, in darkness, when everybody in the house is sleeping.

The soul had to go out to accomplish so heroic and rare a feat—to be united with its divine Beloved outside—because the Beloved is not found except alone, outside, and in solitude. The bride accordingly desired to find Him alone, saying: *Who will give you to me, my brother, that I may find you alone outside and communicate to you my love.* [Ct. 8:1] The enamored soul must leave its house, then, in order to reach its desired goal. It must go out at night when all the members of its house are asleep, that is: when the lower operations, passions, and appetites of its soul are put to sleep or quelled by means of this night. These are the people of its household who when awake are a continual hindrance to the reception of any good and hostile to the soul's departure in freedom from them. Our Saviour declares that a man's enemies are those of his own household. [Mt. 10:36] The operations and movements of these members had to be put to sleep in order not to keep the soul from receiving the supernatural goods of the union of love of God, for this union cannot be wrought while they are awake and active. All the soul's natural activity hinders rather than helps it to receive the spiritual goods of the union of love. All natural ability is insufficient to produce the supernatural goods which God alone infuses in the soul passively, secretly, and in silence. All the faculties must receive this infusion, and in order to do so, they must be passive and not interfere through their own lowly activity and vile inclinations.

It was a sheer grace for this soul that God in this night put to sleep all the members of its household, that is: all the faculties, passions, affections, and appetites which live in its sensory and spiritual parts. God put them to sleep to enable the soul to go out to the spiritual union of the perfect love of God without being seen, that is, without the hindrance of these affections, etc. For these members of the household are put to sleep and mortified in this night, which leaves them in darkness, that they may not be able to observe or experience anything in their lowly, natural way which would impede the soul's departure from itself and the house of the senses.

Oh what a sheer grace it is for the soul to be freed from the house of its senses! This fortune, in my opinion, can only be understood by the man who has savored it. For then a person will become clearly aware of the wretched servitude and the many miseries he suffered when he was subject to the activity of his faculties and appetites. He will understand how the life of the spirit is true freedom and wealth and embodies inestimable goods. In the following stanzas we will specify some of these goods and see more clearly how right the soul is in singing about the journey through this horrendous night as being a great grace.

St. Francis de Sales
1567-1622

The Introduction to the Devout Life *is one of the few masterpieces of spiritual literature. It was written by St. Francis de Sales in response to a need in his time for a clear, simple and sound guide to spiritual perfection. The intention of the author was to instruct those who live in towns, in families, or at court, who are obliged to lead ordinary lives and frequently assume that it is impossible to undertake a devout life. Francis set out to prove to the average Christian layman that he or she can live in the world without being infected by any of its moods.*

Given the life of Francis himself, it is not surprising that his book was immediately recognized as a classic and that it continues to be so today. Francis came from the nobility of Savoy. He studied in Paris and Padua; in both universities he manifested an excellent intellect. Along with obtaining degrees in law and the arts, he became proficient in theology and scripture. From his earliest years he led a life of deep prayer and had but a single goal in life, union with God. By temperament he was gentle, kind, patient and understanding. His family wanted him to enter a state career and even arranged the right marriage for him. Francis chose a clerical life. After several years of missionary activity in a region called the Chablais, Francis became Bishop of Geneva. Were he not famous for his writing, his commitment to the pastoral aspect of the Episcopacy would have established his reputation. He dedicated himself totally to the spiritual growth of his people, both clergy and laity. During his lifetime he preached over 4,000 sermons and wrote over 20,000 letters of counsel. No one who ever came to him for help was refused. His sole intention as Bishop of Geneva was to draw people to God through love and gentleness. He had learned, through his own life of prayer and mission experience, that harshness and cold discipline can never bring humans together with one another or with God. A man knowing no fear, either of self, neighbor or God, he chose to lead his people to God by the positive path of joy and cheerfulness.

The Introduction to the Devout Life *is more than a book. It is the outpouring of the life of an unusual person, whose spiritual life and methodology actually identify. He lived what he wrote on a daily basis. The reader will find* The Introduction *easy to read, its atmosphere warm and gentle, its counsel sound and mature. It is divided into five parts. Part I describes true devotion and presents a brief version of the* Spiritual Exercises *of St. Ignatius of Loyola. It is designed to bring the soul to a moment of decision in the presence of God. Part II is predominantly a treatise on prayer and the sacraments. Part III treats of virtues necessary for spiritual advancement, Part IV deals with various temptations met in the spiritual life, Part V offers instructions designed to repose and renew the spirit.*

Our selection discusses devotion and prayer. True devotion is not a matter of emotion. Rather it consists in a dedicated, firm, prompt will to do what is pleasing to God. Francis exposes the emptiness of external actions which are too often identified as devotion and teaches that living devotion is the love of God which brings the soul's capacity to do good to perfection. Devotion is the right and duty of all Christians, regardless of state in life. "Wheresoever we are, we can and should aspire to a perfect life."

The treatise on prayer walks the Christian through a methodology that is at once simple and enriching. It reveals Francis' unusual understanding of the human condition, as well as his capacity to propose practical means to develop a rich life of prayer.

INTRODUCTION TO THE DEVOUT LIFE

THE FIRST PART OF THE INTRODUCTION

I. THE DESCRIPTION OF TRUE DEVOTION

You aspire to devotion, dearest Philothea, because, being a Christian, you know it to be a virtue extremely pleasing to the Divine Majesty. Since small faults, committed in the beginning of any undertaking, grow in the progress infinitely greater and become in the end almost irreparable, you must above all else know what the virtue of devotion is. There is but one true devotion, and there are many that are false and deceitful. Hence, if you cannot distinguish that which is true, you may easily deceive and distract yourself in following one that is offensive and superstitious.

As Arelius painted all the faces in his pictures in the manner and likeness of the woman he loved, so everyone paints devotion according to his own love and fancy. The man who is addicted to fasting thinks himself very devout if he fasts, though his heart be at the same time filled with rancor. He scruples to moisten his tongue with wine, or even with water, because of his sobriety, but he makes no difficulty of drinking deep of his neighbor's blood by detraction and calumny. Another considers himself devout because he recites daily a multiplicity of prayers, although immediately afterward he utters the most disagreeable, arrogant, and injurious words in his home and among his neighbors. Another cheerfully draws an alms out of his purse to give to the poor, but he cannot draw meekness out of his heart to forgive his enemies. Another readily forgives his enemies, but he never satisfies his creditors except when compelled by the sharp power of the law. All these are commonly esteemed devout, while in reality they are by no means so. Saul's servants sought David in his house, but Michol laid a statue in his bed, covered it over with clothes, and made them believe that it was David himself. In the same manner, many persons by covering themselves with certain external actions belonging to holy devotion make the world believe that they are truly devout, whereas they are in truth nothing but images and phantoms of devotion.

True, living devotion, Philothea, presupposes the love of God, and hence it is nothing else than the love of God. But it is not always love as such. Inasmuch as divine love adorns the soul, it is called grace, which makes us pleasing to His Divine Majesty. Inasmuch as it gives us the strength to do good, it is called charity. When it has arrived at that degree of perfection by which it not only makes us do well but also do this diligently, frequently, and readily, then it is called devotion. Ostriches never fly; hens fly close to the ground, clumsily, and only occasionally; but eagles, doves, and swallows fly aloft, swiftly, and frequently. In like manner, sinners fly not at all toward God, but make their whole course upon the earth and for the earth. Good people who have not as yet attained to devotion fly toward God by their good works, but infrequently, slowly, and clumsily. Devout souls ascend to Him by more frequent, prompt, and lofty flights. In short, devotion is nothing else than that spiritual agility and vivacity by which charity works in us, or we work by her aid, with alacrity and affection. As it is the function of charity to make us observe all of God's commandments in general and without exception, so it is the part of devotion to make us observe them more quickly and with diligence. Wherefore, the man who does not observe all the commandments of God cannot be esteemed either good or devout. For to be good he must be possessed of charity, and to be devout, in addition to charity, he must show a cheerfulness and alacrity in the performance of charitable actions.

As devotion consists in a certain degree of eminent charity, it not only makes us active and diligent in the observance of God's commandments, but beyond this it arouses us to do quickly and lovingly as many good works as we can, both those commanded and those that are merely counseled and inspired. Just as a man newly recovered from an illness walks only as much as is necessary for him, but yet slowly and with difficulty, so a sinner, just healed of his iniquity, walks as far as God commands him but slowly and with difficulty, until such time as he attains to devotion. Then, like a man in sound health, he not only walks but runs and leaps forward in the way of God's commandments. Moreover, he moves and runs in the paths of His heavenly counsels and inspirations. To conclude, charity and devotion differ no more from each other than does the flame from the fire, for charity is a spiritual fire, which, when inflamed, is called devotion. Hence, it appears that devotion adds nothing to the fire of charity but the flame that makes it ready, active, and diligent, not only in the observance of the commandments of God, but also in the execution of His heavenly counsels and inspirations.

II. THE PROPRIETY AND EXCELLENCY OF DEVOTION

The man who discouraged the Israelites from going into the Promised Land told them that it was a country that devoured its inhabitants; or, in other words, that it was impossible to live long there, so malignant was its air, and further that the natives were such monsters that they devoured men like locusts. It is in this manner, my dear Philothea, that the world defames holy devotion. It represents devout persons with peevish, gloomy, and sullen faces, and pretends that devotion begets melancholy and insupportable moods. But just as Joshua and Caleb protested that the Promised Land was not only good and fair but also that possession of it would be sweet and agreeable, so the Holy Spirit by the mouths of all the saints, and our Savior by His own, assure us that a devout life is a life above all others the most sweet, happy, and amiable.

The world sees devout people fast, pray, suffer injuries, serve the sick, give alms to the poor, watch over themselves, restrain their anger, stifle their passions, deprive themselves of sensual pleasures, and perform other actions in themselves and by their own nature and character painful and rigorous. But the world does not discern the interior and heartfelt devotion that renders all these actions agreeable, sweet, and easy. Look at the bees in the midst of thyme. They find there a very bitter juice, yet in sucking it they convert it into honey, because they have the ability to do so. O worldlings! devout souls, it is true, find much bitterness in their exercises of mortification; but in performing them they convert them into the most delicious sweetness. Fire, flame, wheel, and sword seemed flowers and perfumes to the martyrs because they were devout. If devotion can confer a sweetness on the most cruel torments, and even on death itself, what can it not do for virtuous actions?

Sugar sweetens green fruits and corrects whatever is crude or unwholesome in those that are ripe. Now, devotion is that true spiritual sugar which corrects the bitterness of mortification by the sweetness of its consolations. It removes discontent from the poor, and solicitude from the rich; sadness from the oppressed, and insolence from the exalted; melancholy from the solitary, and dissipation from him who is in society. It serves equally for fire in winter and for dew in summer. It knows equally how to use abundance and how to suffer want, and how to render honor and contempt equally profitable. It accepts pleasure and pain with a heart nearly always the same and fills us with an admirable sweetness.

Consider Jacob's ladder, for in it you have a true picture of a devout life. The two sides, between which we ascend and in which the rungs are fixed, represent prayer, which calls down the love of God, and the sacraments, which confer it. The rungs are the various degrees of charity by which we advance from virtue to virtue, either descending by deed to the help and support of our neighbor, or ascending by contemplation to a union of love with God. Now look attentively, I beseech you, upon those who are on this ladder. They are either men who have angelical hearts or angels who have human bodies. They are not young, although they seem so because they are full of vigor and spiritual agility. They have wings to soar up to God by holy prayer, but they have also feet to walk with men in a holy and edifying way of life. Their countenances are fair and cheerful, because they receive all things with sweetness and content. Their legs, their arms, and their heads are bare, because in all their thoughts, affections, and actions they have no other design or motive than that of pleasing God. The rest of their body has no other covering than a fair and light robe. This is to show that although they make use of the world and worldly things, yet they use them in a most pure and moderate manner, not taking more of them than is necessary for their condition. Such are devout persons.

Believe me, dear Philothea, devotion is the delight of delights and the queen of virtues, for it is the perfection of charity. If charity be milk, devotion is its cream; if it be a plant, devotion is its flower; if it be a precious stone, devotion is its luster; if it be a rich balm, devotion is its odor; yea, the odor of sweetness, which comforts men and rejoices angels.

III. THAT DEVOTION IS COMPATIBLE WITH EVERY VOCATION AND PROFESSION

In the creation God commanded the plants to bring forth their fruits, each one after its kind. So does He command all Christians, who are the living plants of His Church, to bring forth the fruits of devotion, each according to his character and vocation. Devotion must be exercised in different ways by the gentleman, the workman, the servant, the prince, the widow, the maid, and the married woman. Not only this, but the practice of devotion must be also adapted to the strength, the employment, and the duties of each one in particular. I ask you, Philothea, is it fit that a bishop should lead the solitary life of a Carthusian? Or that married people should lay up no greater store of goods than the Capuchin? If a tradesman were to remain the whole day in church, like a member of a religious order, or were a religious continually exposed to encounter difficulties in the service of his neighbor, as a bishop is, would not such devotion be ridiculous, unorganized, and insupportable? Nevertheless, this fault is very common. Hence, the world, which does not distinguish, or does not wish to distinguish, between real devotion and the indiscretion of those who imagine themselves to be devout, murmurs at devotion and censures it, as if it were unable to prevent these disorders.

No, Philothea, true devotion does no harm whatever, but rather gives perfection to all things. But when it goes contrary to our lawful vocation, then without doubt it is false. "The bee," says Aristotle, "extracts honey from flowers without injuring them," and leaves them as whole and fresh as she found them. True devotion does still better. It not only does no injury to any vocation or employment, but on the contrary it adorns and beautifies it. Every kind of precious stone receives a greater luster when cast into honey, each according to its color. So also every vocation becomes more agreeable when united with devotion. The care of the family is rendered more peaceable, the love of the husband and wife more sincere, the service of the prince more faithful, and every type of employment more pleasant and agreeable.

It is an error, or rather a heresy, to try to banish the devout life from the regiment of soldiers, the shop of the mechanic, the court of princes, or the home of married folk. It is true, Philothea, that a purely contemplative, monastic, and religious devotion cannot be exercised in such ways of life. But besides these three kinds of devotion, there are several others adapted to bring to perfection those who live in the secular state. Abraham, Isaac, and Jacob, David, Job, Tobias, Sarah, Rebecca, and Judith bear witness of this in the Old Testament. As for the New Testament, St. Joseph, Lydia, and St. Crispin were perfectly devout in their workshops; St. Anne, St. Martha, St. Monica, Aquila, and Priscilla in their families; Cornelius, St. Sebastian, and St. Maurice in the army; Constantine, Helena, St. Louis, Blessed Amatus, and St. Edward on the throne. It has even happened that many have lost perfection in solitude, which is none the less so desirable for perfection, and have preserved it among the multitude, which seems so little favorable to it. "Lot," says St. Gregory, "who was so chaste in the city, defiled himself in the wilderness." Wheresoever we are, we can and should aspire to a perfect life.

IV. OF THE NECESSITY OF A GUIDE FOR BEGINNING AND PROGRESSING IN DEVOTION

Young Tobias, when commanded to go to Rages, answered, "I know not the way." "Go then," replied his father, "and seek some man to conduct thee." I say the same thing to you, my Philothea. Would you walk in earnest toward devotion? Seek some good man who will guide and conduct you. This is the greatest of all words of advice. "Though you search for the will of God," says the devout Avila, "you shall never so assuredly find it as in the way of humble obedience, so much recommended and practiced by all holy persons who have aspired to devotion."

When the blessed Mother Teresa saw the Lady Catherine of Cardona perform some rigorous penances, she desired anxiously to imitate her. This was contrary to the advice of her confessor, who forbade her to do them. The saint was much tempted to disobey him in this matter, and God said to her: "Daughter, thou art in a good and safe way. Dost thou see the penance that she does? I value more thine obedience." Hence, she loved so much this virtue that besides that which she owed to her superiors, she vowed a particular obedience to a certain excellent man. She bound herself to follow his directions and charges, and by this she was infinitely consoled. So also were many other devout souls, both before and after her, who submitted their wills to those of God's servants in order to subject themselves more completely to God Himself. St. Catherine of Siena in her *Dialogues* highly praises this obedience. The devout princess, St. Elizabeth, submitted herself with an entire obedience to the learned Master Conrad. The advice given by the great St. Louis to his son, a little before his death, was this: "Confess often; choose a good confessor, a wise man, who may safely teach thee to do the things that shall be necessary for thee."

"A faithful friend," says Holy scripture, "is a strong defence; and he that hath found him hath found a treasure. A faithful friend is the medicine of life and immortality; and they that fear the Lord shall find Him." These words, as you perceive, refer to a happy immortality. For the attainment of this, it is necessary that we have above all else this faithful friend, who by his advice and counsels may guide us in our actions and protect us from the ambushes and deceits of the wicked one. He will be to us a treasure of wisdom and consolation in our afflictions, our sorrows, and our failures. He will serve as a medicine to ease and comfort our hearts in our spiritual disorders. He will guard us from evil, and make our good still better. Should any infirmity befall us, he will assist in our recovery and prevent its being unto death.

Who shall find this friend? "They that fear the Lord," answers the wise man; that is, the humble, who earnestly desire their spiritual advancement. Since it concerns you so much, Philothea, to travel with a good guide on this holy road to devotion, beseech God with the greatest insistence to furnish you with one who may be according to His own heart. You may be assured that He who sent an angel from heaven, as He did to young Tobias, will give you one that is good and faithful.

Now, such a guide ought always to be an angel to you. That is, when you have found him, do not look upon him as a mere man. Do not place your confidence in his human learning, but in God who befriends you and speaks to you by means of this man, putting in his heart and in his mouth whatever shall be requisite for your happiness. Hence, you ought to pay as much attention to him as to an angel who would come down from heaven to conduct you thither. Open your heart to him with all sincerity and fidelity, manifesting clearly and explicitly the state of your conscience without fiction or dissimulation. By this means your good actions will be examined and approved and your evil ones will be corrected and remedied. You will be comforted and strengthened in your afflictions, and moderated and regulated in your consolations. Place great confidence in him, but let it be united with a holy reverence, so that the reverence may not diminish the confidence nor the confidence oppose the reverence. Confide in him with the respect of a daughter for her father; respect him with the confidence of a son in his mother. In a word, your friendship for him ought to be strong and sweet, entirely holy, entirely sacred, entirely divine, and entirely spiritual.

"For this end, choose one among a thousand," says Avila. I say, "Choose one amongst ten thousand," for there are fewer than can be imagined who are capable of this office. He must be full of charity, knowledge, and prudence. If any one of these three qualities is wanting in him, there is danger. But I say to you again: Ask him of God. Having found him, bless His Divine Majesty, remain constant, and seek no other, but proceed on with sincerity, humility, and confidence, for you will make a most happy journey.

V. THAT WE MUST BEGIN BY PURIFYING THE SOUL

"The flowers have appeared in our land, the time of pruning is come." What else are the flowers of our hearts, O Philothea, but good desires? Now, as soon as they appear

we must put our hand to the pruning knife, to remove from
our conscience all dead and superfluous works. Before she
could marry an Israelite, an alien maid was obliged to put
off the garment of her captivity, pare her nails, and shave her
hair. So also the soul that aspires to the honor of being the
spouse of the Son of God must "put off the old man, and put
on the new," by forsaking sin, and removing and cutting away
every obstacle which may prevent her union with God. The
beginning of a good state of health is to be purged of our sinful
humors.

St. Paul in a single moment was cleansed with a perfect
purgation. So also were St. Catherine of Genoa, St. Mary
Magdalen, St. Pelagia, and certain others. But this kind of
purgation is as miraculous and extraordinary in the order of
grace as the resurrection of the dead is in that of nature, and
therefore we ought not to expect it. The ordinary purification
and healing, whether of the body or of the mind, takes place
only little by little, by passing from one degree to another
with labor and patience. The angels upon Jacob's ladder had
wings; yet they flew not, but ascended and descended in order
from one step to another. The soul that rises from sin to devotion may be compared to the dawning of the day, which at its
approach does not expel the darkness instantaneously but only
little by little. The cure, says the aphorism, which is made
slowly is always the surest. The diseases of the heart, as well
as those of the body, come posting on horseback but depart
slowly and on foot.

Courage and patience, Philothea, are necessary in this
enterprise. Alas! how much are those souls to be pitied who,
perceiving themselves still subject to many imperfections after
having exercised themselves in devotion for a little while, begin
to be dissatisfied, troubled, and discouraged, and suffer their
hearts to be almost overcome with the temptation of forsaking
all and returning to their former course of life. On the other
hand, are not those souls also in extreme danger who, by a
contrary temptation, believe themselves quite purified from
their imperfections the first day of their purgation, who think
themselves perfect, though as yet scarcely formed, and who
presume to fly without wings? O Philothea! in what danger are

they of relapsing, being so soon out of the physician's hands? "It is vain for you to rise before light," says the prophet, "rise after you have sitten." He himself practiced this lesson, for having been already washed and cleansed, he desired to be washed and cleansed still more and more.

The exercise of purifying the soul neither can nor should end unless with our life itself. Let us not be disturbed at the sight of our imperfections, for our perfection consists in fighting against them. And how can we fight against them without seeing them, or overcome them without encountering them? Our victory consists not in being unconscious of them, but in refusing to consent to them, and not to consent to them is to be displeased with them. It is absolutely necessary for the exercise of our humility that we should sometimes suffer wounds in this spiritual warfare. But we are never overcome, unless we lose either our life or our courage. Imperfections or venial sins cannot deprive us of our spiritual life, for this is lost only by mortal sin. It only remains that we do not lose our courage. Save me, O Lord! said David, from cowardice and discouragement. It is happy for us that in this warfare we shall always be victorious, provided that we are willing to fight.

VI. OF THE FIRST PURGATION, WHICH IS THAT OF MORTAL SIN

The first purgation that must be made is that of sin; the means to make it is the holy sacrament of penance. Seek the best confessor you can find. Then procure some of those books which have been composed for assisting sinners to make a good confession, such as Granada, Bruno, Arias, or Auger. Read them carefully, and remark, from point to point, in what you have offended from the time you came to the use of reason to the present hour. Should you distrust your memory, write down what you have observed. Having thus prepared and collected together the peccant humors of your conscience, detest and renounce them with the greatest contrition and sorrow that your heart can conceive. Have in mind these four things: that by sin you have lost the grace of God; that you have given up your place in paradise; that you have chosen the eternal pains of hell; and that you have renounced the eternal love of God.

You see, Philothea, that I speak of a general confession of your whole life. I grant freely that this is not absolutely necessary. Yet I look upon it as exceedingly profitable in the beginning, and therefore, I earnestly advise it. It frequently happens that the ordinary confessions of those who lead a common, worldly life are full of considerable defects, for they often make little or no preparation and do not have sufficient contrition. Nay, it too frequently happens that they go to confession with a tacit determination of returning to sin. This is apparent from their subsequent unwillingness to avoid the occasions of sin and to make use of the means necessary for the amendment of their life. Beyond this a general confession calls us to the knowledge of ourselves. It excites in us a wholesome shame for our past life. It makes us marvel at the mercy of God, who has so patiently waited for us. It calms our hearts, composes our minds, excites us to good resolutions, affords occasion to our spiritual father to give us advice more suitable to our condition, and opens our heart to declare ourselves with more confidence in our succeeding confessions.

Since I speak of a general renovation of your heart and of a universal conversion of your soul to God by undertaking a devout life, it appears necessary, Philothea, to exhort you to this general confession.

VII. OF THE SECOND PURGATION, WHICH IS THAT OF AFFECTION FOR SIN

Although all the Israelites departed in effect out of the land of Egypt, yet they did not all depart in affection. For this reason many of them regretted in the wilderness their want of the onions and fleshpots of Egypt. In like manner, there are penitents who in effect depart from sin, but do not quit it in affection. They propose to sin no more, but it is with a certain reluctance of heart that they deprive themselves of, or abstain from, an unhappy pleasure in sin. Their heart renounces sin and shuns it, but it often looks back upon it, as Lot's wife did toward Sodom. They abstain from sin, as sick men do from melons. These they forbear to taste because the physician threatens them with death if they eat them, but it is with the utmost reluctance that they refrain from them. They talk of

them incessantly and are unwilling to believe them hurtful.
They wish at heart to smell them, and they think those who
may eat them to be happy. Such is the case with weak and lazy
penitents; they abstain for some time from sin, but it is with
regret. They would rejoice if they could sin and still not be
damned. They speak of sin with a certain petulance and with
relish for it, and think those who sin are at peace with themselves. The man who was resolved to be revenged on another
changes his mind in confession. Shortly afterward you may
find him among his friends, talking with pleasure to them of
his quarrel and saying, "Had it not been for the fear of God,
he would have done this or that," and that "the divine law in
this matter of forgiving is hard—would to God it were allowed
to revenge oneself!" Ah! who does not see, that although he
be delivered from the sin, he is still entangled by an affection
for it. He is in effect out of Egypt, but he is still there in affection, longing after its garlic and onions, with which he once
glutted himself. He is like a woman who has detested her impure love but is nevertheless pleased with being courted and
followed. Alas, in how great danger are all such people!

XVI. THE EIGHTH MEDITATION—ON PARADISE

PREPARATION

1. Place yourself in the presence of God.
2. Beseech Him to inspire you with His grace.

CONSIDERATIONS

1. Consider a beautiful, clear night, and reflect how
delightful it is to behold the sky bespangled with all that
multitude and variety of stars. Next, join this beautiful sight
with that of a fine day, so that the brightness of the sun may
not prevent the clear view of the stars or of the moon. Then
say boldly that all this beauty put together is nothing when
compared with the excellence of the great paradise. Oh how
lovely, how desirable is this place! Oh, how precious is this
city!

2. Consider the glory, the beauty, and the number of the
citizens and inhabitants of this happy country: those millions

of millions of angels, of cherubim and seraphim; those bands of apostles, prophets, martyrs, confessors, virgins, and holy women. The multitude is innumerable. O how glorious is this company! The least of them is more beautiful to behold than the whole world. What a sight then will it be to behold them all! But, O my God! how happy are they! Unceasingly they sing the sweet song of eternal love! They always enjoy a constant happiness. They give to one another unspeakable contentment and live in the consolation of a happy and indissoluble union.

3. In fine, consider how happy the blessed are in the enjoyment of God. He favors them forever with a sight of His lovely presence and therby infuses into their hearts a depth of delights. How great a felicity must it be to be united to their first principle! They are like happy birds, who fly and sing perpetually in the air of His divinity, which encompasses them on all sides with incredible pleasure. There everyone does his utmost and sings without envy the praises of his Creator. Blessed be Thou forever, O sweet and sovereign Creator and Savior, who art so good, and who dost communicate to us so generously the everlasting treasures of Thy glory! And God likewise blesses with an everlasting blessing all His saints. Blessed forever be ye, He says, My beloved creatures, who have served Me and who will praise Me eternally with such great love and zeal.

AFFECTIONS AND RESOLUTIONS

1. Admire and praise this heavenly country. O how beautiful art thou, my dear Jerusalem, and how happy are thy inhabitants!

2. Reproach your heart with the lack of courage with which it has hitherto strayed so far away from the path leading to this glorious dwelling. Oh! why have I gone so far from my sovereign happiness? Ah! wretch that I am, for these false and trifling pleasures I have a thousand and a thousand times turned my back upon those eternal and infinite delights. Was I not mad to despise such precious blessings for such empty and contemptible desires?

3. Aspire with fervor to this most delightful abode. Ah! my good and sovereign Lord; since it has pleased Thee at length to direct my steps into Thy ways, never hereafter will I turn back from them. Let us go, O my dear soul, let us go toward this blessed land which is promised us! What are we doing in Egypt?

4. I will therefore unburden myself of everything that may divert or retard me on this journey.

5. I will perform such and such things as may conduct me thither. Give thanks; offer; pray.

THE SECOND PART OF THE INTRODUCTION

I. OF THE NECESSITY OF PRAYER

1. Prayer places our understanding in the divine brightness and light and exposes our will to the warmth of heavenly love. There is nothing that so effectually purges our understanding of its ignorance and our will of its depraved affections. It is the holy water that by its flow makes the plants of our good desires grow green and flourish, that cleanses our souls of their imperfections, and that quenches the thirst of passion in our hearts.

2. Above all, I recommend to you mental prayer, the prayer of the heart, and particularly that which concerns the life and Passion of our Lord. By making Him often the subject of your meditation, your whole soul will be filled with Him. You will learn His ways and frame all your actions according to His model. He is "the light of the world." It is, therefore, in Him and by Him and for Him that we must be instructed and enlightened. He is the tree of desire, in whose shade we must refresh ourselves. He is the living fountain of Jacob, in which we may wash away all our stains. In fine, little children, by hearing their mothers talk, lisp at first and learn at length to speak their language. So also by keeping close to our Savior, by meditation and by observing His words, actions, and affections, by the help of His grace, we shall learn to speak, to act, and to will like Him.

Here we must stop, Philothea, as we cannot find access to God the Father except through this gate. Just as the glass in a mirror could never stop our eyes unless the back were tinned or leaded, so we could never by our own efforts contemplate in this world the godhead, had it not been united to the sacred humanity of our Savior, whose life and death is the most suitable, delightful, sweet, and profitable object that we can choose for our ordinary meditation. Not for nothing did our Savior call Himself "the bread that came down from heaven." As bread is to be eaten with all sorts of meat, so our Savior should be the subject of our meditation, consideration, and imitation in all our prayers and actions. For the purpose of meditation, His life and death have been disposed and distributed into distinct points by several authors. Those whom I recommend to you are St. Bonaventure, Bellintani, Bruno, Capilia, Granada, and Du Pont.

3. Employ an hour every day before dinner in this spiritual exercise, or, if convenient, early in the morning, when your mind will be less distracted, and more fresh after the repose of the night. Do not extend it beyond an hour, unless your spiritual director expressly tells you to do so.

4. If you can perform this exercise in church, and if you find there sufficient tranquillity, that is the most convenient and comfortable place possible. The reason is that neither father nor mother, nor wife nor husband, nor anyone else, could well prevent you from spending one hour in church. On the other hand, being perhaps under obligation to them, you could not promise yourself so free an hour at home.

5. Begin all your prayers, whether mental or vocal, in the presence of God. Abide by this rule without exception and you will soon see how profitable it is to you.

6. If you follow my advice, Philothea, you will say your *Pater,* your *Ave,* and your *Credo* in Latin. At the same time learn perfectly to comprehend the meaning of the words in your own language, so that while saying them in the common language of the Church, you may at the same time relish the wonderful and delicious meaning of those holy prayers. These prayers must be said with a deeply fixed attention and with your affections aroused by the sense of their words. Do not hasten to say many things, but strive to speak from your

heart. For one single *Pater* said with feeling has greater worth than many said quickly and in haste.

7. The rosary is a very useful form of prayer, provided you know how to say it properly. To do this, procure one of those little books which teach the manner of reciting it. It is good also to say the litanies of our Lord, of our Lady, and of the saints, and other vocal prayers, which may be found in approved manuals and books of hours. However, if you have the gift of mental prayer, you should always give it the first place. If you cannot say your vocal prayers, either through multiplicity of duties or some other cause, you must not be troubled on that account. Rest content with saying simply, either before or after your meditation, the Lord's Prayer, the Angelic Salutation, and the Apostles' Creed.

8. If during vocal prayer you feel your heart drawn and invited to mental prayer, do not refuse to take it up. Let your mind turn gently that way, without being concerned at not finishing the vocal prayers you intended to say. The choice you have made is more pleasing to God and more profitable to your soul. I except the Divine Office, if you are obliged to say it. In that case you must fulfill your obligation.

9. If it should happen through a pressure of business or some other cause that your entire morning should pass away without allowing you leisure for the exercise of mental prayer—and this you should not let happen if it is possible to prevent it—try to repair this loss at some remote hour after dinner. By doing it immediately after dinner before digestion is advanced, you would be drowsy and your health might be injured. But if in the whole course of the day you cannot do this, you must repair this loss by multiplying your ejaculatory prayers, reading some book of devotion, or performing some penance, which may prevent the ill consequences attending this failure. Along with this, make a firm resolution to return to your custom the following day.

II. A SHORT METHOD FOR MEDITATION: AND FIRST OF THE PRESENCE OF GOD, WHICH IS THE FIRST POINT OF THE PREPARATION

Perhaps, Philothea, you do not know how to pray mentally. Unfortunately this is a thing that few in our age know how to do. For this reason I give you a short and plain method, until by practice or by reading some of the many good books that have been composed on this subject, you may be more fully instructed. I shall explain to you first the preparation. This consists of two points: first, to place yourself in the presence of God; and second, to invoke His assistance, to assist you to place yourself in the presence of God, I propose four principal means which you will be able to use in this beginning.

The first consists in a lively and attentive apprehension of God's absolute presence. That is, that God is in all things and in every place. There is not a place in the world in which he is not most truly present. Just as birds, wherever they fly, always meet with the air, so we, wherever we go, or wherever we are, always find God present. Everyone knows this truth, but everyone does not fully reflect upon it. Blind men, who do not see a prince who is present among them, behave themselves with respect when they are told of his presence. However, because they do not see him, they easily forget that he is present, and having forgotten it, they still more easily lose their respect for him. Alas, Philothea, we do not see God, who is present with us. Although faith assures us of His presence, yet because we do not behold Him with our eyes, we too often forget Him and behave as though He were very far away from us. Although we well know that He is present in all things, because we do not reflect upon it we act as if we did not know it. That is why before prayer we must always excite in our souls a lively thought and apprehension of the presence of God. This was the mind of David when he exclaimed: "If I ascend up into heaven, O my God, Thou art there; if I descend into hell, Thou art there!" Thus we should use the words of Jacob, who when he saw the sacred ladder said: "Oh, how terrible is this place! Indeed the Lord is in this place, and I knew it not." He meant that he did not reflect on His presence, for he could not have been ignorant that God was present everywhere. Therefore, when you come to prayer, you must say with your whole heart and in your heart: O my heart, my heart, God is truly here!

The second means to place yourself in His sacred presence is to reflect that God is not only in the place in which you are, but that He is, in a most particular manner, in your heart and in the very center of your spirit. This He enlivens and animates by His divine presence, being there as the heart of your heart and as the spirit of your spirit. For just as the soul, being diffused through the whole body, is present in every part thereof and yet resides in a special manner in the heart, so likewise God is present to all things and yet resides in a more particular manner in our spirit. For this reason David calls him "the God of his heart." And St. Paul says that it is in God "we live, and move, and are." Therefore, in consideration of this truth, excite in your heart a profound reverence towards God, who is there so intimately present.

A third means is to consider our Savior in His humanity, looking down from heaven on all mankind, but especially on Christians, who are His children, and more particularly on such as are at prayer, whose actions and behavior He observes. This is by no means a mere imagination, but a very truth. Although we see Him not, yet it is true that He beholds us from above. It was thus that St. Stephen saw Him at the time of his martyrdom. Thus we may truly say with the Spouse: "Behold he standeth behind our wall, looking through the windows, looking through the lattices."

A fourth method consists in making use of the imagination, by representing to ourselves our Savior in His sacred humanity, as if He were near us, as we sometimes imagine a friend to be present, saying, "I imagine that I see him who has done this or that," or "It seems to me that I see him," or something similar. If the Most Holy Sacrament of the Altar is present, then this presence is real and not purely imaginary. The species and appearances of bread are like a tapestry behind which our Lord, being really present, sees and observes us, although we cannot actually see Him.

Hence, you will employ one of these four means of placing yourself in the presence of God before prayer. Do not use them all at once, but one at a time, and that briefly and simply.

III. OF INVOCATION, THE SECOND POINT OF THE PREPARATION

The invocation is made in the following way. Your soul knows that it is in the presence of God and prostrates itself before Him with the most profound reverence. It acknowledges itself most unworthy to appear before so sovereign a Majesty. Yet knowing that this same goodness wills that it should do so, it implores His grace to serve and adore Him well in this meditation. For this end you may use some short, burning words, such as these words of David: "Cast me not, O God, away from Thy face; and take not Thy Holy Spirit from me." "Make Thy face to shine upon Thy servant," "and I will consider the wondrous things of Thy law. Give me understanding, and I will search Thy law; and I will keep it with my whole heart. I am Thy servant: give me understanding," and similar words. I would also advise you to invoke your guardian angel, as well as the holy saints who had part in the mystery on which you meditate. For example, in meditating on the death of our Lord, you may invoke our Lady, St. John, the Magdalen, and the good thief, begging that the affections and interior movements which they then conceived may be communicated to you. Also, in meditating on your own death you may invoke your guardian angel, who will then be with you, beseeching him to inspire you with proper considerations; and so of other mysteries.

IV. ON PROPOSING THE SUBJECT OF THE MYSTERY, THE THIRD POINT OF PREPARATION

After these two general points in the preparation, there remains a third, which is not common to every kind of meditation. It is the one that some call "the composition of place" and others "the interior lesson." This is nothing else but to represent to your imagination the whole of the mystery on which you desire to meditate as if it really passed in your presence. For example, if you wish to meditate on our Lord on the Cross, imagine that you are on Mount Calvary, and that you there behold and hear all that was done or said on the day of the Passion. Or, if you prefer it, for it is all one, imagine that in the very place where you are they are crucifying our Lord in the manner described by the holy evangelists. I say the same thing when you meditate on death, as I have noted in the meditation upon it, and so also on hell, or on any like mystery in which visible and sensible objects form a part of the subject. As to other mysteries, such as relate to the greatness of God, the excellency of the virtues, or the end for which we were created, which are invisible things, there is no question of using this kind of imagination. It is true that we may use some similitude or comparison to assist us in the consideration of these subjects, but this is attended with some difficulty. My intention is to instruct you in so plain and easy a manner that your mind may not be burdened too much with making such devices.

By means of the imagination we confine our mind within the mystery on which we meditate, that it may not ramble to and fro, just as we shut up a bird in a cage or tie a hawk by his leash so that he may rest on the hand. Some may perhaps tell you that it is better to use the simple thought of faith and to conceive the subject in a manner entirely mental and spiritual in the representation of the mysteries, or else to imagine that the things take place in your own soul. This method is too subtle for beginners. Therefore, until God raises you higher, Philothea, I advise you to remain in the low valley which I have shown you.

V. OF CONSIDERATIONS, THE SECOND PART
OF MEDITATION

After the act of the imagination there follows the act of the understanding, which we call meditation. This is nothing other than one or more considerations made in order to raise up our affections to God and heavenly things. Hence, meditation is different from study and other thought and reflections which do not have the love of God or our spiritual welfare for their object, but some other end or purpose, such as to acquire learning, to write, or to dispute. Having confined your mind within the limits of the subject on which you desire to meditate, as I have already said, either by means of the imagination, if the matter be sensible, begin to form considerations on it according to the models I have proposed to you in the foregoing meditations. Should your mind find sufficient savor, light, and fruit in any one of them, occupy yourself in it without going further. Do like the bees, who never quit a flower so long as they can extract any honey from it. If, after a little hesitation and trial, you do not succeed with one consideration according to your wishes, proceed to another. But go calmly and tranquilly in this matter without hurrying yourself.

VI. OF AFFECTIONS AND RESOLUTIONS, THE THIRD PART OF MEDITATION

Meditation produces pious motions in the will, or affective part of our soul, such as the love of God and of our neighbor, a desire for paradise and glory, zeal for the salvation of souls, imitation of the life of our Lord, compassion, admiration, joy, the fear of God's displeasure, of judgment, and of hell, hatred of sin, confidence in the goodness and mercy of God, and deep sorrow for the sins of our past life. In these affections our hearts should open themselves and expand as much as possible. If you wish to be aided in this, take in hand the first volume of the *Meditations* of Dom Andrea Capilia and consult its preface. In it he shows the manner of enlarging these affections. Père Arias does this more largely in his *Treatise on Prayer*.

Yet you must not dwell upon these general reflections, Philothea, without determining to reduce them to special and particular resolutions for your own correction and amendment. For example, the first word that our Lord spoke on the Cross will doubtless excite in your soul a holy desire to imitate Him, namely, a desire to pardon your enemies and to love them. But I now say that this will avail you little if you do not add to the desire a special resolution of this sort: "Well, then, I will not hereafter be offended at the vexatious words that such and such a man or such and such a woman, my neighbor, man or woman, my servant or my maid, may say to me; nor at some contemptuous treatment offered me by this one or that, nor resent in order to win him and soften him." And thus also of the others. By this means, Philothea, you will correct your faults in a short time, whereas by affections only, your amendment will be but slow and attended with great difficulty.

VII. OF THE CONCLUSION AND SPIRITUAL BOUQUET

Last of all, we must conclude our meditation by forming three acts, which must be done with the utmost humility. The first is the act of thanksgiving: returning thanks to God for the affections and resolutions that He has given us, and for His goodness and mercy, which we have discovered in the mystery meditated upon. The second is the act of offering. By this we offer to God His own goodness and mercy, the death, the Blood, and the virtues of His Son, and in union with them our own affections and resolutions. The third act is that of supplication. By this we beseech God and implore Him to communicate to us the graces and virtues of His Son and to bless our affections and resolutions so that we may faithfully execute them. We then pray for the Church, our pastors, relatives, friends, and others, imploring for that end the intercession of our Lady, of the angels, and of the saints. Lastly, as I have already observed, we conclude by saying the *Pater Noster* and the *Ave Maria*, which are the general and necessary prayers of all the faithful.

Besides all this, as I have already told you, you must gather a little devotional bouquet. This is what I mean. Those who have been walking in a beautiful garden do not willingly depart without gathering in their hands four or five flowers to smell and keep for the rest of the day. Thus ought we, when our soul has been entertaining itself by meditating on some mystery, to select one or two or three of those points in which we have found most relish and which are most proper for our advancement, to think frequently on them, and to smell them spiritually during the course of the day. This is to be done in the place in which we have been meditating, either remaining there apart, or walking by ourselves for some time after.

VIII. CERTAIN PROFITABLE INSTRUCTIONS ON THE SUBJECT OF MEDITATION

Above all things, Philothea, when you rise from meditation, remember the resolutions and decisions you have made and carefully put them into practice on that very day. This is the great fruit of meditation, without which it is often not only unprofitable but even hurtful. Virtues meditated upon but not practiced sometimes puff up our spirits and courage and make us imagine that we really are such as we have thought and resolved to be. This is doubtless true when our resolutions are lively and solid; they are not so, but rather vain and dangerous, when they are not put into practice. Therefore, we must by all means strive to practice them and to seek every occasion, little or great, to do so. For example, if I have resolved to gain by mildness the hearts of such as offend me, I will seek this very day an opportunity to meet them and greet them kindly. If I should not meet them, at least I will speak well of them and pray to God in their behalf.

After finishing this mental prayer be careful not to disturb your heart, lest you spill the precious balm it has received. My meaning is that you must for some time, if possible, observe silence and gently remove your heart from prayer to your other employments. Retain as long as you can the feeling and the affections that you have conceived. When a man has received some precious liquid in a porcelain vase and carries it home, he walks gently. He does not look aside but generally before him, for fear of stumbling against a stone or making a false step, and sometimes he looks upon the dish he carries, for fear of spilling the liquor. You must do the same thing when you finish your meditation. Do not let anything distract you, but look forward with caution. Or, to speak more plainly, should you encounter anyone with whom you are obliged to enter into conversation, there is not help for that and it is necessary to adjust yourself to it. However, you must watch over your heart, so that as little of the liquor of holy prayer as possible may be spilt.

You must even accustom yourself to know how to pass from prayer to those occupations which your state of life justly and lawfully requires, even though they are very different from the affections that you have received in prayer. I mean that the lawyer must learn to pass from prayer to pleading, the merchant to commerce, and the married woman to the care of her family, with so much ease and tranquillity that their minds may not be disturbed. Since prayer and the duties of your state of life are both in conformity with the will of God, you must learn to pass from the one to the other in the spirit of humility and devotion.

You must also know that it sometimes happens that immediately after the preparation you will feel your affections moved toward God. In this case, Philothea, you must yield to the attraction without following the method I have given you.

Generally speaking, consideration precedes affections and resolutions. However, when the Holy Spirit gives you the affections before the consideration, you must not then seek the consideration, since it is used for no other purpose than to arouse the affections. In a word, whenever affections present themselves, we must expand our hearts to make room for them, whether they come before or after considerations. Although I have placed the affections after all the considerations, I have done so merely to distinguish more plainly the parts of prayer. Otherwise, it is a general rule never to restrain the affections, but to let them have a free course whenever they present themselves. I say this not only with regard to the other affections, but also in respect of thanksgiving, oblation, and petition, which may likewise be used in the midst of the considerations. They must be restrained no more than the other affections, though afterward, for the conclusion of the meditation, they must be repeated. As for resolution, they are always to be made after the affections and just at the end of the whole meditation, before the conclusion. The reason is that in these we represent to ourselves particular and familiar objects. Hence, they would put us in danger of distractions, should we mingle them with our affections.

While we are forming our affections and resolutions, it is good to use colloquies, and to speak, sometimes to our Lord, sometimes to the angels and the persons represented in the mysteries, to the saints, to ourselves, to our own hearts, to sinners, and even to insensible creatures, as we see David do in his Psalms, and other saints in their prayers and meditations.

IX. OF THE DRYNESS WHICH WE SOMETIMES EXPERIENCE IN MEDITATION

Should it happen, Philothea, that you feel no relish or comfort in meditation, I urge you not to disturb yourself on that account, but sometimes open the door of your heart to vocal prayer. Lament your condition to our Lord, confess your unworthiness, and beseech Him to assist you. Kiss His image if you have it at hand, saying to Him those words of Jacob, "I will not let Thee go, O Lord! till Thou hast given me Thy blessing," or those of the Canaanean woman, Yea, Lord, I am a dog, for the whelps also eat of the crumbs that fall from the table of their masters. At other times, take up some spiritual book and read it with attention until your spirit is awakened and restored in you. Sometimes you may arouse your heart by some position or action of exterior devotion, such as prostrating yourself on the ground, crossing your hands before your breast, or embracing a crucifix, provided you be alone or in some private place.

If after all this you should receive no comfort, do not be disturbed, no matter how excessive the dryness may be, but continue to remain in a devout posture in the presence of God. How many courtiers enter a hundred times a year into the prince's presence chamber without hope of speaking to him, but merely to be seen by him and to pay him their homage. So ought we, my dear Philothea, to come to holy prayer, purely and merely to do our duty and to testify our fidelity. Should it please the Divine Majesty to speak to us and aid us by His holy inspirations and interior consolations, it would certainly be a great honor and the sweetest delight. But should it not please Him to grant us this favor, and should He leave us without speaking to us any more than if He did not see us or we were not in His presence, we must not on that account depart. On the contrary, we must continue with respect and devotion in the presence of His adorable Majesty. Unfailingly will He be pleased at our patience. He will note our diligence and perseverance, so that when we again come before Him, He will favor us with His consolations and make us experience the sweetness of His holy prayer. Yet if He should not do so, let us assure ourselves, Philothea, that it is an exceeding great honor for us to stand before Him and in His sight.

XIV. OF THE MOST HOLY MASS AND HOW WE OUGHT TO HEAR IT

1. Hitherto I have said nothing of the sun of all spiritual exercises, which is the most holy, sacred, and most sovereign Sacrament and Sacrifice of the Mass, the center of the Christian religion, the heart of devotion, and the soul of piety, and ineffable mystery that comprises within itself the abyss of divine charity and by which God really communicates Himself

to us and in a special manner replenishes our souls with His graces and favors.

2. When prayer is united to this divine Sacrifice, Philothea, it becomes so unspeakably efficacious as to cause the soul to flow with heavenly delights, "leaning upon her Beloved." He fills her with so much spiritual sweetness that she resembles, as it is said in the Canticle, "a pillar of smoke, of aromatic perfume and alspices, of myrrh· and frankincense, and of all the powders of the perfumer."

3. Endeavor, therefore, to assist at Holy Mass every day, that you may jointly with the priest offer up the Sacrifice of your Redeemer to God, His Father, for yourself and for the whole Church. "The angels," says St. John Chrysostom, "always attend in great numbers in order to honor this adorable mystery." By associating ourselves with them, with one and the same intention, we cannot but receive many favorable influences from such a society. The choirs of the Church triumphant and those of the Church militant unite themselves to our Lord in this divine action, so that with Him, in Him, and through Him, they may ravish the heart of God the Father and make His mercy all our own. What happiness it is to a soul devoutly to contribute her affections in order to obtain so precious and so desirable a treasure!

4. Should some strict duty prevent you from assisting in person at the celebration of this sovereign Sacrifice, endeavor at least to transport your heart to it and to assist at it by a spiritual presence. Sometime during the morning enter the church in spirit, if you cannot go otherwise, unite your intention with that of all Christians, and make the same interior acts of devotion in the place you are that you would make if you were really present in a church at the offering of Holy Mass.

5. To hear Mass in a proper manner, either actually or mentally: (1) From the beginning until the priest goes up to the altar, make your preparation with him. This consists in placing yourself in the presence of God, acknowledging your unworthiness, and begging pardon for your sins. (2) From the time he goes up to the altar until the Gospel, consider the birth and the life of our Lord in this world, by a simple and

general consideration. (3) From the Gospel until after the *Credo*, consider the preaching of our Savior and protest that you resolve to live and die in the faith and obedience of His holy word and in the communion of the holy Catholic Church. (4) From the *Credo* to the *Pater Noster* apply your heart to the mysteries of the Passion and death of our Redeemer. They are essentially represented in this Holy Sacrifice, and with the priest and the rest of the people, you must offer them to God the Father for His honor and for your own salvation. (5) From the *Pater Noster* to the Communion, strive to excite a thousand desires in your heart, ardently wishing to be united forever to our Savior by an everlasting love. (6) From the Communion to the end, return thanks to Jesus Christ for His incarnation, life, Passion, and death; and also for the love He testifies to us in this Holy Sacrifice. Implore Him to be forever merciful to you, to your parents, to your friends, and to the whole Church. Humbling yourself with your whole heart, receive devoutly the benediction which our Lord gives you through the ministry of His officer.

Should you prefer to meditate during Mass on the mystery you proposed for your consideration on that day, it is not necessary that you should change your thoughts to make all these particular acts. At the beginning, direct your intention to adore and offer up this Holy Sacrifice by the exercise of your meditations and prayer. In all meditations the aforesaid acts may be found either expressly or tacitly and equivalently.

John Henry Newman
1801-1890

John Henry Newman was born in London on February 21, 1801. He came from a comfortable Protestant family whose roots were Dutch and French. In 1816 he entered Trinity College, Oxford, where he won a scholarship at the end of his first year. He was ordained into the Anglican priesthood in 1825. Newman's intellectual and spiritual journey eventually led him into the Catholic Church (1845) and the Catholic priesthood (1847). A lifetime of preaching and writing have assured him a lasting place among the influential leaders of Catholicism in England. Criticized by Anglicans and Catholics alike, he knew the loneliness of a great mind that is often misunderstood. At the age of 78, he was made a cardinal by Pope Leo XIII, an action which vindicated much of his life's work. For the remaining ten years of his life he continued to live simply and quietly. He died in Birmingham, England in 1890.

Newman is already recognized for the tremendous influence he has had on the literature of the English language. It may be generations before the full impact of his theological vision and personal spirituality are adequately evaluated.

In 1833, Newman wrote "Lead Kindly Light," the brief three stanza poem that is perhaps the most famous of all his writings. It reveals much of the man's profundity. His was a life anchored in the sureness of Light as revelation of the God Who led him through the darkness of time and the human condition toward home. The sense of God's presence which had accompanied him from his adolescent years comes through in the poem. The awareness of God, with whom he could dialogue so personally, was the foundation for all that Newman wrote.

The following selection is taken from Newman's Apologia pro vita sua. *The original work, written in 1864, was composed of seven pamphlet size articles written for a weekly newspaper. They were a response to a Charles Kingsley, who alleged that Newman and all the Roman clergy taught that truth has no value. Actually the* Apologia *is far more than a mere response. It contains, in beautiful and eloquent language, the story of Newman's spiritual pilgrimage. Parts I and II of the book are concerned with Mr. Kingsley; Parts III through VI are the history of his religious opinions from childhood to age 44. The book concludes with a final answer to Mr. Kingsley.*

Newman writes clearly, directly and honestly. He speaks of his early education and religious formation, of the great revolution of mind that occurred within him and the pain of separation that necessarily accompanied it, of the death-bed atmosphere that surrounded his relationship to the Anglican Church from 1841 till his conversion in 1845.

Now, more than a hundred years since the writing of Newman's Apologia, *another dimension of the book's greatness has begun to surface. Newman was sensitive to the tragedy of the modern world and sought to address it. His themes of Christian rebirth, service, meekness, passiveness and innocence are all crucial to today's renewal of faith. Newman realized, more than most Christian thinkers, that one arrives home only by living such themes while completing the journey through the darkness to Light.*

APOLOGIA PRO VITA SUA

PART VI

HISTORY OF MY RELIGIOUS OPINIONS—1841-1845

From the end of 1841, I was on my death-bed, as regards my membership with the Anglican Church, though at the time I became aware of it only by degrees. I introduce what I have to say with this remark, by way of accounting for the character of this remaining portion of my narrative. A death-bed has scarcely a history; it is a tedious decline, with seasons of rallying and seasons of falling back; and since the end is foreseen, or what is called a matter of time, it has little interest for the reader, especially if he has a kind heart. Moreover, it is a season when doors are closed and curtains drawn, and when the sick man neither cares nor is able to record the stages of his malady. I was in these circumstances, except so far as I was not allowed to die in peace,—except so far as friends, who had still a full right to come in upon me, and the public world which had not, have given a sort of history to those last four years. But in consequence, my narrative must be in great measure documentary. Letters of mine to friends have come to me since their deaths; others have been kindly lent me for the occasion; and I have some drafts of letters, and notes of my own, though I have no strictly personal or continuous memoranda to consult, and have unluckily mislaid some valuable papers.

And first as to my position in the view of duty; it was this:—1. I had given up my place in the Movement in my letter to the Bishop of Oxford in the spring of 1841; but 2. I could not give up my duties towards the many and various minds who had more or less been brought into it by me; 3. I expected or intended gradually to fall back into Lay Communion; 4. I never contemplated leaving the Church of England; 5. I could not hold office in her, if I were not allowed to hold the Catholic sense of the Articles; 6. I could not go to Rome, while she suffered honours to be paid to the Blessed Virgin and the Saints which I thought incompatible with the Supreme, Incommunicable Glory of the One Infinite and Eternal; 7. I desired a union with Rome under conditions, Church with Church; 8. I called Littlemore my Torres Vedras, and thought that some day we might advance again within the Anglican Church, as we had been forced to retire; 9. I kept back all persons who were disposed to go to Rome with all my might.

And I kept them back for three or four reasons; 1, because what I could not in conscience do myself, I could not suffer them to do; 2, because I thought that in various cases they were acting under excitement; 3, while I held St. Mary's, because I had duties to my Bishop and to the Anglican Church; and 4, in some cases, because I had received from their Anglican parents or superiors direct charge of them.

This was my view of my duty from the end of 1841, to my resignation of St. Mary's in the autumn of 1843. And now I shall relate my view, during that time, of the state of the controversy between the Churches.

As soon as I saw the hitch in the Anglican argument, during my course of reading in the summer of 1839, I began to look about, as I have said, for some ground which might supply a controversial basis for my need. The difficulty in question had affected my view both of Antiquity and Catholicity; for, while the history of St. Leo showed me that the deliberate and eventual consent of the great body of the Church ratified a doctrinal decision, it also showed that the rule of Antiquity was not infringed, though a doctrine had not been publicly recognised as a portion of the dogmatic foundation of the Church, till centuries after the time of the apostles. Thus, whereas the Creeds tell us that the Church is One, Holy, Catholic, and Apostolic, I could not prove that the Anglican communion was an integral part of the One Church, on the ground of its being Apostolic or Catholic, without reasoning in favour of what are commonly called the Roman corruptions; and I could not defend our separation from Rome without using arguments prejudicial to those great doctrines concerning our Lord, which are the very foundation of the Christian religion.

The *Via Media* was an impossible idea; it was what I had called "standing on one leg;" and it was necessary, if my old issue of the controversy was to be retained, to go further either one way or the other.

Accordingly, I abandoned that old ground and took another. I deliberately quitted the old Anglican ground as untenable; but I did not do so all at once, but as I became more and more convinced of the state of the case. The Jerusalem bishopric was the ultimate condemnation of the old theory of the *Via Media;* from that time the Anglican Church was, in my mind, either not a normal portion of that One Church to which the promises were made, or at least in an abnormal state, and from that time I said boldly, as I did in my protest, and as indeed I had even intimated in my letter to the Bishop of Oxford, that the Church in which I found myself had no claim on me, except on condition of its being a portion of the One Catholic Communion, and that that condition must ever be borne in mind as a practical matter, and had to be distinctly proved. All this was not inconsistent with my saying that, at this time, I had no thought of leaving that Church; because I felt some of my old objections against Rome as strongly as ever. I had no right, I had no leave, to act against my conscience. That was a higher rule than any argument about the notes of the Church.

Under these circumstances I turned for protection to the note of sanctity, with a view of showing that we had at least one of the necessary notes, as fully as the Church of Rome; or, at least, without entering into comparisons, that we had it in such a sufficient sense as to reconcile us to our position, and to supply full evidence, and a clear direction, on the point of practical duty. We had the note of life,—not any sort of life, not such only as can come of nature, but a supernatural Christian life, which could only come directly from above. In my article in the *British Critic,* to which I have so often referred, in January 1840 (before the time of Tract 90), I said of the Anglican Church that "she has the note of possession, the note of freedom from party titles, the note of life,—a tough life and a vigorous; she has ancient descent, unbroken continuance, agreement in doctrine with the Ancient Church." Presently I go on to speak of sanctity: "Much as Roman Catholics may denounce us at present as schismatical, they could not resist us if the Anglican communion had but that one note of the Church upon it,—sanctity. The Church of the day [fourth century] could not resist Meletius; his enemies were fairly overcome by him, by his meekness and holiness, which melted the most jealous of them." And I continue, "We are almost content to say to Romanists, account us not yet as a branch of the Catholic Church, though we be a branch, till we are like a branch, provided that when we do become like a branch, then you consent to acknowledge us," etc. And so I was led on in the article to that sharp attack on English Catholics for their shortcomings as regards this note, a good portion of which I have already quoted in another place. It is there that I speak of the great scandal which I took at their political, social, and controversial bearing; and this was a second reason why I fell back upon the note of sanctity, because it took me away from the necessity of making any attack upon the doctrines of the Roman Church, nay, from the consideration of her popular beliefs, and brought me upon a ground on which I felt I could not make a mistake; for what is a higher guide for us in speculation and in practice, than that conscience of right and wrong, of truth and falsehood, those sentiments of what is decorous, consistent, and noble, which our Creator has made a part of our original nature? Therefore I felt I could not be wrong in attacking what I fancied was a fact,— the unscrupulousness, the deceit, and the intriguing spirit of the agents and representatives of Rome.

This reference to holiness as the true test of a church was steadily kept in view in what I wrote in connection with Tract 90. I say in its Introduction, "The writer can never be party to forcing the opinions or projects of one school upon another; religious changes should be the act of the whole body. No good can come of a change which is not a development of feelings springing up freely and calmly within the bosom of the whole body itself; every change in religion" must be "attended by deep repentance; changes" must be "nurtured in mutual love; we cannot agree without a supernatural influence;" we must come "together to God to do for us what we cannot do for ourselves." In my letter to the bishop I said, "I have set myself

116

against suggestions for considering the differences between ourselves and the foreign Churches with a view to their adjust-
ment." (I meant in the way of negotiation, conference, agitation, or the like.) "Our business is with ourselves,—to make
ourselves more holy, more self-denying, more primitive, more
worthy of our high calling. To be anxious for a composition of
differences is to begin at the end. Political reconciliations are
but outward and hollow, and fallacious. And till Roman Catholics renounce political efforts, and manifest in their public
measures the light of holiness and truth, perpetual war is our
only prospect."

According to this theory, a religious body is part of the
One Catholic and Apostolic Church, if it has the succession
and the creed of the apostles, with the note of holiness of life;
and there is much in such a view to approve itself to the direct
common sense and practical habits of an Englishman. However,
with events consequent upon Tract 90, I sunk my theory to a
lower level. What could be said in apology, when the bishops
and the people of my Church not only did not suffer, but
actually rejected primitive Catholic doctrine, and tried to eject
from their communion all who held it? after the Bishops'
charges? after the Jerusalem "abomination?" Well, this could
be said; still we were not nothing: we could not be as if we
never had been a church; we were "Samaria." This then was
that lower level on which I placed myself, and all who felt
with me, at the end of 1841.

To bring out this view was the purpose of four sermons
preached at St. Mary's in December of that year. Hitherto I
had not introduced the exciting topics of the day into the pulpit; on this occasion I did. I did so, for the moment was urgent;
there was great unsettlement of mind among us, in consequence
of those same events which had unsettled me. One special
anxiety, very obvious, which was coming on me now, was, that
what was "one man's meat was another man's poison." I had
said even of Tract 90, "It was addressed to one set of persons,
and has been used and commented on by another;" still more
was it true now, that whatever I wrote for the service of those
whom I knew to be in trouble of mind, would become on the
one hand matter of suspicion and slander in the mouths of my

opponents, and of distress and surprise to those, on the other hand, who had no difficulties of faith at all. Accordingly, when I published these four sermons at the end of 1843, I introduced them with a recommendation that none should read them who did not need them. But in truth the virtual condemnation of Tract 90, after that the whole difficulty seemed to have been weathered, was an enormous disappointment and trial. My protest also against the Jerusalem bishopric was an unavoidable cause of excitement in the case of many; but it calmed them too, for the very fact of a protest was a relief to their impatience. And so, in like manner, as regards the four sermons, of which I speak, though they acknowledged freely the great scandal which was involved in the recent episcopal doings, yet at the same time they might be said to bestow upon the multiplied disorders and shortcomings of the Anglican Church a sort of place in the revealed dispensation, and an intellectual position in the controversy, and the dignity of a great principle, for unsettled minds to take and use, which might teach them to recognise their own consistency, and to be reconciled to themselves, and which might absorb into itself and dry up a multitude of their grudgings, discontents, misgivings, and questionings, and lead the way to humble, thankful, and tranquil thoughts;—and this was the effect which certainly it produced on myself.

The point of these sermons is that, in spite of the rigid character of the Jewish law, the formal and literal force of its precepts, and the manifest schism, and worse than schism, of the ten tribes, yet in fact they were still recognised as a people by the Divine Mercy; that the great prophets Elias and Eliseus were sent to them, and not only so, but sent to preach to them and reclaim them, without any intimation that they must be reconciled to the line of David and the Aaronic priesthood, or go up to Jerusalem to worship. They were not in the Church, yet they had the means of grace and the hope of acceptance with their Maker. The application of all this to the Anglican Church was immediate;—whether a man could assume or exercise ministerial functions under the circumstances, or not, might not clearly appear, though it must be remembered that England had the apostolic priesthood, whereas Israel had no priesthood at all; but so far was clear, that there was no call at all for an Anglican to leave his Church for Rome, though he did not believe his own to be part of the One Church:—and for this reason, because it was a fact that the kingdom of Israel was cut off from the Temple; and yet its subjects, neither in a mass, nor as individuals, neither the multitudes on Mount Carmel, nor the Shunammite and her household, had any command given them, though miracles were displayed before them, to break off from their own people, and to submit themselves to Judah.

It is plain that a theory such as this, whether the marks of a divine presence and life in the Anglican Church were sufficient to prove that she was actually within the covenant, or only sufficient to prove that she was at least enjoying extraordinary and uncovenanted mercies, not only lowered her level in a religious point of view, but weakened her controversial basis. Its very novelty made it suspicious; and there was no guarantee that the process of subsidence might not continue, and that it might not end in a submersion. Indeed, to many minds, to say that England was wrong was even to say that Rome was right; and no ethical reasoning whatever could overcome in their case the argument from prescription and authority. To this objection I could only answer that I did not make my circumstances. I fully acknowledged the force and effectiveness of the genuine Anglican theory, and that it was all but proof against the disputants of Rome; but still like Achilles, it had a vulnerable point, and that St. Leo had found it out for me, and that I could not help it;—that, were it not for matter of fact, the theory would be great indeed, it would be irresistible, if it were only true. When I became a Catholic, the editor of a magazine who had in former days accused me, to my indignation, of tending towards Rome, wrote to me to ask which of the two was now right, he or I? I answered him in a letter, part of which I here insert, as it will serve as a sort of leave-taking of the great theory, which is so specious to look upon, so difficult to prove, and so hopeless to work.

"Nov. 8, 1845. I do not think, at all more than I did, that the Anglican principles which I advocated at the date you mention, lead men to the Church of Rome. If I must specify what I mean by 'Anglican principles,' I should say, *e.g.* taking

Antiquity, not the *existing Church,* as the oracle of truth; and holding that the *Apostolical Succession* is a sufficient guarantee of Sacramental Grace, without *union with the Christian Church throughout the world.* I think these still the firmest, strongest ground against Rome—that is, *if they can be held.* They *have* been held by many, and are far more difficult to refute in the Roman controversy, than those of any other religious body.

"For myself, I found *I could not* hold them. I left them. From the time I began to suspect their unsoundness, I ceased to put them forward. When I was fairly sure of their unsoundness, I gave up my Living. When I was fully confident that the Church of Rome was the only true Church, I joined her.

"I have felt all along that Bp. Bull's theology was the only theology on which the English Church could stand. I have felt, that opposition to the Church of Rome was *part* of that theology; and that he who could not protest against the Church of Rome was no true divine in the English Church. I have never said, nor attempted to say, that any one in office in the English Church, whether Bishop or incumbent, could be otherwise than in hostility to the Church of Rome."

The *Via Media* then disappeared for ever, and a new theory, made expressly for the occasion, took its place. I was pleased with my new view. I wrote to an intimate friend, Dec. 13, 1841, "I think you will give me the credit, Carissime, of not undervaluing the strength of the feelings which draw one [to Rome], and yet I am (I trust) quite clear about my duty to remain where I am; indeed, much clearer than I was some time since. If it is not presumptuous to say, I have . . . a much more definite view of the promised inward Presence of Christ with us in the Sacraments now that the outward notes of it are being removed. And I am content to be with Moses in the desert, or with Elijah excommunicated from the Temple. I say this, putting things at the strongest."

However, my friends of the moderate Apostolical party, who were my friends for the very reason of my having been so moderate and Anglican myself in general tone in times past, who had stood up for Tract 90 partly from faith in me, and certainly from generous and kind feeling, and had thereby shared an obloquy which was none of theirs, were naturally surprised and offended at a line of argument, novel, and, as it appeared to them, wanton, which threw the whole controversy into confusion, stultified my former principles, and substituted, as they would consider, a sort of methodistic self-contemplation, especially abhorrent both to my nature and to my past professions, for the plain and honest tokens, as they were commonly received, of a divine mission in the Anglican Church. They could not tell whither I was going; and were still further annoyed, when I would view the reception of Tract 90 by the public and the Bishops as so grave a matter, and threw about what they considered mysterious hints of "eventualities," and would not simply say, "An Anglican I was born, and an Anglican I will die." One of my familiar friends, who was in the country at Christmas 1841-2, reported to me the feeling that prevailed about me; and how I felt towards it will appear in the following letter of mine, written in answer:—

"Oriel, Dec. 24, 1841. Carissime, you cannot tell how sad your account of Moberly has made me. His view of the sinfulness of the decrees of Trent is as much against union of Churches as against individual conversions. To tell the truth, I never have examined those decrees with this object, and have no view; but that is very different from having a deliberate view against them. Could not he say *which* they are? I suppose Transubstantiation is one. A.B., though of course he would not like to have it repeated, does not scruple at that. I have not my mind clear. Moberly must recollect that Palmer thinks they all bear a Catholic interpretation. For myself, this only I see, that there is indefinitely more in the Fathers against our own state of alienation from Christendom than against the Trientine Decrees.

"The only thing I can think of [that I can have said] is this, that there were persons who, if our Church committed herself to heresy, *sooner* than think that there was no Church anywhere, would believe the Roman to be the Church; and therefore would on faith accept what they could not otherwise acquiesce in. I suppose it would be no relief to him to insist upon the circumstance that there is no immediate danger. Individuals can never be answered for of course; but I should think lightly of that man, who, for some act of the Bishops, should all at once leave the Church. Now, considering how the Clergy really are improving, considering that this row is even making them read the Tracts, is it not possible we may all be in a better state of mind seven years hence to consider these matters? and may we not leave them meanwhile to the will of Providence? I *cannot* believe this work has been of man; God has a right to His own work, to do what He will with it. May we not try to leave it in His hands, and be content?

"If you learn anything about Barter, which leads you to think that I can relieve him by a letter, let me know. The truth is this—our good friends do not read the Fathers; they assent to us from the common sense of the case: then, when the Fathers, and we, say *more* than their common sense, they are dreadfully shocked.

"The Bishop of London has rejected a man, 1. For holding *any* Sacrifice in the Eucharist. 2. The Real Presence. 3. That there is a grace in Ordination.

"Are we quite sure that the Bishops will not be drawing up some stringent declarations of faith? is this what Moberly fears? Would the Bishop of Oxford accept them? If so, I should be driven into the Refuge for the Destitute [Littlemore]. But I promise Moberly, I would do my utmost to catch all dangerous persons and clap them into confinement there."

Christmas Day 1841. "I have been dreaming of Moberly all night. Should not he and the like see that it is unwise, unfair, and impatient to ask others, What will you do under circumstances which have not, which may never come? Why bring fear, suspicion, and disunion into the camp about things which are merely *in posse?* Natural, and exceedingly kind as Barter's and another friend's letters were, I think they have done great harm. I speak most sincerely when I say, that there are things which I neither contemplate, nor wish to contemplate; but, when I am asked about them ten times, at length I begin to contemplate them.

"He surely does not mean to say, that *nothing* could separate a man from the English Church, *e.g.* its avowing Socinianism; its holding the Holy Eucharist in a Socinian sense. Yet, he would say, it was not *right* to contemplate such things.

"Again, our case is [diversing] from that of Ken's. To say nothing of the last miserable century, which has given us to *start* from a much lower level and with much less to *spare* than a Churchman in the 17th century, questions of *doctrine* are now coming in; with him, it was a question of discipline.

"If such dreadful events were realised, I cannot help thinking we should all be vastly more agreed than we think now. Indeed, is it possible (humanly speaking) that those, who have so much the same heart, should widely differ? But let this be considered, as to alternatives. *What* communion could we join? Could the Scotch or American sanction the presence of its Bishops and congregations in England, without incurring the imputation of schism, unless indeed (and is that likely?) they denounced the English as heretical?

"Is not this a time of strange providences? is it not our safest course, without looking to consequences, to do simply *what we think right* day by day? shall we not be sure to go wrong, if we attempt to trace by anticipation the course of divine Providence?

"Has not all our misery, as a Church, arisen from people being afraid to look difficulties in the face? They have palliated acts, when they should have denounced them. There is that good fellow, Worcester Palmer, can whitewash the Ecclesiastical Commission and the Jerusalem Bishopric. And what is the consequence? that our Church has, through centuries, ever been sinking lower and lower, till good part of its pretensions and professions is a mere sham, though it be a duty to make the best of what we have received. Yet, though bound to make the best of other men's shams, let us not incur any of our own. The truest friends of our Church are they who say boldly when her rulers are going wrong, and the consequences; and (to speak catachrestically) *they* are most likely to die in the Church, who are , under these black circumstances, most prepared to leave it.

"And I will add, that, considering the traces of God's grace which surround us, I am very sanguine, or rather confident (if it is right so to speak), that our prayers and our alms will come up as a memorial before God, and that all this miserable confusion tends to good.

"Let us not then be anxious, and anticipate differences in prospect, when we agree in the present.

"P.S. I think, when friends [i.e. the extreme party] get over their first unsettlement of mind and consequent vague apprehensions, which the new attitude of the Bishops, and our feelings upon it, have brought about, they will get contented and satisfied. They will see that they exaggerated things. . . . Of course it would have been wrong to anticipate what one's feelings would be under such a painful contingency as the Bishops' charging as they have done—so it seems to me nobody's fault. Nor is it wonderful that others" [moderate men] "are startled" [i.e. at my Protest, etc., etc.] ; "yet they should recollect that the more implicit the reverence one pays to a Bishop, the more keen will be one's perception of heresy in him. The cord is binding and compelling, till it snaps.

"Men of reflection would have seen this, if they had looked that way. Last spring, a very high churchman talked to me of resisting my Bishop, of asking him for the Canons under which he acted, and so forth; but those, who have cultivated a loyal feeling towards their superiors, are the most loving servants, or the most zealous protestors. If others became so too, if the clergy of Chester denounced the heresy of their diocesan, they would be doing their duty, and relieving themselves of the share which they otherwise have in any possible defection of their brethren.

"St. Stephen's [December 26]. How I fidget! I now fear that the note I wrote yesterday only makes matters worse by *disclosing* too much. This is always my great difficulty.

"In the present state of excitement on both sides, I think of leaving out altogether my re-assertion of No. 90 in my Preface to Volume 6, and merely saying, 'As many false reports are at this time in circulation about him, he hopes his well-wishers will take this Volume as an indication of his real thoughts and feelings: those who are not, he leaves in God's hand to bring them to a better mind in His own time.' What do you say to the logic, sentiment, and propriety of this?"

There was one very old friend, at a distance from Oxford, afterwards a Catholic, now dead some years, who must have said something to me, I do not know what, which challenged a frank reply; for I disclosed to him, I do not know in what words, my frightful suspicion, hitherto only known to two persons, as regards my Anglicanism, perhaps I might break down in the event, that perhaps we were both out of the Church. He answered me thus, under date of Jan. 29, 1842: "I don't think that I ever was so shocked by any communication, which was ever made to me, as by your letter of this morning. It has quite unnerved me. . . . I cannot but write to you, though I am at a loss where to begin. . . . I know of no act by which we have dissevered ourselves from the communion of the Church Universal. . . . The more I study Scripture, the more am I impressed with the resemblance between the Romish principle in the Church and Babylon of St. John. . . . I am ready to grieve that I ever directed my thoughts to theology, if it is indeed so uncertain, as your doubts seem to indicate."

While my old and true friends were thus in trouble about me, I suppose they felt not only anxiety but pain, to see that I was gradually surrendering myself to the influence of others, who had not their own claims upon me, younger men, and of a cast of mind uncongenial to my own. A new school of thought was rising, as is usual in such movements, and was sweeping the original party of the Movement aside, and was taking its place. The most prominent person in it was a man of elegant genius, of classical mind, of rare talent in literary composition:—Mr. Oakeley. He was not far from my own age; I had long known him, though of late years he had not been in residence at Oxford; and quite lately he has been taking several signal occasions of renewing that kindness which he ever showed towards me when we were both in the Anglican Church. His tone of mind was not unlike that which gave a character to the early Movement; he was almost a typical Oxford man, and, as far as I recollect, both in political and ecclesiastical views, would have been of one spirit with the Oriel party of 1826-1833. But he had entered late into the Movement; he did not know its first years; and, beginning with a new start, he was naturally thrown together with that body of eager, acute, resolute minds who had begun their Catholic life about the same time as he who knew nothing about the *Via Media,* but had heard much about Rome. This new party rapidly formed and increased, in and out of Oxford, and, as it so happened, contemporaneously with that very summer when I received so serious a blow to my ecclesiastical views from the study of the Monophysite controversy. These men cut into the original Movement at an angle, fell across its line of thought, and then set about turning that line in its own direction. They were most of them keenly religious men, with a true concern for their souls as the first matter of all, with a great zeal for me, but giving little certainty at the time as to which way they would ultimately turn. Some in the event have remained firm to Anglicanism, some have become Catholics, and some have found a refuge in Liberalism. Nothing was clearer concerning them, than that they needed to be kept in order; and on me who had had so much to do with the making of them, that duty was as clearly incumbent; and it is equally clear, from what I have already said, that I was just the person, above all others, who could not undertake it. There are no friends like old friends; but of those old friends, few could help me, few could understand me, many were annoyed with me, some were angry, because I was breaking up a compact party, and some as a matter of conscience, could not listen to me. I said, bitterly, "You are throwing me on others, whether I will or no." Yet still I had good and true friends around me of the old sort, in and out of Oxford too. But on the other hand, though I neither was so fond of the persons, nor of the methods of thought, which belonged to this new school, excepting two or three men, as of the old set, though I could not trust in their firmness of purpose, for, like a swarm of flies, they might come and go, and at length be divided and dissipated, yet I had an intense sympathy in their object and in the direction of their path, in spite of my old friends, in spite of my old life-long prejudices. In spite of my ingrained fears of Rome, and the decision of my reason and conscience against her usages, in spite of my affection for Oxford and Oriel, yet I had a secret longing love of Rome the mother of English Christianity, and I had a true devotion to the Blessed Virgin, in whose college I lived, whose altar I served, and whose immaculate purity I had in one of my earliest printed sermons made much of. And it was the consciousness of this bias in myself, if it is so to be called, which made me preach so earnestly against the danger of being swayed by our sympathy rather than our reason in religious inquiry. And moreover, the members of this new school looked up to me, as I have said, and did me true kindnesses, and really loved me, and stood by me in trouble, when others went away, and for all this I was grateful; nay, many of them were in trouble themselves, and in the same boat with me, and that was a further cause of sympathy between us; and hence it was, when the new school came on in force, and into collision with the old, I had not the heart, any more than the power, to repel them; I was in great perplexity, and hardly knew where I stood; I took their part; and, when I wanted to be in peace and silence, I had to speak out, and I incurred the charge of weakness from some men, and of mysteriousness, shuffling, and underhand dealing from the majority.

Now I will say here frankly, that this sort of charge is a matter which I cannot properly meet, because I cannot duly realise it. I have never had any suspicion of my own honesty; and, when men say that I was dishonest, I cannot grasp the accusation as a distinct conception, such as it is possible to encounter. If a man said to me, "On such a day and before such persons you said a thing was white, when it was black," I understand what is meant well enough, and I can set myself to prove an alibi or to explain the mistake; or if a man said to me, "You tried to gain me over to your party, intending to take me with you to Rome, but you did not succeed," I can give him the lie, and lay down an assertion of my own as firm and as exact as his, that not from the time that I was first unsettled, did I ever attempt to gain any one over to myself or to my Romanising opinions, and that it is only his own coxcombical fancy which has bred such a thought in him: but my imagination is at a loss in presence of those vague charges, which have commonly been brought against me, charges which are made up of impressions, and understandings, and inferences, and hearsay, and surmises. Accordingly, I shall not make the attempt, for, in doing so, I should be dealing blows in the air;

what I shall attempt is to state what I know of myself and what I recollect, and leave its application to others.

While I had confidence in the *Via Media,* and thought that nothing could overset it, I did not mind laying down large principles, which I saw would go further than was commonly perceived. I considered that to make the *Via Media* concrete and substantive, it must be much more than it was in outline; that the Anglican Church must have a ceremonial, a ritual, and a fullness of doctrine and devotion, which it had not at present, if it were to compete with the Roman Church with any prospect of success. Such additions would not remove it from its proper basis, but would merely strengthen and beautify it: such, for instance, would be confraternities, particular devotions, reverence for the Blessed Virgin, prayers for the dead, beautiful churches, rich offerings to them and in them, monastic houses, and many other observances and institutions, which I used to say belonged to us as much as to Rome, though Rome had appropriated them, and boasted of them, by reason of our having let them slip from us. The principle, on which all this turned, is brought out in one of the letters I published on occasion of Tract 90. "The age is moving," I said, "towards something; and most unhappily the one religious communion among us, which has of late years been practically in possession of this something, is the Church of Rome. She alone, amid all the errors and evils of her practical system, has given free scope to the feelings of awe, mystery, tenderness, reverence, devotedness, and other feelings which may be especially called Catholic. The question then is, whether we shall give them up to the Roman Church or claim them for ourselves. . . . But if we do give them up, we must give up the men who cherish them. We must consent either to give up the men, or to admit their principles." With these feelings I frankly admit, that, while I was working simply for the sake of the Anglican Church, I did not at all mind, though I found myself laying down principles in its defence, which went beyond that particular defence which high-and-dry men thought perfection, and though I ended in framing a sort of defence, which they might call a revolution, while I thought it a restoration. Thus, for illustration, I might discourse upon the "Communion of Saints" in such a manner (though I do not recollect doing so) as might lead the way towards devotion to the Blessed Virgin and the saints on the one hand, and towards prayers for the dead on the other. In a memorandum of the year 1844 or 1845, I thus speak on this subject: "If the Church be not defended on establishment grounds, it must be upon principles, which go far beyond their immediate object. Sometimes I saw these further results, sometimes not. Though I saw them, I sometimes did not say that I saw them; so long as I thought they were inconsistent, *not* with our Church, but only with the existing opinions, I was not unwilling to insinuate truths into our Church, which I thought had a right to be there."

To so much I confess; but I do not confess, I simply deny that I ever said anything which secretly bore against the Church of England, knowing it myself, in order that others might unwarily accept it. It was indeed one of my great difficulties and causes of reserve, as time went on, that I at length recognised in principles which I had honestly preached as if Anglican, conclusions favourable to the Roman Church. Of course I did not like to confess this; and, when interrogated, was in consequence in perplexity. The prime instance of this was the appeal to Antiquity; St. Leo had overset, in my own judgment, its force in the special argument for Anglicanism; yet I was committed to Antiquity, together with the whole Anglican school; what then was I to say, when acute minds urged this or that application of it against the *Via Media?* it was impossible that, in such circumstances, any answer could be given which was not unsatisfactory, or any behaviour adopted which was not mysterious. Again, sometimes in what I wrote I went just as far as I saw, and could as little say more, as I could see what is below the horizon; and therefore, when asked as to the consequences of what I had said, had no answer to give. Again, sometimes when I was asked, whether certain conclusions did not follow from a certain principle, I might not be able to tell at the moment, especially if the matter were complicated; and for this reason, if for no other, because there is great difference between a conclusion in the abstract and a conclusion in the concrete, and because a conclusion may be modified in fact by a conclusion from some opposite principle. Or it might so happen that I got simply confused by the very clearness of the logic which was administered to me, and thus gave my sanction to conclusions which really were not mine; and when the report of those conclusions came round to me through others, I had to unsay them. And then again, perhaps I did not like to see men scared or scandalised by unfeeling logical inferences, which would not have touched them to the day of their death, had they not been made to eat them. And then I felt altogether the force of the maxim of St. Ambrose, "Non in dialecticâ complacuit Deo salvum facere populum suum;"—I had a great dislike of paper logic. For myself, it was not logic that carried me on; as well might one say that the quicksilver in the barometer changes the weather. It is the concrete being that reasons; pass a number of years, and I find my mind in a new place; how? the whole man moves; paper logic is but the record of it. All the logic in the world would not have made me move faster towards Rome than I did; as well might you say that I have arrived at the end of my journey, because I see the village church before me, as venture to assert that the miles, over which my soul had to pass before it got to Rome, could be annihilated, even though I had had some far clearer view than I then had, that Rome was my ultimate destination. Great acts take time. At least this is what I felt in my own case; and therefore to come to me with methods of logic had in it the nature of a provocation, and, though I do not think I ever showed it, made me somewhat indifferent how I met them, and perhaps led me, as a means of relieving my impatience, to be mysterious or irrelevant, or to give in because I could not reply. And a greater trouble still than these logical mazes was the introduction of logic into every subject whatever, so far, that is, as it was done. Before I was Oriel, I recollect an acquaintance saying to me that "the Oriel Common Room stank of Logic." One is not at all pleased when poetry, or eloquence, or devotion, is considered as if chiefly intended to feed syllogisms. Now, in saying all this, I am saying nothing against the deep piety and earnestness which were characteristics of this second phase of the Movement, in which I have taken so prominent a part. What I have been observing is, that this phase had a tendency to bewilder and to upset me, and, that instead of saying so, as I ought to have done, in a sort of easiness, for what I know, I gave answers at random, which have led to my appearing close or inconsistent.

I have turned up two letters of this period, which in a measure illustrate what I have been saying. The first is what I said to the Bishop of Oxford on occasion of Tract 90:

"March 20, 1841. No one can enter into my situation but myself. I see a great many minds working in various directions and a variety of principles with multiplied bearings; I act for the best. I sincerely think that matters would not have gone better for the Church, had I never written. And if I write I have a choice of difficulties. It is easy for those who do not enter into those difficulties to say, 'He ought to say this and not say that,' but things are wonderfully linked together, and I cannot, or rather I would not be dishonest. When persons too interrogate me, I am obliged in many cases to give an opinion, or I seem to be underhand. Keeping silence looks like artifice. And I do not like people to consult or respect me, from thinking differently of my opinions from what I know them to be. And (again to use the proverb) what is one man's food is another man's poison. All these things make my situation very difficult. But that collision must at some time ensue between members of the Church of opposite sentiments, I have long been aware. The time and mode has been in the hand of Providence; I do not mean to exclude my own great imperfections in bringing it about; yet I still feel obliged to think the Tract necessary.

"Dr. Pusey has shown me your Lordship's letters to him. I am most desirous of saying in print anything which I can honestly say to remove false impressions created by the Tract."

The second is part of the notes of a letter sent to Dr. Pusey in the next year:

"October 16, 1842. As to my being entirely with A.B., I do not know the limits of my own opinions. If A.B. says that this or that is a development from what I have said, I cannot say Yes or No. It is plausible, it *may* be true. Of course the fact that the Roman Church *has* so developed and maintained, adds great weight to the antecedent plausibility. I cannot assert that it is not true; but I cannot, with that keen perception which some people have, appropriate it. It is a nuisance to me to be *forced* beyond what I can fairly accept."

There was another source of the perplexity with which at this time I was encompassed, and of the reserve and mysteriousness of which it gave me the credit. After Tract 90 the Protestant world would not let me alone; they pursued me in the public journals to Littlemore. Reports of all kinds were circulated about me. "Imprimis, why did I go up to Littlemore at all? For no good purpose certainly; I dared not tell why." Why, to be sure, it was hard that I should be obliged to say to the editors of newspapers that I went up there to say my prayers; it was hard to have to tell the world in confidence, that I had a certain doubt about the Anglican system, and could not at that moment resolve it, or say what would come of it; it was hard to have to confess that I had thought of giving up my living a year or two before, and that this was a first step to it. It was hard to have to plead, that, for what I knew, my doubts would vanish, if the newspapers would be so good as to give me time and let me alone. Who would ever dream of making the world his confidant? yet I was considered insidious, sly, dishonest, if I would not open my heart to the tender mercies of the world. But they persisted: "What was I doing at Littlemore?" Doing there? have I not retreated from you? have I not given up my position and my place? am I alone, of Englishmen, not to have the privilege to go where I will, no questions asked? am I alone to be followed about by jealous prying eyes, who note down whether I go in at a back door or at the front, and who the men are who happen to call on me in the afternoon? Cowards! if I advanced one step, you would run away; it is not you that I fear: "Di me terrent, et Jupiter hostis." It is because the Bishops still go on charging against me, though I have quite given up: it is that secret misgiving of heart which tells me that they do well, for I have neither lot nor part with them: this it is which weighs me down. I cannot walk into or out of my house, but curious eyes are upon me. Why will you not let me die in peace? Wounded brutes creep into some hole to die in, and no one grudges it them. Let me alone, I shall not trouble you long. This was the keen heavy feeling which pierced me, and, I think, these are the very words that I used to myself. I asked, in the words of a great motto, "Ubi lapsus? quid feci?" One day when I entered my house, I found a flight of undergraduates inside. Heads of houses, as mounted patrols, walked their horses round those poor cottages. Doctors of divinity dived into the hidden recesses of that private tenement uninvited, and drew domestic conclusions from what they saw there. I had thought that an Englishman's house was his castle; but the newspapers thought otherwise, and at last the matter came before my good Bishop. I insert his letter, and a portion of my reply to him:—

"April 12, 1842. So many of the charges against yourself and your friends which I have seen in the public journals have been, within my own knowledge, false and calumnious, that I am not apt to pay much attention to what is asserted with respect to you in the newspapers.

"In a " [newspaper], "however, of April 9, there appears a paragraph in which it is asserted, as a matter of notoriety, that a 'so-called Anglo-Catholic Monastery is in process of erection at Littlemore, and that the cells of dormitories, the chapel, the refectory, the cloisters all may be seen advancing to perfection, under the eye of a Parish Priest of the Diocese of Oxford.'

"Now, as I have understood that you really are possessed of some tenements at Littlemore—as it is generally believed that they are destined for the purposes of study and devotion—and as much suspicion and jealousy are felt about the matter, I am anxious to afford you an opportunity of making me an explanation on the subject.

"I know you too well not to be aware that you are the last man living to attempt in my Diocese a revival of the Monastic orders (in anything approaching to the Romanist sense of the term) without previous communication with me—or indeed that you should take upon yourself to originate any measure of importance without authority from the heads of the Church—and therefore I at once exonerate you from the accusation brought against you by the newspaper I have quoted, but I feel it nevertheless a duty to put it in my power to contradict what, if uncontradicted, would appear to imply a glaring invasion of all ecclesiastical discipline on *your* part, or of in-excusable neglect and indifference to my duties on *mine.*"

* * * * *

"Nov. 25, 1845. I hope you will have anticipated, before I express it, the great gratification which I received from your Eminence's letter. That gratification, however, was tempered by the apprehension, that kind and anxious well-wishers at a distance attach more importance to my step than really belongs to it. To me indeed personally it is of course an inestimable gain; but persons and things look great at a distance, which are not so when seen close; and, did your Eminence know me, you would see that I was one, about whom there has been far more talk for good and bad than he deserves, and about whose movements far more expectation has been raised than the event will justify.

"As I never, I do trust, aimed at anything else than obedience to my own sense of right, and have been magnified into the leader of a party without my wishing it or acting as such, so now, much as I may wish to the contrary, and earnestly as I may labour (as is my duty) to minister in a humble way to the Catholic Church, yet my powers will, I fear, disappoint the expectations of both my own friends, and of those who pray for the peace of Jerusalem.

"If I might ask of your Eminence a favour, it is that you would kindly moderate those anticipations. Would it were in my power to do, what I do not aspire to do! At present certainly I cannot look forward to the future, and, though it would be a good work if I could persuade others to do as I have done, yet it seems as if I had quite enough to do in thinking of myself."

Soon, Dr. Wiseman, in whose vicariate Oxford lay, called me to Oscott; and I went there with others; afterwards he sent me to Rome, and finally placed me in Birmingham.

I wrote to a friend:—

"January 20, 1846. You may think how lonely I am. 'Obliviscere populum tuum et domum patris tui,' has been in my ears for the last twelve hours. I realise more that we are leaving Littlemore, and it is like going on the open sea."

I left Oxford for good on Monday, February 23, 1846. On the Saturday and Sunday before, I was in my house at Littlemore simply by myself, as I had been for the first day or two when I had originally taken possession of it. I slept on Sunday night at my dear friend's, Mr. Johnson's, at the observatory. Various friends came to see the last of me; Mr. Copeland, Mr. Church, Mr. Buckle, Mr. Pattison, and Mr. Lewis. Dr. Pusey too came up to take leave of me; and I called on Dr. Ogle, one of my very oldest friends, for he was my private tutor when I was an undergraduate. In him I took leave of my first college, Trinity, which was so dear to me, and which held on its foundation so many who have been kind to me both when I was a boy, and all through my Oxford life. Trinity had never been unkind to me. There used to be much snapdragon growing on the walls opposite my freshman's rooms there, and I had for years taken it as the emblem of my own perpetual residence even unto death in my University.

On the morning of the 23rd I left the observatory. I have never seen Oxford since, excepting its spires, as they are seen from the railway.

St. Thérèse of Lisieux
1873-1897

"Love can only be repaid by love." This motto, which concludes the first part of Thérèse of Lisieux's Autobiography, suitably describes her life and spirituality. She was the little child totally dependent upon her loving Father God, totally dedicated to her loving Spouse Christ, and totally immersed in the love of the Spirit. Thérèse simply understood the meaning of love and lived it. She emptied herself completely of all self-interest and poured out her entire existence for God.

The life of Thérèse of Lisieux is as simple as the style of spirituality with which her name is identified. She lived 24 years, a brief lifetime by man's measure, yet enough to astound the world of Christianity. Thérèse was born in Alencon, France, in 1873. After the death of her mother in 1877, the Martin family moved to Lisieux. There Thérèse lived the remainder of her life. She entered the Carmel of Lisieux at the age of fifteen. Her years of quiet prayer and hidden suffering ended on September 30, 1897.

The autobiography of Thérèse, by which her life and spirituality became known to the world, was written between January 1895 and September 1896. Actually it is composed of three letters. The first was dedicated to her sister Pauline who, in the Carmel, was the Reverend Mother Agnes of Jesus. The second was written to her sister Marie, in religion Sister Marie of the Sacred Heart. The third was dedicated to the Reverend Mother Marie de Gongague. Thérèse relates her memories and interpretations of her childhood and life in Carmel. After the death of Thérèse, an edited version of the autobiography was circulated among Carmel convents. Mother Agnes had done the editing. Within a few years the story of little Thérèse had spread from one religious group to another. The cause for her beatification was introduced to the Holy See in 1914. She was beatified in 1923 and declared a saint in 1925.

The concept of God's Fatherhood is basic to Christianity. Thérèse took the concept literally and responded to it with a life of filial dependence. Spiritual Childhood, the term which best summarizes her life, is an uncomplicated but highly demanding way to perfection. It requires absolute confidence in God, unshakeable faith in the revelation of God's will through one's superiors and a corresponding total obedience, a recognition of and conviction of one's own nothingness. Love must be lived in all of its dimensions, the joyous and the sad, the bright and the dark, the extraordinary and the all too common. There is no room for sentimentality, weakness, or discouragement. One must begin each day anew with the resilience of a child.

By living all of this, Thérèse became a kind of sign to the twentieth century that there still is room in a world hardened by war and terror for the simplicity and naiveté of the child, and that the pressures created by the drive for efficiency and progress can be counterbalanced by the gathering of flowers.

The following selections from the Autobiography of a Saint *are taken from the complete and authorized text of the manuscript which was made available to the public in 1952.*

AUTOBIOGRAPHY OF A SAINT

CHAPTER XVI

INTERIOR PROGRESS

Hitherto, my life had been moving within the limits of a narrow circle, and now God had found the means to extricate me from it. It's with heart-felt gratitude that I look back over the way he made me travel; but even now, it has to be admitted, although I'd taken the big step forward, there were plenty of things I'd got to leave behind me. Here was I delivered from scruples, cured of that deplorable touchiness I've spoken of; but by now my mind was opening out. The sublime, the beautiful, had always appealed to me, but it wasn't till this period of my life that I was seized with a great desire for knowledge. Lessons and exercises were all very well, but they weren't enough for me; I took to reading on my own, especially in the two departments of history and science. Other subjects left me cold, but these two really gripped me, and in quite a short time I had amassed more knowledge than had come my way in the whole course of my schooling. Oh, it's quite true that this was 'frustration and lost labour, all of it'; that chapter of the *Imitation* where it talks about unnecessary curiosity was always coming back to my mind, but I went on all the same, persuading myself that I was of the right age for study, so there couldn't be any harm in it. And indeed, however much waste of time there may have been, I don't think God grudged it me; I was always careful to devote so many hours to reading and no more, so as to keep my itch for acquiring information within due limits.

The fact is, I was at the dangerous moment of girlhood, but God was looking after me. He might have applied to me the words he addresses to Jerusalem in the prophecy of Ezechiel: 'Who but I came upon thee, as I passed on my way? And already thou wert ripe for love; my troth I plighted to thee, and thou wert mine. Cloak of mine should be thrown about thee; oil I brought to anoint thee, clad thee with embroidery; a collar for that neck, on thy head a crown magnifical. Of wheat and honey and oil was thy nourishment; matchless beauty was thine, such beauty as brought thee to a throne.' Yes, that's what our Lord did for me; I could take up every word of what I've just written, and show how appropriately it describes his treatment of me; but the graces I've already mentioned are sufficient proof of it. Let me only say something about the *nourishment* he gave me, and gave me in such good measure.

For a long time past, what had kept me going was the wholemeal bread you get in *The Imitation of Christ*: I found nothing else really useful, until I began to discover the treasures hidden in the gospels. Dear *Imitation!* I knew nearly all the chapters by heart, but nothing would part me from my little book; it lived in my pocket during the summer, and in my muff during the winter, so that it had become quite an institution; it was a favourite joke at my aunt's to open it at random and 'put me on' at the first chapter you came to. But I was fourteen now, and developing a taste for wider reading; and God saw fit to supplement this dry bread with 'oil and honey' that would content me. I got that from Abbé Arminjon's book, *Fin du monde présent et mystères de la vie future*. The dear Carmelites had lent this book to Papa; I didn't ordinarily read his books, but I made an exception in this case and got his leave to have a look at it. Here was another great grace in my life; I can still see myself reading it at my school-room window, but the impression it made on me was something so intimate, so exquisite, that I can't attempt to describe it.

All the tremendous truths of religion, all the mysteries of eternity, came flooding into my soul with a feeling of happiness that had nothing to do with this world. I was getting a foretaste, already, of 'the welcome God has prepared for those who love him'—yes, heart can feel what eye has never seen; and realising that there is no proportion between those heavenly rewards and the cheap sacrifices we make in this life, I longed to love our Lord, love him passionately, shew him, while life still offered its unique chance, a thousand proofs of my love. I copied out several passages, about perfect love, and about the welcome

God means to give us at that moment when he himself becomes our rich, eternal reward; I repeated to myself, again and again, the tender words which had so entwined themselves round my heart.

Céline was by now the privileged confidante of my thoughts. Ever since Christmas we had been able to understand one another; the difference of age didn't matter, because I'd grown so much in size and still more because I'd grown so much in grace. In earlier days, I'd often complained because she wouldn't tell me her secrets, and she assured me I was too tiny; I'd have to grow 'by the whole height of that stool' before she could trust me. I was fond of getting up on to the magical stool in question, close to her side, and asking her to talk to me in confidence; but all my pains were wasted—there was still a barrier between us. But now our Lord wanted us to go forward side by side, so he united us by a bond closer than any ties of blood; we were to be sisters in spirit. We were like the maidens in the Canticle of St. John of the Cross, where the Bride cries out to her Lover:

'Tracking your sandal-mark,
The maidens search the roadway for your sign
Yearning to catch the spark
And taste the scented wine
Which emanates a balm that is divine.'

Light of foot we followed in our Lord's footsteps: the sparks of life which he spread so generously in our souls, the strong, satisfying wine which he gave us to drink, made transitory things vanish from our sight; our lips breathed tender aspirations which he, no other, had communicated to us.

Those were wonderful conversations we had, every evening, upstairs in the room with a view. Our eyes were lost in distance, as we watched the pale moon rising slowly above the height of the trees. Those silvery rays she cast on a sleeping world, the stars shining bright in the blue vault above us, the fleecy clouds floating by in the evening wind—how everything conspired to turn our thoughts towards heaven! How beautiful it must be if this, the obverse side of it, was so calm and clear! Perhaps it's silly of me, but that opening-up of our hearts has always reminded me of St. Monica and her son at Ostia, rapt in ecstasy as they contemplated the wonderful works of their Creator. I feel as if we'd received graces belonging to the same high order as some of those bestowed on the great Saints: as the *Imitation* says, God has two ways of making himself manifest; he shews himself to some people in a blaze of light, to others under a considerate veil of symbols and figures. Well, of course it was only this second kind of revelation he saw fit to give to Céline and me, but how light and transparent it seemed, this veil which hid him from our sight! How could there be room for doubt, how could there be any need of faith or hope? It was love that taught us to find, here on earth, the Bridegroom we searched for. 'He came upon us alone, and greeted us with a kiss: henceforward we need fear no contemptuous looks.'

Graces like these, as you would expect, bore abundant fruit in our lives; so that the path of holiness came easy and natural to us. At first, there would sometimes be a struggle, and I would make a wry face over it; but gradually that feeling disappeared, and I could renounce my own will, from the first, without difficulty. 'If a man is rich,' our Lord says, 'gifts will be made to him, and his riches will abound.' And so it was with me; if I would only correspond faithfully with each grace that was given me, a multitude of others would follow. He gave himself to me in Communion, at the time I'm speaking of, oftener than I'd have dared to hope. I made a rule of going whenever my confessor would let me, but allowing him to judge for himself, not asking it of him as a favour. (Nowadays, I should be more plucky, and take the opposite line; I'm quite sure that if a soul feels drawn towards frequent Communion, the confessor ought to be told about it. After all, our Lord doesn't come down from heaven every day just to wait there in a gold ciborium; he has found a much better heaven for his resting-place; a Christian soul, made in his own image, the living temple of the Blessed Trinity.)

Anyhow our Lord, finding me so eager and so well-disposed, saw to it that my confessor should encourage me to make my Communion four times a week all through that May; and when May was over, he raised it to five times in any week when a great feast came along. It was with tears of happiness that I left the confessional; our Lord himself, I felt, was determined to be my Guest. You see, I'd had a short shrift, saying nothing about my interior dispositions; why should I need any other guidance than his, when the way by which he led me was so direct, so clearly lit up? Directors, after all, were only faithful mirrors, to reflect our Lord's will in the conduct of souls; what if God meant to deal with me personally, without making use of any intermediary?

When a gardener takes a great deal of trouble with some fruit he wants to ripen before its time, he doesn't mean to leave it hanging on the tree; it must be served up at a banquet. And it was on the same principle that our Lord lavished his graces on such a tender plant as I was. Once, while he was on earth, he cried out in a transport of joy: 'Father, I give thee praise that thou hast hidden all this from the wise and the prudent, and revealed it to little children.' And now, just because I was so helpless and insignificant, he saw in me the opportunity for a startling exercise of his mercy. He brought himself down to my level, and taught me, all unobserved, the lesson of love. Oh dear, those learned people who spend a whole lifetime in getting up their subjects! How surprised they'd have been to hear that there was a secret which all their scientific method couldn't discover for them, the secret of perfection! It wasn't to be understood except by the poor in spirit; and here was a girl of fourteen who was ready to tell them about it.

CHAPTER XXIV

FIRST IMPRESSIONS OF CARMEL

Today, as yesterday, the whole family was there; we all heard Mass and went to Communion. Together, we made our Lord welcome in his sacramental presence; there was sobbing all around me, nobody but myself was dry-eyed. My own sensation was a violent beating of the heart which made me wonder whether I'd find it possible to move when we were beckoned to the convent door. I did just manage it, but feeling as if it might kill me; it's the sort of experience one can't understand unless one's been through it. There was no outward sign of all this; all the other members of the family kissed me good-bye, and then I knelt down and asked for a blessing from the best of fathers, who knelt down too, and blessed me with tears in his eyes. I think the angels smiled down on us, rejoicing at the sight of an old man giving up his daughter, in the very spring-time of life, to the service of God.

A few moments more, and then the doors of God's Ark shut behind me, and I was being embraced by all those dear nuns who had so long been mothers to me, whose example I was to take henceforward as my rule of living. No more waiting now for the fulfilment of my ambitions; I can't tell you what a deep and refreshing sense of peace this thought carried with it. And, deep down, this sense of peace has been a lasting possession; it's never left me, even when my trials have been most severe. Like all postulants, I was taken off to the choir as soon as I'd entered; the light there was dim, because the Blessed Sacrament was exposed, and I was conscious of nothing at first except a pair of eyes—the eyes of dear, holy Mother Geneviève resting upon me. I knelt for a moment at her feet, thanking God for the grace of being allowed to know a Saint; and then I went on with Mother Marie Gonzague.

In all the different parts of the convent, everything charmed me; it seemed so completely cut off from the world; and above all, how I loved my little cell! But there was nothing agitating about this delight I experienced, it was quite calm; as if the breeze was too light to rock my little boat on the water's surface, the sky too bright to admit of a single cloud. All that difficult time I'd gone through had been worth it after all, and I could go about saying to myself: 'I'm here for good, now, here for good!' There's nothing transitory about joy of this kind; it doesn't fade away with the honeymoon illusions of the noviciate. And indeed, I'd no illusions at all, thank God, when I entered Carmel; I found the religious life exactly what I'd expected it to be. The sacrifices I had to make never for a moment took me by surprise—and yet, as you know, Mother, those first footsteps of mine brought me up against more thorns than roses! Suffering opened her arms to me, and I threw myself into them lovingly enough. In the interrogation which is made before a nun is professed, I declared in the presence of the sacred Host that I'd come there to save souls, and above all to pray for priests. Well, if you want to secure any object, no

matter what it is, you've got to find the right steps for attaining
it. And our Lord let me see clearly that if I wanted to win souls
I'd got to do it by bearing a cross; so the more suffering came
my way, the more strongly did suffering attract me.

For the next five years, it was this way of suffering I had
to follow, and yet there was no outward sign of it—perhaps it
would have relieved my feelings a bit if other people had been
conscious of it, but they weren't. There'll be a lot of surprises at
the Last Judgement, when we shall be able to see what really
happened inside people's souls; and I think this way of suffering
by which God led me will be a revelation to the people who
knew me. Indeed, I can prove it; two whole months after I
entered, our director, Père Pichon, came down for the profession
of Sister Marie of the Sacred Heart; and he told me then that he
was astonished at God's dealings with my soul; he'd been looking
at me the evening before when I was praying in choir, and got
the impression that my fervour was still the fervour of childhood, and the way by which I was being led was one of unruffled
calm.

I derived a great deal of comfort from my interview with
this holy priest, but it was through a mist of tears, because I
found it so difficult to explain the state of my soul to him. All
the same, I made my general confession, the most thorough-
going I'd ever made; and at the end of it he used an expression
which echoed in my inward ear as nothing else ever had. 'In the
presence of Almighty God,' said he, 'and of the Holy Virgin,
and of all the Saints, I assure you that you've never committed a
single mortal sin.' Then he added: 'You must thank God for the
mercy he's shewn you: if he left you to yourself, you wouldn't
be a little angel any longer, you'd be a little demon.' I'd no
difficulty in believing that; I knew well enough how weak and
imperfect I was. But my gratitude knew no bounds; I'd always
been terrified that I might, somehow, have soiled the robe of
my baptismal innocence; and an assurance like this, coming
from a director after St. Teresa's own heart, so wise, so holy,
seemed to me to come straight from our Lord himself. Some
other words of his remained deeply imprinted on my heart: 'My
child, there's one Superior, one Novice-master you must always
obey—Jesus Christ.'

As it proved, that's what happened; and our Lord had to be my Director as well. I don't mean that I kept the state of my soul a secret from those who had charge of it; on the contrary, I wanted it to be an open book to them. But Reverend Mother was often ill, and couldn't devote much time to me. I know she was very fond of me, and said the nicest things about me; but God saw to it that she should treat me very severely without meaning to. I hardly ever met her without having to kiss the ground in penance for something I'd done wrong; and it was the same on the rare occasions when she gave me spiritual direction. This was a grace beyond all price; quite unmistakably, God was acting like this through his earthly representative. I don't know what would have become of me if I'd been treated as the pet of the community—which is what the outside world naturally supposed. Instead of learning to see my superiors as the expression of our Lord's will, I might have become interested in them as persons, and so my heart, which had always been fancy-free when I was in the world, might have been entangled by human attachments in the cloister. From all that I was mercifully preserved; actually I was very fond of Reverend Mother, but my affection for her was quite disinterested, pointing always upwards to the claims of a divine lover upon my soul.

Our Novice-mistress was a real saint, of the type they produced in the early days of Carmel. I was with her all day, because she had to teach me my work, and she was kindness itself to me; but somehow I could never open out to her. It was always an effort to me to take spiritual advice, simply because I'd no practice in talking about the affairs of my soul, and had no idea how to express what was going on inside me. One of the older nuns put her finger on this when she said to me with a smile, one day at recreation: 'Dear child, I can't imagine you have a great deal to confide to your superiors.' 'What makes you say that, Mother?' 'Why, there's such a simplicity about your soul. Of course, the nearer you approach perfection, the simpler you will become; nearness to God always makes us simple.' I think she was right, but my difficulty in opening out, whether it arose from simplicity or not, was a great trial to me. I realise that now, having become, since then, not less simple, but more capable of giving expression to my thoughts.

I said just now that our Lord was also my Director. Immediately upon entering Carmel I came to know the priest who was meant to help me in this way, but he'd scarcely had time to take me under his charge when he was sent overseas, and I lost him as soon as I'd found him. All I could do was to write a letter to him once a month, and get a letter back once a year. No wonder if I turned to him who is the Director of all those entrusted with the direction of souls and learned from him that secret which he hides from the wise and prudent, and reveals to little children.

How was it to thrive, this little wild flower planted out on the hill-side of Carmel? Only under the shadow of the Cross, watered by our Lord's tears and his precious blood, with his adorable Face for its sun, that Face overcast with sorrow. Till then, I'd never realised the depth of meaning there was in devotion to the Holy Face; it's to you, Mother, that I owe my fuller knowledge of it. Just as you were the first of us to join Carmel, so you were the first of us to sound the mystery of that love which the face of Jesus Christ conceals and reveals; and now you called me to your side, and I understood it all. I understood the true object of human ambition; our Lord hadn't wanted any kingdom in this world, and he shewed me that 'if you want to learn an art worth knowing, you must set out to be unknown, and to count for nothing:' you must find your satisfaction in self-contempt. If only my face could be hidden away, like his, pass unrecognised by the world; to suffer and to remain unnoticed, that was all I longed for. God has always shewn such mercy in the paths by which he has led me; he makes me want something badly, and then he proceeds to give it me—that's why the bitterest cup he puts to my lips always tastes delicious.

CHAPTER XXVI

THE EVE OF PROFESSION

So the days wore on, the days of my betrothal, and a long engagement it seemed to me! At the end of the statutory year I was warned not to think, at present, of asking to be professed, because the Father Superior was certain to refuse his consent; I must wait another eight months. Here was a sacrifice which didn't, at first sight, seem easy to make; but it wasn't long before I saw things in a clearer light. At that time, I remember, I was using as my meditation-book Père Surin: *On the Foundations of the Spiritual Life*. And it was borne in upon me during my prayer that this eagerness to make my profession was mixed up with a good deal of self-love. After all, I'd given myself over to our Lord for his pleasure, his satisfaction, not mine; and here was I trying to see if I could get him to do my will, not his. Another thing occurred to me too; a bride's got to have a trousseau against her wedding-day, and what sort of trousseau had I got? So I told our Lord: 'I'm not going to ask you to hurry on my profession; I'm ready to wait just as long as you want me to; only it mustn't be through any fault of mine that this union between us has to be put off. In the meantime, I'll work hard at trying to make myself a lovely wedding-dress, all set with jewels; and when you see that it's ready, I know quite well that nothing in heaven or earth will prevent you from coming to me, and making me, once and for ever, your bride.'

Ever since taking the habit, I'd been seeing my way much clearer towards perfection, especially where the vow of poverty is concerned. While I was still a postulant, it didn't worry me, always having the best of everything for my use and finding everything I wanted close to hand. Our Lord was directing me, and he let all that go on, because in the ordinary way he doesn't let us into the whole of his secret at one blow, he illuminates our minds gradually. In the early days of my own spiritual life, when I was about thirteen or fourteen, I used to wonder what further heights there could still be for me to climb; I didn't see how I could possibly get a clearer idea of what perfection meant. But of course I realised before long that the further you go along that road, the more conscious you are of the distance between you and the goal, and by now—well, by now I'm resigned to seeing myself always far from perfect; even glad, in a way, to see how much more there is to do.

But what was I saying? Oh yes, about the direction our Lord used to give me at this time. One evening after Compline I went to look for my bedroom lamp on the shelf where such things were kept, and it wasn't there; the Greater Silence had started, so there was no chance of getting it back; obviously one of the other sisters had picked it up by mistake for her own. I needed it badly, but somehow I didn't find myself repining over the loss of it; I counted it as a privilege, because after all, I said to myself, poverty doesn't mean just going without luxuries, it means going without necessities. All was dark around me, but there was a fresh infusion of light within. It was at this time that I developed a positive taste for ugly things and inconvenient things, so that I was really delighted when somebody took away the pretty little jug that used to stand in my cell, and replaced it by a big one that was badly chipped. I resisted, too, not without effort, the temptation to make excuses for myself; and it was all the harder for me because I didn't like having any secrets from my Novice-mistress. Here is the story of my first success in that direction, which really did cost me something, though it sounds petty enough. A little vase on a window-sill had got broken, and the Novice-mistress thought I must have swept it off; so she called my attention to it and told me to be more careful another time. And I kept my own counsel, simply kissing the floor and promising to be tidier in future. I was so far from being well grounded in good habits that little humiliations of this sort came difficult to me, and I had to console myself with the reflection that all these things would come out at the Day of Judgement. In the meantime, it appeared, you got no thanks for doing your duty, unless you were prepared to stick up for yourself, whereas the mistakes you made became public property at once!

I tried my best to do good on a small scale, having no opportunity to do it on a large scale; I would fold up the mantles which the sisters had left lying about, and make myself useful in ways of that sort. I had a real love of mortification, but I'm afraid it was a hunger which only came from undernourishment: I wasn't allowed to do anything in that line—when I was in the world, I never rested against the back of the chair I was sitting in, but now I was told this gave me a stoop. I expect if my superiors had prescribed a whole lot of penances for me, I should have lost my enthusiasm in no time. As it was, all I could do was to take such opportunities of denying myself as came to me without the asking; that meant mortifying self-love, a much more valuable discipline than any kind of bodily discomfort.

The refectory, in which I started work as soon as I had taken the habit, was always giving me the chance of putting my self-love where it belonged—that is, trampling it underfoot. It's true, dear Mother, that I had the comfort of sharing my work with you, and learning at first hand from your good example; but even this partnership had its drawbacks, because the rule had to be observed, and I wasn't in a position to tell you everything, to open my heart to you, as in the old days; this was Carmel, not Les Buissonnets. Anyhow, our Lady helped me with my wedding-dress, and as soon as it was ready all the obstacles disappeared; the Bishop sent his leave, the community agreed to take me, and the ceremony of my profession was fixed for September the 8th. Of course, dear Mother, all this brief account of myself which I've been giving you would have called for pages and pages if I'd set it out in detail, but those pages will never be written on earth. Before long, I shall be able to tell you about these things when we meet in our Father's house, in the heaven we so long for, you and I.

My wedding-dress was set with jewels, some old, one of them quite new and sparkling. By jewels I mean trials; Papa's wretched situation was already bad enough, and now it was complicated by a minor set-back as far as I was concerned—a small thing in itself, but a bitter disappointment. For some time dear Papa's health had been a little better; he was taken out for carriage-exercise, and there was even some question of his facing a railway journey to come and see us. Céline, I need hardly say, was all for its happening on the day when I took the veil. 'I won't tire him out,' she wrote, 'by making him follow the whole ceremony; I'll go and fetch him at the end of it and bring him up quietly to the grille, so that Thérèse can have his blessing.' How like dear Céline! 'Love never pleads inability; everything seems possible and everything seems allowable'—so different from human prudence, which hesitates at every turn and walks warily! This time, God allowed human prudence to have its way, as a suitable means of chastening me. So I had to go through my wedding ceremony as an orphan; I could only look upwards and appeal, with more confidence than before, to my Father in heaven.

Before mentioning all this, I ought really to have said something about the retreat I made before my profession; it brought no consolation with it, only complete dryness and almost a sense of dereliction. Once more, our Lord was asleep on the boat; how few souls there are that let him have his sleep out! He can't be always doing all the work, responding to all the calls made upon him; so for my own part I am content to leave him undisturbed. I dare say he won't make his presence felt till I start out on the great retreat of eternity; I don't complain of that, I want it to happen. It shews, of course, that there's nothing of the saint about me; I suppose I ought to put down this dryness in prayer to my own fault, my own lukewarmness and want of fidelity. What excuse have I, after seven years in religion, for going through all my prayers and my thanksgivings as mechanically as if I, too, were asleep? But I don't regret it; I think of little children lying asleep, under the loving eyes of their parents; I think of the surgeons who put their patients under an anaesthetic—in a word, I remember how God knows the stuff of which we are made, and can't forget that we are only dust. Anyhow, my profession retreat, like all the retreats I've made since, was a time of great dryness; and yet I felt that all the time, without my knowing it, God was shewing me the right way to do his will and to reach a high degree of holiness. You know, I always have the feeling that our Lord doesn't supply me with provisions for my journey—he just gives me food unexpectedly when and as I need it; I find it there without knowing how it got there. It simply comes to this, that our Lord dwells unseen in the depths of my miserable soul, and so works upon me by grace that I can always find out what he wants me to do at this particular moment.

Some days before I made my profession, I had the satisfaction of receiving the Holy Father's blessing. I'd asked for this favour through kind Brother Simeon, for Papa and for myself; I was very glad to have this opportunity of repaying the spiritual debt which I owed Papa for my journey to Rome. When the great day came, my wedding-day, there was no cloud on my horizon; on the eve of it, my soul had been in such tumult as I had never before experienced. Till then, I'd never known what it was to have a doubt about my vocation, and this was the ordeal I now had to face. That evening, as I made the Stations of the Cross after Mattins, my vocation seemed to me a mere dream, a mere illusion; I still saw life at Carmel as a desirable thing, but the devil gave me the clear impression that it wasn't for me; I should only be deceiving my superiors if I tried to persevere in a way of life I wasn't called to. Darkness everywhere; I could see nothing and think of nothing beyond this one fact, that I'd no vocation. I was in an agony of mind; I even feared (so foolishly that I might have known it was a temptation of the devil's) that if I told my Novice-mistress about it she'd prevent me taking my vows. And yet I did want to do God's will, even if it meant going back to the world; that would be better than doing my own will by staying at Carmel. Anyhow, I did get hold of the Novice-mistress, and stood there covered with confusion, trying to explain what I felt like. Fortunately she knew her way about better than I did, and set my doubts completely at rest; indeed, they disappeared the moment I had given expression to them—perhaps the devil had hoped I wouldn't bring myself to do it, and was defeated by my act of humility. Meanwhile I was determined that the act of humility should be complete, so I told Reverend Mother about this strange temptation, and she only laughed at me.

CHAPTER XXVII

PROFESSION: MOTHER GENEVIÈVE

On the morning of September the 8th, I seemed to be carried along on a tide of interior peace; and this sense of peace 'which surpasses all our thinking' accompanied the taking of my vows. This wedding of my soul to our Lord was not heralded by the thunders and lightning of Mount Sinai, rather by that 'whisper of a gentle breeze' which our father Elias heard there. I set no limit to the graces I asked for that day; I felt that I had the privileges of a queen, who can use her influence to set prisoners free, and reconcile the king to his rebellious subjects; I wanted to empty Purgatory, and convert sinners everywhere. I prayed so hard for my mother, for my dear sisters, for all the family; but especially for my poor father, now so sorely tried and still so holy. I offered myself to our Lord, asking him to accomplish his will in me and never let any creature come between us.

(Here, between the pages of the manuscript, is inserted the *billet de profession*, composed by the Saint and worn on her heart, according to custom, when she took her vows.)

September 6, 1680

Jesus, my heavenly Bridgegroom, never may I lose this second robe of baptismal innocence; take me to yourself before I commit any wilful fault, however slight. May I look for nothing and find nothing but you and you only; may creatures mean nothing to me, nor I to them—you, Jesus, are to be everything to me. May earthly things have no power to disturb the peace of my soul; that peace is all I ask of you, except love; love that is as infinite as you are, love that has no eyes for myself, but for you, Jesus, only for you. Jesus, I would like to die a martyr for your sake, a martyr in soul or in body; better still, in both. Give me the grace to keep my vows in their entirety; make me understand what is expected of one who is your bride. Let me never be a burden to the community, never claim anybody's attention; I want them all to think of me as no better than a grain of sand, trampled under foot and forgotten, Jesus, for your sake. May your will be perfectly accomplished in me, till I reach the place you have gone to prepare for me. Jesus, may I be the means of saving many souls; today, in particular, may no soul be lost, may all those detained in Purgatory win release. Pardon me, Jesus, if I'm saying more than I've any right to; I'm thinking only of your pleasure, of your content.

Well the great day passed, as all days must, joyful or sorrowful; even in our greatest moments of happiness, there's a morrow to look forward to. But this time, as I laid my wreath down at the feet of our Lady's statue, I did it without any feeling of anti-climax, because I realised that I'd now come into possession of a joy which time couldn't take away from me. Our Lady's Nativity was a wonderful day for my heavenly wedding; you see, everything was to scale—our Lady just born into the world, making the present of a flower still in bud to the Child Jesus, a day of small things. Only there was nothing small about the graces I received, and the sense of peace that went with them; it was with quiet happiness that I looked up that night at the stars glittering overhead, and reflected that before long heaven would open to my eager gaze, and I should be united to this heavenly Bridegroom of mine in joy everlasting.

I took the veil on the 24th, but a veil hangs over the memory of it; it passed in a mist of tears. Papa could not be there to give a last blessing to his little princess. Père Pichon was already in Canada. The Bishop had arranged to come over and go to dinner at my uncle's, but he was ill and couldn't manage it. Altogether it was a sad disappointment; and yet it left an after-taste of peace. Our Lord allowed me to give way to tears that day, which caused some astonishment; I'd learned by then to put up·with worse set-backs without crying over them, but that was due to a special grace, whereas on this 24th of September, he left me to my own resources, and very inadequate they proved to be.

Eight days afterwards my cousin Jeanne got married. I can't tell you, dear Mother, how anxious I was to learn, from her example, about all the little attentions which a bride ought to lavish on her bridegroom; I wanted to know all I could about it, because surely my attitude towards our Lord ought not to be less carefully studied than Jeanne's towards her husband—an excellent creature, but only a creature all the same. I even amused myself by sketching out a wedding invitation of my own, modelled on hers; this was the way it ran:

Letter of invitation to the wedding of Sister Thérèse of the Child Jesus and of the Holy Face.

Almighty God, Creator of heaven and earth, Lord of the whole world, and the glorious Virgin Mary, queen of the heavenly court, invite you to take part in the wedding of their Son Jesus Christ, King of Kings and Lord of Lords, to Thérèse Martin, now invested by right of dowry with two freedoms, those of the Sacred Infancy and of the Passion, her title of nobility being derived from the Child Jesus and the Holy Face.

Monsieur Louis Martin, the Heir-in-chief of all Misfortune and Humiliation, and Madam Martin, Lady-in-waiting at the Court of Heaven, invite you to take part in the wedding of their

daughter Thérèse to Jesus, the Word of God, Second Person of
the Blessed Trinity, now by the operation of the Holy Spirit
made Man, and Son of Mary, the Queen of heaven.

Since it was impossible to invite you to the ceremony of
the nuptial blessing, to which only the Court of Heaven was
admitted, on the 8th of September, 1890, you are asked to be
present at their return from the marriage tour, which will take
place

To-morrow, that is, the day of eternal reckoning, when
Jesus Christ, Son of God, will come on the clouds of heaven in
all the splendour of his majesty to judge the living and the dead.

The hour of this being still uncertain, you are asked to
hold yourself in readiness and be on the watch.

And now, dear Mother, have I anything left to tell you? I
thought I'd finished, but it occurs to me that I've said nothing
about the happiness of knowing Mother Geneviève. That was,
surely, an inestimable grace; God, who had given me so much
already, allowed me to live under the same roof with a Saint—
and not the sort of saint who defies imitation; hers were hidden,
unobtrusive virtues. I owe her a debt for many graces received
through her. In particular, I remember one Sunday when I went
as usual to pay her a short visit, and found she had two sisters
with her; we weren't allowed to visit three at a time, so I just
smiled at her and prepared to go out of the room. But she
looked at me as if she had some inspired message to convey, and
said this: 'Listen, my child, I've got a word to say to you. When
you come here, you always want a spiritual keepsake to take
away with you, and here's one for to-day. Serve God with peace
and with joy; remember, always, that our God is a God of
peace.' Well, I thanked her and went out, but I went out almost
in tears, fully convinced that God had revealed to her the state
of my soul. All that day I'd been ill at ease, and on the verge of
melancholy, being in such deep spiritual darkness that I even
doubted God's love for me. You can imagine, then, what consolation her words brought me. The next Sunday, when I asked
Mother Geneviève what revelation had been made to her, she
said none at all; and this made me admire her more than ever—I
could see that all she did and said really came from our Lord
living in her; and that's the truest and the best kind of sanctity,

the kind I would most like to attain, because there's no danger of illusion about it.

On the day of my profession, I was greatly encouraged by hearing from Mother Geneviève's own lips that she'd been through exactly the same temptation as I had, before she took her vows. And you, dear Mother, will remember what a comfort she was to us at the time of our greatest distress. Altogether, it's a fragrant memory that she has left in my heart. On the day when she went to her reward, I was deeply touched by this first experience I had had of a death-bed, and could watch the slightest movement of the dying Saint. I spent two hours like that, telling myself that I ought to be overcome with feelings of devotion, and yet finding that it was just the other way about—I was quite numb, quite insensible. And then, at the very moment when her soul was re-born into eternity, my whole attitude suddenly changed; I was conscious of a joy and a fervour which I can't describe to you. It was just as if Mother Geneviève had communicated to me a part of the happiness she was experiencing at that moment; I find it impossible to doubt that she went straight to heaven. I remember saying to her one day: 'There won't be any Purgatory for you, Mother,' and her gentle reply: 'It's what I'm hoping for.' Hope, tempered by humility, was no doubt the chief quality God saw in her; the favours we've received through her are proof of it.

How eager we were, all of us, to preserve some relic of her! You know what it is that I treasure. During her last agony, I saw a tear shining like a diamond on her eye-lashes, the last she would ever shed. It didn't fall; I could see it still shining there when she lay in choir, and as nobody had removed it, I went in quietly that evening with a piece of fine linen, and took this for my relic—the last tear of a saint. Since then, I've always carried it in the little locket in which my vows are enclosed.

I don't attach much importance to my dreams, and indeed I seldom have any dreams of the kind that could mean anything. Why is it that when I've been thinking about God all day he disappears from my mind during sleep? In the ordinary way I dream of woods and flowers and brooks and the sea; nearly always, I see dear little children about me, and spend my time catching butterflies and strange birds; a poet's dreams, if you like, but as you see not the dreams of a mystic! Only I did have a more comforting experience one night, soon after Mother Geneviève died. I dreamt that she was making her will, and left some keepsake to each of the sisters, but when it came to my turn it looked as if I should get nothing, because there was nothing left. But she raised herself in bed, and repeated three times, in a curiously penetrating voice: 'To you, I leave my heart.'

CHAPTER XXVIII

THE INFLUENZA
MOTHER AGNES PRIORESS

A month after this saintly mother of ours left us, an epidemic of influenza broke out among the community, and only three of us were left on our feet. I saw many new sights, gained many new impressions about life and about this passing world. My nineteenth birthday was marked out by a death, and two others followed before long. By now I was alone in the sacristy, because the senior sacristan was in a very bad way; it was I who had to arrange for the funerals, to open the choir grille at Mass, and so on. God was very good to me in supplying me with the strength I needed; I still can hardly imagine how I shrank so little from the work that came my way. Death seemed everywhere in the ascendant; the worst cases of all had to be nursed by nuns who could scarcely drag themselves across the room, and the moment a sister was dead, her body had to be left unattended. I had a presentiment as I was getting up one morning that Sister Madeleine was dead; finding the passage all dark, and nobody coming or going between the cells, I went into Sister Madeleine's (the door had been left open) and there she was, sure enough, lying on her mattress fully dressed. I wasn't at all frightened; I just went off and got a candle and a rose-wreath for her.

On the evening when our sub-Prioress died, I was alone in the infirmary; nobody can imagine the state to which the community was reduced, except those of us who kept our feet through it all, and yet, desolate as we were, I felt that God was watching over us all the time. Those who died seemed to pass from this world to a better without the least struggle; immediately after death a look of joy and peace settled on their features, as if they lay comfortably asleep. And so they did; once the fashion of this world has passed away, they will wake up to enjoy, eternally, the happiness of God's elect. While the community was going through these searching trials, I had the unspeakable consolation of making my Communion every day. That was wonderful; and our Lord went on spoiling me even after the epidemic, because I was still allowed to receive him every day when those others, his more faithful servants, no longer had the same privilege. It was also a great happiness to be able to touch the sacred vessels, and prepare the altar linen for our Lord's coming; I felt that a great deal of devotion was expected of me now, and often repeated to myself the charge given to deacons at their ordination: 'Keep yourselves unsullied, you that have the vessels of the Lord's worship in your charge.'

I can't say that my thanksgivings after Communion have often brought with them any strong access of devotion; indeed, I don't know that there's any moment at which I experience so little. But then, that's not to be wondered at; I've been offering myself to our Lord as a hostess ready to receive him, not for her own satisfaction but simply to please him. I picture my soul at such times as a vacant site, with some rubbish lying about, only I ask our Lady to clear all that away; then I ask her to erect a great tent, worthy of the occasion, and furnish it with all the finery she has at her disposal; and then I ask all the Saints and Angels to come and make music there. I think this is all the welcome our Lord expects when he comes to visit my soul, and if he's satisfied I'm satisfied too. Only, of course, all this exercise of the imagination doesn't prevent my being distracted and dozing off over my prayers. When my thanksgiving's over, I realise what a bad one I've made, and resolve to turn the rest of the day into a thanksgiving after Communion.

You can see for yourself, Mother, that the path by which I travel isn't one of scrupulous fear; anything but that. I can always find some reason to be glad of my failures and make the best of them, and our Lord doesn't seem to mind; or why does he encourage me to follow that path? I remember one day when I was rather worried about going to Communion, a thing which very seldom happened to me; I felt as if God found something wanting in me, and I remember saying to myself: 'Now, if for some reason I'm only given half of a Sacred Host to-day, it will worry me; I shall take it as a sign that our Lord is coming to me with reluctance.' So I went up to the grille and, believe it or not, for the first time in my life I saw the priest take up two Hosts instead of one, two quite separate Hosts, and give them to me. There were tears of joy in my eyes at this providential coincidence.

It was in the year after my profession, about two months before Mother Geneviève died, that I received great graces during the retreat. In the ordinary way public retreats are even more of a disappointment to me than the ones I make by myself, but it wasn't so this time. I'd made a novena beforehand and prayed hard over it, in spite of a conviction that this retreat father was very unlikely to understand me; his reputation was for dealing with great sinners, not so much with religious. But it was God himself who was my Director, and he wanted me to know it; so it was this priest he chose for his instrument, although I think I was the only person who really appreciated the choice. I'd been going through a bad time spiritually in every way, even to the point of asking myself whether heaven really existed. But I didn't feel inclined to say anything about these intimate doubts of mine, because I wasn't sure that I could express them properly. Then I went into the confessional, and immediately my heart opened out. Almost as soon as I'd begun, I felt that the priest understood me, with an insight that was surprising, almost uncanny.

My soul had become an open book, in which this priest who was a stranger to me could read better than I could myself. He launched me in full sail on that sea of confidence and of love on which I'd been afraid to venture, though it attracted me so strongly. He told me that my faults were not such as to merit God's displeasure. 'Speaking to you as God's representative,' said he, 'and in his name, I assure you that he is well satisfied with what you are doing for him.' Imagine what a consolation those words were to me—nobody'd ever suggested to me that one could have faults which nevertheless didn't offend God; I could bear all the home-sickness of this earthly exile as long as I felt sure of that! And at the same time I was conscious, deep down in my heart, that what he said was true; after all, God is more tender to us than any mother could be, and you, Mother, are always so ready to forgive those little indiscretions of which I am guilty without meaning to be. Again and again I have found that a single caress from you has had more effect on me than any reprimand you could have uttered. I suppose I'm made like that—when I'm frightened, I simply curl up; when I'm appealed to by love, I can go ahead at full speed.

This feeling that love was winging my feet has been with me specially since that golden day when you were elected Prioress— that Pauline should stand, in my life, for our Lord's earthly representative! Not that I hadn't realised, for a long time, what wonderful things our Lord was doing through your influence; your example taught me that it's only through suffering we can achieve spiritual motherhood, and more than ever I could appreciate the hidden force of our Lord's words: 'Believe me when I tell you this; a grain of wheat must fall into the ground and die, or else it remains nothing more than a grain of wheat; but if it dies, then it yields rich fruit.' What a harvest you've won! You've sowed with tears, but before long you'll see the reward of your labours; you'll come back rejoicing, carrying your sheaves with you. And somewhere among these abundant sheaves, a little white flower is hidden away; later on, in heaven, a voice will be given me to put on record all the tenderness and the holiness which I've marked in you, day after day, as we passed through the dark and silent days of our earthly exile.

In these last two years, I've been making plenty of discoveries. God has been merciful to me exactly as he was to King Solomon, and granting *all* my wishes; not only my aspirations towards holiness, but my desire for mere earthly shadows as well—and of course I knew they were only that, even before I had the experience of attaining them. You were always my ideal, Mother, and I wanted to be exactly like you; so when I found you could paint lovely pictures, or make up charming poetry, I would say to myself: 'How wonderful to have the gift of painting like that, to have the art of expressing oneself in verse, and to help souls in that way.' I wouldn't have dreamed of praying for such natural gifts, so that these desires were buried away in the depths of my heart. But then our Lord himself condescends to dwell in the depths of my heart, and he must have welcomed the opportunity of assuring me that 'All man does beneath the sun is frustration, and labour lost.' To the surprise of the community, I was told to paint, and God allowed me to make good use of the lessons my Mother gave me; I found myself capable of writing poetry after your model, and making up prayers which some people admired. Solomon found, didn't he, that when he looked round at all he had done, that ungrateful drudgery was no better than frustration and labour lost, and I had the same experience. I found that true happiness consists in hiding oneself, in being content to go without any expert knowledge of creatures. I realised that without love nothing we do can be worth anything, even if we dazzle the world's imagination by raising the dead to life, or converting whole nations. So these gifts which came to me unasked haven't encouraged me to be vain; they carry me straight back to him, and I reflect that he alone is unchanging, he alone can satisfy the limitless desires of our hearts.

And there are plenty of quite different ways in which our Lord has seen fit to humour me; I mean, over childish hopes like that wish to have snow on the ground when I took the habit. Flowers, for instance—you know how fond I've always been of them; and when I shut myself up in the cloister at fifteen, I felt I was renouncing for ever the happiness of running about in the fields when they were bright with the treasures of spring. And yet it's a fact that I've never had so many flowers passing through my hands as in these years since I entered Carmel. A bridegroom can always be trusted to make presents of this kind, and our Lord hasn't forgotten me; he's sent me any amount of cornflowers, marguerites, poppies and so on, all the ones I like best. There's even a little flower that goes by the name of corn-cockle, which I'd never managed to find since we moved to Lisieux; and I did so want to see it again, with all its memories of our childhood at Alencon. Well, there it was at Carmel, looking brightly up at me as if to assure me that God repays us a hundredfold, in small things as in great, if we give up everything for him. But there was one wish I cherished beyond all others, and I used to think I should never see it realised.

CHAPTER XXIX

CÉLINE ENTERS CARMEL
VICTIMS OF LOVE

This cherished dream was that Céline should enter Carmel, our Carmel. It seemed like a dream, too good to be true, that I should ever be able to live under the same roof again with my childhood's playmate, share once more her joys and her sorrows. So I'd made a complete cut; I'd entrusted Céline's future entirely to our Lord, quite ready to see her take ship for the other side of the world, if that was her destiny. The only thing I felt I couldn't bear was the idea that she, in her turn, shouldn't become the bride of Christ; I loved her like myself, and the thought that she might give herself to an earthly husband just couldn't find room in my mind. It went to my heart to think of her being exposed to all the spiritual dangers I had escaped; it was a mother's rather than a sister's feeling I had for her since I had joined Carmel. I remember one day when I knew she was going out to an evening party, and it worried me so much that the tears came to my eyes, a thing which wasn't usual with me now, and I entreated our Lord to see that she didn't dance. My prayer was heard; in the ordinary way she was an accomplished dancer, but that evening she found it impossible, and the partner who was in attendance on her simply couldn't get her to take the floor. There was nothing for it but to take her back to her place, and there, in some embarrassment, he left her, and didn't come back the whole evening. This extraordinary inhibition of hers increased my confidence that our Lord had set his seal on her forehead, as on mine.

On the 29th of July last year, God saw fit to release a most faithful servant of his from the bonds of mortality, and when Papa was thus called away to his heavenly reward, it was the signal for Céline's release from the last links which bound her to the world. She had been our representative in looking after the father we all loved so well, and had acquitted herself like an angel. The Angels, when they have fulfilled the task God has given them, go straight back to his presence; that is why we think of them as always posed for flight. And Céline, like the angel she was, took wing; she would have gone anywhere in obedience to our Lord's call, but, as it proved, she had only a short journey to take. It was enough for him that she had given her consent to a sacrifice whose nature was kept secret for two whole years, greatly to my distress and, for that matter, to hers. But in the end dear Papa, who was always for getting things done at once during his life-time, saw to it that Céline's affairs were quickly arranged, and the 14th of September saw us re-united once more.

I remember one day, when the obstacles seemed quite insuperable, saying to our Lord during my thanksgiving: 'You know how I long to be reassured that Papa has gone straight to heaven. I don't ask for a word from you about this, only for a sign. If Sister A. de J. gives her consent to Céline being admitted to Carmel, and makes no difficulties about it, then that will be my answer, I shall know that Papa went straight to join you.' You'll remember, dear Mother, that this particular Sister thought three of us was quite enough, and wasn't anxious to admit a fourth. But God holds our hearts in his hand, and does what he likes with them; he did so on this occasion. The first person I met after I'd finished my thanksgiving was this identical Sister, who called me to her side in a most friendly way and took me up to your room, where she talked to me about Céline with the tears standing in her eyes. No, I can never thank our Lord enough for the way in which he has satisfied all my ambitions.

And now I have no wishes left at all, except the wish to love our Lord to distraction; those childish desires of mine seem to have vanished. To be sure, I still enjoy putting flowers out on the altar of the Child Jesus; but it hasn't the same importance for me since I realised my ambition of offering dear Céline, fresh and graceful as a nosegay of flowers, to the same Master's service. What is there left for me to desire? Not suffering or death, though both have their appeal for me; only love really attracts me. It used not to be so; I thought at one time that to suffer was to skirt along the coasts of heaven; I made sure that I was to be carried off by an early death. Now, resignation is my only guide, the only compass I have to steer by; there's nothing I can pray for eagerly except the fulfilment of God's will for my soul, unhindered by any intrusion of created things. I can say, with our father St. John of the Cross:

'Deep-cellared is the cavern
Of my love's heart, I drank of him alive:
Now, stumbling from the tavern,
No thoughts of mine survive,
And I have lost the flock I used to drive. . . .

My spirit I prepare
To serve him with her riches and her beauty.
No flocks are now my care,
No other toil I share,
And only now in loving is my duty.'

And he writes elsewhere:

'Since I knew Love, I have been taught
He can perform most wondrous labours.
Though good and bad in me are neighbours,
He turns their difference to naught
Then both into Himself. . . .'

Oh what a comfort it is, Mother, this way of love! You may stumble on it, you may fail to correspond with grace given, but always love knows how to make the best of everything; whatever offends our Lord is burnt up in its fire, and nothing is left but a humble, absorbing peace deep down in the heart.

I can't tell you how much illumination I've found before now in the works of that great father of ours, St. John of the Cross. When I was seventeen or eighteen, it was all the spiritual food I needed. After that, I found that all spiritual books left me as dry as ever, and I'm still like that. I've only to open one—even the finest, even the most affecting of them—to find my heart shut up tight against it; I can't think about what I'm reading, or else it just gets as far as my brain without helping me to meditate at all. I can only escape from this inhibition of mine by reading Holy Scripture and the *Imitation of Christ*; there you have solid, wholemeal nourishment. But above all it's the gospels that occupy my mind when I'm at prayer; my soul has so many needs, and yet this is the one thing needful. I'm always finding fresh lights there; hidden meanings which had meant nothing to me hitherto. It's an experience that makes me understand what's meant by the text, 'The kingdom of God is here, within you.' Our Lord doesn't need to make use of books or teachers in the instruction of souls; isn't he himself the Teacher of all teachers, conveying knowledge with never a word spoken? For myself, I never heard the sound of his voice, but I know that he dwells within me all the time, guiding me and inspiring me whenever I do or say anything. A light, of which I'd caught no glimmer before, comes to me at the very moment when it's needed; and this doesn't generally happen in the course of my prayer, however devout it may be, but more often in the middle of my daily work.

Dear Mother, after receiving such graces, do you wonder that I should echo the words of the Psalmist: 'Give thanks to the Lord; the Lord is gracious, his mercy endures for ever'? I believe that if all creatures had received these same graces, there would be nobody left serving God under the influence of fear; we should all love him to distraction, and nobody would ever do him an injury, not because we were afraid of him but simply because we loved him. Still, I realise that we aren't all made alike; souls have got to fall into different groups, so that all God's perfections may be honoured severally. Only for me his infinite mercy is the quality that stands out in my life, and when I contemplate and adore his other perfections, it's against this background of mercy all the time. They all seem to have a dazzling outline of love; even God's justice, and perhaps his justice more than any other attribute of his, seems to have love for its setting. It's so wonderful to think that God is really just, that he takes all our weakness into consideration, that he knows our frail nature for what it is. What reason can I have for fear? Surely he who pardons, so graciously, the faults of the Prodigal Son will be equally just in his treatment of myself, who am always at his side.

On the 9th of June this year, the feast of the Holy Trinity, I was given the grace to see more clearly than ever how love is what our Lord really wants. I was thinking about the souls who offer themselves as victims to the divine justice, with the idea of turning aside and bringing upon themselves the punishments decreed against sinners. I felt that this kind of self-immolation was a fine gesture, a generous gesture, but it wasn't at all the one I wanted to make. The cry of my heart was something different: 'My God, why should only your Justice claim victims; why should there be no victims of your merciful Love? Everywhere that Love is misunderstood and thrust on one side; the hearts upon which you are ready to lavish it turn away towards creatures instead, as if happiness could be found in such miserable attachments as that; they won't throw themselves into your arms and accept the gift of your infinite Love. Must this rejected Love of yours remain shut up in your own Heart? If only you could find souls ready to offer themselves as victims to be burnt up in the fire of your love, surely you would lose no time in satisfying their desire; you would find a welcome outlet, in this way, for the pent-up force of that infinite tenderness which is yours. If your justice, which finds its scope on earth, demands to take its course, how much stronger must be the impetus which impels your merciful love to take possession of souls! Your mercy, we are told, reaches up to heaven itself. Jesus, grant me the happiness of being such a victim, burnt up in the fire of your divine love!'

It was you, dear Mother, who gave me leave to offer myself in this way, and you know all about the streams of grace, or perhaps I ought to say the seas of grace, which have come flooding into my soul since then. Ever since that memorable day, love seems to pierce me through and wrap me round, merciful love which makes a new creature of me, purifies my soul and leaves no trace of sin there, till all my fear of Purgatory is lost. To be sure, no merits of my own could even win me entrance there; it is only for the souls of the redeemed. But at the same time I felt confident that the fire of love can sanctify us more surely than those fires of expiation; why should our Lord want us to suffer unnecessary pain? Why should he inspire me with this ambition to become a victim, if he doesn't mean to satisfy it? No, there's nothing that can bring us comfort like this way of love; for me, nothing matters except trying to do God's will with utter resignation.

There, Mother, that's all I can tell you about the life of your youngest sister. You yourself know far better than I do what I am, and what our Lord has done for me, so you won't mind my having compressed my life as a religious within such narrow limits. How is it going to end, this story which I've called the story of a little white flower? Perhaps it will be picked, still fresh; perhaps it will be replanted in some distant soil; I can't tell. But I know that the mercy of God will always go with me, and that I shall never cease to bless you for giving me to our Lord. For all eternity, I shall rejoice to think that I am one flower in the wreath you have earned; to all eternity I shall echo your song, that song of love which can never lose the freshness of its inspiration.

Joseph Columba Marmion

1858-1923

The life of Joseph Columba Marmion was a simple and quiet one. He was born in Dublin of an Irish father and French mother. After several years of seminary studies in Ireland, he went to Rome. Ordained a priest in 1881, he returned to Ireland, worked in a parish, taught in a seminary and then, in 1886, entered the Benedictine monastery of Maredsous in Belgium. For the last fourteen years of his life he was abbot of the monastery. Coincidentally these years span the years of the First World War. His life was also incredibly apostolic, for he spent his monastic years preaching retreats, guiding a monastery, keeping up an extensive correspondence and writing books. The simplicity and quiet sustained his apostolate; the knowledge of the human spirit that he obtained through the apostolate nourished his monastic life. He is recognized as a master of the spiritual life.

The writings of Marmion are the fruit of much reflection and prayer. They read easily and are almost too good to be true. Marmion sees no need to make the life of spiritual perfection a difficult and impossible one. He avoids complicating things unnecessarily, does not bog down in too much detail or subtle refinements. His objective is "to fix the eyes and the hearts of my readers on Jesus Christ and on His word. He is the Alpha and Omega of all sanctity and His word is the divine seed, from which all sanctity springs." (from the foreword, Christ, the Life of the Soul) *Marmion sought to discover and communicate God's message according to the simplicity of the divine plan, for he regretted that over the Christian centuries men had complicated that message with too many conceptions of their own.*

Thus, his is a spirituality of recall, of return to origins, to the Gospels and the scriptural literature surrounding them. He admits a preference for Paul. Though he insisted on pushing back to foundations, he was aware of the riches of the Christian theological tradition and used it well in his meditation of scripture.

Marmion's central theme is Christ, true God and true man, Sanctifier of souls, Exemplar of all holiness, Cause of salvation, Mediator, Source of all grace, life and holiness. Christ is not merely one subject of meditation among many; he is the only subject.

The book from which we have taken our selection, Christ, the Life of the Soul, *beautifully develops this theme. It begins with a reflection on God's plan for mankind as revealed in the sacred scriptures. "God chose us in Christ." That brief phrase contains the entire mystery. God, by loving choice, pours limitless divine life into mankind through Christ. Holiness consists in the human receiving, keeping and increasing that life by means of evergrowing union. To be human is to be the adopted child of God. He who comes to realize this basic fact of divine liberality can only burst out in a song of thanksgiving and praise.*

One must know God in order to be one with Him. Such knowledge is possible only through Christ who is the revelation of the Father. Faith is the first attitude of soul, the foundation of the supernatural life, the precondition of union with God in Christ. Baptism, the sacrament of adoption, incorporates man into the death and life of Christ. The signs of incorporation are gratitude, joy and confidence.

Marmion's great hope was that the twentieth century would allow the two divine principles, namely, Christ and His word, to be active as they were in the early ages of Christianity and thus work wonders among men.

CHRIST, THE LIFE OF THE SOUL

I. THE DIVINE ECONOMY

I. THE DIVINE PLAN OF OUR ADOPTIVE PREDESTINATION IN JESUS CHRIST

God chose us in Christ "before the foundation of the world, that we should be holy and unspotted in His sight in charity. Who hath predestinated us unto the adoption of children through Jesus Christ unto Himself, according to the purpose of His Will: unto the praise of the glory of His grace, in which He hath graced us in His beloved Son."

These are the terms in which the Divine plan is set forth by the Apostle St. Paul, who had been caught up to the third heaven, and was chosen by God to bring to light, as he himself says, the economy of the mystery which hath been hidden from all eternity in God. We see the great Apostle labouring unceasingly to make known this eternal plan, established by God Himself for the sanctification of our souls. Why do all the efforts of the Apostle tend, as he carefully points out, to bring to light this Divine dispensation?

Because God, Who is the Author of our salvation, and the first source of our sanctity, could alone make known to us what He desires of us in order that we may attain to Him.

Among the souls who seek God, some hardly succeed in reaching Him.

Some have no precise idea of what holiness is; being ignorant of the plan traced out by Eternal Wisdom, or setting it aside, they make holiness consist in such or such a conception formed by their own intelligence, they only wish to be guided by themselves; attached to those purely human ideas they have framed, they go astray; if they make great strides, it is outside the true way marked out by God; they are the victims of those illusions against which St. Paul warned the first Christians.

Others have clear notions on points of detail, but lack a view of the whole; losing themselves in these *minutiae*, and not having any synthetic view, they are always going over the same ground; their life becomes a real labour, subject to incessant difficulties, without zest, without expansion, and often without much result, because these souls attach too much importance to their acts, or give them less value than they should relatively have.

It is therefore extremely important, as St. Paul says, to run in the race, "not as at an uncertainty", as one beating the air, but so as to obtain the prize: *Sic currite ut comprehendatis*; to know as perfectly as possible the Divine idea of holiness; to examine with the greatest care, so as to adapt ourselves to it, the plan traced out by God Himself, whereby we may attain to Him: it is only at this price that our salvation and sanctification can be realized.

In so grave a matter, in so vital a question, we must look at and weigh things, as God looks at and weighs them. God judges all things in the light, and His judgment is the test of all truth. "We must not judge things according to our own liking," says St. Francis of Sales, "but according to that of God; this is the great secret. If we are holy according to our own will, we shall never be truly holy, we must be so according to God's Will." Divine Wisdom is infinitely above human wisdom; God's thoughts contain possibilities of fruitfulness such as no created thought possesses. That is why God's plan is so wise that it cannot fail to reach its end because of any intrinsic insufficiency, but only through our own fault. If we leave the Divine idea full freedom to operate in us, if we adapt ourselves to it with love and fidelity, it becomes extremely fruitful and may lead us to the most sublime sanctity.

Let us contemplate in the light of Revelation God's plan for us. This contemplation will be a source of light, strength and joy for our souls.

I am going to give you, first of all, a general idea of the Divine plan; we will then study it in detail, following the words of St. Paul quoted at the beginning of this conference.

Joseph Columba Marmion

I

It can be demonstrated by human reason that there exists a Supreme Being, the First Cause of every creature, the Providence of the world, the Sovereign Rewarder and the Last End of all things. From this rational knowledge and from the relations it manifests between creatures and God, proceed for us certain duties towards God and towards our neighbour, duties which form what is called the natural law, and the observance of which constitutes natural religion.

But our reason, powerful though it is, has been unable to discover anything, with certainty, of the intimate life of the Supreme Being: the Divine life appears to natural reason to be infinitely distant, far off in solitude: *Lucem inhabitat inaccessibilem.*

Revelation has come to us, bringing its light.

It teaches us that there is an ineffable paternity in God. God is a Father: that is the fundamental dogma which all the others suppose, a magnificent dogma which leaves the reason confounded, but ravishes faith with delight and transports holy souls.

God is a Father. Eternally, long before the created light rose upon the world, God begets a Son to Whom He communicates His Nature, His perfections, His beatitude, His life, for to beget is to communicate being and life: *Filius meus es tu, ego hodie genui te; ex utero ante luciferum genui te.* In God then is life, life communicated by the Fathr and received by the Son. This Son, like in all things to the Father, is the only Son of God: *Unigenitus Dei Filius.* He is so because He has, with the Father, one same and indivisible Divine Nature, and both, although distinct from one another (on account of their personal properties "of being Father" and "of being Son"), are united in a powerful, substantial embrace of love, whence proceeds that Third Person, Whom Revelation calls by a mysterious name: the Holy Ghost.

Such is, as far as faith can know it, the secret of the inmost life of God; the fulness and the fruitfulness of this life are the source of the incommensurable bliss that the ineffable society of the three Divine Persons possesses.

And now God—not in order to add to His plenitude, but by it to enrich other beings—extends, as it were, His Paternity. God decrees to call creatures to share this Divine life, so transcendent that God alone has the right to live it, this eternal life communicated by the Father to the Only Son, and by them to the Holy Spirit. In a transport of love which has its source in the fulness of Being and Good that God is, this life overflows from the bosom of the Divinity to reach and beatify beings drawn out of nothingness, by lifting them above their nature. To these mere creatures God will give the condition and sweet name of children. By nature God has only one Son; by love, He wills to have an innumerable multitude: that is *the grace of supernatural adoption.*

Realized in Adam from the dawn of creation, then crossed by the sin of the first of human kind, who drew after him into disgrace all his race, this decree of love is to be restored by a marvellous invention of justice and mercy, of wisdom and goodness. The Son of God, Who dwells eternally in the Bosom of the Father, unites Himself in time, to a human nature, but in so close a manner that this nature, while being perfect in itself, belongs entirely to the Divine Person to Whom it is united. The Divine life, communicated in its fulness to this humanity makes it the very humanity of the Son of God: that is the wonderful work of the *Incarnation*. It is true to say of this Man Who is called Jesus, the Christ, that He is God's own Son.

But this Son, Who by nature is the only Son of the Eternal Father, *Unigenitus Dei Filius*, appears here below only to become the Firstborn of all who shall receive Him, after having been redeemed by Him: *Primogenitus in multis fratribus.* Alone born of the Father in eternal splendour, alone Son by right, He is constituted the head of a multitude of brethren, on whom, by His redeeming work, He will bestow the grace of Divine life.

So that the same Divine life which proceeds from the Father into the Son and from the Son into the humanity of Jesus, will circulate, through Christ in all who will accept it; it will draw them even into the Bosom of the Father, where Christ has gone before us, after having paid, with His Blood, the price of this divine gift.

Hence all holiness is to consist in this: to receive the Divine life from Christ and by Christ, Who possesses its fulness and Who has been constituted the One Mediator; to keep this Divine life and increase it unceasingly by an ever more perfect adhesion, an ever closer union with Him Who is its source.

Holiness then, is a *mystery of Divine life communicated and received*: communicated in God, from the Father to the Son by an ineffable generation; communicated by the Son to humanity, which He personally unites to Himself in the Incarnation; then restored to souls by this humanity, and received by each of them in the measure of their special predestination: *secundum mensuram donationis Christi*, so that Christ is truly the life of the soul because He is the source and giver of life.

Communication of this life will be made to men within the Church until the day fixed by the eternal decrees for the achievement of the Divine work upon earth. On that day, the number of the children of God, of the brethren of Jesus, will have reached its perfection. Presented by Christ to His Father, the innumerable multitude of these predestined souls will surround the throne of God, to draw an endless beatitude from the fountains of life, and to exalt the splendours of the Divine goodness and glory. Union with God will be eternally consummated, and "God will be all in all".

Such is the Divine Plan in its general outline.

When in prayer, we consider this liberality and these advances towards us on the part of God, we feel the need of prostrating ourselves in adoration, and of singing a song of thanksgiving to the praise of the Infinite Being Who stoops towards us to give us the name of children. "O Lord, how great are Thy works; Thy thoughts are exceeding deep!" *Nimis profundae factae sunt cogitationes tuae*. "Thou hast multiplied Thy wonderful works, O Lord, my God; in Thy thoughts there is no one like to Thee." "In the works of Thy hands I shall rejoice." "I will sing to the Lord as long as I live, I will sing praise to my God while I have my being. Let my mouth be filled with praise that I may sing Thy glory!" *Repleatur os meum laude ut cantem tibi gloriam tuam.*

II

Let us now resume our exposition in detail, being guided by the text of the Apostle. This exposition will inevitably lead to some repetition, but I have confidence that your charity will bear with it on account of the importance of such vital questions.

We cannot sufficiently appreciate the greatness of these dogmas and their profit to our souls unless we contemplate them at some length.

In every science, there are, as you know, first principles, fundamental points which must first be grasped, because on them all the ulterior developments and final conclusions depend.

These first elements have to be gone into so much the more deeply and require so much the more attention in as far as their consequences are the more important and extended. Our minds, it is true, are so made, that they are easily wearied in the analysis or meditation of fundamental notions. All initiation in a science, such as mathematics, in an art, such as music, in a doctrine, such as that of the inner life, requires an attention from which the mind is prone to wander. In its impatience, it wishes to hasten to the development to admire its sequence, and to the applications in order to gather and taste the fruits. But it is greatly to be feared that if the mind does not carefully fathom the principles, it will lack solidity in the conclusions that it will afterwards draw from them, however brilliant these may appear to be.

God wills us to be saints: that is His eternal Will; it is for that He has chosen us: *Elegit nos. . . . Ut essemus sancti et immaculati in conspectu ejus.* "For this is the will of God, your sanctification." St. Paul says again: *Haec est voluntas Dei sanctificatio vesira.*

God desires, with an infinite will, that we should be holy; He wills it because He is Himself holy; because it is in this holiness that He has placed the glory He expects from us, and the joy with which He desires to satisfy us.

But what is "being holy"? We are creatures, our holiness only consists in a participation in God's holiness; to understand what it is, we must then consider what sanctity is in God. He alone is holy by essence, or rather, He is holiness itself.

Holiness is the Divine perfection which is the object of the eternal contemplation of the Angels. Open the Scriptures. You will see that twice only, the gates of Heaven were partly opened, in the sight of two great prophets, the one of the Ancient alliance, the other of the New Isaias and St. John. What did they see? What did they hear? Both saw God in His glory, both saw the angelic choir surrounding His throne, both heard them ceaselessly praising, not the beauty of God, nor His mercy, nor His justice, nor His greatness, but His holiness: *Sanctus, Sanctus, Sanctus, Dominus Deus exercituum; plena est omnis terra gloria ejus.*

Now in what does holiness in God consist?

In God, all is simple; His perfections are, in Him, really identical with Himself; besides, the notion of sanctity can only be applied to Him in an absolutely transcendent manner; we have no term which can adequately render the reality of this Divine perfection. However, it is permitted us to employ a human language. What then, is holiness in God?

According to our manner of speaking, it seems to us that it is composed of a double element: first, infinite distance from all that is imperfection, from all that is created, from all that is not God Himself.

This is only a "negative" aspect. There is another element which consists in this: that *God adheres, by an immutable and always present act of His will, to the Infinite Good which is Himself,* in order to conform Himself entirely to all that this Infinite Good is. God knows Himself perfectly. His All-Wisdom shows Him His own essence as the supreme norm of all activity. God cannot will, do, or approve anything which is not ruled by His supreme wisdom, according to this ultimate norm of all good, which is the Divine essence.

This immutable adhesion, this supreme conformity of the Divine Will to the infinite Essence considered as the ultimate norm of activity could not be more *perfect*, because in God the will is really identical with the essence.

Divine holiness is, therefore, the most perfect love and the supremely unchanging fidelity with which God loves Himself infinitely. And as His supreme Wisdom shows God that He is the All-Perfect, the only necessary Being, it causes Him to refer all to Himself and His own glory. That is why Sacred Scripture grants us to hear the angels' song: "Holy, holy, holy ... Heaven and earth are full of Thy glory." It is as if the Angels said: "Thou art the All-Holy, O God, Thou art Very Holiness, because with Sovereign Wisdom, Thou dost glorify Thyself worthily and perfectly."

Hence the Divine holiness serves as the first foundation, the universal exemplar and the one source of all created holiness. You understand that, necessarily loving Himself with infinite perfection, God also necessarily wills that every creature should exist for the manifestation of His glory, and that, remaining in the rank of creature, it should only act conformably to the relations of dependence and of end that the Eternal Wisdom finds in the Divine Essence.

Our holiness will be the higher according as there is in us more loving dependence on God and conformity of our free will to our ultimate end (which is the manifestation of the Divine Glory). The more *we adhere to God* by detaching ourselves from all that is not God, the more this dependence, conformity, adhesion, and detachment are *firm and stable*.

III

Human reason can arrive at establishing the existence of this holiness in the Supreme Being, holiness which is an attribute, a perfection of the Divine nature considered in itself.

But Revelation brings us a new light.

Here we must reverently raise the eyes of our soul even to the sanctuary of the Adorable Trinity, we must hear what Jesus Christ, both to nourish our piety and to exercise our faith, has Himself willed to reveal to us, or to teach us through His Church, about the intimate life of God.

There are, as you know, Three Divine Persons in God, the Father, the Son, and the Holy Ghost, three distinct Persons, but all three having one and the same Nature or Divine Essence. Being infinite Intelligence, the Father perfectly knows His perfections, He expresses this knowledge in One Word, the living, substantial Word, the adequate expression of what the

Father is. In uttering this Word, the Father begets the Son, to Whom He communicates all His Essence, His Nature, His Perfections, His Life: *Sicut Pater habet vitam in semetipso, sic dedit et Filio habere vitam in semetipso*. The Son also belongs entirely to His Father, is entirely given up to Him by a total donation which pertains to His nature as Son. And from this mutual donation of one and the same love, proceeds, as from one principle, the Holy Spirit Who seals the union of the Father and the Son by being Their substantial and living Love.

This mutual communication of the three Persons, this infinite loving union between themselves assuredly constitutes a new revelation of holiness in God: it is the ineffable union of God with Himself in the unity of His Nature and the Trinity of Persons.

God finds all His essential beatitude in this inexpressibly unique and fruitful life. To exist, God has only need of Himself and all His infinite perfections; finding all felicity in the perfections of His nature, and in the ineffable society of His Persons, He has no need of any creature; He refers to Himself, in Himself, in His Trinity, the glory which springs from His infinite perfections.

God has decreed, as you know, to make us enter into participation of this intimate life proper to Himself alone; He wills to communicate to us this infinite, endless beatitude, which has its source in the fulness of the Infinite Being.

Therefore—and this is the first point of St. Paul's exposition of the Divine Plan—our holiness is to consist in *adhering to God, known and loved*, not only as the Author of creation, *but as He knows and loves Himself* in the bliss of His Trinity; this is to be united to God to the point of sharing His intimate life. We shall soon see in what a marvellous manner God realizes His design. Let us for a moment consider the greatness of the gift He makes us. We shall get some idea of it if we look at what takes place in the natural order.

Look at minerals; they do not live; there is no interior principle in them as source of activity, they possess a participation in being, with certain properties, but their mode of being is very inferior. Then there is the vegetable kingdom; plants grow and live in accordance with fixed laws, and progress towards the

THE CATHOLIC TRADITION: Spirituality

perfection of their being, but this life is at the bottom of the scale, for the plant is destitute of knowledge. Although superior to that of plants, the life of animals is yet limited to sensibility and the necessities of the instinct. With man we rise to a higher sphere: reason and free-will characterize the life proper to a human being; but man is also matter. Above him is the angel, a pure spirit, whose life reaches the highest degree in the scale of creation. Infinitely surpassing all these created lives received in participation, is the Divine life, life uncreated, fully autonomous and independent, above the strength of any creature, a necessary life, subsistent in itself. God being unlimited intelligence, apprehends, by an eternal act, both the infinite and every being of which the prototype is found in Him. Being the Sovereign Will, He attaches Himself in the fulness of His strength to the Supreme Good which is none other than Himself. In this Divine life in which is all plenitude, is found the source of all perfection and the principle of all bliss.

It is this life which God wills to communicate to us; it is a share in this life which forms our holiness. And as, for us, there are degrees in this participation, the more this participation is extended, the higher will be our holiness.

And let us never forget that it is only out of love that God has resolved, *proposuit sibi Deus*, to give Himself thus. The ineffable communications of the Divine Persons with each other are all that is necessary in God. These mutual relations belong to the very Essence of God; it is the life of God. All other communications that God makes of Himself are the outcome of a love supremely free. But as this love is divine, the gift of it makes us so likewise. God loves divinely; He gives *Himself*. We are called to receive this Divine communication in an ineffable measure. God intends to give Himself to us, not only as supreme beauty, to be the object of our contemplation, but to unite Himself to us so as to make Himself, as far as possible, one with us. Holy Father, said Jesus Christ at the Last Supper, let My disciples be one in Us, as Thou and I are one, so that they may find in this union the endless joy of Our own beatitude. *Ut habeant gaudium meum impletum in semetipsis.*

180

IV

How does God fulfil this magnificent design by which He wills us to have a part in this life which exceeds the capacities of our nature and surpasses its rights and proper energies, which none of its exigences require, but which, without destroying this nature, fill it with bliss unimagined by the human heart? How will God cause us to enter into the ineffable "fellowship" of His Divine life so that we may partake of eternal beatitude? By adopting us as His children.

With a Will infinitely free, but full of love: *Secundum propositum voluntatis suae*, God has predestined us to be not only creatures, but His children: *Praedestinavit nos in adoptionem filiorum*, thus to share in His Divine Nature: *Divinae consortes naturae*. God adopts us as His children. What does St. Paul mean by this.

What is human adoption?

It is the admission of a stranger into a family. By adoption the stranger becomes a member of the family, he takes the name and receives the titles of this family, he has the right to inherit its possessions. It is necessary for the one who is adopted to be of the same race as the one who adopts. To be adopted by man, it is necessary to be a member of the human race. Now we, who are not of the race of God, who are poor creatures, by nature further from Him than the animal is from man, we who are infinitely distant from God, *hospites et advenae*, how can we be adopted by Him?

Here is a marvel of the Divine Wisdom, power, and goodness. God gives us a mysterious share in His Nature which we call "grace": *Efficiamini divinae consortes naturae*.

Grace is an *interior quality*, produced in us by God, inherent to the soul, adorning it and making it pleasing to God, just as in the natural domain, beauty and strength are qualities of the body, genius and science are qualities of the mind, loyalty and courage are qualities of the heart.

According to St. Thomas, this grace is a "participated similitude" of the Divine nature. *Participata similitudo divinae naturae*. Grace makes us sharers in the nature of God in a way we cannot fathom. We are raised above our nature by grace; we become, in some manner, gods. We do not become equal, but like to God; that is why Our Lord said to the Jews: "Is it not written in your law: I said: you are gods?" *Nonne scriptum est in lege vestra: quia ego dixi: Dii estis?*

For us, participation in this Divine life is brought about by grace, in virtue of which our soul becomes capable of knowing God as God knows Himself, of loving God as God loves Himself, of enjoying God as He is filled with His own beatitude, and thus living the life of God Himself.

Such is the ineffable mystery of our Divine adoption. But there is a profound difference between Divine and human adoption. The latter is only exterior, fictitious. Certainly, it is established by a legal document, but it does not penetrate the nature of the one who is adopted. On the contrary, in adopting us, in giving us grace, God penetrates to the depths of our nature; without changing what is essential to the order of this nature, He raises it by this grace to the point of making us truly children of God. This act of adoption has so much efficacy that we really become, through grace, partakers of the Divine nature. And as participation in the Divine life constitutes our holiness, this grace is called *sanctifying*.

The consequence of this Divine decree of our adoption, of this loving predestination by which God wills to make us His children, is to give a special character to our holiness.

This character is that our holiness is *supernatural*.

The life to which God raises us is supernatural, that is to say, exceeding the capacities, the strength and the exigences of our nature. Hence, it is no more as simple human creatures that we must be holy, but *as children of God, by acts animated and inspired by grace*.

Grace becomes the principle of the Divine life in us. What is it *to live*? For us, to live is to move in virtue of an interior principle, the source of actions which tend to the perfection of our being. Another life is engrafted, so to speak, upon our natural life, a life of which grace is the principle; grace becomes in us the source of actions and operations which are supernatural, and tend towards a Divine end, namely, one day to possess God, to rejoice in Him, as He knows Himself and rejoices in His perfections.

This point is of capital importance. God might have been content to accept from us the homage of a natural religion; it would have been the source of a human, natural morality, of a union with God conformable to our nature as reasonable beings, founded upon our relations as creatures with our Creator, and our relations with our kind.

But God did not wish to limit Himself to this natural religion. We have all met with men who were not baptized, but who were, however, straightforward, loyal, upright, equitable, just and compassionate, but that can only be a natural goodness. Without rejecting this (on the contrary), God is not content with it. Because He has decided to make us share in His infinite life, in His own beatitude—which is for us a supernatural end— because He has given us His grace, God demands that our union with Him should be a supernatural union, a holiness which has His grace for principle.

Apart from this plan, there is, for us, only eternal loss. God is Master of His gifts, and He has decreed from all eternity that we shall only be *holy* in His sight, *by living through grace as children of God.*

O Heavenly Father, grant that I may preserve within my soul the grace that makes me Thy child! Keep me from all evil that might separate me from Thee! . . .

V

As you know, it is from the time of the creation of the first man that God has realized His design. Adam received for himself and for his race, the grace that made of him a child of God; but by his sin, he lost this Divine gift for himself as well as for his race. Since his revolt, we are all born sinners, deprived of the grace which would have made us children of God; we are, on the contrary, *Filii irae*, enemies of God, and children of wrath. Sin crossed God's plan.

But, as the Church says, God has shown Himself ever more wonderful in the restoration of His designs than He had been in the creation: *Deus qui humanae substantiae dignitatem mirabilter condisti* MIRABILIU *reformasti.* How is this done?—*What is this Divine marvel?*

This mystery is the *Incarnation.*

It is through the Incarnate Word that God will restore all things. Such is the "mystery which hath been hidden from eternity," in the thoughts of God, and which St. Paul reveals to us. Christ, the Man-God, will be our Mediator; He it is Who will reconcile us with God and restore grace to us. And as the great design has been foreseen from all eternity, it is with good reason that St. Paul speaks of it as an ever-present mystery. It is the last great feature of the Divine Plan made known to us by the great Apostle.

Let us listen to him with faith, for here we touch the very heart of the Divine work.

The Divine design is to constitute Christ the Head of all the redeemed, of all that is named in this world and in that which is to come: *Quod nominatur non solum in hoc saeculo sed in futuro*, in order that by Him, with Him, and in Him, we may all arrive at union with God, and realize the supernatural holiness which God requires of us.

There is no thought more clearly expressed in the Epistles of St. Paul, none of which he is more convinced, or that he places in higher relief. Read all his Epistles and you will see that he continually returns to this, to the extent of making it almost all the substance of his doctrine. In this passage of the Epistle to the Ephesians that I quoted at the beginning what does he tell us? It *is in Christ* that God has chosen us, that we should be holy; He has predestinated us to be His adopted children, *through Jesus Christ.* . . . "He hath graced us *in His beloved Son.*" It is in His Son, Jesus, that God has resolved "to re-establish all things". *Instaturare omnia in Christo*, or rather, according to the Greek text, "to gather together all things under Christ, as under one only Head". Christ is always foremost in the Divine idea.

How is this realized?

The Word Whose eternal generation we adore in the Bosom of the Father, *in sinu Patris*, is made flesh: *Et Verbum caro factum est.* The most Holy Trinity has created a humanity like to ours, and from the first instant of His creation has united it in an ineffable and indissoluble manner to the Person of the Word, of the Son, of the Second Person of the Holy Trinity. This God-Man is Jesus Christ. This union is so close that there is only one single Person, that of the Word. Perfect God, *Perfectus Deus*, by His Divine nature, the Word becomes, by His Incarnation, perfect Man: *Perfectus homo*. In making Himself man, He remains God: *Quod fuit permansit, quod non erat assumpsit*: the fact of having taken a human nature in order to unite it to Himself has not lessened the Divinity.

In Jesus Christ, the Incarnate Word, the two natures are united without admixture or confusion, they remain distinct while being united in the unity of the Person. On account of the personal character of this union, Christ is the very Son of God, He possesses the life of God: *Sicut Pater habet vitam in semetipso, sic dedit et Filio habere vitam in semetipso*. The same Divine life subsists in God and fills the Sacred Humanity of Jesus. The Father communicates His life to the Word, to His Son, and the Word communicates it to the Humanity which He has personally united to Himself. That is why, in looking upon Our Lord, the Eternal Father recognizes Him as His own Son: *Filius meus es tu, ego hodie genui te*. And because He is His Son, because this Humanity is the Humanity of His Son, it possesses a full and entire communication of all the Divine perfections. The soul of Christ is filled with all the treasures of God's knowledge and wisdom: *In quo sunt omnes thesauri sapientiae et scientiae*. In Christ, says St. Paul, "dwelleth all the fulness of the Godhead corporally". *In ipso inhabitat omnis plenitudo divinitatis corporaliter*; the Holy Humanity is filled with grace and truth.

The Word made flesh is, therefore, adorable in His Humanity as in His Divinity, because beneath this Humanity is veiled the Divine life. O Jesus Christ, Incarnate Word, I cast myself down before Thee, because Thou art the Son of God, equal to the Father. Thou art indeed the Son of God, *Deum de Deo, lumen de lumine, Deum verum de Deo vero*. Thou art the beloved Son of the Father, in Whom He is well pleased. I love and adore Thee! *Venite adoremus!*

But, this Divine life which is in Jesus Christ is to overflow from Him upon us, upon the whole human race. This is a wonderful revelation which fills us with joy.

The Divine Sonship which is in Christ by nature, and makes Him God's own and only Son, *Unigenitus qui est in sinu*

Patris, is to be extended to us by grace, so that in the thought of God, Christ is the First-born of many brethren, who are by grace what He is by nature, sons of God: *Praedestinavit nos conformes fieri imaginis Filii sui ut sit ipse primogenitus in multis fratribus.*

We are here at the central point of the Divine Plan: *it is from Jesus Christ, it is through Jesus Christ that we receive the Divine adoption.* "God sent His Son", says St. Paul, "that we might receive the adoption of sons"; *Deus misit Filium suum factum ex muliere, ut . . . adoptionem filiorum reciperemus.* The grace of Christ the Son of God is communicated to us so as to become in us the principle of adoption; it is from this fulness of Divine life and grace of Jesus Christ that we must all draw. After having said that the fulness of the Divinity dwells corporally in Christ, St. Paul adds immediately by way of conclusion: *Et estis in illo repleti, qui est caput omnis principatus et potestatis.* Behold in Him you have all, because He is your Head. And St. John says likewise, after having shown us the Word, full of grace and truth: "And of His fulness we have all received." *Et de plenitudine ejus nos omnes accepimus.*

Thus, not only has the Father chosen us from all eternity in His Christ: *Elegit nos in ipso*—note the expression *In ipso*: all that is apart from Christ does not exist, so to speak, in the Divine thought—but it is also by Jesus Christ that we receive grace, the means of the adoption He destines for us: *Qui praedestinavit nos in adoptionem filiorum per Jesum Christum.* We are sons, like Jesus, we by grace, He by nature; He, God's own Son, we His adopted sons: *Et ipse filius et nos filii; ille proprius, nos adoptivi, sed ille salvat et nos salvamur.* It is by Christ that we enter into God's family, it is from Him and by Him that grace and consequently Divine life come to us: *Ego sum vita . . . ego veni ut vitam habeant et abundantius habeant.*

Such is the very source of our holiness. As everything in Jesus Christ can be summed up in His Divine Sonship, thus everything in the Christian can be summed up in his participation of his sonship, by Jesus Christ, and in Jesus Christ. *Our holiness is nothing else but this: the more we participate in the Divine life through the communication Jesus Christ makes to us of the grace of which He ever possesses the fulness, the higher is the degree of our holiness.* Christ is not only holy in Himself, He is *our* holiness. All the holiness God has destined for our souls has been placed in the Humanity of Christ, and it is from this source that we must draw.

"O Jesus Christ", we sing with the Church in the *Gloria* of the Mass: "Thou only art holy": *Tu solus sanctus, Jesu Christe.* Only holy, because Thou dost possess the fulness of the Divine life; only holy, because it is from Thee alone that we look for our holiness: Thou hast become, as the great Apostle says, *our* justice, *our* wisdom, *our* redemption, *our* holiness: *Estis in Christo Jesu qui factus est nobis sapientia a Deo et justitia et sanctificatio et redemptio.* In Thee we find all; in receiving Thee, we receive all; for in giving Thee to us, Thy Father, Who is our Father, as Thou hast Thyself said, has given us all: *Quomodo non etiam cum illo omnia nobis donavit?* All the graces of salvation and forgiveness, all riches, all the supernatural fruitfulness with which the world of souls abounds, come from Thee alone: *In Christo habemus redemptionem . . . secundum divitias gratiae ejus quae superabundavit in nobis.* Let all praise be given to Thee, O Christ; and by Thee may all praise ascend to Thy Father for the unspeakable gift He has made us of Thee!

VI

We must all be partakers of the holiness of Jesus. Christ excludes no one from the life He has brought, and, by it, He renders us children of God: *Pro omnibus mortuus est Christus*; Christ has re-opened the gates of eternal life to all humanity. As St. Paul says: He is the first-born, but of a multitude of brethren: *In multis fratribus.* The Eternal Father wishes to constitute Christ His Son, Head of a Kingdom, the Kingdom of His children. The Divine Plan would not be complete if Christ was isolated. It is His glory, as it is the glory of the Father, *In laudem gloriae gratiae suae,* to be at the head of an innumerable company, which is his complement, πήλρωμα and without which, so to say, He would not be complete.

St. Paul distinctly says this in his Epistle to the Ephesians, where he traces out the Divine Plan: God has made Christ to sit "on His right hand in the heavenly places, above all principality and power and virtue and dominion, and every name that is named not only in this world, but also in that which is to come: And He hath subjected all things under His feet, and hath made Him head over all the Church which is His body." It is this company, this Church that Christ has acquired, according to the words of the same Apostle, that it may be at the last day, without "spot or wrinkle, but holy and without blemish": *Ut exhiberet ipse sibi gloriosam Ecclesiam, non habentem maculam, aut rugam, aut aliquid hujusmodi, sed ut sit sancta et immaculata.* This Church, this Kingdom is being formed even here below. It is only entered by Baptism. On earth we live in it by grace, in faith, hope, and charity, but the day will come when we shall contemplate its perfection in heaven; that will be the kingdom of glory in the light of vision, the rejoicing in unending possession and union. That is why St. Paul said that "the grace of God is life everlasting, in Christ Jesus, our Lord."

This is the great mystery of God's design. *Si scires donum Dei!* If you but knew the gift of God! Gift ineffable in itself, ineffable above all in its source, which is *love*.

It is because He loves us that God wills us to make us share, as His children, His own beatitude: *Videte qualem caritatem dedit nobis Pater ut filii Dei nominemur et simus.* The love which makes us such a gift is infinite, for, says St. Leo: "the gift surpassing all gifts is that God calls man His child, and that man calls God his Father". Each of us can say in all truth: It is by a special act of love and kindness that God has created and called me by Baptism to Divine adoption, for in His penitude and infinite riches, God has no need of any creature: *Genuit nos voluntarie verbo veritatis suae.* By a special act of love and complacency God has chosen me, *Elegit nos*, to be raised infinitely above my natural condition, to enjoy eternally His own beatitude, to be the realization of one of His Divine thoughts, to be a voice in the concert of the elect, to be one of those brethren who are like to Jesus, and share for ever His heavenly inheritance.

This love is manifested with special splendour in the way the Divine plan is fulfilled "in Jesus Christ" *in Christo Jesu.*

"By this hath the charity of God appeared towards us, because God hath sent His only-begotten Son into the world, *that we may live by Him.*" Yes, God loves us so much, that to show us this love He has given us His only-begotten Son: *Sic Deus dilexit mundum ut Filium suum Unigenitum daret*; He has given us His Son, so that His Son may become our Brother, and that we may one day be His co-heirs, and share in the riches of His grace and glory: *Ut ostenderet . . . abundantes divitas gratiae sua in bonitate super nos in Christo Jesu.*

Such is then in its majestic range and merciful simplicity God's plan for us. *God wills our holiness*, He wills it because He loves us infinitely, and we ought to will it with Him. He wills to make us saints *in making us participate in His very life*, and for that end, He *adopts us as His children*, and the heirs of His infinite glory and eternal beatitude. *Grace* is the principle of this holiness, supernatural in its source, in its acts, and in its fruits. But God only gives us this adoption *through His Son, Jesus Christ*. It is in Him, and by Him, that God wills to unite Himself to us, and that we should be united to Him: *Nemo venit ad Patrem nisi per Me.* Christ is the Way, the only way, to lead us to God, and without Him we can do nothing: *Sine Me nihil potestis facere.* Our holiness has no other foundation than that same one which God has established, that is to say, union with Jesus Christ *Fundamentum aliud nemo potest ponere, praeter id quod positum est, quod est Christus Jesus.*

Thus, God communicates the fulness of His Divine life to the Humanity of Christ, and through it, to all souls in the measure of their predestination in Jesus Christ: *Secundum mensuram donationis Christi.*

We must understand that we can only be saints according to the measure in which the life of Jesus Christ is in us: that is the only holiness God asks of us; there is no other. We can only be holy in Jesus Christ, otherwise we cannot be so at all. There is not an atom of this holiness in creation; it proceeds from God by a supremely free act of His Almighty Will, and that is why it is supernatural.

St. Paul returns more than once to the gratuitousness of the Divine Gift of adoption, and also to the eternity of the ineffable love which determined Him to make us partakers of it, and to the wonderful means of realizing it through the grace of Jesus Christ. He bids his disciple, Timothy, remember that God has "called us by His holy calling, not according to our works, but according to His own purpose and grace, which was given us in Christ Jesus before the times of the world". By grace you are saved through faith, he wrote to the faithful of Ephesus, "and not through your own works, that no man may glory".

VII

It is to God that all glory must be referred. This glory is the end of the Divine work. St. Paul shows us this when he concludes his exposition of the Divine Plan in these words: *In laudem gloriae gratiae suae.*

If God adopts us as His children; if He realizes this adoption through the grace of which the plenitude is in His Son Jesus; if He wills to make us partakers in Christ's eternal inheritance, it is for the exaltation of His glory.

Remark how insistently St. Paul dwells upon this point in exposing the Divine Plan to us in the words I quoted at the beginning: God "has predestinated us . . . unto the praise of the glory of His grace": *In laudem gloria gratiae suae.* He twice returns to this point further on: "In Whom we who are called . . . being predestinated unto the praise of His glory": *Ut simus in laudem gloriae ejus.*

The first expression of the Apostle is particularly remarkable. He does not say unto the glory of His grace, but "unto the praise of the glory of His grace"; which means that this grace will be surrounded with the splendour attached to a triumph. Why does St. Paul speak thus? It is because in order to restore to us the Divine adoption, Christ has had to triumph over the obstacles created by sin. But these obstacles have only served to make the Divine marvels in the work of our supernatural restoration shine out the more in the sight of the whole world: *Mirabiliter condidisti et mirabilius reformasti.* Each of the elect is the fruit of the Blood of Jesus, and of the wonderful operations of His grace; all the elect are so many trophies won by this Divine Blood, and that is why they are all like a glorious praise to Christ and to His Father: *Ut simus in laudem gloriae ejus.*

I said at the beginning that the Divine perfection of which the Angels especially sing the praise is holiness: *Sanctus, Sanctus, Sanctus.* But what is the outburst of praise which rises from the choir of the elect in heaven? What is the uninterrupted canticle of that immense multitude that constitutes the kingdom of which Christ is the Head? "O Lamb that wast slain, Thou hast redeemed us, Thou hast made us to our God a kingdom: to Thee and to Him that sitteth on the Throne, praise and honour and glory and power for ever and ever." That is the song of praise with which heaven resounds to exalt the triumph of the grace of Jesus: *In laudem gloriae gratiae suae.*

We enter, then, into the eternal designs, if, even here below, we join in this canticle. When St. Paul writes this wonderful Epistle to the Ephesians, he is a prisoner; but at this moment when he is preparing to reveal to them the mystery hidden from the beginning, he is so transported with the greatness of the mystery of the Divine adoption in Jesus Christ, he is so dazzled with the "unfathomable riches" brought by Christ, that, in spite of his privations, he cannot refrain from exclaiming at the very beginning of this letter, in an outburst of praise and thanksgiving: "Blessed be the God and Father of Our Lord Jesus Christ Who hath blessed us with spiritual blessings in Christ." Yes, blessed be the Eternal Father Who has called us to Himself from all eternity to make us His children, and partakers of His own life and His own beatitude; Who, in order to fulfil His designs, has given us in Jesus Christ, all good, all riches, all treasures, so that in Him nothing is wanting to us: *Ita ut nihil vobis desit in ulla gratia!*

This is the Divine Plan.

All our holiness consists in entering more and more deeply, by the light of faith, into this *Sacramentum absconditum*, in entering into the design of God and realizing the eternal economy in ourselves.

He Whose Will it is to save us and to make us holy has traced out the plan with a wisdom only equalled by His goodness. Let us adapt ourselves to this Divine design by which God wills that we should find our holiness in our conformity to Christ Jesus. Once again, there is no other way; we shall only be pleasing to the Eternal Father—and is not that the whole substance of sanctity: to be pleasing to God?—if He recognizes in us the features of His Son. We must, by grace and by our virtues, be so identified with Christ that the Father, in looking down upon our souls, will recognize us as His true children and be well pleased with us as He was when contemplating Jesus Christ during His earthly life. Christ is His Beloved Son, and it is in Him that we shall be filled with all blessing which will lead us to the fulness of our adoption in the beatitude of heaven.

How good it is to repeat now, in the light of these truths, the prayer that Jesus Himself, the Beloved Son of the Father, has placed on our lips, which, coming from Him, is pre-eminently the prayer of the child of God: O Holy Father, Who dwellest in Heaven, we are Thy children, since Thou dost will to be called Our Father! May Thy Name be hallowed, honoured, glorified! May thy perfections be praised and exalted more and more upon earth! May we manifest in ourselves, by our works, the splendour of Thy grace! Extend then Thy reign; may Thy Kingdom ever increase, this Kingdom which is also that of Thy Son, since Thou hast made Him the head of it. May Thy Son be truly the King of our souls, and may we testify to His kingship over us by the perfect accomplishment of Thy Will! May we, like Him, ever seek to adhere to Thee by fulfilling Thy good pleasure, Thy eternal designs for us, so as to be like to Jesus in all things, and through Him, worthy children of Thy love!

II. CHRIST THE ONLY MODEL OF ALL PERFECTION

When we read the Epistles of St. Paul to the Christians of his time, it is striking to see with what insistency he speaks of the mystery of Our Lord Jesus Christ. He constantly returns to this subject which has taken such possession of him that Christ is his very life: *Mihi vivere Christus est*. He spends himself, without counting the cost, for Christ and His members: *Ego autem libentissime impendam, et superimpendar ipse pro animabus vestris*.

Chosen and instructed by Jesus Himself to be the herald of His mystery throughout the world, he has penetrated so deeply into its depths and glories, that his one desire is to unveil it and make the adorable Person of Christ known and loved. He writes to the Colossians that he is filled with joy in the midst of his tribulations in the thought that it has been given to him to announce "the mystery which hath been hidden from ages and generations but now is manifested to His saints, to whom God

192

would make known the riches of the glory of this mystery ...
which is Christ".

See how when he is in prison he is told that others besides
himself are preaching Christ; some are doing this out of a spirit
of contention in opposition to him; others with good intentions.
Does he feel trouble or jealousy? Quite the contrary. Provided
Christ is preached, what does it matter to him? "So that by all
means, whether by occasion, or by truth, Christ be preached,
in this also I rejoice, yea and will rejoice": *Et in hoc gaudeo, sed
et gaudebo.* Thus he refers all his knowledge, all his preaching,
all his love, all his life to Jesus Christ: *Non enim judicavi me
scire aliquid inter vos nisi Jesum Christum.* In the labours and
struggles of his apostolate, one of his joys is to think that he is
"in labour"—it is his own expression—to form Christ in souls.

The Christians of the first ages understood the doctrine
the great apostle set forth to them. They understood that God
has given His only Son Christ Jesus that He may be for us "our
wisdom, justice, sanctification and redemption"; they understood the divine plan: namely, that God has given to Christ the
fulness of grace that we may find all in Him. They lived by this
doctrine, *Christus . . . vita vestra*, and that is why their spiritual
life was at once so simple and bore so much fruit.

Now let us remind ourselves that, in these our days, the
Heart of God is not less loving nor his arm less powerful. God
is ready to shed His graces upon us, I do not say as extraordinary
in their character, but as abundant and as useful as those He
shed upon the first Christians. He does not love us less than He
loved them. All the means of sanctification that they had, we
too possess; we have besides the examples of the saints who
have followed Christ to encourage us. But we are too often like
Naaman the leper who came to consult the prophet and beg his
cure; he was on the point of not obtaining it because he found
the remedy too simple.

That is the case with some of those who undertake the
spiritual life; people are to be met with who are so attached to
their own way of seeing things that they are scandalized at the
simplicity of the divine plan. And this scandal is not without
harm. These souls that have not understood the mystery of
Christ lose themselves in a multiplicity of details and often weary

themselves in a joyless labour. Why is this? Because all that our human ingenuity is able to create for our inner life serves for nothing if we do not base our edifice upon Christ: *Fundamentum aliud nemo potest ponere praeter id quod positum est, quod est Christus Jesus.*

This explains the change that sometimes takes place in certain souls. For years, their lives have been as it were cramped, they have been often depressed, hardly ever contented, for ever finding new difficulties in the spiritual life. Then one day God gives them the grace of understanding that Christ is our All, that He is the *Alpha* and *Omega*, that out of Him we have nothing, that in Him we have everything, for everything is summed up in Him. From that moment all is, as it were, changed for these souls; their difficulties vanish like the shades of night before the rising sun. As soon as Our Lord, the true Sun of our lives, *Sol justitiae*, fully illumines these souls, they unfold, mount upwards and bear much fruit of holiness.

Doubtless, trials are not absent from the lives of such souls; they are often the very condition of inward progress; collaboration with Divine grace will also remain attentive and generous, but all that narrows the soul and leads to discouragement disappears. Such souls live in the light; they dilate in it. *Viam mandatorum tuorum cucurri cum dilatasti cor meum*; their life becomes simplified. They understand the poverty of the means they had themselves created and so often renewed, hoping by them to prop up their own spiritual edifice. They grasp the truth of these words: *Nisi Dominus aedificaverit domum, in vanum laboraverunt qui aedificant eam.* Unless Thou, O Lord, dost build Thyself a dwelling in us, we shall never be able to form a habitation worthy of Thee! It is in Christ, and no longer in self, that these souls seek the source of their holiness. They know this holiness is supernatural in its principle, its nature and its end; and that the treasures of sanctification are only to be found gathered up in Jesus, so that we may share in them: they understand that they are only rich with the riches of Christ.

These riches, according to the word of St. Paul, are unsearchable: *Investigables divitiae.* We can never exhaust them and all we can say of them will always remain far below the praises of which they are worthy.

There are, however, three aspects of the mystery of Christ, which we must contemplate when we speak of Our Lord as the source of our sanctification. We borrow the idea from the doctrine of St. Thomas, the prince of theologians, in what he has written of the sanctifying causality of Christ.

Christ is at once the exemplary cause, the meritorious cause and the efficient cause of all our holiness. Christ is the sole Model of our perfection—the Author of our redemption and the infinite Treasury of grace—and the efficient cause of our sanctification.

These three points sum up perfectly what we have to say of *Christ* Himself as the *life of our souls*. Grace is the principle of that supernatural life of children of God that forms the foundation and substance of all holiness. Now this grace is found in its fulness in Christ, and all the works we accomplish through grace have their model in Jesus—next, Christ has merited this grace for us by the satisfactions of His life, passion and death—lastly, Christ Himself produces this grace in us by the contact we have with Him through faith.

But these truths contain so much that we must contemplate each one separately. In this conference, we will consider Our Lord as our Divine Model in all things, as the Exemplar towards which we must tend. The first thing to be considered is the end we must attain. Once this end is clearly understood, the application of the means proper to its realization will follow quite naturally.

I

We have seen that holiness for us is only a participation in the Divine holiness. We are holy if we are children of God and if we live as true children of the Heavenly Father, worthy of our supernatural adoption. St. Paul says: "Be ye therefore followers of God as most dear children": *Estate imitatores Dei sicut filii carissimi*. Jesus Himself tells us: *Estote perfecti*, "Be you therefore perfect"—and it is to all His disciples He speaks—not with any kind of perfection, but *sicut Pater vester coelesti perfectus est*, "as also your heavenly Father is perfect". And why? Because "noblesse oblige". God has adopted us as His children, and children ought to resemble their father in their lives.

But in order to imitate God, we must know Him. And how are we to know God? He "inhabiteth light inaccessible", says St. Paul. *Lucem inhabitat inaccessibilem.* "No man, says St. John, "hath seen God at any time," *Deum nemo vidit unquam.* How then can we reproduce and imitate the perfections of One Whom we do not see?

St. Paul gives us the answer to this question. *Illuxit nobis in facie Christi Jesu.* God has revealed Himself to us by His Son and in His Son Jesus Christ. Christ Jesus is "the brightness of His glory", "the image of the invisible God", perfectly like to His Father, capable of revealing Him to men, for He knows Him as He is known: "No one knoweth the Father," Jesus says, "but the Son, and he to whom it shall please the Father to reveal Him." Christ Jesus Who is always *in sinu Patris*, tells us: "I know My Father", *Ego agnosco Patrem*; and He knows Him in order to reveal Him to us. *Ipse enarravit.* Christ is the revelation of the Father.

And how does the Son reveal the Father? By becoming incarnate. The Word, the Son, is incarnate, is made man, and in Him, by Him, we know God. Christ is God brought within our reach under a human expression. It is the Divine perfection revealed to us under earthly forms; it is holiness itself appearing sensibly before our eyes during thirty-three years so as to be rendered tangible and imitable. We can never think too much about this: Christ is God made man, living among men so as to teach them by His words and above all by His life how men ought to live in order to imitate God and please Him. We have then first of all, if we wish to live as children of God, only to open our eyes with faith and love and contemplate God in Jesus.

There is in the Gospel a very simple and yet magnificent episode. You know it, but here is the place to recall it. It was the eve of the passion of Jesus. Our Lord had been speaking, as He alone could speak, of His Father to His disciples, and these, carried out of themselves, desired to see and know the Father. The apostle Philip exclaims: "Lord, show us the Father and it is enough for us." *Ostende nobis Patrem et sufficit nobis.* And Christ Jesus answers: "Have I been so long a time with you, and have you not known Me? Philip, he that seeth Me, seeth the

Father also." *Qui videt me, videt et Patrem.* Yes, Christ is the revelation of God, His Father. As God, He makes only one with Him, and he who contemplates Him, sees the revelation of God.

When you contemplate Christ abasing Himself in the poverty of the crib, recall this word: *Qui videt me, videt et Patrem.* When you see the Youth of Nazareth, full of obedience, toiling in the humble workshop until the age of thirty, say to yourself "He that seeth Him, seeth His Father", to contemplate Him is to contemplate God. When you see Christ passing through the villages of Galilee, everywhere doing good, healing the sick, announcing the good tidings; when you see the Crucified, dying for love of men, the object of the derision of His executioners, it is He Who says to you: *Qui videt me, videt et Patrem.* "He that seeth Me, seeth the Father also."

These are so many manifestations of God, so many manifestations of the Divine perfections. The perfections of God are in themselves as incomprehensible as the Divine nature. Which of us, for example, could comprehend what Divine love is? It is an abyss surpassing all we could imagine. But when we see Christ, Who, as God, is "one" with His Father, Who has in Him the same Divine life as the Father, instruct men, die upon a cross, give His life for love of us; when we see Him institute the Eucharist, we then understand the greatness of God's love.

So is it with each of God's attributes, with each of His perfections; Christ reveals them to us; and according to the measure we advance in His love, He makes us enter more deeply into His mystery: *Qui autem diligit me, diligetur a Patre . . . ego diligam eum et manifestabo ei meipsum.* Which amounts to saying: If anyone loves Me, receives Me in My humanity, he shall be loved of My Father, and I also will love him and will manifest Myself to him in My divinity. I will disclose its secrets to him.

"The life was manifested," writes St. John, "and we have seen and do bear witness, and declare unto you the life eternal, which was with the Father, and hath appeared to us," in Christ Jesus. So that to know and imitate God, we have only to know and imitate His Son Jesus, Who is the expression at once human and divine of the infinite perfections of His Father: *Qui videt me, videt et Patrem.*

II

But how and in what is Christ, the Incarnate Word, our Model, our exemplar?

Christ is doubly our Model: in His Person and in His works; in his *state* of Son of God, and in His human *activity*, for He is at the same time Son of God and Son of man, perfect God and perfect man.

Christ is God, perfect God, *Perfectus Deus*.

Let us go in spirit to Judea, at the time of Christ. He has already fulfilled one part of His mission, journeying through Palestine, teaching and accomplishing the "works of God". Behold Him after a day of apostolic labour, gone apart from the multitude, surrounded only by His disciples. He asks them: "Whom do men say that the Son of man is?" The disciples echo all that is noised abroad concerning Him.

"Some John the Baptist, and others Elias, and others Jeremias, or one of the prophets." "But whom do you say that I am?" Jesus asks. Then Peter answering says to Him: "Thou art Christ, the Son of the living God." And Our Lord, confirming the testimony of His apostle, responds: "Blessed art thou . . . because flesh and blood (natural intuition) hath not revealed it to thee, but My Father Who is in heaven."

Christ is then the Son of God, God of God, Light of Light, very God of very God, as the *Credo* expresses it. Christ, says St. Paul, "thought it not robbery" to call Himself equal with the Father: *Non rapinam arbitratus est esse se aequalem Deo.*

Thrice, moreover, the voice of the Eternal Father made itself heard to the world, and each time it was to glorify Christ by proclaiming Him to be His Son, the Son in Whom He is well pleased: *Hic est Filius meus dilectus in quo mihi bene complacui, ipsum audite.* Let us prostrate ourselves like the disciples who heard this voice of the Father on Thabor, and with Peter, inspired from on high, let us say to Jesus: Yes, Thou art the Christ, the Incarnate Word, true God, equal to Thy Father, perfect God, possessing all the Divine attributes; Thou art, O Jesus, with Thy Father and the Holy Ghost, the Almighty; Thou art the Eternal; Thou art infinite Love. I believe in Thee, and I adore Thee "my Lord and my God!"

Son of God, Christ is also Son of man, perfect Man: *Perfectus homo.*

The Son of God is made flesh; He remains what He is— perfect God. But He unites Himself to a human nature, complete like ours, integral in its essence, with all its native properties. Like all of us Christ is "made of a woman". He belongs authentically to our race. Often in the Gospel, He calls Himself "the Son of man"; eyes of flesh have seen Him, human hands have touched Him. Even on the morrow of His glorious resurrection, He makes the incredulous Apostles verify the reality of His human nature: *Palpate et videte quia spiritus carnem et ossa non habet sicut me videtis habere.*

Like each of us, He has a soul, created directly by God; a body formed of the substance of a woman, an intelligence to know, a will to love and choose; all the faculties that we have, memory and imagination. He has passions in the philosophical, elevated, and noble sense of the word, in the sense excluding all disorder and all weakness; for in Him these passions are perfectly subject to reason and only moved by an act of His will. His human nature is then similar in everything to that of his brethren: *Debuit per omnia fratribus similari,* says St. Paul, excepting sin: *Absque peccato.* Jesus has not known sin, nor that which is the source and consequence of sin—ignorance, error, sickness, all things unworthy of His wisdom, His dignity and His divinity.

But our Divine Saviour willed, during His mortal life, to bear our infirmities, all those infirmities compatible with His sanctity. The Gospel clearly shows us this. There is nothing in the nature of man that Jesus has not sanctified; our labours, our sufferings, our tears. He has made all these His own. See Him at Nazareth: during thirty years He spent His life in the obscure toil of an artisan, inasmuch that when He began to preach, His compatriots were astonished, for up to this time they had only known Him as the son of the carpenter: *Unde huic omnia ista? Nonne hic est fabri filius?*

Like us Our Lord has felt hunger; after having fasted in the desert "He was hungry": *Postea esuriit.* He has suffered thirst: did He not ask the Samaritan woman to give Him to drink, *Da mihi bibere?* and upon the cross did He not cry: "I thirst." *Sitio?* Like us He has felt fatigue; He was often fatigued by His long journeyings throughout Palestine. When at Jacob's well, He asked for water to quench His thirst. St. John tells us that He was wearied; it was the hour of noon, and after having walked far and being wearied, He sat down on the side of the well: *Fatigatus ex itinere, sedebat sic supra fontem. Hora erat quasi sexta.* Thus then, in the words of St. Augustine in the wonderful commentary he has given us on this beautiful evangelical scene, "He Who is the very Strength of God is overwhelmed with lassitude": *Fatigatur Virtus Dei.* Slumber has closed His eyelids; He slept in the boat when the tempest arose: *Ipse vero dormiebat.* He really slept, so the apostles fearing to be engulfed by the angry waves, had to awaken Him. He wept over Jerusalem, His own city which He loved despite its ingratitude; the thought of the disasters that, after His death, were to fall upon it drew tears from His eyes: "If thou hadst also known . . . the things that are to thy peace!" *Flevit super illam.* He wept at the death of Lazarus, as we weep over those we cherish, so that the Jews who witnessed this sight said to one another: "Behold how He loved Him! Christ shed tears because His Heart was touched; He wept for him who was His friend; the tears sprang from the depth of His Heart. Several times too it is said of Him in the Gospel that His Heart was touched with compassion.

Still more than this, He has felt sadness, heaviness and fear: *Coepit pavere et taedere, et moestus esse*; in His agony in the Garden of Olives, His soul is overwhelmed with sorrow: *Tristis est anima mea usque ad mortem*; anguish penetrated His soul to the point of wringing from it "a strong cry and tears". All the mockeries, all the outrages with which He was saturated in His Passion, the being buffeted and spit upon, all these insults, far from leaving Him insensible, caused Him intense suffering. His nature being more perfect, His sensibility was the greater and more delicate. He was plunged in an abyss of suffering. Lastly, after having shown Himself to be truly man, like to us in all things, He willed to endure death like all the sons of Adam: *Et inclinato capite tradidit spiritum.*

It is then both as Son of God and Son of man, that Our Lord is our Model—but He is so first of all as Son of God. This *state* of Son of God is properly speaking what is essential and fundamental in Christ, and it is in this we must first of all resemble Him.

And how can we do so?

The Divine Sonship of Christ is the type of our supernatural sonship; His condition, His "being" the Son of God is the exemplar of the state in which we must be established by sanctifying grace. Christ is the Son of God by nature and by right, in virtue of the union of the Eternal Word with human nature; we are so by adoption and grace, but we are so really and truly. Christ has, moreover, sanctifying grace; He possesses the fulness of it; from this fulness it flows into us more or less abundantly, but, in its substance, it is the same grace that both fills the created soul of Jesus and deifies us. St. Thomas says that our divine filiation is a resemblance of the eternal filiation: *Quaedam similitudo filiationis aeternae.*

Such is the primordial and supereminent manner in which Christ is first of all our example: in the Incarnation He is constituted, by right, the Son of God; we should become so by being partakers of the grace derived from Him which, deifying the substance of our souls, constitutes us in the state of children of God. That is the first and *essential* characteristic of the likeness we must have to Christ Jesus; it is the condition of all our supernatural activity. If first and above all we do not possess in us this *sanctifying grace* which is the *fundamental sign of similitude with Jesus,* the Eternal Father will not recognize us for His own; and all we do in our lives without this grace is of no merit to make us partakers of the everlasting inheritance: we shall only be coheirs with Christ if we are His brethren by grace.

III

Christ is also our Model *in His works.*

We have seen how truly He *was* man, we must now see how truly He *acted* as man.

In this again, Our Lord is for us a perfect, and yet an accessible model of all holiness. In an incomparable degree, He practised all the virtues that can adorn human nature, all those at least that were compatible with His Divine nature.

You know that with sanctifying grace, there was given to the Soul of Christ the magnificent array of virtues and gifts of the Holy Spirit. These virtues flowed from grace as from a fountain-head, they were expressed in all their perfection in the course of the life of Jesus.

Evidently He had not faith. This theological virtue only exists in a soul not yet enjoying the vision of God. The Soul of Christ contemplated God face to face; It could not exercise faith in regard to this God Whom it saw; but it had that submission of the will necessary to the perfection of faith, that reverence, that adoration of God, the first and infallible Truth. This disposition was in the highest degree in the Soul of Christ.

Neither had Jesus, properly speaking, the virtue of hope: it is no longer possible to hope for what is already possessed. The theological virtue of hope makes us desire the possession of God, whilst giving us the confidence of receiving the graces necessary to arrive at this possession. Through its union with the Word, the Soul of Christ was filled with the Divinity; It could not then have hope; this virtue only existed in Christ in the sense that He could desire, and indeed did desire, the glorification of His holy Humanity, the accidental glory that was to come to Him after His Resurrection: *Clarifica me, Pater*. He possessed in Himself, from the moment of His Incarnation, the source and root of this glory; He allowed it to appear for an instant at His Transfiguration on Thabor, but His mission on earth among men obliged Him to veil its splendour until His death. There were also certain graces Christ asked from His Father; for example, at the resurrection of Lazarus we hear Him addressing these words to His Father with the most absolute confidence: *Pater ego sciebam quia semper me audis.*

As to charity, He practised it to a supreme degree. The Heart of Christ is an immense furnace of love. The great love of Christ is that which He bears towards His Father. All His life can be summed up in these words: "I do always the things that please My Father."

Let us meditate these words in our prayer; only thus shall we be able to penetrate a little into their secret. This unspeakable love, this tending of the Soul of Christ towards His Father is the necessary consequence of His hypostatic union. The Son is altogether *Ad Patrem*, as the theologians say: this is, if I may thus express it, His essence: the holy Humanity is carried along by this divine current; having become, by the Incarnation, the Humanity of the Son of God, it therefore belongs entirely to the Father. The fundamental disposition, the primary and habitual sentiment of the Soul of Christ is necessarily this: I live for My Father, "I love My Father." It is because He loves His Father that Jesus gives Himself up to all He wills; His first act on coming into the world is an act of love towards Him: "Behold I come to do Thy will." It may be said that His whole existence here below was only to be the continued expression of this initial act. . . . During His life, He loves to repeat that His meat is to do the will of His Father; therefore He always did the things that pleased Him: *Quae placita sunt ei facio semper*. All that His Father had decreed for Him, He fulfilled to the least detail. Lastly, it was out of love for His Father that He was made obedient to the death of the cross: *Ut cognoscat mundus quia diligo Patrem, sic facio*. Never let us forget this: If Christ was able to say "Greater love than this no man hath than to lay down his life for his friends", if it is of faith that He died for us and for our salvation, *Propter nos et propter nostram salutem*, it remains true that it was before all, out of love for His Father, that Our Lord laid down His life. In loving us, it is His Father He loves; He sees us, He finds us in His Father: *Ego pro eis rogo . . . quia tui sunt*. These are His own words: "I pray for them . . . because they are Thine." Yes, Christ loves us, because we are the children of His Father, because we belong to His Father. He loves us with an ineffable love, surpassing all we can imagine, to such a point that each of us can say with St. Paul: *Dilexit me et tradidit semetipsum pro me*, "Who loved me, and delivered Himself for me".

Our Lord possessed too all the other virtues. Meekness and humility: "Learn of Me because I am meek and humble of Heart"; He, the Saviour, before Whom every knee bows in heaven and on earth, kneels before His disciples to wash their feet. Obedience: He is subject to His Mother and St. Joseph; one word of the Gospel sums up His hidden life at Nazareth: *Et erat subditus illis*. He obeys the Mosaic law; He goes assiduously to the assemblies in the Temple; He submits Himself to the powers lawfully established, declaring it necessary to "render to Caesar the things that are Caesar's"; He Himself pays the tribute money. Patience: how many testimonies has He not given of this especially during His bitter Passion! His infinite mercy towards sinners: with what kindness He welcomes the Samaritan woman and Mary Magdalen! As the Good Shepherd, He hastens to seek the straying sheep and bring it back to the fold. He is full of ardent zeal for the glory and interests of His Father; it is because of this zeal He drives out the sellers in the Temple and flings anathemas at the hypocrisy of the Pharisees. His prayer is continual: *Erat pernoctans in oratione Dei*. What shall we say of those sublime communications between the Incarnate Ward and His Father, of the spirit of religion and adoration with which Our Lord was animated?

In Him then every virtue blossomed in its season for the glory of God and for our salvation.

You know that the ancient patriarchs, before leaving this world, used to give to their eldest son a solemn blessing that was like the pledge of heavenly prosperity for his descendants. Now we read in the book of Genesis that the patriarch Isaac, before giving this solemn blessing to his son Jacob, kissed him, and smelling the perfume of his garments cried out in joy: "Behold the smell of my son is as the smell of a plentiful field, which the Lord hath blessed," *Ecce odor filii mei sicut odor agri pleni, cui benedixit Dominus*. And immediately, carried out of himself, he called down on his son's head the richest blessings from on high: "God give thee the dew of heaven, and of the fatness of the earth, abundance of corn and wine. And let peoples serve thee, and tribes worship thee; be thou lord of thy brethren. . . . Cursed be he that curseth thee; and let him that blesseth thee be filled with blessings!"

This scene is an image of the delight the Father has in contemplating the humanity of His Son Jesus, and of the spiritual blessings He sheds on those united to Him. Like a field enamelled with flowers, the soul of Christ is decked with every virtue that can embellish human nature. God is infinite. As such, His exigencies are infinite; and yet the least action of Jesus was the object of His Father's complacency. When Christ Jesus worked in the humble workshop at Nazareth, when He conversed with men or sat at meat with His disciples—things apparently so simple—His Father looked upon Him and said: "This is My beloved Son in

Whom I am well pleased": *Hic est Filius meus dilectus in quo mihi complacui.* And He adds: "Hear ye Him", *Ipsum audite*, that is to say, contemplate Him in order to imitate Him: He is your Model, follow Him: He is the Way and no one cometh to Me but by Him, no one has a share in My blessings but in Him, for I have given Him the fulness of them, as I have given Him the nations of the earth for His inheritance. Why does the heavenly Father take this infinite delight in Jesus? Because Christ accomplished everything perfectly, and His actions were the expression of the most sublime virtues; but especially because all the actions of Christ, whilst being in themselves human actions, were divine in their principle.

O Christ Jesus, full of grace and Model of every virtue, beloved Son in Whom the Father is well pleased, be the one object of my contemplation and love. May I regard all passing things "as dung" so as to place my joy in Thee alone; may I seek to imitate Thee so as to be, by Thee and with Thee, pleasing to Thy Father in all things!

IV

When we read the Gospel of St. John, we notice the insistency with which Jesus repeats: "My doctrine is not Mine"; "The Son cannot do anything of Himself"; "I cannot of Myself do anything"; "I do nothing of Myself".

Is this to say that Christ had neither human intelligence, nor will nor activity? In no wise; it would be heresy to think so; but the humanity of Jesus, being hypostatically united to the Word, there was not in Christ a human Person to which His faculties could be attached, there was in Him only one Person, that of the Word doing all in union with the Father; all was in the most absolute dependence on the Divinity, all His activity emanated from the one Person that was in Him, that of the Word. This activity, although immediately exercised by the human nature, was divine in its root, in its principle; and therefore the Father received from it infinite glory and found in it utmost delight.

Can we imitate this? Yes, since by sanctifying grace, we share in the divine filiation of Jesus; by this, our activity is enhanced and as it were made divine in its principle. It goes without saying that in the order of *being*, we always keep our own personality; we always remain, by nature, purely human creatures; our union with God by grace, however close and intimate it may be, remains an accidental not a substantial union. But it is so much the greater in as far as the autonomy of our personality, in the order of activity, is effaced before the Divinity.

If we wish nothing to interpose between us and God, nothing to hinder our union with Him, if we wish Divine blessings to flow in upon our souls, we must not only renounce sin and imperfection, but moreover despoil ourselves of our personality *in so far as it constitutes an obstacle to perfect union with God*. It constitutes an obstacle to perfect union when our judgment, our self-will, our self-love, our susceptibilities, make us think and act otherwise than according to the desires of our Heavenly Father. Believe me, our faults of frailty, our miseries, our human limitations, hinder our union with God infinitely less than that habitual attitude of the soul which, so to speak, wills to keep in everything the proprietorship of its activity. We must therefore not annihilate our personality—which is neither possible nor yet willed by God—but bring it to an entire capitulation before God. We must lay it down at God's feet and ask Him to be by His Spirit—as He is for the humanity of Christ—the supreme mover of all our thoughts, of all our feelings, of all our words, of all our actions, of all our life.

When a soul arrives at the state of having stripped itself of all sin, and all attachment to self and the creature; of having destroyed in itself, as far as possible, all purely natural and human springs of action in order to surrender itself completely to the Divine action; of living in absolute dependence of God, on His will, His commandments, on the spirit of the Gospel; of referring everything to the Heavenly Father, then it can truly say: *Dominus regit me*; "The Lord ruleth me; everything in me comes from Him, I am in His hands". This soul has attained to the perfect imitation of Christ to the point that its life is the very reproduction of that of Christ: *Vivo ego, jam non ego, vivit vero in me Christus*. God directs it; it is in everything, moved under divine impulsion: that is sanctity, the most perfect imitation of Christ in His *being*, in His *state* of Son of God, as in His primordial disposition of belonging altogether to His Father, in His person and in His *activity*.

Do not think it is presumption on our part to wish to attain so sublime an ideal: no, it is God's own desire; it is His eternal design for us: *Praedestinavit nos conformes fieri imaginis Filii sui*. The more we are conformed to His Son, the more the Father loves us, because we are more closely united to Him. When He sees a soul fully transformed in His Son, He surrounds it with His special protection, the most tender cares of His providence; He showers His blessings upon it, He places no limit to the communication of His graces: that is the secret of God's extraordinary gifts.

Let us thank our Father in Heaven for having given us His Son, Christ Jesus, as our Model, so that we have only to look at Him to know what we have to do: *Ipsum audite*. Christ has told us: "I have given you an example, that as I have done to you, so you do also." *Exemplum enim dedi vobis ut quemadmodum ego feci vobis, ita et vos faciatis*. He has left us His example that we may walk in His footsteps: *Vobis relinquens exemplum, ut sequamini vestigia ejus*. He is the only way we must follow: *Ego sum via*; he who follows Him does not walk in the darkness, but comes to the light of life. That is the Model faith reveals to us, a transcendent and yet an accessible Model: *Inspice et fac secundum exemplar*.

The soul of Our Lord contemplated at every moment the divine essence. With one and the same glance, His Soul saw the ideal conceived by God for humanity, and each of His actions was the expression of this ideal. Let us then lift up our eyes, let us love to know Christ Jesus more and more, to study His life in the Gospel, to follow His mysteries in the wonderful order established by the Church herself in her liturgical cycle from Advent to Pentecost; let us open the eyes of our faith and live in such a way as to reproduce in ourselves the features of this Exemplar, to conform our lives in accordance with His words and acts. This model is divine and visible and shows us God acting in the midst of us and sanctifying in His humanity all our actions, even the most ordinary; all our sentiments, even the most intimate; all our sufferings, even the deepest.

Let us contemplate this Model with faith. We are at times tempted to envy the contemporaries of Jesus, who were able to see Him, to follow Him and listen to Him. But faith renders Him also present to our souls with a presence not less efficacious for us. Christ has said Himself: *Beati qui non viderunt et crediderunt*: "Blessed are they that have not seen and have believed." This was to make us understand that it is not less advantageous for us to live in contact with Jesus by faith than to have seen Him in the flesh. He, Whom we see living and acting when we read the Gospel or when we celebrate His mysteries, is the very Son of God. We have said everything when we have said of Christ: "Thou art the Son of the Living God", and that is the fundamental aspect of the Divine Model of our souls. Let us contemplate Him, not with an abstract contemplation, exterior, theoretic and cold, but with a contemplation full of love attentive to grasp, in order to reproduce them in our lives, every feature of this Model and above all that fundamental and primordial disposition of Christ, of living for His Father. All His life was resumed in this disposition; all the virtues of Christ are the effect of this orientation of His Soul towards the Father, and this orientation is itself only the fruit of that ineffable union by which, in Jesus, all humanity is drawn into that Divine impulse which draws the Son towards His Father.

It is this which properly constitutes the Christian: first of all to share *by sanctifying grace*, in the Divine filiation of Christ: that is the imitation of Jesus in *His state* of Son of God; and next to reproduce *by our virtues* the characteristics of this unique archetype of perfection: that is the imitation of Jesus *in His works*. St. Paul points out this when he tells us we must form Christ in us, put on Christ, and bear in us the image of Christ.

Christianus, alter Christus: "The Christian is another Christ." That is the true definition of a Christian given by tradition, if not in the same words, at least equivalently. "Another Christ", because the Christian is first of all, by grace, a child of the heavenly Father and brother of Christ here below in order to be His co-heir above; "another Christ", because all his activity—thoughts, desires, actions—plunges its root in this grace, to be exercised according to the thoughts, desires, sentiments of

Jesus, and in conformity with the actions of Jesus: *Hoc enim sentite in vobis quod et in Christo Jesu.*

Émile Mersch
1890-1940

The twentieth century prides itself for its spirit of individual freedom and expression. Even the world of Christian spirituality is permeated by it. One of the strengths of the individual freedom approach is the fact that it invites and encourages a great amount of creativity and variety, thus rendering possible an enrichment of the spiritual life. Accompanying this, of course, is a weakness inherent to individualism, viz., the increased possibility of misunderstanding the foundations of Christian spirituality and the consequent impoverishment of that same spiritual life. The doctrine of the Mystical Body, properly incorporated into the Church's life, can serve to guide the members of the church to fullness of perfection in Christ while permitting the greatest possible freedom of individual expression.

Among the most significant contributors to the development of the doctrine of the Mystical Body in the twentieth century was Father Émile Mersch. He was born in Belgium in 1890. At the age of seventeen he entered the Society of Jesus. He was a student of theology during the years of the First World War and, during the years between the two great wars, taught philosophy and theology. He died in France, the victim of a bomb attack, in 1940.

Father Mersch dedicated himself to a study of the mystery of Christ. He called the mystery a prodigy of unity which permeates the whole of existence. He saw a natural unity underlying all mankind and was convinced that God, through and in Christ, had elevated this to supernatural perfection. Mankind's unity with Christ is the principle of all else. Christ is the cause of all holiness, purity, and justice. In Him and in Him alone is the restoration and the ennobling of man. One and the same holiness flows through all humanity. Unity in Christ calls for a deepened interior life, a deification of mankind, an obligation to rise above oneself, a new and purer code of morality, and the virtues of Christian holiness, chastity and charity. The mystery of Christ is a miracle of God's goodness and mankind's transformation.

The Whole Christ was Father Mersch's effort, by way of history, to explore this fundamental insight. In it, he studied the doctrine of the Mystical Body in Sacred Scripture (Part One), in the Greek Fathers of the Church (Part Two), and in the Western Tradition (Part Three). The selection presented below is from Part Three. It is a survey of the doctrine of the Mystical Body in the French School of the Spiritual Life, and a statement on the doctrine in our own day (pre-1940). Mersch saw the doctrine as making rapid progress at the present time. He believed that it could overcome the naturalism of our century, serve as a remedy for the sickness of nationalism, and correct misguided individualism and socialism. He further believed that the doctrine could be the driving force for all social, political and economic progress in our world.

"Each Christian has his own personal grace; yet in all who possess grace, all these individual graces remain united in their common source, which is Christ, the Head of the Church." Mersch realized that the spirituality of the Church, while concretized and lived through individual Christians, could come to full maturity only when all individuals return their lives to the one source of holiness, Christ.

THE WHOLE CHRIST

CHAPTER X

THE FRENCH SCHOOL. THE MYSTICAL BODY AND THE
SPIRITUAL LIFE

The theology of our incorporation in Christ. Pierre de Bérulle. Religion is the center of all, and the heart of religion is Jesus Christ. Comparison with the Greek Fathers. Christ is the life of souls, "a divine capacity for souls." The Eucharist. The mysteries of Christ's life are present and perpetual.

II. *Spirituality based on this theology.* The ideal: to be in the same relation to the humanity of Jesus as His humanity is to the Word: that is, we should be without subsistence of our own, continuing in Him the divine mission of the Word. Obedience, contemplation, adherence to God.

III. *Rigorism of the doctrine,* especially as proposed by Condren and Olier. The sternness of Bérulle's teaching. The Jansenist theory of grace and of the Mystical Body. Sources and characteristics of the theory of the Mystical Body as taught by Condren; by Olier. Both manifest a certain disdain for human nature. We are loathsome in the eyes of God, and even in the eyes of Jesus Christ. We ought to feel a like detestation for ourselves. To lose and to annihilate self.

IV. This rigorism is belied by their true spirit of Christian charity.

I

The energy and richness which the doctrine of the Mystical Body loses at the hands of the Schoolmen is restored by the masters of the French Oratory and of St. Sulpice. These are Cardinal Pierre de Bérulle, founder and first general of the Congregation of the Oratory of Jesus Christ, Père Charles de Condren, disciple and successor of Bérulle in the office of general, and Jean-Jacques ("Monsieur") Olier, the founder of St. Sulpice. It is not our purpose here to tell the story of their lives, but simply to discover what they have to say of the Mystical Body in their doctrine of the spiritual life; for all three, and especially Condren and Olier, must be classed as spiritual writers rather than as theologians. Our task will be easy and fruitful, for the doctrine of the Mystical Body occupies a prominent place in their writings; it will be a simple task as well, since the teaching of all three is very much the same, and may be studied as one. Consequently, we shall restrict ourselves to a summary of the doctrine of Bérulle, who is first both in time and in theological importance. Toward the end of the chapter, when we shall have to turn our attention to a secondary though important feature, the rigorism and the negative side of the doctrine, we shall also quote from Condren and Olier, in whose writings this tendency is more pronounced. In this way we shall have an opportunity to indicate the characteristics proper to these two masters.

In speaking of Bérulle, we should first consider the reasons which led him to take a special interest in the truth of the Mystical Body. Unfortunately, however, we can make only conjectures on this point. His method of prayers, together with the assistance of grace, seems to have been one of his sources of information concerning our incorporation in the Incarnate Word. But his biographers have so crowded their accounts with other developments that it is impossible to determine the exact nature of the spiritual lights which he thus received. These were probably only the first germ of the doctrine which he was to develop through profound meditation and laborious study. His teaching is marked by a blend of deep sincerity and bookish profusion that appears to indicate some such combination of divine light, personal work, and dogged assimilation at the beginning. Moreover, he had excellent opportunity to improve his knowledge of the subject, by reason of his association with several mystics, with various theories of mysticism, and perhaps also with the masters of the School of Salamanca on the occasion of his visits to Spain. We know that he went to Spain in order to make arrangements for bringing the Carmelites of St. Theresa to France. And, as a matter of fact, St. Theresa lays much stress upon our incorporation in Christ. Not that she makes use either of the idea or of the expression as such, but she frequently speaks of the life of Christ in the soul, which is a corollary of our incorporation in Him. However, we are not told whether or not Bérulle was impressed by this aspect of Teresian spirituality.

Though the contributing influences are not so easily distinguishable as we might wish, the doctrine is sufficiently complete to explain itself. We shall indicate its principal elements here.

The summit of all is God; the foundation of all our duties is religion, worship, the adoration of God. The center and bond of all is Christ, God like the Father and man like ourselves, who unites heaven and earth in Himself and who is Himself our religion. To adore God in Christ and through Christ is, we may say, the sole preoccupation of the founder of the Oratory, and the résumé of his spirituality.

Personally, he would have wished to count for naught in his own works, and let Jesus be everything in them. He would have preferred to remain silent and not to write, in order that the one Master should speak to souls. According to the testimony of Père Bourgoing, he sought to have no sentiment or thought or activity outside of Jesus; he united himself with Jesus in every undertaking, and, after transacting the most important business, he could return within himself to Jesus, the sole object of his life, with as much ease and tranquillity as if he had spent the entire time in contemplation.

As he lived it and as he presents it to his readers, the Christ-life is a limitless dependence; he loved to call it his "slavery"; often he speaks of it as an attachment, a belonging to Christ, an incorporation. This life comes to us wholly from the Incarnate Word, since according to the idea and the explanation that he borrows from the Greek Fathers, the Incarnation has stored up in Christ the life of all humanity.

> Jesus is Life in a threefold manner: in His eternal nature, in His divine Person, and in His new nature, which is His humanity. In His eternal nature, for the divinity is not simply the source of life, but Life itself; in His Person, for to be Life is His proper

215

and personal prerogative, by virtue of His eternal generation: in His humanity, since He vivifies it and makes it the plenitude and inexhaustible source of life.

The Father is the principle of all life, the First Principle. The Word is likewise a principle of life, but He is a principle generated by the Father. The human nature assumed by the Word is also a principle by reason of its assumption, but it is a dependent principle. It is the principle in the order of grace and of the second creation, as God is the Principle of the first creation. It was made such by God, of course; it was even created for this purpose. As Bérulle tells us, it was created to be our very own:

> Christ is ours by reason of His office (*par état*), and not merely because of certain actions; He is ours by birth, and not simply in virtue of His office: "He was born for us" (Isa. 9:6). He is ours forever, and not merely for a time; He is ours for all our needs and for all our uses; He is ours by the same power whereby the Father generates Him in Himself.

At the same time that the Word places His humanity in an order apart and draws it to the Father, He also makes that humanity our life, and causes it to reach out toward men; it becomes a universal Life, of which we are all "begotten and derived," and in which we are all vivified. The Saviour, declares Bérulle, is "a divine capacity for souls."

> *Jesus is a divine capacity for souls, and He is the source of the life whereby they live in Him.*
>
> There are in Jesus two wonderful capacities. By the one He is rendered capable of divinity, capable of the fullness of the divinity and of equality with God, though with dependence. The second is a capacity for souls; this He possesses in Himself, in His authority, in His power. For, if He has a capacity for the divinity, there is all the more reason why He should have a capacity for creatures. Our Lord receives this second capacity from the fullness of the divinity that is in Him: it makes Him a capacity for souls just as God is

a capacity for His creatures: a capacity that contains, preserves, protects, and places souls in a continual and profound dependence upon Jesus and upon God. And it pleased Jesus Christ to institute the sacrament of His body in order to bind our souls to Himself, and to draw them into the plenitude of the divinity that abides in Him, by means of His lovable and adorable capacity to contain them and to give them life and subsistence in Himself. Thus we have a representation of that wondrous chain composed of three links, of which the Fathers speak. The first link binds the only Son to the eternal Father by the bond of consubstantiality and unity of essence. The second binds the Son to our nature by the unity of His sacred Person. The third binds this deified humanity, this Man-God, to the person of each of us, by the efficacious and singular virtue of the Sacrament of His body, which incorporates us in His sacred humanity and causes us to live in Him, to share His life as His members, and to live with Him in His Father. Thus man ascends to this deified flesh and even to God, while God descends to the flesh and even to us.

These limitless perspectives are the joy of the founder of the Oratory.

Jesus is all, and He must be all in us. And we must be nothing, treat ourselves as nothing, be nothing in ourselves, and be only in Him. . . . This is the work that we must begin on earth, and which will be consummated in heaven, where Jesus shall be all in all.

We must quote Bérulle's rather lengthy development of this thought, entitled, *Of the life of the Christian in Jesus,* and addressed "to the Carmelites of the Convent of N."

Jesus is the crowning perfection (*accomplissement*) of our being; we subsist in Him alone, more truly than the body has its life and its perfection only in the soul, and the branch in the vine, and the part in the whole. For we are part of Jesus, and He is our all; all our good is to be in Him, as the branch exists and draws life and fruit from the vine. The truth is more real and more important than the reality of the branch in the vine; the latter is but a shadow and figure of the true reality.

We must regard our being as something defective and imperfect, as an empty space that needs to be filled, as a part that needs to be completed, as a piece of silver that awaits the stamp of the mint, or as a painting that has yet to receive the final life-like touches from the brush of a great artist.

Bérulle's sentences are labored and heavy, to be sure, but how insistent he is!

We should look upon Jesus as our consummation (*accomplissement*). This He is, and this He wills to be, as the Word is the consummation of the human nature that subsists in Him. . . .

Jesus alone is our consummation. We must attach ourselves to Him, who by His divinity is the foundation of our being, and who by His humanity is the bond that unites our being to God. He is the life of our life, the fullness of our capacity. Our first lesson should be a realization of our incomplete and imperfect condition, and our first step should be toward Jesus, who is our consummation. In this search for Jesus, in this adherence to Jesus, in this continual and profound dependence upon Jesus, lie our life, our rest, our strength, and all our power of action. Never must we act except united with Him, directed by Him, and drawing life from Him.

Since He was created Head of human nature, we have a relationship with Him, a proportion with Him, an aptitude for Him; we wait to be actuated by Him and to be filled by Him. . . . We are a capacity, a pure capacity for Him; none can actuate and fill it but He. . . .

We must not suffer ourselves to be in ourselves, except to see to it that Jesus Christ be living in us, and that He may use and enjoy possession of all that is within us.

Echoing the words of St. Cyril of Alexandria, Bérulle explains that Jesus exercises this possession of us by means of the Eucharist. Through this sacrament,

> we are joined to this divine substance in a real and substantial union, which approaches very nearly to the unity of the divine Persons, and which is a perfect imitation of that unity. This union I ought to recognize as a masterpiece of the divinity, a masterpiece which is itself divine. This union I ought to contemplate as a portrait drawn from life by a great Master, Jesus Christ, according to a model as divine, as perfect, and as incomparable as is the union, or rather, the unity, of the divine Persons of the Most Holy Trinity.

Not only the Person of Jesus, but, as Bérulle says in concert with the Fathers and the Scholastics, all His mysteries, all His dispositions, and all His sentiments affect us and vivify us. Past though they are in execution, His acts and His virtues are "perpetual" in their effects. One of his treatises bears the title:

> *Of the perpetuity of the mysteries of Jesus Christ.*
>
> We must consider the infinity which is communicated to these mysteries by the infinite Person who performs them in His human nature. We must weigh, as it were, the perpetuity of these mysteries. They took place under certain circumstances in the past, yet they continue and are present and perpetual in a new manner.
>
> They are past in execution, but present by their virtue. . . . The Spirit of God by whom this mystery was wrought, the interior disposition of the outward mystery, the efficacy and virtue whereby this mystery lives and acts in us, this virtuous state and disposition, the merit by which He acquired us for the Father and merited heaven, His life, and His very self, the actual

taste and sentiments He experienced when He accomplished the mystery—all this is ever living, actual, and present to Jesus. So that, if it were necessary or pleasing to God His Father, He would be ready to suffer anew and to accomplish once more this work, this action, this mystery. Therefore we must treat the things of Jesus and His mysteries, not as things that are past and dead, but as things that are living and present, yea eternal, from which we too should reap fruit that is present and eternal.

Perpetually then, according to Bérulle, "the Incarnation is a mystery binding God to man and man to God, a mystery to which we must bind ourselves"; perpetually the childhood of Jesus confers the grace of innocence and of docile obedience to direction, and the wound of the Sacred Side of the Crucified is an eternal mark of love. We cannot forego the pleasure of quoting the beautiful page which Bérulle devotes to this "Eternal Wound."

> Let us note that the living Heart of Jesus is already wounded deeply enough by love. Therefore the blow of the lance is reserved for His dead Heart; it is as if the wound of love was so great that the steel could inflict no deeper wound until He was dead. His Heart is eternally open, eternally wounded; His glory does not efface this wound, for it is a wound of love; the mark of the lance is but the symbol of the true and eternal wound of His Heart. This wound of the Side belongs to Jesus alone; it is proper neither to crucifixion nor to other men that are crucified; it is an eternal wound. It is a torment or wound inflicted upon a dead man, but it will endure unto eternal life, a wound that began in death but remains in life. This is not the case for others who are wounded, for their wounds do not survive death and will not be permanent in the resurrection. Give thanks to the eternal Father, who in decreeing the torment of the Cross for His humiliation, also decreed for Him this wound which is not proper to crucifixion, in order that we may abide in His Heart for all eternity.

Christ willed all the mysteries and all the events of His life, in order that He might thus elevate and "deify" in Himself all the conditions in which men may find themselves. In Jesus, childhood is deified; death is deified; even penance, shame, and sorrow are deified. For, as the cardinal explains:

> The Incarnation of the Word is the basis and foundation of the supreme dignity, which is not only the sanctification, but also the deification of all the dispositions and mysteries that enter into the life and pilgrimage of the Son of God on earth. All these dispositions and mysteries are deified. Therefore they have a divine dignity, a supreme power, a holy operation; and they are accomplished for the glory of God and for our particular good. . . . It is God's plan that all these dispositions should be honored, appropriated, and applied to our souls. As He distributes His gifts and graces, so also He distributes His dispositions and His mysteries among men and even among the angels.

It is the duty of each Christian to fulfill his own proper part in these mysteries. One is made partaker of His humiliations, another of His authority; but always and through all, it is the Incarnation that acts upon the faithful.

> In all these various states and conditions He gives Himself to all. He gives us His Heart, His grace, His Spirit. He incorporates us in Himself. He makes Himself our own, and appropriates us to Himself. He communicates Himself to us and incorporates us in Himself. He makes us His own, living in Him, of Him, and by Him, as forming part of His body, of His Spirit, and of Himself, in a manner that is far more efficacious and important than that whereby our members form part of our own body and of ourselves.

When the true nature of our Christ-life is represented in such a light, one immediately sees what rules of conduct it must impose upon us.

II

The Holy Scriptures and the earliest of the Fathers had already represented our incorporation in Christ as a first principle that should govern all our conduct. We recall, for instance, how Paul drew from it exhortations to charity, union, chastity, patience. This concern for practical applications is more characteristic of Latin than of oriental theology, but with the masters of the French School it attains its highest development. Their doctrine of the Mystical Body is primarily spiritual. Others use it merely on occasion, but with these writers it becomes a sort of system of spirituality.

The general principle, sometimes called "the fundamental equation," is that Christ our Head, who gives us life and movement, is likewise the norm of our activity, and that our relations with Him and with God are similar to those which unite His humanity to the divinity.

Thus, explains Bérulle, since Christ's human nature lacked a human personality, we too must cease to be a complete and self-sufficient whole. Christ's humanity subsists only in the personal existence of the Word; therefore we must live and act in total dependence upon Christ, placing ourselves in the same relation to Him as His humanity is in relation to, and dependent upon His divinity.

Such a manner of existence demands, first of all, a total abnegation. However, for the sake of better order, we shall reserve this particular point until later in the chapter. Another consequence is the supernatural nobility and dignity that is conferred upon the flesh and the soul of Christ by the hypostatic union. Christ's humanity becomes strictly divine and the source of supernatural life, while we are divinized and animated with a new life. And, just as all holiness is given to the humanity of Christ by its union with the divinity, so our new life obliges us to supernatural goodness, purity, and virtue.

The humanity of Christ was the instrument of the Word in working out the salvation of the world. In like manner, we too must be docile instruments in the hands of Christ for the sanctification of the world. However, it is not often that the cardinal speaks of this nobility and of our function as instru-

Émile Mersch

ments of God; he sees the entrance of God into us, rather than our assimilation and transfiguration at His hands.

By its personal union with the Word, the activity of the sacred humanity of Jesus shares in the mission on which the Father still continues to send His Incarnate Son. So it is also with the Christians, when they act as Christians. Their activity is a prolongation of Christ's activity; therefore it unites them with the same mission, which emanates from the Father and which sends forth the only-begotten Son.

> This divine mission is fundamental to all other missions. All others must adore it, depend upon it, and imitate it particularly in this point: that as the Son of God did not come into this world to do the work of the Father, worthy and important as that work was, without being sent by His Father, so no one must enter into the field of Jesus Christ, which is His Church, without justifying His mission and proving that it originates from that first mission.

But the mission of the Word is itself united with His eternal procession from the Father. So, too, for the Christians: whatever they do in Christ has a connection and a relation, through Christ, with the eternal generation of the Second Person of the Trinity.

> The divine action whereby, without any change, the Father generates His Son, is the origin of the mystery of the Incarnation, in which He gives His Son to human nature and begets Him anew in this second nature. The same divine action is also the origin of the union of the Son, in His twofold nature, with us all, uniting us to Him, giving us life in Him, and making us part of Him as the branch is part of the vine.

Thus we are brought back to the Trinity; the masters of the Oratory refuse to stop short of this goal. Since our life and activity as Christians is the prolongation of the Incarnation, it is joined through Christ to the eternal generation of the Word, who is the sole principle of the personality of the indivisible Christ. Therefore our actions have God, not only as their first beginning, but also as their first exemplar and ultimate norm. To know what the conduct of a Christian should be, we must in the first place consider, not the Christian himself—he is merely a participation—nor the relation between the two natures in Christ—this is simply a mediation indicating a higher principle—instead, we must first study the relations that unite the three divine Persons in the inner life of the Trinity.

So, our authors tell us, the prime reason for all obedience is the bond that unites the Son to the Father. Since the Son is only a subsistent relation, the Christian must have no existence, no will, no tendency except toward God. This Christian obedience must be wholly transformed into love, free of all servility, just as the term of the union between the Father and the Son is the Spirit of Love. In the Trinity there is order and love, but no domination. Hence our authors require that superiors exercise authority only for the sake of charity and never for their selfish ends.

Another conclusion which they draw from the generation of the Word is this: every Christian is essentially consecrated to the contemplative life, through faith and prayer here below and through the beatific vision in heaven.

> I say that the Christians are called to contemplation, not only by [a special] inspiration, but by the very state and condition of life and of grace that they have received in baptism. This grace elevates them and binds them to God through Jesus Christ His Son, who is His Word, His Thought, His Contemplation.

Again, as the Person of Christ united with the Father is the sole principle of the Holy Spirit, so the faithful must be principles of holy and spiritual works. This they cannot be except through union with God, through adherence to Him and dependence upon Him.

> We must adhere to Jesus. In this adherence to His divine Person—which is continually active in the production of the Holy Spirit who proceeds from Him—and in imitation of Him, we must be constantly occupied with spiritual and eternal things, directing

our every act to God. The Son of God is ever acting with God His Father in the production of the Holy Spirit; He operates with His Father in such a manner that He is one and the same Principle with the Father. This model we must both adore and imitate in our own activity, never acting alone, but conjointly with God our Father, in dependence upon Him yet in a union so intimate that we may be one principle and one spirit with Him. "He that cleaveth to the Lord is one spirit with Him" (1 Cor. 6:17).

Comparisons and arguments of this kind are very frequent in the writings of our masters, and most of all in the works of Cardinal de Bérulle. We know of no other author who has drawn so calmly and intrepidly the last consequences of our incorporation in the Incarnate Word. Especially in the matter of practical applications, none other has given us so sublime and so faithful a commentary of the words of Jesus Christ recorded by St. John: Thou in Me, and I in Thee, that they may be one in Us, as We are one" (John 17:21, 23). Small wonder that at these lofty heights Bérulle's thought and vocabulary betray a certain hesitancy; the more finely the point is drawn, the more flexible it becomes. Not a few of the cardinal's expressions demand explanation. The same remark is even more true of Père de Condren and Monsieur Olier. But the explanation is not hard to find; the context itself is usually a sufficient indication of the orthodox sense in which the passage should be understood.

Their teaching is extremely rich, as the reader will have been able to judge; it constitutes a considerable contribution to the doctrine of the Mystical Body. We believe that they have been more successful than others in effecting the synthesis between Christology and spirituality, and in proposing the truth of our incorporation in Christ as a code of perfection; they have also been more successful than anyone else in the Latin Church, in bringing out the divine and transcendent aspect of the life that is given us in Christ, and the elevation of soul that is demanded of us in consequence.

They have restored to the Latin doctrine of the Mystical Body the vigor of expression that it had lost in the works of the

Schoolmen. No longer has it any reason to envy the teaching of the Greek Fathers, except for one thing: it lacks a certain supernatural optimism. We must now turn our attention to this last point.

III

The reader will have observed that the holy cardinal proposes a most exacting spirituality. His constant refrain is "adherence, dependence, a manner of acting derived from Jesus," a complete stripping off of self in order to be a capacity, a pure capacity for Jesus, distrust of self in order to experience to the full the influence of Jesus. The supernatural life comes to us, not from a living God, but from a dying God—what the author means is clear; it is therefore a grace of self-annihilation, a spirit of death, an operation wherein God "confiscates" our whole being.

This note of sternness is presented even more vividly by Père Charles de Condren and Monsieur Jean-Jacques Olier. However, in order to understand their teaching properly, we must first of all consider the circumstances of the period in which they wrote.

In this seventeenth century a chill breath of rigorism reaches even to the highest summits of spirituality. Protestantism had been condemned, it is true, together with its doctrine of contempt for our nature and for our liberty, while the Church, aided here and hampered there by the secular power, was laboring to win back souls from heresy. Yet, so deep seated was the poison that it now gave rise, within the Church, to errors and heresies that were simply new manifestations, less virulent but even more dangerous, of the same morbid disease. What was worse, the new heretics were obstinate in their determination to remain in the Church. We need mention only a few names: Baius, who died in 1589; Jansenius, in 1638; Saint-Cyran, in 1643; Molinos, in 1697; and Quesnel, in 1719; and we may recall the long survival of Jansenism. One is struck by the profound resemblance that exists between these several errors, despite their many differences. Each is a different way of professing the same contempt for human nature. All teach that man's part in the work of salvation is to abstain from acting, to withdraw, to do nothing. They look upon all human love, all natural spontaneity, all affection for creatures, all joy and all gaiety, all seeking for personal happiness, and even all initiative, as sins, or at least as shortcomings and deviations from virtue; all these things appear to them as so many encroachments of man upon the universal domain of God.

True, they do not adopt the attitude of the Protestants, but there is a strong resemblance. They do not say with the Reformers that sin has vitiated the very substance of our nature; in fact, they consider this nature to be capable of true sanctification. But they do agree with the Reformers, when they maintain that this holiness cannot be the effect of our own acts, except insofar as these are acts of abstention; the less we have to do with our sanctification the better it will succeed. Their chief anxiety, it would seem, is to keep the human element at the greatest possible distance from the divine. Was not this also the chief anxiety of the Protestants?

What had man done during those centuries to deserve this treatment? How explain such contemptuousness? Was it an infiltration of Protestant ideas? Possibly it was; but, in our opinion, the reasons for the spread of the contagion lay rather in the general unhealthy condition and the intellectual decadence of the period. In speaking of Protestantism, we noted how the great metaphysical tradition had lost much of its vigor and breadth; many minds had chosen the simplest, and at the same time the most misleading concept of God and creature, representing them as two extremities of the same category. Consequently, the only way now remaining to exalt the Infinite was to annihilate the finite.

Had the monarchist conceptions of the day anything to do with this mentality? We are rather inclined to believe so. Absolute monarchy and enlightened despotism were beginning to assert themselves in politics; the deference and self-effacement of courtiers in the presence of human majesties offered a convenient illustration of the proper attitude to be taken before the King of Kings At all events, rigorism was in vogue; nature had to be degraded, all but crushed, lest it spoil God's work.

Quite naturally, it was impossible for the doctrine of the Mystical Body to develop freely in this atmosphere of constraint. Before we return to the masters of the French School, let us give one example. The truth of the Mystical Body is not, of course, quite so open a contradiction in the Jansenist doctrine as it is in Protestantism; nevertheless it still suffers from the same internal opposition. It could be prominent enough on occasion, as happened at the time of the Reformation, to compromise the Mystical Body in the eyes of many, and even to give heresy an appearance of piety. But the truth has been misrepresented in such cases. The whole Mystical Body is indeed described as really living, for according to the Jansenist doctrine human nature is truly sanctified and vivified by grace, at least in the few fortunate souls that are chosen by God. Yet it is only half alive. Though they are sanctified, the just remain passive under the impulses and delectations that they receive from God. There is no spontaneity, no initiative, no life proceeding from ourselves. We are like spectators, looking on while another acts within our own being. In this doctrine, grace leaves our natural activity just as tightly bound up in its insignificant nothingness as grace itself is distributed with a miserly hand. Grace enters into us, but only to drive out our will, our liberty, our natural love for ourselves, all that is most personal to us. It enters like a sword, not like the root which, while absorbing, also transforms us. So inseparable are the physical body of the Saviour and His Mystical Body that this conception of the action of grace reminds us of that style of crucifix in which the immense appeal of the outstretched arms of Christ is reduced to a gesture of rejection.

This brief sketch is necessary, not simply to give one more example of a false and heretical theory of the Mystical Body, but to throw proper light on the pages that follow. We shall be obliged to emphasize deficiencies and to point out certain unfortunate resemblances to these false ideas in the theology of the masters of the Oratory and of St. Sulpice. The first part of this chapter should make it clear that these deficiencies are by no means their own doing, but rather the invasion of a disease proper to their time. In fact, they themselves, less seriously infected than others, have helped to eliminate the evil from Christian thought.

With Père Charles de Condren the doctrine of the French
School takes on a special character. Cardinal de Bérulle had
made the virtue of religion the center of all, and had synthesized
all Christian life in the religion of Christ. His disciple and
successor introduces still greater unity into the doctrine by
centering all that pertains to the religion of Christ round the
immolation of Golgotha, the final act in which He offered His
entire self to the glory of His Father. Thus the Cross and the
Mass, rather than the person of the Man-God, make up the
essence of Christianity, for it is in these that the person of the
Man-God is found in its fullest actuality. Hence the chief Christian virtue is not religion, since this is merely a general disposition, but rather the spirit of oblation, of mortification, of
sacrifice. One feels at once that this is an austere and exacting
doctrine; nor is that first impression altered by what is to
follow.

What was it that led Pere de Condren to insist on this
aspect of the spiritual life? To judge from the remarks of his
biographer and confidant, Père Denis Amelotte, the answer is
to be sought in his ardent piety, and also in his character and
intellectual preoccupations. The following incident is significant. When he was about twelve years of age, writes Père
Amelotte,

> It happened that one day, while studying in
> his chamber and keeping watch at the door of wis-
> dom, as he was wont ever to do in a spirit of sacri-
> fice, converting all his reading into motives of ado-
> ration—

One moment. Condren, we notice, does not appear before God as a *tabula rasa;* he will naturally interpret the grace
he is now to receive in the light of his previous dispositions. So,
while he was studying and reflecting, in a spirit of sacrifice and
adoration,

> his spirit was suddenly surrounded with an extraor-
> dinary light, in which the divine majesty appeared
> to him, so immense and so infinite that it seemed
> this pure Being alone could subsist, and that the
> entire universe must be immolated to His glory. He

229

saw that God had no need of any of His creatures, and that even His Son, who was all His joy, had to sacrifice His life; that only the annihilation of ourselves and of all things with the dying Christ can give honor to the divine infinity, and that our love for Him is not great enough unless we have the desire to be consumed together with His Son in proof of our love.

So pure and powerful was this light that it made an impression as of death in his soul, never to be effaced. He gave himself whole-heartedly to God, to be reduced to nothingness in His presence and to live henceforth in a spirit of death. Then he knew that the whole world was condemned to the flames for the sins of men, in which all creatures are accomplices, and that the holy, pure, just God feels an utter aversion toward them. . . . He saw that almost all men, even Christians, were filled with sentiments and affections opposed to those of God: that they loved passionately what He condemns and that there was scarcely one who was not possessed by the spirit of the world, which is an abomination in the eyes of God.

This is the negative side. Now, in growing contrast, appears the positive side of the doctrine.

As he was in the abyss of his nothingness in presence of the divine holiness, ardently desiring to be sacrificed to His glory, he experienced an incomparable joy in the reflection that the Son of God is ever offering Himself to His Father as Victim, and that the saints in heaven and the priests on earth likewise offer Him up incessantly in honor of the holiness and all the perfections of God. He understood that the sacrifice of Jesus Christ is both the consummation and the supplement of the zeal of those who, passionately desirous of immolating themselves, feel that their own sacrifice is wholly incapable of giving due honor to God. He understood that infinite praise is offered to God's holiness, to His justice, to His essential and absolute independence, in a word, to His infinity, when we present His dead Son to Him, protesting that not only the universe but even this Son had to be destroyed in His divine presence. He understood that nothing is worthy of God except this unique sacrifice of Jesus Christ, that it is the foundation and support of the new creation, the bond of union between heaven and earth, the accomplishment of all that God desires for Himself and for His children, the refuge of all the saints in their helplessness, the perfection of all virtues and the inexhaustible source of eternal life.

This is indeed a wonderful vision, and yet—perhaps the reader may have a different impression—there is something frightening about it, like an immense desert landscape. The constant repetition of our nothingness, but most of all the peculiar glory that God is said to take in the fact that His Son is offered to Him dead, are depressing details. If I may venture an opinion, these elements do not appear quite wholesome; in this complex vision they seem to proceed from Condren's previous disposition rather than from the grace itself. In reading the masters of the French School, true men of God though they are, it is often necessary to draw this same distinction between the Christian piety that they profess, and the way in which, owing to the evils of their times, they sometimes conceive this piety. We wished to make the point very dear before examining this phase of their doctrine. With the reader's permission, we shall not repeat the caution each time that the circumstances might warrant it; we shall mention it again at the end of the chapter, adding the necessary explanations.

Much the same criticism may be made concerning Monsieur Olier. He, too, had his attention drawn by certain interior experiences, though less tragic, to our union with Christ. One of these made a profound impression upon him, and certainly exerted considerable influence on his doctrine. He heard our Lord Himself say: "I am really present to souls." Père de Condren, who was his spiritual director at the time, urged him to make this assurance the center of his spiritual life. The mention of Père de Condren is significant: grace was not acting wholly alone in Olier, either.

At all events, these words do give the distinctive note of his spirituality. For Olier, as for Bérulle and Condren, the religion of Christ and the sacrifice of Christ are the center of Christianity; but since Olier is more directly intent upon showing how this religion and this sacrifice are ever present to us, he considers them where they are perpetuated; namely, in the Host that prolongs the Sacrifice of the Mass and where Christ remains always at the center of His religion. Therefore he sees the Christlife primarily as a union with the Eucharistic Christ, as a sacramental and spiritual communion by which the religion and the sacrifice of Christ pass into us. He is quite as exacting as Condren, except that he speaks rather of effacement than of immolation: one is reminded more of a candle burning itself out than of a victim being slaughtered. Apart from this, his doctrine presents exactly the same rigor as that of Condren, and we explain the two as one doctrine. We prefer to quote Olier. His developments are less strained and less brief than Condren's, and less cumbersome than Bérulle's; of the masters of the French School, he is not the greatest theologian, for that is Bérulle; nor the most vigorous, for that is Condren; but he is the most readable and the most classical. In his writings the tradition of the School is clear and calm.

Here again the point of departure is a too contemptuous view of human nature. We repeat that it is not the Protestant or the Jansenistic view. Our masters declare that our nature is capable of true sanctity and of efficacious co-operation with grace. But they do say that our nature is so despicable, so wounded by sin, that its activity must always remain suspect and that the wisest course is to limit, as much as possible, its sphere of operation. In the words of Père de Condren:

> Were God to treat us as we deserve, we should
> have no other thoughts but those of the devils and of
> sin, like the damned, for we should be in the same
> condition as they.

By "sin," Monsieur Olier tells us, he means the whole life of the flesh.

Originally God had formed man in a perfect state; He had imprinted in him His own image and resemblance, and had made him a partaker of His nature and of all His perfections. When sin came, this pure and holy likeness of God within us was effaced, and man became so perverted and corrupt that now he has almost nothing of what he had received from God. True, the image of the divinity is still there, but its chief beauty is spoiled and stained. . . . [The soul still possesses its natural being.] But, before it is restored through baptism, it is in sorry disorder and in total opposition to God, since in itself, in its interior and exterior faculties it is wholly covered with sin. It seems we may say that in a sense it has lost even its natural being, for, whereas it was once a most pure spirit, it has become flesh by entering into an alliance with the body and by plunging into the abyss of fleshy sentiments.

Such pessimism cannot be truly Christian. In fact, as we shall see, it prevents one from viewing either the Incarnation in all its truth, or the Christ-life in all its hopeful assurance.

At the sight of our ignoble nature, God in His holiness can feel only an infinite revulsion. All this revulsion has passed into the God-Man. To show this, our authors recall how human nature is treated in Him. The Incarnation leaves it without a subsistence of its own; in the redemption it is crushed with opprobrium; finally, in its very glorification it is forever annihilated, so to speak, since it is all but absorbed in the divine splendor. Even now in the Eucharist it disappears beneath the Sacred Species, and comes upon the altar only to be a victim for the sacrifice. Thus, in the Incarnate Word, God is quite as remote from the world as ever, and when Christ comes to dwell in our souls in Holy Communion, "He lives in us with horror of us, and with condemnation for us." Therefore we, too, must feel a like revulsion toward ourselves; human holiness must consist, like the holiness of God and Christ, in fleeing from human nature.

Our principal function in the work of our perfection is to withdraw from ourselves. Bérulle had described asceticism not as a matter of prudent strategy and sustained effort, though he admitted the necessity of these, but as an adherence and attachment to Christ, to His mysteries and His dispositions. The source of all virtues is Christ; hence the essential thing is to attach ourselves to that source, in order that the life stream may flow into us. Condren and Olier likewise insist upon this self-abdication. Our first act in prayer should be to renounce ourselves and our own intentions. If we are to grow in the eyes of God, we must first annihilate ourselves and "have a tendency and an inclination to nothingness."

> Death must always precede life. This is nothing else than the entire ruin of our whole selves, in order that whatever is opposed to God in us may be destroyed, and that His Spirit may abide within us in the purity and holiness of His ways."

Once we shall have wholly emptied ourselves of ourselves. God can at last be all in us; the gentlest breath of the Spirit can instantly elevate the soul that is no longer weighed down by anything of earth. We shall then be a pure capacity, where Jesus fills all and does all; we shall be true Christians:

> There is nothing greater, nothing more august, nothing more glorious; such a soul is Jesus Christ, living on earth.

The conclusions are magnificent and beautifully expressed. But, since we have already explained these in the first part of the chapter, we need not dwell upon them here. What interests us at present is the path by which our masters arrive at these conclusions. In order to indicate the route with greater completeness, we think it best to quote a lengthy passage from Monsieur Olier's *Catéchisme de la vie intérieure:*

> *In order to be a Christian, is it enough to have the dispositions that you have explained to me thus far?*
>
> No. Christians must also take part in all the mysteries of Jesus Christ; for our lovable Redeemer performed them in His person precisely in order that they might be the source of the most abundant and most special graces in His Church.

Émile Mersch

Did each mystery obtain a special grace for the Church?

Yes. Each mystery obtained for the Church sanctifying grace and a variety of dispositions and special graces which God confers upon purified souls when He pleases, but particularly at the times when the mysteries are solemnly commemorated. . . .

What grace is wrought in us by the mystery of the incarnation?

The grace of annihilation to all self-interest and all self-love.

What is meant by annihilation to all self-interest and self-love?

It means that, as by the sacred mystery of the Incarnation our Lord's sacred humanity was annihilated in its own person, in such wise that it no longer sought itself, no longer had any interest of its own, no longer acted for itself, since for its own personality another Person had been substituted, namely, the personality of the Son of God, who sought only the interests of His Father whom He saw always and in all things—so we too must be annihilated to all our own designs, to all our own interests, and entertain only those of Jesus Christ, who is present within us in order to live in us for His Father. "Just as My Father, in sending Me to earth, cut away every root of self-seeking, when instead of giving Me a human personality, He united Me to a divine Person in order to make Me live for Him; so when you eat Me, you will live wholly for Me and not for yourselves, for I shall live in you. I shall fill your souls with My desires and My life, which will consume and annihilate in you all that is your own, so that it will be I, not you, that live and desire all things in you; and, thus annihilated in yourselves, you will be wholly clothed in Me."

Is this putting on of Christ another grace of the Incarnation?

Yes, for besides the fact that the mystery of the Incarnation, properly speaking, effects in us a complete stripping off and renunciation of ourselves, it likewise clothes us with our Lord, by a total consecration to God; just as on the day of the Incarnation our Lord wholly consecrated Himself and all His members to His Father, thereby sanctifying in advance each individual occasion which He and His members should ever have of serving and glorifying God.

On the most holy day of the Incarnation, did our Lord Jesus Christ offer His life and the lives of all His members to God His Father?

Yes, He offered them, and He still continues to make the same offering. He is still living in the same dispositions that He had during His whole life. He never interrupts them, and He is ever offering Himself to God, in Himself and in all His members, in all the occasions that they have to serve, honor, and glorify Him. Our Lord in His divine Person is an altar, upon which all men are offered to God with all their actions and all their sufferings. This is that golden altar (Apoc. 8:3), on which every perfect sacrifice is consummated. The human nature of Jesus Christ and of all the faithful is the victim, His spirit is the fire, and the offering is made to God the Father, who is thus adored in spirit and in truth.

Certainly there exists no easier road to such sublime heights of spirituality. But at this altitude, how far man is left behind, and how little he matters! And yet Olier is speaking here only of the dignity which grace confers on our nature. What would he say if he were expressly treating of our misery and sinfulness?

We wish to make ourselves perfectly clear. It is not the precepts of renunciation and of austerity that we find too severe; one who follows a crucified Head can never practice too much abnegation. We find fault only with the manner in which these precepts are laid down, and which, we repeat, betrays a certain contempt for human nature—not a Protestant or Jansenistic contempt, certainly as we have already observed. Thanks be to God, our authors have themselves helped to counteract the malady. But human nature is a very essential part of Christianity, and too great a contempt of the part must inevitably influence one's attitude toward the whole.

After all, human nature is also present, truly and fully, in Christ. One who has little esteem for that nature will be inclined to belittle it even in Him. Yet Christ is Head precisely in His human nature, a fact that is difficult to explain in such a view. Our authors have much to say in praise of the humanity of the Saviour, and in what they say we perceive a new tone which at once betrays their intense love and their profound meditation on the subject. But unfortunately, all that is purely human in Christ appears to them so despicable that even in these moments their chief care is to represent the humanity of Christ, not as humanity, but as the subsistent religion of men, as a holocaust offered to God, or as a total annihilation before the Most High. The abasement of the Incarnation, the ignominy of Calvary, the very glory of heaven, and the mystery of the tabernacle are all regarded as a kind of sacred annihilation, obscuring their vision of the most sweet humanity and gentle goodness through which the Word has made Himself accessible to the children of men. They have little to say of His life, of His human actions, of the wonderful yet familiar proximity that He ever sought to have with us. Lastly, the hypostatic union, as they conceive it, does not make Christ's humanity human, more human even than it would otherwise have been, but rather absorbs that humanity, so to speak, into a glory and a function that are divine.

These are delicate points, and we regret that we have had to express them in a way that makes them appear more serious than they actually are. But as we see, the very idea of the Mystical Body is here at stake. The Saviour's humanity is raised to the Headship of our race precisely because of its supernatural and mysterious proximity to us, and because of its extremely perfect manner of being man, true man. Once this fact is lost sight of, the very concept of the Mystical Christ must suffer.

Once more, what we have said of the Head is true of the members, so great is their solidarity. The same concept of our nature makes it impossible for our authors to explain clearly the supernatural dignity which makes us the body of Christ. What nobility can there be in poor nothings and poor sinners such as we are? Out of respect for the dignity of God and for the holiness of Christ, out of respect for the very justification that we are to receive, they tell us that our activity must be restricted. Their most beautiful pages are marred by the idea, which amounts almost to an obsession, of annihilation; the word is ever on their lips, and they keep repeating that our worship must consist essentially in offering to God His lifeless Son; our prayer must consist in renouncing our own desires, and our virtue must consist in stripping ourselves entirely of ourselves and of our acts. As with the Head, so with the members, the part of human nature in the supernatural life is certainly not denied, but it is minimized.

One cannot help thinking of the great Scholastics. For all their seeming abstraction, they were more human and also, we believe, more Christian. They saw nothing in mere annihilation that could give honor to Him who is. Therefore, out of respect for the Creator and out of love for the Word made flesh, they refuse to admit that the least of even material creatures will return to nothingness, if it is capable of lasting forever.

We must remember that the great metaphysical tradition has meanwhile lost much of its early vigor. Upon the systems of philosophy and theology there has fallen a certain pessimism; this it is that prevents the free development of the doctrine of the Mystical Body in the works of the founders of the French School. Its effects, alas, were far more disastrous in other instances.

IV

However, this pessimism did not succeed in conquering the spirit that inspired them. We have read many beautiful thoughts in the preceding pages, and, in order not to leave an unfavorable and false impression of our authors, we wish to conclude with a brief consideration of one of the most human and most Christian aspects of their doctrine; namely, their teaching concerning charity toward the neighbor. We do not mean their systematic teaching, for that is poor; their slight esteem for human nature was not apt to induce them to assign a prominent place in their system of spirituality to a humble and devoted love for men. But it is to their living teaching, their practical counsels, and their example that we refer; in these they continue the urgent precept of the Gospel to love one's brethren before all else. This doctrine is forcibly expressed in manuscripts that were discovered among Monsieur Olier's papers after his death.

> We must hold as certain that Jesus Christ abides in the Church of God, and therefore in the faithful, by His spirit, His graces, His gifts, His virtues. All that is of Jesus Christ is holy, great, divine, and hence it merits our adoration and our homage. The duty of a Christian toward the whole Church and toward each of her members is in consequence a duty of cult and of honor. . . .
>
> The vow of servitude obliges us so to love all the members of Jesus Christ that we enter into their interests, and even prefer their interests to our own. . . . We shall make it our study to please them in all things. . . . and lastly, we shall treat them as a servant treats his master.

These are not empty words. "I give myself to God, that I may belong to all who come to me," said Père de Condren in his "vow of servitude." And, for fear of taking back that offering, he dared not send away the most exasperating visitor. "Since I am the servant of all," he explained, "everyone has the right to order me about." His very office as general he regarded as "a universal servitude that obliges me to serve all my subjects," so that, when harassed by the importunate, by disappointments and humiliations, he would say with a smile: "I haven't a chance to do my own will in this world."

Such perfect graciousness is the most eloquent commentary on any rigidity of doctrine. Their attitude is somewhat passive perhaps; but so human, so deferential, and so supernatural a love for the neighbor is the best possible recognition of the incorporation of men in Christ and of the dignity which God has conferred upon our nature.

For such heroes of charity, rigoristic formulas can be only superficial and incidental, traces of an evil to which their Christian souls, are opposed and which their disciples succeed in eliminating, simply by remaining faithful to their teaching.

But they themselves remain inimitable. Now that the Church has spoken clearly, it is easy to avoid certain errors that were less perceptible in their day. Yet there are some things concerning our incorporation in Christ that can be earned best only from their lips. Too great a gap would have been left in our studies if we had not examined their doctrine rather carefully.

CHAPTER XI

THE DOCTRINE OF THE MYSTICAL BODY TODAY

I. *Resurgence of the doctrine of the Mystical Body,* freed from the pessimism of the masters of the French School; this progress is apparently due to the influence of the same French School and to the advance of positive theology.

II. *Naturalism and the doctrine of the Mystical Body.* Cardinal Pie. Human nature united with God in Christ. All creation supernaturalized. The life of Christ prolonged in men, and even in material things. The doctrine of the Mystical Body as compared with naturalistic pantheism.

III. *The Vatican Council.* According to the *Schema De Ecclesia,* the Church is essentially the Mystical Body of Christ. From this principle the document deduces the Church's visibility, necessity, and unfailing unity. Generally favorable reception of this *Schema.*

IV. *The Popes.* Leo XIII repeats the doctrine of the Church as the Mystical Body of Christ, which had been formulated in the *Schema De Ecclesia.* Pius X points out that the Blessed Virgin Mary is the Mother of the members of the Mystical Body. Catholic Action and the Mystical Body. In the encyclical *Miserentissimus Redemptor,* His Holiness Pope Pius XI explains how our works of expiation and satisfaction have their value: through their union with the expiation and satisfaction of Christ. Redemption in the Mystical Body.

V. *The antidote for modern heresies,* especially for Modernism.

Émile Mersch

I

In our own day, the doctrine of the Mystical Body is making rapid progress. Indeed, one of the distinctive notes of present-day theology is a tendency to broaden more and more the scope of our doctrine. We cannot ignore the part which the French School has taken in this progress. The Congregation of the Oratory, and to an even greater extent the Congregation of St. Sulpice, have devoted themselves to the formation of the clergy. It was inevitable that their spiritual teaching, which insists so strongly on our incorporation in Christ, should have made a profound impression on the minds of the many eminent bishops and priests who were trained in their seminaries.

Another factor contributing to this growth was the development of positive theology. The inspired writers and the Fathers are not studied merely as sources whence arguments may be drawn in support of a thesis; they are being read more and more for the sake of becoming familiar with their way of thinking and with their concept of Christianity. But since these sources speak forcibly of the Mystical Body, as is abundantly clear from the foregoing studies, it is quite natural that a more objective exposition of Scriptural and patristic theology should lead to a more realistic doctrine of the Mystical Body.

Whatever may have been the causes, the effect is visible enough. Not only is the doctrine more widely accepted, but it has been set free from the pessimism that enshrouded it in the teaching of the French School. It retains its note of austerity, to be sure, but it has taken on a more optimistic and cheerful spirit.

So many theologians are now teaching it that we shall make no attempt to enumerate them, much less to class them into schools. Again, its proponents are so recent that it is as yet too early to devote a historical study to them. We intend here only to examine a few documents which appear to possess greater authority.

II

Let us mention in the first place Cardinal Pie, bishop of Poitiers, friend of Pius IX, and one of the most influential among the Fathers of the Vatican Council. He has written with vigor and eloquence of our unity in Christ, for he recognized this doctrine as the providential remedy for the error of his day—and alas, of our own as well; that error is Naturalism.

Naturalism claims that man is sufficient unto himself; he has neither need nor knowledge of any higher reality that transcends his own sphere. This pride in human nature and this assumption of man's ability to do without supernatural assistance are, after all, only a perversion of a moral attitude which is in itself quite legitimate; namely, respect for human nature. Hence the error can be best refuted, not so much by lowering man in his own eyes as by letting him see his true dignity. Realizing this, the bishop of Poitiers chose the doctrine of the Mystical Body as the means of showing the inadequacy of the teachings of naturalism. They tell us man is sufficient unto himself. That might be true, answers our author, if there were question of his being simply a man. But other perspectives open before our eyes: God invites us to a union with His only Son, so intimate that one is almost tempted to call it identification. This, he observes, is an error to be avoided, but

keeping this necessary qualification in mind, our deification in Jesus Christ is one of the fundamental truths of Christianity. In it are our title to nobility for the present and our assurance of happiness and glory for the future. And, since this doctrine reaches to the inmost depths of our being, since it is bound up with our whole destiny, present and future, since it is at once our charter of rights and our code of duty, this article of our faith can never be impressed deeply enough on the minds of the faithful; it must often be presented to them and explained from every possible point of view. The deeper the darkness in which naturalism envelops the sphere of profane knowledge, the greater the light which sacred theology must throw upon the whole Christ, that is, upon that mystery in which human nature is deified hypostatically in the individual person of Jesus Christ, and deified by adoption in all the elect, who are the members of the body of Jesus Christ. This deification affects the whole of creation, angelic and terrestrial, of which man is the center and the bond of union; it is an obligatory deification, commanded by God, so that he who presents himself without this supernatural gift and without this divine supplement will be found wanting in the heavenly balance.

This deification is obligatory, not simply because God desires its presence in all His works, but also because of the dignity of our human nature; when man voluntarily rejects the supernatural nobility that is offered him, he sins against his own nature.

The Word of God has descended into the very heart of His work; He assumed our humanity, and by means of this nature, which, being at once spiritual and corporal, reaches to both extremities of creation, He has communicated Himself to every part of that creation, vivifying the angelic spirits as well as inferior beings, extending the divine activity to all things in heaven and on earth, bringing to all nature a supernatural consecration and elevating it from its base and profane condition. . . . The Word has come unto His own; can it be optional for them to receive Him or to reject Him as they please? . . . Still more important is this question: if Jesus Christ has been given us by God, in order to raise us up to a glory and a beatitude that transcend all the exigencies and all the ambitions of our nature, can we be free to select a more humble destiny and propose to ourselves a purely natural end? Ah, it is here that the Scriptures break down the very foundations of naturalism.

Far from belittling our human nature, this doctrine is a message of respect. Human nature was made to be united to God in Christ, because the humanity of Christ was made that it might penetrate all things, *ut impleret omnia* (Eph. 4:10). For, as the bishop of Poitiers observes, with careful precision:

There is no question here of His presence as God, for as God He has always been present, but of His presence both as God and as man.

This presence embraces our whole nature:

The history of humanity, the history of nations, of peace and of war, and especially the history of the Church, is but the history of the life of Jesus filling all things, *ut impleret omnia.*

Over and above the life that Jesus led in Judea, there is another life, mystical and real, written by each of the faithful, not on pages of parchment but on the living tables of the heart; "in all that goes to make up what we may call the equipment or the organism of the Christ-life, the divine Youth of Nazareth is still living and growing on this earth."

Nor is this all. It is not to our nature alone that this theandric dignity is offered. The entire universe is likewise destined for this glory, because of its relation to us. Naturalism would cut it off from God, set it up as a self-sufficient whole, and make of it a kind of god. This is naturalistic pantheism, a more subtle error, yet allied with the first. But the doctrine of the Mystical Body confutes and destroys this theory also. They tell us of a God striving to be God, of an immense "becoming" that is destined to produce something divine.

Indeed, yes! All that is true, provided it is understood not of the eternal and changeless God who is God by nature and essence, but of this God who is united in Jesus Christ with the very heart of the divinity, and yet extends throughout the world in time and space. These sacrilegious counterfeiters, these instruments of him whom Tertullian calls "the ape of truth," have merely put a horrible blasphemy in the place of an adorable truth; they have substituted the absurd and the impossible for the masterpiece of the wisdom and power and love of the heavenly Father who has called us to His eternal glory in Jesus Christ, and who, having discovered a way to make men partakers of His divine nature, has caused this deification to flow into every part of the universe in greater or less abundance according as each part concurs more or less directly in the operations of the supernatural order, as St. Paul writes to the early Christians: "All things are yours, and you are Christ's and Christ is God's" (1 Cor. 3:23).

As grace transcends nature, so this teaching transcends that of naturalism, and it expresses in addition the full and expansive optimism of the doctrine of the Mystical Body.

III

Cardinal Pie was not the only one who looked on this doctrine as the remedy for the religious ills of the present time. The entire episcopate shared his view, as may be seen from what the Fathers of the Vatican Council have to say on the subject of our incorporation in Christ. The *Schema De Ecclesia Christi* which was distributed to the bishops on January 21, 1870, states that the primary characteristic, the very essence of the Church is her quality as the Mystical Body of the Saviour.

Times have changed: heresy no longer strikes at the visibility of the Church, as it did in the days of the Reformers. Naturalism takes a bolder step, and denies the hidden life and mystical presence of Christ which makes His supernatural society an organism of salvation. These, therefore, are the truths that must now be insisted upon; from them, if possible, must be deduced the chief prerogatives of the Church: her holiness, her indefectibility, her necessity, and even her visible unity. The *Schema* does just this; in its opening lines, it states that the whole of Christ's work on earth and the entire economy of salvation consist in the building up of the Mystical Body.

That the Church is the Mystical Body of Christ.
The only-begotten Son of God, who enlighteneth every man that cometh into the world (John 1:9), and who has never failed to come to the aid of the unfortunate children of Adam, did, in the fullness of time appointed by the eternal decree, become like unto men. Assuming the form of our body, He appeared in visible guise in order that earthly and carnal men, putting on the new man who is created according

245

to God in justness and holiness of truth (Eph. 4:24), might make up a Mystical Body of which He Himself should be the Head. To effect this union of the Mystical Body the Lord Christ instituted the sacred waters of regeneration and renewal, whereby the sons of men, once so sadly divided among themselves and especially corrupted by sin, might be purified from every stain of their sins and so become members one of the other, and that being united to their divine Head by faith, hope, and charity, they might all be vivified by the one Spirit and filled with heavenly graces and spiritual gifts. We can never commend too highly to the consideration of the faithful, or impress too deeply on their minds this remarkable [visible] feature (*species*) of the Church, whereby she has as her Head Christ, "from whom the whole body, welded and compacted together throughout every joint of the system, part working in harmony with part, deriveth its increase, unto the upbuilding of itself in charity" (Eph. 4:16).

From such a principle it is easy to deduce the other properties of the Church. The *Schema* begins with her visibility.

Since such is the nature of the true Church of Christ, we declare that the visible and perceptible society whereof we speak is the very same as that Church of the divine promises and mercies which Christ was pleased to distinguish and enrich with so many prerogatives and privileges.

Her constitution is so clearly determined that none of those societies which have withdrawn from the unity and communion of her body can in any sense be called a part or a member. She is not divided or dismembered by the different societies that call themselves "Christian"; she is one whole, gathered together and closely united within herself (*totam in se collectam penitusque cohaerentem*), and her conspicuous unity is the outward manifestation of that undivided and indivisible body which is the Mystical Body of Christ Himself.

The same principle explains why membership in the Church is a necessary means of salvation.

Hence let all understand how necessary for salvation is this society, this Church of Christ. She is as necessary as attachment to and union with Christ and the Mystical Body are necessary. . . . This is why we teach that membership in the Church is not a matter of option, as if it made no difference whether one knows the Church or not, whether he enters her or not, as far as salvation is concerned, but that it is a matter of necessity, not only in virtue of the precept whereby the Lord commanded every nation to enter the Church, but also as a means. For in the economy of salvation which Providence has established, none can receive the communication of the Holy Spirit, and none can partake of truth and of life except in the Church and through the Church, whose Head is Christ.

The Church's vitality, her perpetuity, all her prerogatives become just as evident when one considers her as the body of Christ.

Although the Church grows—and God grant that she may ever continue to grow in faith and charity in order that the body of Christ may be built up!—and although her development varies in different ages and according to the changing circumstances in which she leads her ever militant existence, she always remains intrinsically the same, adhering immutably to the constitution given her by Christ. Therefore the Church of Christ can never lose her attributes and her qualities, her sacred *magisterium,* her ministry, and her power of jurisdiction, for Christ must remain forever and for all men, by means of His visible body, the way, the truth, and the life.

Lastly, we are told that even the Church's right to possess property follows from the same general principle.

This right is more sacred and more sublime in the Church than elsewhere, since the goods in question belong to the Mystical Body of Christ, and are therefore consecrated in a more special manner to Christ.

The *Schema* is not a definition, of course; it was not even publicly discussed at the Council. Its framers were not bishops but theologians, consultors of the theologico-dogmatic Commission. Nevertheless it does indicate what these scholars regarded as definable doctrine. Nor were these men ordinary theologians; they were the most eminent of their time, selected by the central commission of the Council, and their appointment was approved by the Pope.

They were unanimous in making the truth of the Mystical Body the first principle of the doctrine concerning the Church. The records of their discussions indicate no divergence of view on this subject.

While the Council itself passed no final judgment on the *Schema,* the motivated opinions of a considerable number of its members are on record. Copies of the *Schema* has been distributed to all beforehand, in order to give them an opportunity to examine it and to hand in their comments and criticisms before March 4, as was requested. There were about 639 Fathers in Rome at the time of the Council; this was the number that assisted at the general session of March 18. About 230, or a little better than a third, presented their written opinions either on the *Schema* as a whole or on those parts that have the most direct reference to the Mystical Body; namely, the beginning and the first chapter. Of this number only four expressed regret at the mention of the Mystical Body in such a document. They considered that the doctrine was vague, ill understood, too mystical. Of the twenty-five others who objected, though less vigorously, to its mention, about twenty wished to substitute the term "kingdom of God" or "society"; in short, they desired a simpler, more practical definition of the Church. A good hundred approved the manner in which the doctrine was presented, some making certain reservations, some suggesting slight modifications, some openly expressing their satisfaction. Seventy of the Fathers fail to mention the Mystical Body in their comments. If, as is frequently the case, we may presume that those who are satisfied deem it unnecessary to say so, we might count these seventy, as well as the four hundred who gave no opinion, with the hundred who said they approved of the *Schema*. The resulting majority of six sevenths in favor of the mention of the Mystical Body would of course be an exaggeration, and we cannot base any argument upon it. But this tabulation at least shows that a majority of the bishops, the greater part of the ordinary *magisterium,* did not object to centering the treatise on the Church round the doctrine of the Mystical Body.

The reservations that were made cannot be said to concern the doctrine as such. The most unsympathetic did not say that this manner of presentation was false, but that it was too complicated, obscure, vague. Most of the criticisms deal with certain inadequacies, some of which are undeniable, in the way the doctrine was expressed. The following are the most common objections. First, it is certain that the concept of the Mystical Body does not coincide perfectly with that of the Church. This point is important. It may be disputed, for instance, whether sinners and fervent catechumens are members of the Mystical Body; yet it is beyond doubt that the former are members of the Church, while the latter are not. One may also regret, with certain bishops, that the *Schema* fails to state clearly that this "body" of Christ possesses both a visible and an invisible character, corresponding to what are termed "the body of the Church" and "the soul of the Church." He may likewise regret the absence of a complete and accurate Scholastic definition of the Church. The fact that so prominent a place was accorded to the idea of the Mystical Body was no excuse for this omission; on the contrary it made a positive and scientific explanation all the more necessary.

Accordingly a second project was drawn up by Father Kleutgen, S. J., in which the suggestions offered by the Fathers were taken into account. The principle now becomes a scientific definition of the Church, and the idea of the Mystical Body passes into the background. However, the latter still remains very much in evidence, for, as Father Kleutgen observes, "not only is the Mystical Body very frequently and very explicitly spoken of in Scripture, but it also helps very much to an understanding of the properties of the Church."

It is impossible to say whether this new *Schema* would have satisfied the Council. It was not examined by the Fathers of the deputation whose business it was to pass on questions concerning the faith, nor was it submitted to the bishops. We think that some, perhaps many, of the latter would have regretted the summary treatment of a concept which in the first *Schema* they had considered so useful and so true. Is it not significant that almost all the other projects proposed by bishops to take the place of the original formula give far greater prominence to the Mystical Body than does the project of Father Kleutgen?

Whether these suppositions be true or false, we may note, in summing up what we have said of the Council, that the majority of the bishops and the most noted theologians have rendered an important testimony to the doctrine of our incorporation in Christ.

IV

After the suspension of the Council, the doctrine was not hidden away in the archives along with the documents that contained it. Within a few short years, we find it expressed in solemn ecclesiastical pronouncements.

Leo XIII, who had assisted as cardinal at the sessions of the Council, formulates the doctrine in his famous encyclical *Satis Cognitum,* in which he speaks of the Church. It is interesting to note the resemblance between the words of the encyclical and the teaching contained in the *Schema De Ecclesia Christi.* The Pope declares, as the *Schema* had done, that the doctrine of the Mystical Body is the résumé of all that can be said of the Church.

> It is because of all these reasons that in Scripture the Church is so often called a body, or the body of Christ: "You are all the body of Christ" (1 Cor. 12: 27). Because it is a body, it is visible to the eyes of men; because it is the body of Christ, it is a living body, active and growing, for it is sustained and animated by the power which Jesus Christ communicates to it, almost as the vine nourishes and renders fruitful the branches that are united with it.

Émile Mersch

In living beings the vital principle is itself something mysterious and hidden, but it manifests its presence in the movement and activity of the members; in like manner the principle of the supernatural life which animates the Church is made known to all by the effects which it produces.

Again like the *Schema De Ecclesia,* the Pope proceeds to show, from what Christ is, what the Church must be, and what Christ Himself must, therefore, be in His Mystical Body.

The Church is not a dead thing; she is the body of Christ, alive with His supernatural life. Christ, her Head and Model, is not complete if we regard either His visible nature alone, as the Photinians and Nestorians do, or His invisible nature alone, as the Monophysites are wont to do; He is one by the union of both natures, visible and invisible. In the same way, His Mystical Body is the true Church simply because her parts derive their life and strength from supernatural gifts and other invisible sources.

Hence there can be but one Church.

Moreover, the Son of God decreed that the Church should be His Mystical Body, and He willed to be united with it as Head, as His human head is joined naturally with the human body which He took in the Incarnation. Therefore, just as He assumed only one mortal body, to be delivered up to torment and death in order to pay the price of man's redemption, so too He has but one Mystical Body, in which and by means of which He makes men partakers of sanctification and of eternal salvation: "[God] hath made Him Head over all the Church, which is His body" (Eph. 1:22, 23, D. V.).

Members that are isolated and dispersed cannot be united to one and the same head, or form a single body. . . . Members that withdraw from the other members cannot be attached to the same head. . . . To make the unicity of the Church more manifest, God presents it in the form of a living body, whose members can have life only on condition that they be attached to the head, and draw their vital energy (*vim vitalem*) from it. . . .

He, therefore, who thinks that there can be any other Church besides that which is the body of Christ, must look for some other head like Christ; he must look for some other Christ.

The Christ who willed that there should be but one Church, willed also that it should possess unity, in order that all who are destined to be its members should together form a single body. . . . Nay, He desired His disciples to be so intimately and so perfectly united that their union might be the very image, so to speak, of His own unity with the Father: "I pray . . . that they all may be one, even as Thou, Father, art in Me, and I in Thee" (John 17:21).

Many other statements of Leo XIII might be cited concerning the function of the Holy Ghost or the special significance of the Eucharist with regard to the Mystical Body.

The Eucharist, according to the testimony of the holy Fathers, is to be considered as a continuation and extension of the Incarnation. For through this sacrament the substance of the Incarnate Word is united with each individual man.

Our whole life as Christians centers round the Eucharist, just as the Incarnation is the center toward which God directs everything that pertains to the supernatural order.

But if the Incarnation is continued in the Mystical Body, it follows that the Virgin Mother of God, who served as the instrument of God in the Incarnation, is also used by God as Mediatrix in the prolongation of the Incarnation, the purpose of which is to form Christ in us. This truth was proclaimed by Pius X, early in his pontificate. On February 2, 1904, fifty years after the definition of the dogma of the Immaculate Conception, the Pope wrote of Mary, the Mother of divine grace:

All must accept this principle, that Jesus, the Word made flesh, is also the Saviour of the human race. As the God-Man, He possesses a human body

252

like other men; as the Restorer of our race, He has a spiritual, or mystical body, as it is called, which is the society of those who believe in Christ: "We many are one body in Christ" (Rom. 12:5). But the Virgin did not conceive the Son of God solely in order that, by receiving human nature from her, He should become man, but also that, through the nature which He received from her, He might become the Saviour of men. This is the reason why the angel told the shepherds: "There hath been born to you this day a Saviour, who is Christ the Lord" (Luke 2:11).

Consequently, in the same womb of this most pure Mother, Christ assumed not only mortal flesh but a spiritual body as well, consisting of all those who were to believe in Him. Thus we may say that Mary bore within her womb, not Christ only, but also all those whose life was contained in the life of the Saviour.

Therefore, since we are all united with Christ, and since, as the Apostle says, "we are members of His body, of His flesh, and of His bones" (Eph. 5:30, D. V.), we too have all been born of the womb of the Virgin, as a body united with its head.

Hence it is that in a spiritual and mystical sense we are called children of Mary, and she is called the Mother of us all. "She is spiritually and truly the Mother of us who are the members of Christ." If then the most Blessed Virgin is Mother both of God and of men, who can doubt but that she exerts all her influence with Christ, who is Head of His body, the Church, in order that He may infuse His gifts into us His members, and first of all, in order that we may come to know Him and live by Him?

. . . The source of all these gifts, of course, is Christ, "of whose fullness we have all received" (John 1:16), and "from whom the whole body, welded and compacted together throughout every joint of the system . . . deriveth its increase, unto the upbuilding of itself in charity" (Eph. 4:16). But, as St. Bernard aptly observes, Mary is the channel, or the neck, whereby the body is joined to the Head and through which the Head transmits its virtue and power to the body. "For she is the neck of our Head, through which all spiritual gifts are communicated to His Mystical Body."

While the following words of Pius X do not say much of the Mystical Body as such, they are important and interesting because they appear in one of the first great papal pronouncements on the subject of Catholic Action. From the very beginning of the encyclical, in which he recommends Catholic Action to the bishops of Italy, the Sovereign Pontiff links up the lay apostolate with the doctrine of the Mystical Body:

> All of us in God's Church are called to make up that one body whose Head is Christ; as the Apostle teaches, this body is closely knit and co-ordinated in all its parts by virtue of the functions proper to each member, and thus derives its increase, building itself up little by little in the bond of charity (cf. Eph. 4:16).

> And if, in this work of building up the body of Christ, it is Our first duty to teach, to point out the methods to be followed and the means to be taken, to urge and to exhort as a father, it is also the duty of all Our beloved sons everywhere in the world to receive Our words, to put them into execution first in themselves, and then to co-operate effectively in making others put them into practice, each one according to the grace he has received from God, according to his state and office, and according to the zeal that burns in his heart.

> Here We wish simply to mention the many works of zeal that are being carried out for the good of the Church, of society, and of individuals, and which are commonly referred to as "Catholic Action."

The history of the Church, the Mystical Body of Christ, reproduces the very history of the Saviour. In the words of Pius X:

> Must not the Church become daily more like Christ? Must she not become the living image of Him who bore so much and such bitter suffering?

Not only the Incarnation, but the Redemption as well is being continued in the Church. This doctrine, which has the authority of all Tradition behind it, had been expressed, like that of the Church as the Mystical Body, in the documents drawn up in preparation for the Vatican Council. The proposed decrees *De doctrina christiana,* which were submitted to the Fathers, gives the union of the members with the Head as the reason why Christ's satisfaction is one with the satisfactory works of Christians.

We shall not quote this text, however, since we possess a more solemn and more recent pronouncement on a very similar subject. This is the encyclical *Miserentissimus Redemptor* of His Holiness Pope Pius XI. The doctrine of the Mystical Body is not here treated *ex professo,* for the Pope is speaking directly of devotion to the Sacred Heart of Jesus. However, in developing this theme he is led to mention our union with the Saviour, just when he is denouncing naturalistic rationalism, to which we have made frequent reference in the foregoing pages. In answer to this rationalism, Pius XI lays emphasis upon two truths: the fallen state of our nature and the duty of reparation that is incumbent upon us. He then takes a further step, and exalts the dignity which belongs to our works of reparation by reason of their union with Christ's passion.

> For there exists a wonderful and intimate union of all the faithful with Christ, like to that which joins the head to the other members of the body. Moreover, through the mysterious communion of saints which our Catholic faith professes, all men and all peoples are united not only with one another but also with Him who is the Head, Christ. . . . This is the unity that the Mediator of God and men, Jesus Christ Himself, asked of the Father a few hours before His death: "I in them and Thou in Me, that they may be perfected in unity" (John 17:23).

It is this unity that gives value to our acts of reparation, acts that would otherwise be worthless.

The passion of Christ is renewed, and in some way continued and consummated in His Mystical Body, which is the Church. . . . Therefore Christ, who is still suffering in His Mystical Body, asks us to be His companions in expiation. For that matter, our very union with Him demands this: "You are the body of Christ, and members of member" (1 Cor. 12:27, D. V.). Whatever the Head suffers, the members too must suffer with Him.

This, declares the Pope, is a most timely doctrine for our day, when sin abounds and when society seems to be in rebellion against Christ and His Church.

V

We wish to close our studies with these words, in which Pius XI repeats with his pontifical authority what we have read in the *Schema* of the Vatican Council: the doctrine of the Mystical Body, which the Pope calls "this most beautiful doctrine" (*haec pulcherrima mystici Iesu Christi corporis doctrina*), is peculiarly suited to our modern age.

It is a remedy for the naturalism that is chilling the Christ-life in too many souls and in too many peoples, weakening faith and blinding men's eyes to the true nature of the Church.

May we not generalize the statement, and say that this same truth is the remedy for all the many errors that are rife today?

It is a remedy for the liberal individualism which still isolates the lives and thoughts of so many of the faithful. No one lives alone; the member must be mindful of the good of the other members. A true Christian must be, in spirit at least, a missionary.

It is a remedy for that other still more dangerous and more aggressive egoism which is known as nationalism. "There is neither Jew nor Greek," writes St. Paul, "for ye are all one person in Christ Jesus" (Gal. 3:28). If this catholic concept were only realized, what a transformation it would accomplish! A Christ who unites the men of every tongue and nation and color in the same love and in the same supernatural dignity! What joy and security and good will would then reign, instead of the barbed-wire entanglements and the engines of war that mark our frontiers!

It is a remedy, too, for that false conception of society, be it economic, social, or political, which seeks to strengthen the unity of groups at the sacrifice of the rights, at times even the most essential rights, of the individual. That there should be progress in the unification of human societies, as there is in all things human, we cannot doubt. It is quite natural that this progress should be more rapid in an age such as ours, when a spirit of revolt, engendered by the evils of a system of unbridled economic liberalism, is driving nations into the hands of dictators, and when the necessary interdependence of individuals in human society is making itself felt with unprecedented force. Experience is proving more conclusively each day that a union of all with all, in work and in study, in every enterprise, scientific and moral included, is now more indispensable than ever before. Even the apostolate is taking on a more collective aspect, through the many groups that are being formed in response to the call of Catholic Action. But if social unity must progress more rapidly in our day, there is all the greater need for a careful direction of this advance. Whoever imagines that a greater group unity can be attained by weakening the internal unity that makes each member a person, is evidently pursuing a false course. For how can an attempt on the lives of the members be conducive to the good of the organism?

In its own way the doctrine of the Mystical Body warns men against making such a mistake; it shows them a God-made society, a supernaturally perfect society. This is, of course, an ideal society, unattainable by natural groups, but very instructive nevertheless. In it they can see how the unity of the group goes hand in hand with the intensity of each member's personal life. The same attachment to Christ which reinforces supernaturally the personal unity of each member, unites him at the same time with all the other members in the unity of the whole. Here men can learn an important lesson on the necessity of reconciling the inalienable rights of the individual with the needs of the whole: the two must be united, not so that one destroys the other, but so that each perfects the other. Nor should we be surprised that a supernatural reality should teach a lesson that applies to the natural order. Grace is made to perfect nature, and there seems to be no danger that men will ever exhaust even the social and economic lessons that are contained in the doctrine of the Mystical Body.

It is, lastly and chiefly, a remedy for the heresy of Modernism, for its false views on religion, and for its false doctrine of immanence. Modernism, as we know, is an attempt to make all religion, or at least whatever we can know of religion, something purely subjective. The rest is the Unknowable. Of God, of His nature, even of our immortal soul, we can know nothing. *A fortiori,* the divinity of Christ and the transcendent character of the Christ-life and of the Church are wholly beyond the range of our intelligence. The most that we can attain is something subjective, an interior sentiment, an attraction for the divine, the need for an ideal; these alone can give meaning to religious formulas, and especially to the dogmas and facts of Christianity. Venerable and wonderful as these latter are, all their beauty comes from the light that we bear in our own souls: all that man can discover in them is himself, only himself and his vague but persistent longing for an ideal that is unknowable and perhaps nonexistent.

It takes only a moment to see that such a system is not so much a heresy as the sum total of all heresies. It does away with the very notion of the supernatural, and even of the suprasensible.

That aspiration toward a more interior religion, with which it has tempted certain minds in our present age, will ever appear false, even painfully commonplace to those who have come to know the doctrine of the Mystical Body. What a poor immanence is this, that imprisons man in himself, and how sad this cry that loses itself in the darkness!

Immanence? Certainly. Why abandon a word that heresy has stolen from Truth? But we will have no immanence that robs us of our most precious personal treasure. All life is immanent; the life of man is immanent. But this immanence does not consist in man's isolating himself in himself, but in his aspiring to the supreme Life and Immanence, to the God who is immanent Life. The Christ-life, too, is immanent, but with an immanence far superior to that of unaided man. Since we are all taken up in Christ, we are all united in God. It is the eternal Life, which by vivifying the sacred humanity of the Saviour, vivifies us all in Him. It is a catholic life, universally human as it is eternal and divine. And because it is life, it is an immanence. But what an immanence! It is the presence within us of the Mystical Christ, the intimacy of all that is catholic, the union within the individual, in Christ and through Christ, with all of regenerated humanity and with God.

Each Christian has his own personal grace; yet in all who possess grace, all these individual graces remain united in their common source, which is Christ, the Head of the Church. In the supernatural order there is but one living organism in Christ. This organism grows and develops through the ages and it extends itself to all peoples over the entire face of the earth; yet all of this, all this life, all the good that is wrought in heaven by the saints and by men here on earth, in the whole universe and throughout all time—all this is one Christ, Head and members, *unus Christus amans seipsum.*

Dietrich Von Hildebrand
1889-1977

"Follow me."

For two thousand years, Christians have dedicated their lives to exploring the overtones of this simple, awesome phrase. Spoken originally by Jesus Christ, the words have become the starting point for every person who seeks to go beyond the realm of the ordinary and to discover the mystery of the divine that lies hidden at the very heart of mankind. "Follow me" declares that the origin of the Christian life is God and that the sole, the primary task of man in history is to return to his origin. "Follow me" reveals Christ as the Way back to one's origins, for Christianity takes seriously its claim that authentic human existence is possible only through the process of transformation in Christ.

Dietrich Von Hildebrand, an internationally famous student of the modern intellectual movement known as phenomenology, has dedicated a significant portion of his lifetime to meditation upon the Christian process of transformation. Both in Europe and America, his teaching, lecturing, and writing have been enthusiastically received. His books cover a variety of topics such as ethics, marriage, love, celibacy, and reverence for human life.

The volume from which the following selection is taken is entitled, appropriately, Transformation in Christ *(1948). For Hildebrand, the "Follow me" of Christianity is an invitation to become a new man in Christ, not in some secret way in the depths of one's soul, but by the transformation of one's entire personality. The goal of the Christian life is to identify with "Christ's supernatural wealth of virtue, which in its very quality represents something new and distinct from all merely natural virtue." (Introduction).*

Hildebrand makes the interesting observation that too often Christians minimize and take lightly what God expects from them. This leads into a type of existence that is satisfied with doing the minimum, fulfilling the obligations and letting it go at that. Such an approach to life is hardly Christian. The true Christian life begins with a readiness to become something fundamentally different. The Christian described by Hildebrand is enlivened by the vital rhythm of youth, forceful and daring, stable and fully mature. He dwells in simplicity, humility, patience, meekness and joy. He is free. Though this may sound distant and beyond the grasp of most humans, it actually is not. As the author reminds us, Christ's invitation was to all mankind.

While shaped by contemporary philosophy, Hildebrand is clearly familiar with and in agreement with the great spiritual literature of the Christian tradition. He draws heavily from Sacred Scripture, the Fathers of the Church, St. Augustine and St. Thomas Aquinas. It is his hope that the reader will strive to grasp the height, breadth and depth of the Christian vocation.

TRANSFORMATION IN CHRIST

CHAPTER 1

THE READINESS TO CHANGE

Put off the old man who is corrupted according to the desire of error, and be renewed in the spirit of your mind: and put on the new man, who according to God is created in justice and holiness of truth" (Eph. 4:22-24).

These words of St. Paul are inscribed above the gate through which all must pass who want to reach the goal set us by God. They implicitly contain the quintessence of the process which baptized man must undergo before he attains the unfolding of the new supernatural life received in Baptism.

All true Christian life, therefore, must begin with a deep yearning to become a "new man" in Christ, and an inner readiness to "put off the old man"—a readiness to become something fundamentally different.

Even though he should lack religion, the will to change is not unknown to man. He longs to develop and to perfect himself. He believes he can overcome all vices and deficiencies of his nature by human force alone. All morally aspiring men are conscious of the necessity of a purposeful self-education which should cause them to change and to develop. They, too—as contrasted to the morally indifferent man who "lets himself go" and abandons himself passively to his natural dispositions— reveal a certain readiness to change. But for this, no spiritual and moral growth would exist at all.

Yet, when man is touched by the light of Revelation, something entirely new has come to pass. The revelation of the Old Testament alone suffices to make the believer aware of man's metaphysical situation and the terrible wound inflicted upon his nature by original sin. He knows that no human force can heal that wound; that he is *in need of redemption*. He grasps the truth that repentance is powerless to remove the guilt of sin which separates him from God, that good will and natural moral endeavour will fail to restore him to the beauty of the paradisiac state. Within him lives a deep yearning for the Redeemer, Who by divine force will take the guilt of sin and bridge the gulf that separates the human race from God. Throughout the Old Testament that yearning resounds: "Convert us, O God: and show us thy face, and we shall be saved" (Ps. 79:4); we perceive the desire for purification which enables us to appear before God, and to endure the presence of the unspeakably Holy One: "Thou shalt sprinkle me with hyssop, and I shall be cleansed: thou shalt wash me, and I shall be made whiter than snow" (Ps. 50:9).

The New Testament, however, reveals to us a *call* which far transcends that *yearning*. Thus Christ speaks to Nicodemus: "Amen, amen, I say to thee, unless a man be born again, he cannot see the kingdom of God" (John 3:3).

Christ, the Messiah, is not merely the Redeemer who breaks apart the bond, and cleanses us from sin. He is also the Dispenser of a new divine life which shall wholly transform us and turn us into "new men": "Put off the old man who is corrupted according to the desire of error, and be renewed in the spirit of your mind: and put on the new man, who according to God is created in justice and holiness of truth." Though we receive this new life in Baptism as a free gift of God, it may not flourish unless we cooperate. "Purge out the old leaven, that you may be a new paste," says St. Paul.

A strong desire must fill us to become different beings, to mortify our old selves and re-arise as new men in Christ. This desire, this readiness to "decrease" so that "He may grow in us," is the first elementary precondition for the transformation in Christ. It is the primal gesture by which man reacts to the "light of Christ" that has reached his eyes: the original gesture directed to God. It is, in other words, the adequate consequence of our consciousness of being *in need of redemption* on the one hand, and our comprehension of being *called* by Christ on the other. Our surrender to Christ implies a readiness to let Him fully transform us, without setting any limit to the modification of our nature under His influence.

Dietrich Von Hildebrand

In regard to their respective readiness to change, the difference between the Christian and the natural idealist is obvious. The idealist is suffused with optimism concerning human nature as such. He underestimates the depth of our defects; he is unaware of the wound, incurable by human means, with which our nature is afflicted. He overlooks our impotence to erase a moral guilt or to bring about autonomously a moral regeneration of ourselves. Moreover, his infatuation for activity prevents him from understanding even the necessity of a *basic* renewal. He fails to sense the *essential* inadequacy of all natural morality, as well as the incomparable superiority of virtue supernaturally founded, let alone the full presence of such virtue—holiness. His readiness to change will differ, therefore, from that of the Christian, above all in the following respects. First, he has in mind a relative change only: an evolution immanent to nature. His endeavour is not, as is the Christian's, to let his nature as a whole be transformed "from above," nor to let his character be stamped with a new coinage, a new face, as it were, whose features far transcend human nature and all its possibilities. His object is not to be reborn: to become radically—from the root, that is—another man; he merely wants to perfect himself within the framework of his natural dispositions. He is intent on ensuring an unhampered evolution of these dispositions and potentialities. Sometimes even an express approval of his own nature is implicit therein, and a self-evident confidence in the given tendencies of his nature as they are before being worked upon by conscious self-criticism. Such was, for instance, Goethe's case. Invariably in the idealist, the readiness to change is limited to a concept of nature's immanent evolution or self-perfection: its scope remains *exclusively* human. Whereas, with the Christian, it refers to a basic transformation and redemption of things human by things divine: to a supernatural goal.

A second point of difference is closely connected with this. The idealist's readiness to change is aimed at certain details or aspects only, never at his character as a whole. The aspiring man of natural morality is intent on eradicating *this* defect, on acquiring *that* virtue; the Christian, however, on becoming another man in *all* things, in regard to both what is bad and what is *naturally good* in him. He knows that what is naturally good, too, is insufficient before God: that it, *too,* must submit to supernatural transformation—to a re-creation, we might say, by the new principle of supernatural life conveyed to him by Baptism.

Thirdly, the man of natural moral endeavour, willing as he may be to change in one way or another, will always stick to the firm ground of Nature. How could he be asked to relinquish that foothold, tumbling off into the void? Yet it is precisely this firm ground which the Christian *does* leave. His readiness to change impels him to break with his unredeemed nature as a whole: he *wills* to lose the firm ground of unredeemed nature under his feet and to tumble, so to speak, into the arms of Christ. Only he who may say with St. Paul, "I know in whom I have believed" can risk the enormous adventure of "dying unto himself" and of relinquishing the natural foundation.

Now this radical readiness to change, the necessary condition for a transformation in Christ is not actually possessed by *all* Catholic believers. It is, rather, a distinctive trait of those who have grasped the *full* import of the Call, and without reserve have decided upon an imitation of Christ.

There are many religious Catholics whose readiness to change is merely a conditional one. They exert themselves to keep the commandments and to get rid of such qualities as they have recognized to be sinful. But they lack the will and the readiness to become new men all in all, to break with all purely natural standards, to view all things in a supernatural light. They prefer to evade the act of *metanoia*: a true "conversion" of the heart. Hence with an undisturbed conscience they cling to all that appears to them legitimate by natural standards. Their conscience permits them to remain entrenched in their self-assertion. For example, they do not feel the obligation of loving their enemies; they let their pride have its way within certain limits; they insist on the right of giving play to their natural reactions in answer to any humiliation. They maintain as self-evident their claim to the world's respect, they dread being looked upon as "fools of Christ"; they accord a certain role to human respect, and are anxious to stand justified in the eyes of the world also. They are not ready for a total breach with the world and its standards; they are swayed by certain conventional considerations; nor do they refrain from "letting themselves go" within reasonable limits. There are various types and degrees of this reserved form of the readiness to change; but common to them all is the characteristic of a merely conditional obedience to the Call and an ultimate abiding by one's natural self. However great the differences of degree may be, the decisive cleavage is that which separates the unreserved, radical readiness to change from the somehow limited and partial one. The full readiness to change—which might even better be termed "readiness to become another man"—is present in him only who, having heard the call "Follow me" from the mouth of the Lord, follows Him as did the Apostles, "leaving everything behind." To do so, he is not required literally to relinquish everything in the sense of the evangelical counsels: this would be in answer to another, more special call. He is merely required to relinquish his old self, the natural foundation, and all purely natural standards, and open himself entirely to Christ's action—comprehending and answering the call addressed to *all* Christians: "Put on the new man, who according to God is created in justice and holiness of truth."

Readiness to change, taken in this sense, is the first prerequisite for the transformation in Christ. But, in addition thereto, more is needed: a glowing desire to "become a new man in Christ"; a passionate will to give oneself over to Christ. And this, again, presupposes a state of "fluidity," as it were: that we should be like soft wax, ready to receive the imprint of the features of Christ. We must be determined not to entrench ourselves in our nature, not to maintain or assert ourselves, and above all, not to set up before hand—however unconsciously—a framework of limiting or qualifying factors for the pervasive and re-creative light of Christ. Rather we must be filled with an unquenchable thirst for regeneration in all things. We must fully experience the bliss of flying into Christ's arms, Who will transform us by His light beyond any measure we might ourselves intend. We must say as did St. Paul on the road to Damascus: "Lord, what wilt thou have me to do?"

But the unreserved readiness to change, as here outlined, is not merely the condition for embarking on our journey towards our supernatural goal. It also constitutes the permanent basis for continual progress on our road. It is an attitude we must always preserve so long as we are *in statu viae*—until we have reached the safe harbor of the *status finalis*, where there is no longer any "task" proposed to our will, and where our souls will rest unchangeably in the boundless bliss of communion with God. Should that readiness to change and that passionate will to surrender ever cease, we would no longer have the proper religious disposition. That unlimited readiness to change is not only necessary for the transformation in Christ: even as such, it represents the basic and relevant response to God. It reflects our unreserved devotion to God, our consciousness of our infinite weakness before Him, our habitude of living by the Faith, our love and yearning for God. It finds its highest expression in these words of the Blessed Virgin: "Behold the handmaid of the Lord; be it done to me according to thy word" (Luke 1:38).

In his *Discourses for Mixed Congregations,* Cardinal Newman points out the danger inherent in believing oneself to have attained a satisfactory degree of spiritual progress—no matter how high a degree it actually is—and to be entitled now to discontinue the struggle against one's own nature. The example of the saints teaches us that spiritual progress implies no hardening of that "fluidity" of which we have spoken, no weakening of the steady will for transformation by Christ. The more one is transformed in Christ, the deeper and more unlimited his readiness to change beyond the point reached, the more he understands the dimension of depth in which that transformation must extend, and the necessity for him to place himself *anew* in God's hands, again and again, so as to be shaped anew by Christ. Never, *in statu viae,* will he cease to say with Michelangelo, "Lord, take me away from myself, and make me pleasing to Thee." In his earthly life the Christian must never let the process of "dying unto himself" and rising again in Christ come to a standstill: he should always preserve that "inner fluidity" which is an ultimate expression of the situation implied in the *status viae.* Thus spoke the thief on the cross: "We are punished justly, for we receive the due reward of our deeds, but this man hath done no evil. Lord, remember me when thou shalt come into thy kingdom." In that moment, a "bursting through" towards things divine took place in his soul, which bore a connotation of unlimited love. And, because this unlimited surrender was the last act of his life before expiring, in spite of all his imperfections he received this answer from the Lord: "Amen, I say to thee, this day thou shalt be with me in paradise" (Luke 23:42-43).

That unlimited readiness to change is necessary not only for the sinner in the narrower sense of the word, but also for the guarded, the pure, the graced, whom God has drawn unto Himself from youth onwards: not only for a St. Augustine but also for a St. John. The saints are classed sometimes in two categories: on the one hand, the great converts like St. Paul or St. Mary Magdalen; on the other, men and women in whom a continuous slow maturing of grace is clearly observable, such souls as St. John the Evangelist or St. Catherine of Siena. Yet the necessity of what is here described as "readiness to change" applies by no means only to him who has gone through a conversion and who therefore evidently cannot but repent of his former life, but even to such as have never definitely and gravely trespassed against God's commandments. They, too, must be willing to rise above their nature and hold themselves ready for coinage by the spirit of Christ.

However, it would mean a grievous misunderstanding of this indispensable basic attitude to interpret it as a state of "fluidity" as such, a general disposition to change in no matter what direction. In fact, what we have in mind is exclusively the readiness to let ourselves be shaped by Christ, and by whatever speaks of Him and of the "Father of all lights." The change we have in view is merely the change implied in the continual process of "dying unto ourselves," and being re-formed by Christ. Moreover, that state of "fluidity" which makes this process possible is linked, on the other hand, to an attitude of *consolidation in Christ* and in the goods we receive from Him. With the postulate of soft receptiveness susceptible to the formative influences "from above" corresponds, as a logical complement, the postulate of an increasing rigidity in relation to all tendencies towards being changed "from below."

Here the difference between "fluidity" under the sign of the supernatural and the mere natural disposition of "fluidity" becomes clear. Some people, owing merely to their natural temperament are like soft wax, prone to any change whatever. These impressionable persons who yield to all kinds of influences lack solidity and continuity. The "fluidity" which goes with aliveness to the supernatural, on the contrary, has nothing to do with spineless malleability as such. Rather it involves a firm standing in the face of all mundane influences, a character of impermeability in regard to them, and an unshakable solidity on the new base with which Christ supplies us. Even at this early stage we discern that strange *coincidentia oppositorum* which will again and again strike our eyes in the course of our enquiry: that union between attitudes seemingly irreconcilable with each other on the natural level, which is the sign of all supernatural mode of being. Also, that "fluidity" in our relationship with Christ is anything but a state characterized by a continuous flow of change, in the sense that the *change as such* be credited with a value of its own. What the readiness to be transformed by Christ really implies is rather the utter negation both of the worship of "being in a state of movement" as exhibited by the Youth Movement, and of the Goethean ideal of an "abundance of life" based on the concept of continual change. We are far, then, from preaching "fluidity" in general, be it in the sense of a glorification of movement as such, or in the sense of the celebrated verses of Goethe, beautiful though they may be: *Denn solang du das nicht hast, dieses Stirb und Werde, bist du nur ein truber Gast auf der dunkeln Erde* (Unless thou follow the call of Dying and Becoming, thou art but a sad guest on this dark earth). It does not behoove us to cherish variability as such; for, as Christians we give our worship not to change but to the Unchangeable: God, Who in all eternity remains Himself: "They shall perish, but thou remainest" (Ps. 101:26-28). Thus, as Christians we direct our lives towards that moment in which there will be change no longer, and rejoice in the hope of sharing in the unchangeableness of God. We deny our love to the heaving rhythm of life; and the ideal of vitality, seductive to those who see the ultimate reality in Nature, has no attraction for us. Nor can we be intoxicated by any communion with Nature in a pantheistic sense. For we do not believe ourselves to be a part of Nature: we conceive of man as a spiritual person endowed with an immortal soul. We feel that he does not belong as a whole to the natural realm. It is only in respect to our terrestrial situation that we are subject to the rhythm of ebb and flow, the fluctuation of dying and becoming, the law of perishableness. *Non omnis moriar* (I shall not wholly die), says Horace, having in mind earthly fame. But we say it in awareness of our ultimate, our innermost essence. It is part of the blissful message of the Gospel that we are called to participate in the eternal unchangeableness of God. *Yet our life will acquire immutability in the degree in which we are transformed in Christ.* So long as we evade being thus transformed, and insist on maintaining ourselves, this remaining fixed in our own nature cannot but deliver us up to the world of flux and reflux, and the forces of change. Such a solidification would actually mean an imprisonment within the precincts of our own changeable selves: it would prevent us from transcending our limitations as vital beings, and from being drawn into the sphere of divine unchangeableness. In the measure only in which we yield like soft wax to the formative action of Christ, shall we attain genuine "firmness," and grow into a likeness of divine immutability. In that measure, too, shall we rise above the terror which— seeing our status as rational persons distinct from physical nature—the rhythm of death and life's law of transiency portend for us.

A glance at the normal course of human life, considered from a purely natural point of view, will show us a character of comparative "fluidity," in intellectual as in other respects, to be proper to youth. By that we mean not only a love of change for its own sake, but an aspiration towards higher values: an eagerness for education, for enriching and ennobling oneself; such a disposition is the natural gift of youth.

Examine a person enlivened by the vital rhythm of youth, and you will find in him a certain forcefulness and daring which facilitate that aspiration towards higher things. But when men become older and, within the framework of natural tendencies their characters and peculiarities undergo a process of solidification, the natural mobility and urge for change will tend to disappear. Such persons will then become much less accessible to elevating influences, less receptive to fresh stimuli (we are still speaking on purely natural presuppositions). We can no longer expect them to revise their mentality and to re-educate themselves, for they are already cast in a rigid mold. This description does not refer merely to an inveterate habit, owing to the lengthy accumulation of similar experiences, of looking at things in a certain way. What is meant is a general condition different from that which youth implies. The natural readiness to change is gone; its place is taken by the attitude of a person conscious of his maturity, who considers himself to have achieved his period of formation and arrogates to himself the right, as it were, to endure and to settle down in his peculiarities—which may not infrequently be eccentricities—are never so marked during youth. Only at a later period do certain natural tendencies assume such a character of rigidity. From the mere succession of the phases of life one seems to derive the right to be no longer a pupil or an apprentice but a master.

But if we envisage the vital phases of youth and old age from a supernatural point of view, the picture will be different. Here, in fact, an inverse law will appear. The readiness to change, the wax-like receptiveness towards Christ will tend not to vanish but to increase as man grows into a state of maturity. Accidental concerns and complications recede into the background; the pattern of life wins through to simplicity; the great decisive aspects of life become more clearly accentuated. The unrest incident to youth, the vacillating response to disparate appeals, the insatiable hunger for whatever appears attractive or beautiful will subside, and a steady orientation towards the essential and decisive become dominant. This progress towards simplicity, which is part of the spiritual significance of advancing in age, is linked to a "consolidation" in Christ. A number of vital tendencies, longings of all kinds, and a certain ubiquitous unrest fostered by expectations of earthly happiness, recede before that supernatural unrest which attends the supreme yearning for Christ. A liberation from one's own

272

nature becomes apparent. The scriptural words, "Being made perfect in a short space, he fulfilled a long time" (Wisd. 4: 13-14), refer to this true meaning and value of maturity.

Yet this attainment of full maturity also implies "eternal youth" in a supernatural sense. It implies that the readiness to change, the determination to become a "new man," and the unconditional willingness to crucify the old self should increase; that the impatience for Christ should not abate. As he draws nearer to the gates of eternity, such a person will direct his attention to "the one thing necessary," with ever increasing concentration. It is this supernatural youth which is referred to in the Gradual of the Mass, by the words "*qui laetificat juventutem meam*" (Who giveth joy to my youth). Here is, paradoxically speaking, a spiritual intactness increasing with age, inasmuch as throughout the *status viae* we continually enhance our alert readiness to change towards greater proximity to God, so that His features may be engraved upon our souls. And this is equivalent to becoming more and more free from ourselves: ridding ourselves of everything which, though it be rooted in our own nature, stands between our souls and Christ. It may be said without exaggeration that the degree of our inner "fluidity" in relation to Christ, our readiness to "put off our own nature in order to put on Christ," constitutes the standard criterion of our religious progress.

Whenever at some moments we have the specific feeling of being privileged by God and drawn nearer to Him, we must ask ourselves: do we possess this readiness to change?—and how far do we possess it? Unless we can answer that question favorably, we are not in the right religious condition. Yet if, in the moments of inward elevation, we really possess that readiness, our being touched by God will mean more than merely receiving a gift: we are then capable of the cooperation God requires. By the degree of a man's inner readiness to change, his religious level may be decisively judged.

In the unconditional readiness to change, a salutary distrust of one's own self-knowledge is also implied. If I am really intent on becoming "another man" I will not claim the right to determine the limits between what can, and what cannot, be justified in my nature if confronted with Christ. It is He who is to determine them through religious authority. The readiness must be present, on our part, to be changed and shaped to an indefinite degree at the hands of God, wherever He chooses to intervene by the agency of our spiritual director or of our religious superior. *We are not ourselves able or entitled to determine the measure of our transformation.* This is a true sign of the ultimate relevancy, and of the radical "newness" by which a life devoted to the true imitation of Christ is characterized. God will be merciful with those also who possess only a limited readiness to change; but he alone whose readiness to change and whose spiritual plasticity are unlimited can attain to sanctity.

It must be emphasized that there is no contradiction between the Christian's readiness to change and the principle of moral continuity. Our mental attitude reveals the trait of continuity in so far as we remain aware of the ultimate unity of all truth and all values in God. We must keep in view and continue to recognize whatever valid truth we have seized, whatever genuine value experienced; none of these must sink into oblivion once it is no longer actually present to our eyes. The man who is a prey to discontinuity accords an illegitimate priority to what happens to be present in his consciousness. He neglects more important and more valid impressions for the sake of present ones. He fails to preserve his contact with basic general truths and values beyond the range of mere present interest. He is, therefore, unable to confront the concrete situation of the moment with those truths and values, and to experience it in their light. Because he is submerged in the situation of the moment, he lacks the standard by which to measure and to judge all new impressions. Moreover, the impressions succeed one another in a disconnected flight; one replaces the other as though they were mutually equivalent, with no proportionate attention given to those of greater weight; and thus the valid content of former impressions is trampled under foot, as it were, by the "dynamism" of what is actually present.

Suppose, for instance, that we happen to have gained a deep insight into someone's personality. Meeting him later on a more superficial occasion, our impression is different: we see him this time "from the outside," rather like a casual acquaintance. If we have the *habitus* of continuity we shall not let ourselves be confused by this new impression but keep aware of the former impression, which has been deeper and of greater validity. Whereas, if we lack continuity, the new impression will confuse our judgment and, because of its mere recentness, obscure and displace the older but more relevant one.

Continuity, then, consists in the twofold capacity to maintain our comprehension of basic truths, experiencing all things against a background of these truths, and to maintain particular aspects of great validity as against new ones which happen to be less substantial. Both these aptitudes are in close harmony with the quality of receptiveness towards new truths and values. Legitimate faithfulness to things established does not spring from mere inertia and formal conservatism; it represents rather an adequate response to the immutability of unalloyed truth and genuine value, which is past obsolescence. The selfsame motive which impels the person with continuity to cling imperturbably to truth will equally commit him to be ready to accept every new truth. He will be ready even to renounce what he has held to be truth, should a new and deeper insight actually disprove it. The rectification of a former opinion, in the proper sense of the term, is not opposed to, but on the contrary definitely presupposes, continuity. For what is operative here is by no means the merely psychological advantage of the more recent impression but the subordination of all particular convictions, whether they be formed at an earlier or a later period of time, to eternal truths and objective standards of judgment. Thus, continuity is a condition, not only for stable orientation but also for intellectual progress itself. It is on the basis of continuity that we are able to preserve established truths and at the same time to supplement them with new ones, both in the sense of an extension of the breadth of knowledge, and of a re-interpretation of old truths in the light of insights newly acquired.

It is by the attitude of continuity that we conform to the invariability and the mutual consistency—the intrinsic unity—of all values. It implies, therefore, that the higher value should take precedence of the lower one. In granting priority to a higher value, once it presents itself, we give proof of continuity.

For, in following the higher value we implicitly continue to cherish what was the object of our response in the lower value to which we hitherto adhered unreservedly. Our supreme fidelity is not due to a partial value or good, taken by itself, but to value as such—and ultimately, to God, Who is the *summum bonum* (highest good). Our fidelity to that highest good requires that the objectively higher value should rise above the lower one also in regard to our experience and our conduct.

It is important to avoid all equivocation on this point: that continuity is a prime condition of spiritual growth, and even more, of a transformation in Christ; and that it stands in no opposition to the will to become "another man." Without continuity, on the contrary, there could be no genuine responsiveness to the formative claim of Christ. For, with each step achieved the coinage received from Christ must be preserved and be made into a durable and inherent stamp on our nature. Only we must always remain changeable in the sense of remaining, upon each level securely attained, susceptible of ascent towards yet higher levels along the path of transformation in Christ. But every such act of remodelling refers back to the previous level, and thus has its place in the solid framework of continuity. The previous phase will not be buried or obliterated: its essential content will re-appear on the higher level, although deepened, amplified and transfigured in the context of that higher grade of perfection. Thus shall we keep fidelity to Christ, when we follow His call to penetrate into Him ever deeper, and without reserve. It is one and the same Christ who by successive degrees reveals to us His face more and more fully, and who owns us more and more completely as we become more deeply transformed in Him.

But this requires our capacity to discern whether the "new impression" is really a more valid and relevant one. On the basis of continuity alone shall we be able wisely and fruitfully to confront the new thing with the old, so as to avoid falling back from a higher level to a lower one, or yielding to a new impression when it belongs to a level inferior to the one we have already reached.

Is there not, however, also a duty of fidelity towards our own God-created individuality? Is it right for us to ignore—

in our unlimited readiness for transformation—what we feel to be the particular talents which God has entrusted to us, that ineffable essence which we feel to be our ultimate core?

Certainly, the radical readiness to change in the sense used here does not entail renunciation of the particularity of our personality as willed by God. But this concept, the particular individuality of a person, has a dual meaning. On the one hand, it may designate the character of a person as an empirical whole, including also whatever vices, defects, imperfections, eccentricities, and accidental features his personality may contain. Or else, we mean by "individuality" the particular, unique, and inimitable thought in the mind of God which every human being embodies. It is only in a saint that individuality thus conceived can fully display itself. For it contains, on the one hand, the particular natural character of the person which, however, never implies defects and imperfections as such; and on the other hand, a supernatural transfiguration and elevation of that particular nature. Now the readiness to change, as discussed here, refers in the first place to all the negative and ultimately spurious tendencies in our nature which oppose a barrier to our control by Christ. But it also refers, further, to all that is naturally good in us; for the latter is not destined to remain natural but to become enhanced and transfigured by the re-creative action of the supernatural.

No renunciation of the specific value attaching to individuality, no denial of the person's particular nature as willed by God is implied in this transformation. This is best illustrated by the example of the saints. Though it can be said of each of them alike that "he no longer lives but Christ lives in him," they are individualities with marked contours. Let us only think of St. Francis of Assisi and St. Catherine of Siena—to mention only two of the most obvious examples. It is as legitimate to preserve our individuality in the sense of the particular call of God which it enshrines as it is illegitimate to stick to what we commonly regard as "our nature." The maintenance of our divinely sanctioned particular individuality can never conflict with our transformation by Christ. It cannot involve us in resisting the uplifting force and in shielding any part of "our nature" from Christ. For, so long as we keep immured in our nature, that divinely sanctioned individuality is not yet achieved; it is only when "we live no longer but Christ lives in us" that it can unfold integrally.

The great mystery of our metaphysical situation, that God is nearer to us than we are ourselves, is manifest in the fact that we cannot even be wholly ourselves—in the sense of individuality as a unique divine thought—until we are reborn in Christ. Undoubtedly, the preservation of divinely sanctioned individuality may mean that certain forms or modes of religious life are not appropriate to a given person. Every method is not suitable for everyone. There are several equally valid ways towards God, such as the Benedictine, the Franciscan, the Dominican, and so forth. The specific word of God that has been spoken in every soul; the name by which God has called; us the unique design of God underlying every personality—these must not be forcibly denied or suppressed. Yet, as we have already seen, the uniqueness of every person is something to be carefully distinguished from what is commonly subsumed under the term "individuality," and what most of us are apt to cherish as our particular nature. This so-called individuality originates from various factors, such as the experiences a man has undergone, the wounds that have been inflicted upon him, the false responses that have become ingrained in his mind, the environment in which he has lived, the education he has received, the conventions which surround him, and so forth. Only think how many rash generalizations, built upon a single and perhaps accidental experience, survive in our mind. All these things are incorporated in a person's character; but they need not by any means be consonant with the very essence and ultimate meaning of his individuality. All these forces cannot have worked out so favourably as not to have distorted in a certain way and a certain measure the true individuality as willed by God. What we generally feel to be our individual nature is far remote from the inward word by which God has called us. By our own force alone we cannot even truly discern that word. "Every man lies," says the Psalmist.

What should be relinquished without reserve, therefore, are such elements of personality as do not belong to its proper essence. And yet precisely in regard to these does the tendency to fixation persist. Most men are reluctant to sacrifice those manifold features of their personality which are no part of its inmost essence but derivatives of the various factors we have listed above. They attempt tenaciously to maintain themselves in these very features. This tendency to self-affirmation and petrification, as contrasted to the readiness for being transformed in all these points and for receiving the imprint of the face of Christ instead of the old features, is the antithesis to what we have meant here in speaking of "fluidity."

To sum up—the postulate of a readiness to change does not refer to individuality in the ultimate sense, which is according to divine ordination. Individuality in this sense will be transfigured and sanctified, but by no means foregone or supplanted by another individuality. For the essence of every human person supposes a unique and incommensurable task; it is destined to unfold and to operate in a direction inalienably proper to it.

At this stage, let us signalize two dangers which are naturally apt to arise and which should be avoided.

Sometimes we encounter people of a certain type characterized by a proclivity towards spiritual depression and sloth. Such a man will yield to a mood of inward barrenness. Though possessing a certain modesty, he lacks vigor and eagerness for spiritual elevation. He is unresponsive to what is best in him, and demurs at believing in it. The example of the saints, far from inciting him to emulation, only confirms him in his resignation. "I am a wretched man." In his pusillanimity, such a person leaves unused the talents of which he should make the most; he irresponsibly declines being committed by God's call. People of this kind, when speaking of themselves, even are wont to deny the virtues they naturally possess; such is their lack of confidence. They are bent on lowering their stature as much as possible. Their lack of courage and activity, which causes them to desert their higher potentialities, is most deplorable. On the other hand, their care in avoiding false pretensions deserves a certain credit.

The inverse type of deviation is exemplified by the man who, while not lacking a certain *elan*, refuses to take account of his limitations and is thus driven to magnify his stature artificially. Suppose he is present at some discussion of spiritually relevant topics: he will take part in the debate as though he were fully equipped to do so; he will claim impressions as deep as "the others"; he will not yield to any other man as regards intellectual proficiency or even religious stature. Thus he "works himself up," as it were, to a level which he has not reached in reality—and which he may not even be able to reach, so far as it is a matter of natural capacities. He is not without zeal; but that zeal is nourished at heart by pride. He misjudges the limitations of the natural talents which God has lent him, and consequently lapses into pretence. He is fond of speaking of things which far transcend the limits of his understanding; he behaves as though a mere mental or verbal reference to such subjects (however poorly implemented with actual knowledge and penetration) would by itself amount to their intellectual possession. This cramped attitude of sham spirituality is mostly underlain by an inferiority complex, or by a kind of infantile unconsciousness. Stupidity in its really oppressive form is traceable to this pretension to appear something different from what one is in fact, and by no means to a mere deficiency of intellectual gifts. A person who knows his position and confines himself to themes he does understand will, for all his lack of acumen, never really produce the impression of stupidity, that is to say, his fellow men will not feel embarrassed and exasperated by his intellectual weakness.

Both these attitudes—that of undue depression, and that of forced zeal, to put it briefly—are reprehensible. The supernatural readiness to change steers clear of both these dangers. The man whom it governs is cognizant, at the same time, of his natural limits and of the specific call which God has implanted in his soul. He refuses to flag, and to rest content with the lowest potentialities in his individual nature; but neither does he strain to answer a false idealized concept of himself. While he is conscious of his wretchedness, he will not sink into resignation; for he possesses a *supernatural* zeal for perfection, expecting the supreme fructification of the talents which God has in reality entrusted to him from his transformation in Christ, rather than from his own effort alone. Man must be sufficiently spirited to be ready to don his festive garment.

Whatever his nature be like, he will know that it is possible for him to become "another man" if he is rightly disposed for being created anew by Christ—mindful of the words which the king in the parable addresses to his guest: "Friend, how camest thou in hither not having on a wedding garment?" (Matt. 22:12). The state of "fluidity" in relation to Christ, and the readiness to leave behind everything, particularly one's own self—such is the tissue of which the festive garment is woven.

There are few things more obstructive to that "state of fluidity" than a certain misconstrued ideal of fidelity often to be met with. Some people attribute value to the attitude of stubborn adherence as such (adherence to an idea, or to an intellectual milieu, in particular). Yet in reality it is adherence to truth and to genuine values only which is good; adherence to errors is a bad thing. What claims our faithfulness is the presence of genuine values. Fidelity is but a manifestation of that continuity by virtue of which we pay consideration to the immutability and the eternal significance of truth and of the world of values. To abide by a thing inflexibly, merely because we have once believed in it and have come to love it, is not in itself a praiseworthy attitude. It is only in reference to truth and to genuine value that unswerving loyalty is an obligation, and a virtue. In regard to all errors and negative values (that is, evils in the widest sense of the term, but particularly in a morally relevant sense) we have, on the contrary, the duty to break with what we formerly cherished and to withdraw our allegiance from them, once we know them to be false and negative in value. Indeed, the obligation of fidelity in a formal and automatic sense must not hamper our readiness to separate ourselves from such ideals or convictions, once we have serious reasons to doubt their validity. There is only *one* fidelity to which we are absolutely committed: that is, fidelity towards God, the epitome of all values, and towards everything that represents God and is instrumental to us in approaching Him.

This truth is frequently obscured by considerations of this order: "I should, after all, remain faithful to a person whom I have loved, even though I cannot help discovering many negative values in him." By analogy, it is inferred that an obligation of fidelity exists also in regard to ideas, intellectual milieus, and cultural atmospheres which have formerly meant a great deal to us, and have become traditional with us. In reality, however, the situation is quite different in regard to ideological entities than it is in regard to persons. A person, *in statu viae,* is never something as definitively and univocally fixed (concerning his significance and value) as is an idea or an ideal. A person may grow and unfold, he may reform and perfect himself along lines essentially unlimited in their design. Every human being incarnates a divine thought, and it is to this that my love for him in its decisive spiritual aspect is directed. Hence, I may keep in communion with him even though there be revealed to me an entirely new and higher world: for the latter may make a more basic objective appeal to him also, and that appeal may yet be carried to him actually. Moreover, all relationships between persons involve a kind of immanent "promise" which, however tacit, generates a binding mutual claim; whereas in our relationships with non-personal entities that specific note is naturally absent. All inter-personal relations are fraught with a kind of immanent obligation; the specific character of obligation is different according to the essential quality and the objective meaning of the relationship in question; but in any such relationship a claim to fidelity remains. It is not so with our relations to ideal entities and other non-personal things.

Nevertheless, true fidelity towards a person may on occasion impose on us the duty to withdraw altogether from contact with him. In the case where he would constitute a threat to our fidelity to God, and when we on the other hand feel powerless to help him, our breaking off relations with him is still consistent with our true fidelity towards him: it is destined to promote his spiritual good as well as our own, and is therefore involved in our very love for him so far as love in a higher and ultimate sense implies, above all, responsibility.

Frequently, however, the concept of fidelity towards persons is transferred uncritically to the world of ideas. The unfortunate figure of speech, "the Faith of our fathers," is misleading as to the motive for our fidelity towards the Faith; for what can be decisive in this case is only the *truth* of the Faith, and not the accident that "our fathers" already happened to believe in it. If this were not so, paganism in its turn could or should never have been supplanted by Christianity. Fidelity to ideas as such is neutral in value only so long as we abstract from the question *what* ideas are at stake. In reality, there is only one fidelity which is a strict duty: fidelity to truth, fidelity towards Christ.

Not only is "fidelity" towards errors and false ideals a mistaken attitude; we are also bound to dissolve the bonds that unite us with such cultural or human milieus as cannot withstand the test of confrontation with Christ. Often we cherish certain old and familiar things, ensconcing ourselves in them as in a kind of "home," merely because we have lived so long with them, and particularly because they are connected with many memories of our childhood. Thus, we suffer the world of Christ to penetrate us with its light only so far as it does not interfere with our safe residence in that *putative* "home." There is also the danger of attempting so to redraw and to humanize the face of Christ that it may fit into the features of that "home." Many such humanizations and senti-mental falsifications are to be found in so-called popular piety, and are expressed even in certain hymns. We must have the readiness to relinquish such all-too-human substitutes, however comfortable we may feel them. We must be filled with the desire to look into the unfalsified countenance of Christ as shown by the Church in her liturgy. We must long to be lifted by Christ into His world, not try to drag Him down into ours. Whatever is of genuine value and appropriate to His world we shall receive back from Him transfigured and resplendent with a new light.

On the measure of our readiness to change depends the measure of our transformation in Christ. *Unreserved* readiness is an indispensable precondition of the "conception" of Christ in our souls, and it must endure with undiminished vigour all along the path of our transformation. Beyond that, however, as we have seen, it constitutes a central response to Revelation, to God's epiphany in Christ, and to the call He has issued to us; and therefore, a high virtue by itself. The significance and the value of such an attitude also appear from the fact that the better a man's inward condition and the more he feels touched by God the wider the doors of his heart will be opened and the readier he will show himself for being changed. Whenever, on the contrary, some baser impulse gets the upper hand in a man's soul, he will shut himself up, and the "doors" will close again. He will harden, and attempt to maintain himself. There is a deep nexus between a kind, unrestrained attitude in general, and the state of "fluidity," openness and receptivity to formative action "from above." Still more is the act of free inward surrender to God inseparable from that state of "fluidity" and receptivity; whereas, by bolting ourselves up and entrenching ourselves in our nature we stifle in our souls the growth of the germs implanted by God, and an opposition to higher appeals will consequently arise in all domains. The readiness to change is an essential aspect of the Christian's basic relation with God; it forms the core of our response to the merciful love of God which bends down upon us: "With eternal charity hath God loved us; so He hath drawn us, lifted from the earth, to His merciful heart" (Antiphon of Praise, Feast of the Sacred Heart). To us all has the inexorable yet beatifying call of Christ been addressed: *Sequere me* (Follow Me). Nor do we follow it unless, relinquishing everything, we say with St. Paul: "Lord, what wilt Thou have me to do?" (Acts 9:6).

CHAPTER 4

TRUE CONSCIOUSNESS

The inward progress in the Christian's life is linked to a process of awakening to an ever increasing degree of consciousness. Conversion itself is comparable to an emergence from a state of somnolence. In rising from self-contained worldliness towards the reality of God, in experiencing the metaphysical situation in which God has placed him and the new light in which all things and his own self are now appearing, the person attains to a new level of consciousness. The convert, in Cardinal Newman's words, is like a man ascending from a mine to behold daylight for the first time. He looks back upon his former life as a state of somnolence, a twilight of semi-consciousness.

Again, with our unreserved decision to imitate Christ, a new brand of consciousness will necessarily permeate our life.

However, there are many kinds of consciousness, only one of which will constitute the proper mark of our process of transformation in Christ. There also exists a false kind of consciousness which tends to corrode our interior life, and which is definitely opposed to true consciousness. Before discussing this true Christian consciousness, which indeed marks the "measure of the age of the fullness of Christ" (Eph. 4:13), we must first identify and discard that false way of being conscious.

Its prime characteristic is this. The man who is falsely "conscious" is no longer capable of full response to an object or situation. His mind is no longer able to sense the substance of things or of situations, nor the appeal which emanates from them; the normal contact between subject and object appears severed. We may distinguish two basic forms of this false type of consciousness.

First, there is the mental perversion which consists in the fact that we destroy the attitude of genuine absorption in the object by an excess of reflective self-observation.

Secondly, there is the tendency to over-intellectualism, implying that even in a situation which calls upon us to decide or to act rather than merely to know, we persevere in a purely cognitive attitude.

We begin with the description of the first form of false consciousness. There is a type of person whose glance is always turned back upon his own self, and who is therefore incapable of any genuine conforming to the spirit of an object. If, for instance, he is listening to some beautiful music, he at once develops an awareness of his own reaction, and thus loses the possibility of a genuine response to that beautiful music. It is implicit in the normal manifestations of the human mind, so far as they are directed to the object, that we should do full justice to the given object, and should in experiencing joy and sorrow, enthusiasm and indignation, love and hatred, not glance back upon our own attitude but solely upon the object towards which an attitude is directed. Once this normal rhythm is broken, and we squint back at our own behaviour, we shall be out of touch with the object; it will cease to address us really, and hence our response to it will itself become destroyed. A dramatic work will necessarily fail to move us if we are watching ourselves to the joyful event, we are absorbed by our interest in our own psychic state of joyfulness. When we are thus falsely conscious, we are permanently condemned to be our own spectators. We see ourselves from outside, and thereby poison all genuine life within us. For all genuine entering into an object requires that in a sense we forget ourselves. Only then do we achieve a real contact with things and with their inherent meaning.

The way in which we become conscious of a mental act is intrinsically different from the way in which we become conscious of an object; to the latter only does the phrase "conscious *of* something" properly apply. Our mental movements unfold along two fundamental dimensions: one is the "intentional direction" to an object, an object we grasp meaningfully, an object which confronts us and reveals its character and qualities to us. This is had when we look at a house, for example. On the other hand, there is the consciousness of a cognitive or emotional act which is in no way our object but which takes place inside us, or in which we manifest ourselves—for instance, the act of rejoicing in something. To be sure, our own attitude can itself be made an object subsequently, it can be apprehended in reflection. Yet, while we are performing a mental act we cannot but destroy that act if we withdraw our attention from the object which has elicited it and make our own attitude an object instead. Our attitudes depend on their being kindled by the values of the object. These acts are essentially "intentional," that is to say directed to the object and we must genuinely respond without turning back on ourselves. That is the reason why no one who, instead of being fully absorbed in the beloved person and that person's beauty, is always busied with himself and his own emotion, will ever love in the true sense of the word. This false consciousness of self will cause us to remain "outside" of all situations in which we are involved, excluded from participation in their meaning and content. On occasion this anomaly may attain a pathological degree. This omnipresence of reflection results in a nipping in the bud of all genuine contact with objects. This is particularly true of the hysterical, who are incapable of all genuine object-relationship, because they are continually engrossed in their own attitude.

Psychoanalysis is not only unfit to cure this morbid self-consciousness, it is even apt to increase the evil. For it incites its victims continually to dig for the supposedly hidden motives of their thoughts instead of singly attending to the object. It is most important to note that psychoanalysis does not content itself with resorting to that method in the face of abnormal mental reactions but insists on applying it to completely reasonable, well motivated attitudes too. Men are thus trained to pry about in their psychic entrails and to divest themselves of all receptiveness to the appeal of the object.

This false super-consciousness has a deadly effect on true inward life. It denatures all response to values, and nourishes our pride. For, also in performing a good deed, the person who is in this sense "conscious" will watch himself; he plays the spectator to his entire conduct. He sees himself, from the outside, in his goodness. Here is a source of many temptations to pride. So far as this kind of consciousness is concerned, Christians should be "unconscious." In holy self-forgetfulness we should surrender ourselves to the values and the command that issues from them, according to the words of Christ: "Let not thy left hand know what thy right hand doeth."

The second form of false consciousness arises from a hypertrophy, an excessive predominance, of the cognitive attitude. It is found in persons who, in a situation which requires them to take sides emotionally or to intervene actively, remain confined within the bounds of rational analysis. A man, for instance, is listening to the Ninth Symphony of Beethoven. Instead of allowing his soul to absorb the beauty of the music and to give free rein to its delight, instead of allowing himself to be seized and elevated by that beauty, he dissects the object present to his senses and examines the reasons why it is beautiful. Now, whenever we are concerned with the elucidation of aesthetic problems the rational analysis of the object is fully justified; but if the experience of the beauty of that music is at stake, this attitude is entirely inadequate. Or again, take someone who, in a developing love-relationship, at a moment when he and his beloved should naturally be dominated by the experience of their mutual awareness, turns instead the beloved person into an object of psychological research, observing his behaviour and with great interest registering the results of his observation. Such an attitude, again, is fitting an experimental psychologist confronted with his subject but is entirely out of place in a lover. Another example—suppose a man sees someone in immediate danger of life, and, instead of rushing to his rescue, studies his facial expressions. In all these cases the cognitive attitude predominates in a person so exclusively as to prevent him from giving his attention to the objective theme of a situation and the demand which that situation sends forth. This means a destruction of the true contact with the object, and means, in spite of a seemingly prevalent objectivity, an attitude which is actually *non-objective,* since it is based on a refusal to realize and to conform to the inherent meaning and appeal—the objective *logos.* As in the first-described form of false consciousness, here too we remain outside the intrinsic context of a situation, and restrict ourselves to the status of a mere spectator incapable of being moved by the inner sublimity of values.

Rational knowledge has a twofold function in human life. On the one hand, it is a purpose by itself, a theme in its own right; on the other, it provides a foundation for all our emotions and volitions. It is one of the basic qualities of man as a spiritual person that, alone among terrestrial beings, he is able to participate in the existence of the surrounding world, not merely in the sense of exerting causality on that world but in the sense of "intentional relationship": of intellectual apprehension. Whereas the material things and the merely vital beings are interconnected only through the links of causation, man is equipped to penetrate the essence and qualities of things by the light of knowledge. By virtue of acquiring a knowledge of things he possesses them, as it were, "from above." In this unique, ordered, resplendent consciousness of all the rest of creation, the sovereign status of man as an image of God and a lord of created things is specifically manifested. Whoever denies that knowledge by itself is part of man's destiny, that he is invited to penetrate the cosmos intellectually and to propose to himself as a self-subsistent theme the nature and qualities of existing things, cannot but fail to understand the nature of man.

To our intellect is entrusted the further function, however, of supplying a base for all our emotions, volitions, and conduct. But for our underlying knowledge of being, of "what is," we could not be affected and enriched by the values inherent in objects. We could not give forth an affective response, nor actively influence our environment. Yet, while by our intellect we participate in existence in a uniquely dignified way, this is not the only, not even the supreme, form of our participation. Thus, we are not only called to know God, to form a concept of Him, and in the life to come, to contemplate Him eye to eye; we are also called to adore Him, we are called to love Him and to immerse ourselves in His Love, and thus the streams of love are interpenetrating. The intimate union, the true "wedlock" with being, is ultimately achieved in the act of *frui,* the embrace of full awareness, in the "possession through self-surrender" and in the abandonment implied in the response to value. But knowledge is the indispensable basis of this union.

The type of man whose touch with being is and remains an exclusively intellectual one, who loses interest in everything once he has mastered it intellectually, reveals a special kind of spiritual deformation. He is not filled with a genuine longing for participation in being. Knowledge is not for him a road to such participation but a mere submission to the immanent logic of an unlimited process divorced from the goal of possessing the truth. Hence, such a man cannot even truly understand the *primary* function of the intellect, with the participation in being which it embodies by itself. To such a man the process of acquiring knowledge has become a self-sufficient purpose. What really matters, however, is always the objective theme present in a given situation. Should a profound significance and a high value attach to the contents of such an object or situation, then we are summoned by these to proceed beyond the merely intellectual contact, and beyond and above knowledge, to approach the stage of *frui,* and to evince an emotional and volitional response itself based on knowledge. Certain situations require us to intervene actively. He who is affected with a hypertrophy of the intellect is unable to appreciate the objective theme of a given situation and the demands involved in it. He cannot find his way out of the self-contained process of

289

knowledge, and continues endlessly to dissect the object. Thus, he loses hold of the sense of that specific participation in being which is implicit in knowledge as such. Lacking a genuine touch with reality, he perseveres in asking "Why?"—and the object escapes him more and more. He falls short of that intuition of the essential which evokes a new, a secondary, an emotional and volitional attention to the aspects of a situation. He, too, remains an eternal spectator, without ever being admitted into the full presence, the intimate atmosphere of objects.

This corrosive and pseudo-objective intellectualism, then, is the second form of false super-consciousness. It deprives man of genuine surrender to value, of true union with anything that is. A man of this type, we might say, is forever loitering around all sorts of objects, asking questions unceasingly. Also, he is apt to distrust his every impression; and if anything begins to take hold of him he withdraws from direct contact to watch everything again "from the outside." Nor, in so doing, is he unlikely to yield to the temptation of self-analysis. He will thus lapse into the first category of false self-consciousness.

True consciousness has nothing to do with either of these two states. It means, first, that the rational "intentional" relation to being takes precedence over all mere associations of images and physiologically conditioned reactions. The non-conscious are at the mercy of all kinds of fortuitous impressions. If they had a bad night, for instance, they will consequently see the world in drab and depressing colours. They fail to surmount that purely arbitrary impression, void of all validity; no, they give it credence, and behave accordingly. They are incapable of putting themselves at a proper objective distance from a physiologically conditioned, empty mood; they hand themselves over to the latter, and are disappointed with the surrounding world. That world suddenly appears to them in an entirely changed light, owing to the unreasoned trust they place in that deceptive mood. Or again, a certain situation happens to remind them of some former experience of an unpleasant character; and, in this case they do not heed the fact that in its objective contents the new situation has no kinship whatever with that former one. These people develop a hopeless uneasiness and aversion on the ground of sheer association of images. Accordingly their attitudes lack objectivity and conformity with reality. A person who is "conscious" in the more proper sense of the term will, on the contrary, orientate his essential behaviour so as to answer the objective meaning—the revelant content—of the situation. He is not so fully submerged in himself, not so completely a servant of his nature, as to seriously consider invalid, illegitimate, and incidental aspects. He is able to distinguish valid impressions from invalid ones. Here the mental form of meaningful "intentional" object-reference has asserted itself successfully against psycho-physical impulses or purely associative prejudices. It is, indeed, the prime characteristic of intellectual maturity ("majority") that in our mental life the structural trait of "intentional" reference comes to prevail over the power of mere associations of ideas, and states of mind. In infantile thought, associations and body-conditioned states of mind still play a very great part; more important still, impressions thus gleaned are not then clearly distinguished from impressions legitimately founded in the things themselves. Also, mere images of phantasy freely fuse with, and are more or less assimilated into, the concepts of reality. There is as yet no clear-cut distinction between imagination and fact. To be mentally grown up is to have one's reactions adjusted to the immanent logic, the proper meaning of things; to have established "intentional" object-reference in a ruling position in our mental lives. In this sense, an adult is more conscious than a child. To advance in that consciousness and to overcome all infantilism is a necessary condition for attaining the "measure of the age of the fullness of Christ," and thus imperative for the Christian. A consideration of all things *in conspectu Dei,* and a response to them conceived according to the spirit of Christ necessarily presupposes the supremacy of "intentional" object-reference, of a mode of response directed to the central meaning of things, over all merely associative and physiologically conditioned reactions; in particular, it presupposes the capacity of discrimination between valid and invalid aspects.

Another characteristic of true consciousness is closely connected therewith. It is the awakening to full moral majority, the discovery of the capacity of sanctioning. The behaviour of "unconscious" persons is dictated by their nature. They tacitly identify themselves with whatever response their nature suggests to them. They have not yet discovered the possibility of emancipating themselves, by virtue of their free personal "centre," from their nature; they make no use as yet of this primordial capacity inherent in the personal mode of being. Hence their responses to values, even when they happen to be adequate, will always have something accidental about them. Their attitudes lack that character of explicitness and full consciousness which is a prerequisite of meeting in a really apposite way the demand embodied in the values. For what the values claim of us is not assent pure and simple, an assent which might as well be a fortuitous efflux of our natural dispositions; it is a fully conscious, rational, and explicit assent, given by the free "centre" of our personality. By such an answer alone does a personal being adequately honour the values and their call, which is addressed to each of us in sovereign majesty, irrespective of his individual dispositions.

A truly conscious person has so far advanced over his nature that he no longer agrees implicitly to all its suggestions. Should an impulse of malice or envy surge up in his mind, he, actuated by his free personal "centre," will seclude himself from that impulse, and disavow it. Instead of endorsing it as a free personality, he expressly renounces all solidarity with it. True, such an act of disavowal is not by itself sufficient to render the impulse in question non-existent, or to eradicate it; yet that impulse is invalidated, as it were, and, in a sense, "decapitated," and deprived of its malignant potency. On the other hand, when faced with a genuine value the "conscious" person will not content himself with a contingent response to it, due to its fortuitous consonance with his nature: he also will respond with his free personal centre; his response will bear the *sanction* of this free personal centre.

Obviously enough, it is only such sanctioned responses to value which attain to a full degree of freedom and spiritual reality. It is through that actualization of the free and conscious "centre" of his soul that a person comes of age morally, and acquires the ability to utter that "yes" in the face of God which He demands of us. Not otherwise can our life obtain that inner unity and that establishment in God which elevates it above the accidents of our nature. In this sense, the Christian can never be conscious enough.

With this aspect of true consciousness, a further one is closely associated: that of *continuity*—a subject which has already aroused our attention in Chapter 1. "Unconscious" man gives himself entirely over to the moment's experience. He allows the present impression (which, of course, is conditioned, in an extra-conscious sense, by many anterior experiences) to capture him. The truths he has previously got hold of, and the values he has sensed, are not preserved by him as an imperishable possession; they are swamped under the impact of the present impression; nor is the latter confronted with them. The life of a certain type of "unconscious" man never ceases to change with every change in his milieu. Or again, we have the conservative type: this kind of "unconscious" man remains attached to certain strong impressions of his past and is unreceptive towards new ones, yet he clings to those old impressions not by reason of their ascertained importance and validity, but because they have been the first to affect him, or because he has grown accustomed to them. True continuity however has nothing to do with a mere natural disposition towards conservatism (as predicated, sometimes, of a peasantry), and much less with being a slave to the force of habit.

A person who really has continuity persists in his affirmation of all truths and genuine values once they have become manifest to him. While open to every new truth and every new value, he confronts them (in a self-evident and organic way of procedure) with all those he is already familiar with. He knows that no contradictions exist in the world of being, nor between values; and he longs to see all things in their proper interconnection, that is, ultimately in the light of God. Thus alone can man establish that inward order in his life which makes it possible for him to distinguish between valid and invalid impressions. It is only by virtue of continuity that man can be "objective" in his judgments and his behaviour, for continuity preserves him from attributing to the present an illegitimate priority over the past, and thus makes his decision dependent on the objective content and the relevancy of an experience alone. Above all, the person with continuity is fixed in awareness of the ultimate truths, never sacrificing them to the self-contained dialectic of a transient situation which happens to arrest his attention. He views every event of life in the perspective of man's metaphysical situation, and against the background of eternity. He alone is able in every situation to hang on to the basic truth, and thus to see everything in the light of God. Without continuity, no transformation in Christ is possible. For that transformation requires that the light of Christ should pervade all our life, and that concerning everything we should ask whether it can stand the test before His face. *By confronting all things with Christ we also confront them with one another.* Continuity, too, vouches for the possibility of true penitence. By virtue of continuity, we understand that a human action loses nothing of its relevance merely because it belongs to the past; that the evil inherent in a sin is not decreased by the fact of its chronological remoteness.

Consciousness and continuity are also linked to wakefulness, or alertness—what we might call an attitude of being awake.. "Unconscious" man entrusts himself to the flow of events, without setting them at a distance; therefore he is incapable of surveying them. Though he may have single impressions of great intensity, no single fact will reveal itself to him in its full significance and purport, for each lacks connection with the other, and above all, with the primal cause of being and the ultimate meaning of the world. His life is wrapped in a cloud of obscurity. Perhaps such a person will receive, time and again, a strong religious impression, and in its consequence grasp, for a moment, the metaphysical situation of man; but he fails to "awaken" once for all, and no sooner is his mind distracted by some other impressions than the sphere of ultimate reality has again vanished from his sight. Yet, he who is awake maintains that sphere present, over and above the concerns of the business of the moment. He always takes a synoptic view of things. He does not erect into an absolute the small accidental section of reality which just happens to occupy his mind, but views it against the background of integral reality. This is what wakefulness means: to live *in conspectu Dei;* to interpret everything in the context of our eternal destiny, in its nexus with all our previous valid experiences, and most of all, in its function as a

294

token and a representation of God. "Wakefulness" in this sense and "true consciousness" are closely interrelated. *"Conscious" man, and he alone, avoids being submerged beneath things or living among them in the interstices of reality, as it were: he incorporates everything in the objectively valid order of ultimate reality.* Only the Christian can be truly conscious in the full sense of the term. For he alone has a true vision of reality proper, and a true conception of God and the supernatural realm, from which everything derives its ultimate meaning. All those who have not yet risen to the brightness of the *lumen Christi* are (in this higher and qualified use of the term) still unconscious; they are still asleep. The measure in which someone lives in the light of the Christian revelation, maintains it continually present, and keeps in continuous awareness of it at all moments, determines the degree of his real consciousness.

The wakefulness of the truly conscious person also determines a more real and more significant mode of living. He alone, as we have seen, has a genuine comprehension of values; he recognizes their essential demand, and meets it with an explicit response. That eminently "personal" (and, as it were, sanctioned) form of response not only guarantees a conduct more deeply conceived from the moral point of view; in a direct sense also, it represents a reaction more adequately aimed, more bright with meaning, than is possible on the part of such as lack "consciousness" proper.

The "conscious" person's contact with the objects is not deformed by an over-estimation of accidental features; and an integral, explicit comprehension of values is equally his privilege. In his sanctioned, express, and integrally shaped response to values, and in such a response only, *the whole person is present.* We might almost say that the greater the wakefulness which presides over a man's life the more he "exists" *as a person.*

We are now in a position to appreciate the vast difference between the false and the true kind of consciousness. Whereas the former precludes a real contact with the objects, and condemns its bearer always to watch himself without ever being touched by the *logos* of things that are, true consciousness postulates and establishes that genuine object-relationship. Here, man communes, he "conspires," as it were, with the proper and valid meaning of what is: here, the true dialogue between subject and object takes place. All befogging twilight, all blind yielding to accidental impulses, all forms of determination by things taken as forces of nature instead of as "intentional" objects have disappeared: the response to values becomes clear and explicit, yet all the more intense, and charged with experience.

Finally, true consciousness implies an intimate recognition of our defects (cf. Chapter 3). A person who is thus conscious, who has emancipated himself from his nature and no longer agrees automatically to its suggestions, who is awakened to a sense of his free personal "centre" and of the essential, express, and lasting response which God demands of him, has also cast off his illusions concerning himself. His own being, too, is illuminated by the light of God, and he allows that light to penetrate into all corners of his soul. He spreads out his whole life before the face of Christ, and suffers no hidden currents of life which have escaped a clear recognition by him and a confrontation with Christ, to be active in him. The spiritual vision, illumined by Christ, of his central personality clears up all recesses of his being, and sees through all illusions. Hence, he leads a unified life—in contrast to "unconscious" man in whom disparate currents of life can exist side by side, without his taking note of their essential inconsistency with one another.

Frequently we come across people who reveal entirely disparate aspects of character, of which now one and then another prevails, so that on different occasions such a man or woman may almost strike us as a different person. According to the varying elements of his environment, with their fluctuating appeal to this or that strain in his mental composition, a person of this kind may seem again and again to change his identity. Not so the person with genuine consciousness. He always remains himself; his life is integrated, because he has brought everything to "one denominator," with no hidden particle of his self escaping the formative effect of his basic direction towards Christ. In the highest sense of the term, he has become *simple*.

Dietrich Von Hildebrand

A classic example of true consciousness is St. Augustine in his *Confessions,* confronting all things with God and discussing them with fearless clarity before His face, and thus also attaining full consciousness of them himself.

It must be the purpose of a true Christian that his entire life be suffused by that light of truth, the *lumen Christi.* He must endeavour to become fully capable of personal sanction, to rise to a wakeful conduct of life, to acquire complete continuity. The more we are awake and in possession of continuity, the more we are able to light up even our present life with a ray from that wealth of splendour that shall brighten us in the life to come: "We see now through a glass in a dark manner; but then face to face" (1 Cor. 13:12).

By virtue of consciousness alone can we give the answer which God demands of us. For it is that unconditional and explicit assent on our part, sanctioned by our central personality, which He demands of us; and for the sake of that assent He has endowed man with freedom of will, entailing the enormous risk that man, misusing his freedom, may sin. Thus, in the fact of our consciousness our entire earthly task is, as it were, condensed. For that task consists ultimately in our express assenting to be apprehended and transformed by God. It possesses this "yes" which God, when He awarded us His highest gift of inconceivable sublimity, the incarnation of the Eternal Word, also required to hear from Mary the Blessed Virgin: "Behold the handmaid of the Lord; be it done to me according to thy word" (Luke 1:38). This is the primal word, which God has called upon mankind to utter. God expects each of us individually, and man as the highest and most lavishly endowed of His creatures, to say this word. It is the constitutive core of consciousness; and it cannot be spoken too clearly, too wakefully, too explicitly. It is, therefore, one of the basic tasks imposed on every Christian to rise to a state of true consciousness, thus infusing an integral meaning into his life. Based on that primal word, life attains great simplicity, and with that word alone can we "live in that great secret of the adoration of God which is Christ."

Thomas Merton
1915-1968

When Thomas Merton died suddenly in Bangkok in 1968, the American Catholic church lost one of her most challenging and stimulating personalities. For more than two decades, through his writing, he had generously served post World War II Catholicism in its search for meaning and relevancy in modern America. Though perhaps best known for The Seven Storey Mountain, his autobiography up to the age of 33, he was the author of more than 50 published books, dozens of articles and poems, and writings circulated only at the Trappist Monastery of Gethsemani, Kentucky and among fellow Cistercians.

Merton was born in France in 1915. His mother was American, his father a New Zealander. At age one he was brought to America, lost his mother when he was six, and returned to Europe when he was ten years old. He went to schools in France and England. In 1934, he returned to the United States and attended Columbia University. There he earned his baccalaureate and masters degrees in English. Merton was converted to Catholicism in 1938 and entered Gethsemani on December 10, 1941. The life of solitude and prayer for which he yearned was counterbalanced by an apostolate of the written word throughout his 27 years as a Trappist monk. He received permission from his superiors in 1965 to live a short distance from the monastery as a hermit. Rarely did he travel beyond Gethsemani.

Acceding to the request of various Trappist abbots in 1968, he journeyed to the Far East to attend a conference on monasticism in Bangkok and to visit several Trappist monasteries in the Orient. He died in Bangkok, apparently accidentally electrocuted by a faulty electric fan. The day was December 10, the anniversary date of his entry into Gethsemani.

It is difficult to evaluate a man of Merton's stature with a distance of scarcely more than ten years separating us from his life. Clearly he is a major religious personality of twentieth century America. Perhaps his lasting value will be due more to what he tried to do with his life than to his writings. Yet, in some way, we have access to his life only through his writings.

By entering Gethsemani and living the life of a Trappist monk, he raised the question of the meaning and value of the modern world, with its dominant philosophy of materialism. By writing, he supplied Americans, and particularly Catholic Americans, with rich spiritual nourishment. At times it was inspiring and consoling, at times it was critical, even harsh. He was convinced that God is the ground of the human condition, and that God can be encountered by entering into the depths of the mystery of one's existence. He also strongly believed that the Christian must be attuned to and concerned with his fellow man. Consequently, his writing goes in several directions. He speaks beautifully about the God-man relationship and the life of perfection. He explores the dynamics of the interior life. He looks directly at contemporary issues, such as racism and war.

The essay chosen for inclusion in this volume is The Power and Meaning of Love. *In it, Merton reflects on love as both a creative and religious force. He exposes two contemporary corruptions of love, viz., the liberalism approach to love which totally impoverishes the human, and the legalistic approach which smothers it. For Merton, love is the key to all of life's meaning, the discovery of God in the transformation of mankind into Jesus Christ. Love can lead man to fulfillment, but only if man comes to live in Christ and to see that his fellow man is Christ.*

THE POWER AND MEANING
OF LOVE

CHAPTER I

I. Love as a creative force—and its corruptions

Man has lost Dante's vision of that "love which moves the sun and the other stars," and in so doing he has lost the power to find meaning in his world. Not that he has not been able to understand the physical world better. The disappearance of the simple medieval cosmogony upon which Dante built his structure of hell, purgatory, and heaven, has enabled man to break out of the limitations imposed upon his science by that ancient conception. And now he is prepared to fly out into those depths of space which terrified Pascal—and which continue to terrify anyone who is still human. Yet, though man has acquired the power to do almost anything, he has at the same time lost the ability to orient his life toward a spiritual goal by the things that he does. He has lost all conviction that he knows where he is going and what he is doing, unless he can manage to plunge into some collective delusion which promises happiness (sometime in the future) to all those who have learned to use the implements he has now discovered.

Man's unhappiness seems to have grown in proportion to his power over the exterior world. And anyone who claims to have a glib explanation of this fact had better take care that he too is not the victim of a delusion. For after all, this should not necessarily be so. God made man the ruler of the earth, and all science worthy of the name participates in some way in the wisdom and providence of the Creator. But the trouble is that unless the works of man's wisdom, knowledge and power participate in the merciful love of God, they are without real value for the world and for man. They do nothing to make man happy and they do not manifest in the world the glory of God.

Man's greatest dignity, his most essential and peculiar power, the most intimate secret of his humanity is his capacity to love. This power in the depths of man's soul stamps him in the image and likeness of God. Unlike other creatures in the world around us, we have access to the inmost sanctuary of our own being. We can enter into ourselves as into temples of freedom and of light. We can open the eyes of our heart and stand face to face with God our Father. We can speak to Him and hear Him answer. He tells us not merely that we are called to be men and to rule our earth, but that we have an even more exalted vocation than this. We are His sons. We are called to be godlike beings, and, more than that, we are in some sense called to be "gods." "Is it not written in the law, I said you are gods— and they are gods to whom the words of God are spoken?" (John 10:34-35; Ps. 81:6).

This vocation to be sons of God means that we must learn to love as God Himself loves. For God is love, and it is by loving as He loves that we become perfect as our heavenly Father is perfect (Matt. 5:48). Hence, while being called to govern and cultivate the world that God has given us, we are called at the same time to love everything and everyone in it. Nor is this love a matter of mere sentimental complacency. It has a dynamic spiritual meaning, for by this love we are called to redeem and transform the world in that same power which raised up Christ from the dead (Eph. 1:17-23). That power is the infinite love of the Father for His Son.

Love then is not only our own salvation and the key to the meaning of our own existence, but it is also the key to the meaning of the entire creation of God. It is true, after all, that our whole life is a participation in that cosmic liturgy of "the love which moves the sun and the other stars."

But what is love and how do we come to love as sons of God? Surely love is everywhere; man cannot live without it. If everybody loves, or tries to love, why is it that we are not made happy and redeemed by all this constant effort? The answer is that all that seems to be love is not so in reality.

The reality of love is judged, then, by its power to help man get beyond himself, to renew himself in transcending his present limitations. Though the function of natural love is to perpetuate man in time, the function of spiritual love is much greater still—to give man possession of eternity. This it does not merely by "saving man's soul" as an individual, but by establishing in time the eternal kingdom of God. The function of love is to build this spiritual kingdom of unity and peace, and to make man not only the exploiter of creation but truly its spiritual head and king.

A love that merely enables man to "enjoy himself," to remain at peace in a life of inert comfort and to bring into being replicas of himself is not to be regarded as true love. It does not represent a renewal, a progress, a step forward in building the kingdom of God.

Ture love leads a man to fulfilment, not by drawing things to himself but by forcing him to transcend himself and to become something greater than himself. True spiritual love takes the isolated individual, exacts from him labor, sacrifice, and the gift of himself. It demands that he "lose his life" in order to find it again on a higher level—in Christ.

All true love is a death and a resurrection in Christ. It has one imperious demand: that all individual members of Christ give themselves completely to one another and to the Church, lose themselves in the will of Christ and in the good of other men, in order to die to their own will and their own interests and "rise again" as other Christs. A love that does not tend to this transformation does not fulfil the exacting requirements of true spiritual love, and consequently lacks the power to develop and perpetuate man in his spirituality.

All true love is therefore closely associated with three fundamentally human strivings: with *creative work*, with *sacrifice*, with *contemplation*. Where these three are present there is reliable evidence of spiritual life, at least in some inchoate form. There is reliable evidence of love. And the most important of the three is sacrifice.

Man's essential mystery is his vocation to be the son of God; but one of the deepest aspects of this mystery is precisely the fact that the fundamental temptation, the one to which Adam owes his fall, is the temptation to be "like unto God."

There is a singular necessity for man to be tried in that which is deepest and most essential about himself. And if we understand the meaning of this testing, we will understand the vital importance of love in the life of man. In the story of the fall of Adam, we see the tempter apparently suggesting that man attain to what he already possessed. *Eritis sicut dii.* But man was already "like unto God." For in the very act of creation God had said: "Let us make man to our image and likeness" (Gen. 1:26). Satan offered man what he already had, but he offered it with the appearance of something that he did not have. That is to say, he offered man the divine likeness as if it were *something more* than God had already given him, as if it were something that could be his apart from a gift of God, apart from the will of God, or even against the will of God.

Satan offered man the power to be like God *without loving Him.* And in this consisted what we call the "fall" and "original sin": that man elected to be "like unto a god" and indeed a god of his own, without loving God his Father and without seeking participation, by love, in the life and power and wisdom of God who is Love.

God wished man His son to be truly divine, to share in His own wisdom, power, providence, justice and kingship. And all this depended on one thing: the love by which alone man could participate in the divine life of his Father. Satan offered man a pseudo-divine life in a wisdom, knowledge, prudence, power, justice and kingship which had some reality in them, indeed, but which were only shadows and caricatures of the reality which is contained in and depends on God who is Love.

Love, then, is the bond between man and the deepest reality of his life. Without it man is isolated, alienated from himself, alienated from other men, separated from God, from truth, wisdom and strength. By love man enters into contact first with his own deepest self, then with his brother, who is his other self, and finally with the wisdom and power of God, the ultimate Reality. But love comes to man in the first place from God. Love is the gift which seals man's being with its fullness and its perfection. Love first makes man fully human, then gives him his divine stature, making him a son and a minister of God.

So necessary is love in the life of man that he cannot be altogether without it. But a love that does not seek reality only frustrates man in his inmost being, and this love that does not act as a bond between a man and reality is called sin. All sin is simply a perversion of that love which is the deepest necessity of man's being: a misdirection of love, a gravitation toward something that does not exist, a bond with unreality.

The difference between real and unreal love is not to be sought in the *intensity* of the love, or in its subjective *sincerity*, or in its *articulateness*. These three are very valuable qualities when they exist in a love that is real. But they are very dangerous when they are associated with a love that is fictitious. In neither case are they any sure indication of the nature of the love to which they belong, though it is true that one might expect man to feel an intense, sincere and articulate love only for a real object and not for an unreal one.

The trouble is that love is something quite other than the mere disposition of a subject confronted with an object. In fact, when love is a mere subject-object relationship, it is not real love at all. And therefore it matters little to inquire whether the object of one's love is real or not, since if our love is only our impulsion towards an "object" or a "thing," it is not yet fully love.

The reality of love is determined by the relationship itself which it establishes. Love is only possible between persons as persons. That is to say, if I love you, I must love you as a person and not as a thing. And in that case my relationship to you is not merely the relationship of a subject to an object, but it is analogous to my relationship to myself. It is, so to speak, a relationship of a subject to a subject. This strange-sounding expression is only another way of saying something very familiar: I must know how to love you *as myself*.

There might be a temptation, under the influence of modern philosophies, to misunderstand this subjective quality in love. It by no means signifies that one questions the real existence of the person loved, or that one doubts the reality of the relationship established with him by love. Such an illusion would indeed make Christian love impossible, or at best only a matter of fantasy. On the contrary, the subjectivity essential to love does not detract from objective reality but adds to it. Love brings us into a relationship with an objectively existing reality, but because it is love it is able to bridge the gap between subject and object and *commune in the subjectivity of the one loved.* Only love can effect this kind of union and give this kind of knowledge-by-identity with the beloved—and the concrete interiority and mystery of this knowledge of the beloved is not adequately described by the scholastic term "connaturality."

When we love another "as an object," we refuse, or fail, to pass over into the realm of his own spiritual reality, his personal identity. Our contact with him is inhibited by remoteness and by a kind of censorship which *excludes* his personality and uniqueness from our consideration. We are not interested in him as "himself" but only as another specimen of the human race.

To love another as an object is to love him as "a thing," as a commodity which can be used, exploited, enjoyed and then cast off. But to love another as a person we must begin by granting him his own autonomy and identity as a person. We have to love him for what he is in himself, and not for what he is to us. We have to love him for his own good, not for the good we get out of him. And this is impossible unless we are capable of a love which "transforms" us, so to speak, into the other person, making us able to see things as he sees them, love what he loves, experience the deeper realities of his own life as if they were our own. Without sacrifice, such a transformation is utterly impossible. But unless we are capable of this kind of transformation "into the other" while remaining ourselves, we are not yet capable of a fully human existence. Yet this capacity is the key to our divine sonship also. For it is above all in our relationship with God that love, considered as a subject-object relationship, is utterly out of the question.

It is true that we have to deal with God most of the time as if He were "an object," that is to say, confronting Him in concepts which present Him objectively to us. Yet, as everyone knows, we only really come to know God when we find Him "by love" hidden "within ourselves"—that is to say, "by connaturality." Yet, paradoxically, we cannot find God "within ourselves" by sacrifice. Only a sacrificial love which enables us to let go of ourselves completely and empty ourselves of our own will can enable us to find Christ in the place formerly occupied by our own selfhood. And in this sacrifice we cease, in a certain manner, to be the subject of an act of knowing and become the one we know by love.

When man acts according to the temptation of Satan to be "like unto God," he places himself as the *unique subject* in the midst of a world of objects. He alone is a "person," he alone feels, enjoys, thinks, wills, desires, commands. The manifestations of apparent thought, feeling, and desire on the part of others are of little or no concern to him, except insofar as they represent response to his own acts. He never "becomes" the other. On the contrary, the people around him are only objective manifestations of what goes on subjectively in himself. Hence his relationship with them is, if you like, a relationship with another self, yes, but only in the sense of an *added self*, a *supplementary* self, not in the sense of a different self. The selves of others are nothing except insofar as they are replicas of himself. And when this is carried to its logical extreme (as it is, for example, by the totalitarian dictator), then society at large is made over into the image of the leader. The individuals in such a society cease to have any purpose except that of reflecting and confirming the leader's megalomaniac idea of himself.

Man cannot live without love, and if the love is not genuine, then he must have some substitute—a corruption of real love. These corruptions are innumerable. Some of them are so obviously corrupt that they present no problem to the thinker. The only problem is that of avoiding them in actual behavior. Those which present a problem do so because they can seem, and claim to be, genuine love. These false forms of love base their claim on appeal to an ideal, and their falsity consists precisely in the fact that they tend to sacrifice persons to concepts. And since modern thought has deliberately renounced any effort to distinguish between what exists only in the mind and what exists outside the mind (dismissing he question as irrelevant), love has become more and more mental and abstract. It has become, in fact, a flight from reality and from that interpersonal relationship which constitutes its very essence.

This flight from the personal to the purely mental level occurs in various ways, two of which can be taken as most typical of our time and of our society. One is what we might call a romantic or liberal approach to love; the other, a legalist or authoritarian approach.

What we call the romantic approach is that love of the good which sacrifices the persons and the values that are present and actual, to other values which are always out of reach. Here a shiftless individualism dignifies itself as the quest for an elusive ideal, whether in politics or art or religion or merely in one's relations with other men. Such love is apparently obsessed with "perfection." It passes from one object to another, examining it superficially, playing with it, tempting it, being tempted by it, and then letting go of it because it is not "the right object." Such love is therefore always discarding the real and actual in order to go on to something else, because the real and actual are never quite right, never good enough to be worthy of love.

Such love is really only an escape from love, because it refuses the obligation of entering into a real relationship which would render love at the same time possible and obligatory. Because it hates the idea of obligation, it cannot fully face even the possibility of such a relationship. Its romanticism is a justification of flight. It claims that it will only begin to love when it has found a worthy object—whether it be a person who can "really be loved," or an ideal that can really be believed in, or an experience of God that is definitive and binding.

In its liberal aspect, this love justifies itself by claiming to dispense everyone else from responsibility to love. It issues a general permission for all to practice the same irresponsibility under the guise of freedom. Romantic liberalism thus declares an open season on "perfect objects," and proceeds comfortably to neglect *persons* and realities which are present and actual, and which, in all their imperfection, still offer the challenge and the opportunity of genuine love.

One who attempts this romantic and liberal fight may entirely avoid commitment to any object, cause, or person; or he may, on the other hand, associate himself with other men in dedication to some social or private purpose. But when he does this his idealism tends to become either an excuse for inertia or a source of repeated demands upon his associates. Such demands are implicit accusations of their unworthiness, and invitations to become more worthy under threat of being rejected. The unworthy object is treated with long-suffering attempts at forgiveness and understanding; but each heroic effort in this direction makes the object more and more of an object. And such, indeed, is the purpose of "love" in this context.

One discovers, on investigation, that this liberal idealism is in fact a way of defending oneself against real involvement in an interpersonal relationship and of keeping other persons subdued and humiliated in the status of objects.

Communal life in this event becomes a shelter which, by providing an all-embracing cover of idealistic vagueness, enables us to take refuge from the present "thou" in the comforting generalizations of the less meancing "they."

The authoritarian and legalist corruption of love is also a refusal to love on the ground that the object is not worthy. But here, instead of undertaking a vast exploration in quest of the worthy object (which can never be found), the presence of the unworthy object becomes the excuse for a tyrannical campaign for worthiness, a campaign to which there is practically no end.

The legalist is perfectly convinced that he is right. In fact, he alone is right. Serene in his own subjectivity, he claims to make everyone else conform to his idea of what is right, obey his idea of the law, and carry out his policies. But since what is loved is the law or the state or the party or the policy, persons are treated as objects that exist in order to have the law enforced upon them, or to serve the state, or to carry out the policy.

Here the objectification of personality and of all spiritual values is carried to the extreme. Here is no longer any romantic compromise with personality as an ideal. Here what matters is the law and the state—or the dialectical process in history. To these the person must always be sacrificed, and there is no question of ever considering him as a person at all except hypothetically. Men are treated as objects who might be capable of being considered as persons if the law should ever come to be perfectly enforced, or if the state should come to be all powerful, or if society should come to be perfectly socialized.

The romantic and liberal error seeks the perfect person, the perfect cause, the perfect idea, the perfect experience. The authoritarian error seeks the perfect society, the perfect enforcement of its own law, in exception of that perfect situation which will permit objects to turn into persons. Until then, love is a matter of enforcing the law, or stepping up production, and the kindest thing to all concerned is to exterminate everyone who stands in the way of the policy of the moment.

Two things are especially to be noticed when this authoritarian temper is pushed to its logical extreme and becomes totalitarian. Under a totalitarian regime, it is frankly considered more efficient to discount all individual and personal values and to reduce everyone to a condition of extreme objectivization. Whereas the romantic and liberal attitude is that personality should be reverenced at least in theory and as an ideal, here personality is regarded frankly as a danger, and its potentialities for free initiative are brutally discouraged. Not only is man treated as an object in himself, but he is reduced to servitude to material and economic processes, not for his own good but for the sake of "the state" or the "revolution."

This objectivization is justified, implicitly or explicitly, by doctrines which hold either that most races of men are in fact sub-human, or that man has not yet attained his human stature because of economic alienation. In either event, the question of right, of human dignity and other spiritual values of man is altogether denied any consideration.

For a Nazi to treat a Jew as a man, for a Communist to treat a counter-revolutionary as a human being would not only be a weakness but an unpardonable betrayal of the cause. This is all the more cogent when we realize that at any time, any faithful member of the party is liable without reason and without warning to be designated as a counter-revolutionary and thus forced outside the human pale, as something execrable beyond the power of word or thought. All this in order to pay homage to the collective myth. Such is the dignity and greatness of man when he has become "like unto a god."

In these two corruptions of love, error reaches out to affect everything this love attempts to accomplish. For a romantic, "sacrifice" is, in fact, a word which justifies the rejection of the other person as an "imperfect object" in order to pursue the search of an abstract ideal. "Contemplation" becomes a subjective day-dream concerned only with fantasies and abstractions and protected by the stern exclusion of all real claims upon our heart.

310

For an authoritarian, "sacrifice," "contemplation" and "work" all alike are expressed in ruthless enforcement of the law above all. Everyone, oneself as well as others, must be offered up on the altar of present policy. No other value counts, nothing else is worthy of a moment's concern.

We have seen how these two false forms of love operate in man's secular life. We shall consider, in detail, how they work in the life of the Christian.

II. Love as a religious force—and its corruptions

When Christ founded His Church and gave to men His "new commandment" that we should love one another as He has loved us, He made it clear that the Church could never be a mere aggregation of objects, or a collectivity made up of depersonalized individuals.

In all His dealings with men on earth, the Lord acted and spoke in such a way that He appealed always to the deepest and most inviolate recesses of each person. Even those who met Him in the most casual contacts, who cried out to Him from the roadside, asking His help, would be brought before Him and addressed directly, without hedging: "What dost *thou* ask? Canst *thou* believe?" Even a woman who secretly touched the hem of His garment when a thick crowd pressed against Him on all sides was called to speak to Him face to face. She had appealed to Him secretly, perhaps with an intention that had something in it half magical, regarding Him perhaps as a holy thing, a holy force, rather than as a person. But the power that He had felt go out from Him was the power of His love, the power that had been appealed to in His Person, and that demanded to be recognized in a dialogue of "Thou and I."

The Church is, in fact, the united Body of all those who have entered into this dialogue with Christ, those who have been called by their name, or better still, by a new name which no one knows but He who gave it and he who has received it. It is the Body not only of those who know Christ, who have heard of Him, or who have thought about Him: it is the Body of those who know Him in all His mystical dimensions (Eph. 3:18) and who, in union with one another and "all the saints," know the charity of Christ which surpasses all understanding. It is the Body of those who are "filled unto all the fullness of God" (Eph. 3:19). For the Church is the *pleroma* of Christ, the "fullness of Him who is filled all in all" (Eph. 2:23).

This mysterious expression of St. Paul points to the "sacrament" of the Church as the continuation of Christ's incarnation on earth, as a society which is more than any social organization, a spiritual and supernatural unity whose members form one mystical Person, Christ the Lord.

Christ dwells in each one of His members just as truly as He dwells in the whole Church, and that is why He is said to be "all in all." Each one is, in a certain sense, Christ, insofar as Christ lives in him. And yet the whole Church is one Christ.

Each member of the Church, however, "is Christ" only insofar as he is able to transcend his own individual limitations and rise above himself to attain to the level of the Christ-life which belongs to the entire Church. This mystery of plurality in unity is a mystery of love. For "in Christ" we who are distinct individuals, with distinct characters, backgrounds, races, countries, and even living in different ages of the world, are all brought together and raised above our limited selves in a unity of mystical love which makes us "One"—"One Body and one Spirit. . . . One Lord, one faith, one baptism, one God and Father of all who is above all and through all and in us all" (Eph. 4:4-6). "For by Christ we have access both in one Spirit to the Father" (*ibid.*, 2:18). "That they all may be one as Thou Father in Me and I in Thee, that they may be one in Us" (John 17:21).

Those who are one with Christ are also one with one another. But the New Testament shows us how intransigent the Apostles were in demanding, without compromise, that this unity be maintained on the highest and most personal level. It is of course possible for a human being who is not in the fullest sense a person to be a living and holy member of the Church—as in the case of children who have not yet attained the age of reason. But it is by no means the ideal of the Church that her members should remain at this mental and spiritual level all their lives. On the contrary, St. Paul teaches that spiritual immaturity is equivalent to living on the level of "carnal" men, which is a level of dissension and division.

Thomas Merton

The unity of the Mystical Body depends on its members attaining to maturity in Christ, that is to say, achieving the full stature of spiritual manhood, of personality and responsibility and of freedom, in Christ Jesus (see 1 Cor. 1 and 2, Eph. 3:13 ff., etc). Failure to attain to this maturity means inability to "receive the Spirit of Christ" or to "judge the things of the Spirit." Consequently it means failure to rise above the limitations of individuals or small groups, and inability to meet others on a transcendent plane where all are one in Christ while retaining their individual differences.

One who is not mature, not fully a person "in Christ," cannot understand the real nature of the mystery of Christ as a union of many in one, because he is not yet able to live on the level of Christ's love. Such love is foolishness to him, though he may imagine he understands it. It remains a closed book because he is still not fully a person and he is still not able to enter deeply into that dialogue of love in which he finds himself identified with his brother in the unanimity and love, the "we" which forms the Church, the Mystical Body of Christ.

Those of us today who seek to be Christians, and who have not yet risen to the level of full maturity in Christ, tend unfortunately to take one or other of the corrupt forms of love described above for the action of the Spirit of God and the love of Christ. It is this failure to attain to full maturity in love which keeps divisions alive in the world.

There is a "romantic" tendency in some Christians—a tendency which seeks Christ not in love of those flesh-and-blood brothers whith whom we live and work, but in some as yet unrealized ideal of "brotherhood." It is always a romantic evasion to turn from the love of people to the love of love itself: to love mankind more than individual men, to love "brotherhood" and "unity" more than one's brothers, neighbors, and associates.

This corruption of love can be romantic also in its love of God. It is no longer Christ Himself that is loved and sought, but perhaps an objectivized "experience" of Christ, a degree of prayer, a mystical state. What is loved then ceases to be Christ, but the subjective reactions which are aroused in me by the supposed presence of Christ in thought or love or prayer.

The romantic tendency leads to a substitution of aestheticism, or false mysticism, or quietism, for genuine faith and love, and what it seeks in the Church is not so much reality as a protection against responsibility. Failing to establish a true dialogue with our brother in Christ, this fallacy thwarts all efforts at real unity and cooperation among Christians.

It is not necessary to point out that the danger of substituting legalism for Christian love also exists. This danger is perhaps even more actual than that of the romantic error, and tends to become increasingly so in a totalitarian age. Fortunately, the terrible excesses of totalitarian authoritarianism are there to stimulate in us a healthy reaction and a return to the liberty of the sons of God.

The Church must have her structure of law and discipline, like any other visible society of men on earth. In heaven there will be no Law for the elect but God Himself, who is Charity. In heaven, obedience will be entirely swallowed up in love. On earth, unfortunately, not all are able to live without a Law, though as St. Paul says, there should in reality be no need of a Law for the saints. Not all are able to rise to that level of love which, in all things, is a fulfilment of the Law and therefore needs no Law (Gal. 5:13-23).

It is therefore not "legalism" to insist that we must all fulfil the duties of our state and of our proper vocations with all fidelity and in a spirit of humble obedience. There exists in the Church a juridical authority, a hierarchy of ministers through whom the Holy Spirit manifests the will of God in an easily recognizable way. To reject this authority and still claim to love God and the unity of His Church would be a manifest illusion. It has not infrequently happened in the past that some who have believed themselves inspired by charity have in fact rejected obedience and thus done much to dismember the unity of the Body of Christ.

Nothing could be more tragic than a pseudo-mystical enthusiasm which mistakes strong emotion for the voice of God, and on the basis of such emotion claims a "spiritual" authority to break away from communion with the rest of the faithful and to despise legitimate authority. This is not that strong sacrificial love of God which rises above individual interests and cements divergent groups in a transcendent unity. Such errors savor of the romanticism we have discussed above.

Legalism, on the other hand, is another weak form of love which in the end produces dissension, destroys communion, and for all its talk about unity, tends by its narrowness and rigidity to create divisions among men. For legalism, refusing to see truth in anybody else's viewpoint, and rejecting human values *a priori* in favor of the abstract letter of the law, is utterly incapable of "rising above" its own limitations and meeting another on a superior level. Hence the legalistic Christian (like the legalistic Jew who caused so much trouble to St. Paul), instead of broadening his view to comprehend the views of another, insists on bringing everyone else into the stifling confines of his own narrowness.

Legalism is not synonymous with conservatism or traditionalism. It can equally well be found in those social-minded Christians who, by their contact with Communism in the movement for social justice, have unwittingly contracted a spirit of totalitarian narrowness and intolerance. The temptation to legalism arises precisely when the apparent holiness of a *cause* and even its manifest rightness blinds us to the holiness of individuals and persons. We tend to forget that charity comes first and is the only Christian "cause" that has the right to precedence over every other.

Legalism in practice makes law and discipline more important than love itself. For the legalist, law is more worthy of love than the persons for whose benefit the law was instituted. Discipline is more important than the good of souls to whom discipline is given, not as an end in itself but as a means to their growth in Christ.

The authoritarian Christian does not love his brother so much as he loves the cause or the policy which he wants his brother to follow. For him, love of the brother consists, not in helping his brother to grow and mature in love as an individual person loved by Christ, but in making him "toe the line" and fulfil exterior obligations, without any regard for the interior need of his soul for love, understanding and communion. All too often, for the legalist, love of his brother means punishing his brother, in order to force him to become "what he ought to be." Then, when this is achieved, perhaps the brother can be loved. But until then he is not really "worthy of love."

This is in reality a fatal perversion of the Christian spirit. Such "love" is the enemy of the Cross of Christ because it flatly contradicts the teaching and the mercy of Christ. It treats man as if he were made for the sabbath. It loves concepts and despises persons. It is the kind of love that says *corban* (see Mark 7:9-13) and makes void the commandment of God "in order to keep the traditions of men" (*ibid.*).

The reason why this legalism is a danger is precisely because it can easily be a perversion of true obedience as well as a perversion of love. Authoritarianism has a way of becoming so obsessed with the *concept* of obedience that it ends by disobeying the will of God and of the Church in all that is most dear to the Heart of Christ. It is the obedience of the son who says, "Yes, I go" and afterwards does not go to carry out the command of his father. The obsession with law and obedience as *concepts* and *abstractions* ends by reducing the love of God, and of God's will, to a purely arbitrary fiction.

"Obedience" and "discipline" alone cannot guarantee the unity of the Body of Christ. A living organism cannot be held together by merely mechanical and exterior means. It must be unified by its own interior life-principle. The life of the Church is divine Love itself, the Holy Spirit. Obedience and discipline are necessary to prevent us from separating ourselves, unconsciously, from the guidance of the Invisible Spirit. But merely bringing people to submit to authority by external compulsion is not sufficient to unite them in a vital union of love with Christ in His Church. Obedience without love produces only dead works, external conformity, not interior communion.

Doubtless there are very few Christians who, in actual fact, carry this legalism to a dangerous or scandalous extreme. But there remains a taint of legalism in the spirituality of a great many modern Christians, especially among religious. It is so easy to satisfy oneself with external conformity to precepts instead of living the full and integral life of charity which religious rules are intended to promote.

Here the danger is not one of a malicious and definitive perversion of the Christian spirit, but rather of spiritual immaturity. But the danger of this immaturity must nevertheless not be despised, for, as we have said, it frustrates the spontaneous and fruitful growth of charity in individuals, in religious communities and in the Church herself.

A sincere and invincible ignorance may often be the cause of a great deal of this immaturity: the ignorance of those who lead their Christian lives according to superficial formulas that are poorly understood.

For a great many religious of the present day, "love" and "obedience" are so perfectly equated with one another that they become identical. Love is obedience and obedience is love. In practice, this means that love is cancelled out and all that remains is obedience—plus a "pure intention" which by juridical magic transforms it into "love."

The identification of obedience with love proceeds from a superficial understanding of such dicta as: "Love is a union of wills," "Love seeks to do the will of the beloved." These sayings are all very true. But they become untrue when in practice our love becomes the love of an abstract "will," of a juridical decree, rather than the love of a Person—and of the persons in whom He dwells by His Spirit!

A distinction will be useful here. To say that love (whether it be the love of men or the love of God) is a union of wills, does not mean that a mere external *conformity* of wills is love. The conformity of two wills brought into line with each other through the medium of an external regulation may perhaps clear the way for love, but it is not yet love. Love is not a mere mathematical equation or abstract syllogism. Even with the best and most sincere of intentions, exterior conformity with a regulation cannot be made, by itself, to constitute a union of wills in love. Why? Because unless "union of wills" means something concrete, a union of hearts, a union of spirits, *a communion between persons,* it is not a real enough union to constitute love.

A communion between persons implies interiority and depth. It involves the whole being of each person—the mind, the heart, the feelings, the deepest aspiration of the spirit itself. Such union manifestly excludes revolt, and deliberate mutual rejection. But it also presupposes individual differences—it safeguards the autonomy and character of each as an inviolate and solitary

317

person. It even respects the inevitable ambivalences found in the purest of friendships. And when we observe the real nature of such communion, we see that it can really never be brought about merely by discipline and submission to authority.

The realm of obedience and of regulation, however great its value, however crucial its importance, is something so entirely different that it does little to effect this personal communion one way or the other. It merely removes external obstacles to this communion. But the communion itself implies much more than mere submission or agreement to some practical imperative. Communion means mutual understanding, mutual acceptance, not only in exterior acts to be carried out, but in regard to the inviolate interiority and subjectivity of those who commune with one another. Love not only accepts what the beloved desires, but, above all, it pays the homage of its deepest interior assent to what he *is*. From this everything else follows, for, as we know, the Christian is *Christ*.

Hence, as the Gospel teaches us (Matt. 25:31-46), a Christian loves not simply by carrying out commands issued by Christ, in heaven, in regard to this "object" which happens to be a fellow Christian. The Christian loves his brother because the brother "is Christ." He seeks the mind of the Church because the Church "is Christ." He unites himself in the worship of the Church because it is the worship which Christ offers to His Father. His whole life is lived in the climate of warmth and energy and love and fruitfulness which pervades the whole Church and every member of the Church, because the Church is a Body filled with its own life—filled with the Spirit of Christ.

A good example of the true climate of Christian obedience, a climate most favorable to the growth of love, is found in the Rule of St. Benedict. Benedict of Nursia is not only a lawgiver. More important still is the fact that he is a loving Father. The Rule opens with a characteristically Christian invitation to a dialogue of love between persons, and it is this dialogue which, on every page, elevates Benedictine obedience to the level of charity.

Love is the motive for monastic obedience, not love as an abstract and lifeless "intention," but love flourishing in a warm and concrete contact of persons who know, who understand,

and who revere one another. Here obedience is not for the sake of the law but for the sake of Christ. It is not just "supernaturalized" in the sense of being mentally "offered up." It is totally transfigured by a faith which sees that Christ lives and acts in the *personal relationship,* the mutual respect and love, which form the bond between the spiritual father and his spiritual son. Each, in fact, reveres Christ in the other. Each realizes that what matters is not the exact carrying out of an abstract and formal decree that has no concern for individual cases, but that the important thing is this relationship, which is a union in the Holy Spirit. It is for the sake of this sabbath of monastic peace that the Rule is written. And the sabbath itself exists for the men who keep the Rule.

Christ came not to destroy the Law. But neither did He come merely to *enforce* it. He came to *fulfil* the Law. Everyone knows that this "fulfilment" by Christ means more than that He simply carried out the Law in a way that would not have been possible for everyone else. That, of course, is part of the meaning. Christ satisfied all the exigencies of the Law by "blotting out the handwriting of the decree (the Law) which was contrary to us. And He hath taken the same out of the way, fastening it to the Cross" (Col. 2:14). But more than that, He Himself, in His very Person, is the fulfilment of the Law. That is to say, Christ in us, Christ in His Church, dwelling in the world in the unity of charity that makes men one in Him: this is the fulfilment of the Law.

The community of the primitive Church after Pentecost, in which all the believers were of one heart and of one soul—this was Christ on earth, and the fulfilment of the Law. To attempt to satisfy the exigencies of the Law by a quantity of ritual acts and multiple observances, to abide by the countless regulations and decrees of the Torah, this was a futile and hopeless task, rendered all the more ridiculous by the fact that Christ had already "emptied" all these things of their content by dying on the Cross and rising from the dead. Indeed, to return to all these practices was to return to servitude under the "elements of this world," and St. Paul rightly became angry with his "senseless Galatians" who had been "bewitched so that they *should not obey the truth*" (Gal. 3:1).

Obsession with the works of the Law is, then, disobedience to the truth, and a practical contempt for the Cross of Christ (*ibid.*). Obviously the Christian has to be rich in good works, must bring forth fruit. But how does he bring forth fruit? By "remaining in Christ and in the love of Christ" (John 15:1-8). The community of the Church and the life of the Church is then Christ in the world, and the acts of that community are the acts of Christ.

The Christian who no longer has to worry about servitude to the works of the Law need have but one concern: to remain in the community of the faithful, to remain in that love and warmth and spiritual light which pervade the holy society of the Church, to unite himself in simplicity with the holy yet ordinary lives of his brethren, their faith, their worship and their love—this is all. For to live thus, united with the brethren by love, is to live in Christ who has fulfilled the Law. "They were persevering in the doctrine of the apostles and in the communication of the breaking of bread and in prayers . . . and all that were believers were together and had all things in common. Their possessions and goods they sold and divided them to all according as every one had need. And continuing daily with one accord in the temple and breaking bread from house to house, they took their meat with gladness and simplicity of heart, praising God and having favor with all the people" (Acts 2:42-47).

Christ commanded His disciples to love one another, and this commandment summed up all of His will and contained everything else necessary for salvation.

This was not, however, intended to be another commandment of the same kind as the Decalogue—something difficult to be done, a duty to be performed in order to satisfy the demands of God. This is an entirely different kind of commandment. It is like the commandment by which God says, "Let there be light," or says to man, "Stand up, live, be My son." It is not a demand for this or that work, it is a word of life, a creative word, making man into a new being, making his society into a new creation.

The command to love creates a new world in Christ. To obey that command is not merely to carry out a routine duty; it is to enter into life and to continue in life. To love is not merely righteousness, it is transformation from brightness to brightness as by the Spirit of the Lord.

Here, of course, love and obedience are inseparable, not in the sense that obedience is coextensive with love, but in the sense that he who loves fulfills all the commands of the law by loving. To obey is not necessarily to love, but to love is necessarily to obey.

Why does God desire this love from men? Because by it His mercy and His glory are manifested in the world, through the unity of the faithful in Christ. God desires the unity of the Church in order that "men may see what is the dispensation of the mystery which hath been hidden from eternity in God who created all things. That the manifold wisdom of God may be made known to the principalities and powers in the heavenly places through the Church" (Eph. 3:9-10).

Love is the key to the meaning of life. It is at the same time transformation in Christ and the discovery of Christ. As we grow in love and in unity with those who are loved by Christ (that is to say, all men), we become more and more capable of apprehending and obscurely grasping something of the tremendous reality of Christ in the world, Christ in ourselves, and Christ in our fellow man.

The transcendent work of Christian love is also at every moment a work of faith: not only faith in dogmas proposed to our obedient minds by holy Church, not only faith in abstract propositions, but faith in the present reality of Christ, faith in the living dialogue between our soul and Christ, faith in the Church of Christ as the one great and central reality which gives meaning to the cosmos.

But what does this faith imply? Here again the familiar phrase "seeing Christ in my brother" is subject to a sadly superficial interpretation. How many Christians there are, especially priests and religious, who do not hesitate to assert that this involves a sort of mental sleight-of-hand, by which we deftly do away with our neighbor in all his concreteness, his individuality, his personality with its gifts and limitations, and replace him by a vague and abstract presence of Christ.

Are we not able to see that by this pitiful subterfuge we end up by trying to love, not Christ in our brother, but Christ *instead* of our brother? It is this, in fact, which explains the painful coldness and incapacity for love that are sometimes found in groups of men or women most earnestly "striving for perfection." It also accounts for so many avoidable failures in the apostolate on the part of those who are so sincere, so zealous, and yet frighten people away from Christ by the frozen rigidity and artificiality of their lives.

Our charity is intended to give glory to God, not by enabling us to multiply meritorious acts on an imaginary "account" recorded for us in a heavenly bank, but by enabling us to see Christ and find Him where He is to be found, in our brother and in the Church.

The purpose of charity is not only to unite us to God in secret but also to enable God to show Himself to us openly. For this we have to resolutely put away our attachment to natural appearance and our habit of judging according to the outward face of things. I must learn that my fellow man, just as he is, whether he is my friend or my enemy, my brother or a stranger from the other side of the world, whether he be wise or foolish, no matter what may be his limitations, *"is Christ."* No qualification is needed about whether or not he may be in the state of grace. Jesus in the parable of the sheep and the goats did not stop to qualify, or say: "Whenever you did it to one of these My least brethren, *if he was in the state of grace,* you did it to Me." Any prisoner, any starving man, any sick or dying man, any sinner, any man whatever, is to be regarded as Christ—this is the formal command of the Savior Himself.

This doctrine is far too simple to satisfy many modern Christians, and undoubtedly many will remain very uneasy with it, tormented by the difficulty that perhaps, after all, this particular neighbor is a bad man and is foredoomed to hell, and therefore cannot be Christ. The solution of this difficulty is to unite oneself with the Spirit of Christ, to start thinking and loving as a Christian, and to stop being a hair-splitting pharisee.

Our faith is not supposed to be a kind of radio-electric eye which is meant to assess the state of our neighbor's conscience. It is the needle by which we draw the thread of charity through our neighbor's soul and our own soul and sew ourselves together in one Christ. Our faith is given us not to see *whether or not* our neighbor is Christ, but to recognize Christ in him and to help our love make both him and ourselves more fully Christ.

One of the themes that has constantly recurred throughout this article is that corrupt forms of love wait for the neighbor to "become a worthy object of love" before actually loving him. This is not the way of Christ. Since Christ Himself loved us when we were by no means worthy of love and still loves us with all our unworthiness, our job is to love others without stopping to inquire whether or not they are worthy. That is not our business and, in fact, it is nobody's business. What we are asked to do is to love; and this love itself will render both ourselves and neighbor worthy if anything can.

Indeed, that is one of the most significant things about the power of love. There is no way under the sun to make a man worthy of love except by loving him. As soon as he realizes himself loved—if he is not so weak that he can no longer bear to be loved—he will feel himself instantly becoming worthy of love. He will respond by drawing a mysterious spiritual value out of his own depths, a new identity called into being by the love that is addressed to him.

Needless to say, only genuine love can draw forth such a response, and if our love fails to do this, perhaps it is because it is corrupted with unconscious romanticism or legalism and, instead of loving the brother, is only manipulating and exploiting him in order to make him fit in with our own hidden selfishness.

If I allow the Holy Spirit to work in me, if I allow Christ to use my heart in order to love my brother with it, I will soon find that Christ loving in me and through me has brought to light Christ in my brother. And I will find that the love of Christ in my brother, loving me in return, has drawn forth the image and reality of Christ in my own soul.

This, then, is the mystery of Christ manifesting Himself in the love which no longer regards my brother as an object or as a thing, which no longer treats him merely as a friend or an associate, but sees in him the same Lord who is the life of my own soul. Here we have a communion in a subjectivity that transcends every object of knowledge, because it is not just the climate of our own inner being, the peculiar silence of our own narrow self, but is at once the climate of God and the climate of all men.

Once we know this, then we can breathe the sweet air of Christ, a divine air, which is the breath of Christ.

This "air" is God Himself—the Holy Spirit.

Pierre Teilhard de Chardin
1881-1955

Few modern Christian intellectuals have dared to voyage through human history as adventurously as did Pierre Teilhard de Chardin. Born and educated in France, he became a citizen of the universe. His travels took him to Egypt, China, America, Africa. As he moved from country to country and from continent to continent, his constant and single aim was to discover how to "reconcile, and provide mutual nourishment for, the love of God and the healthy love of the world, a striving towards detachment and a striving towards the enrichment of our human lives." (The Divine Milieu.) *Father Teilhard de Chardin (he entered the priesthood and the Society of Jesus) was a Christian to the very center of his being, a human with a passionate love for the world, a scientist internationally respected in geology, anthropology and palaeontology, a poet unusually qualified to voice the praise of both God and the world.*

Convinced that a reconciliation was possible between cosmic love of the world and heavenly love of God, he dedicated his entire life to bringing it about. It was this dedication that grounded his scientific research as well as his theological explorations. He wrote prolifically, though the greater portion of his theological writings were published posthumously. Because of the vow of obedience to which he submitted his entire life, he allowed the brilliance of his wonderful discoveries to remain almost unknown and unnoticed until after his death.

Teilhard succeeds in seeing the mystery of Christianity and the modern scientific insight of evolution as interpenetrating. For him, the one cannot be without the other. He understands evolution as a dynamic current within which matter moves from simple to more complex organisms. At every level of material being, a consciousness is present, and is in evidence according to the level of complexity of matter. The key to understanding evolution is the human who, through the capacity of reflective consciousness, is a critical point in the evolutionary process. The human is both the end point in the process, insofar as it brings matter, life and consciousness together in a unique manner, and the starting point, by clarifying the direction that evolution has taken toward spiritualization, socialization, unification in person. Mankind stands at that moment in history where the cosmic is about to magnify the Christic and the Christic is about to "amorize" the cosmic (i.e., permeate the universe with love)! The Omega Point is that event of convergence and radical identification toward which all science and all faith is madly rushing. Through love, the evoluationary energy, the process of billions of years, is coming to maturity. And mankind is invited to rejoice at the total penetration of matter by God, to orient all of its energy toward the fulfillment of evolution.

One can see how a Christian with less vision than a Teilhard de Chardin would be lost in the face of this invitation. It calls for tremendous maturity, freedom, risk. He himself sensed this. The Divine Milieu, from which our reading selection was made, was written to reassure those who might fear that the Christian religious ideal and the best aspirations of modern times cannot joyously embrace one another. Teilhard invites the reader to see God invading the universe of modern man, to realize that God's presence does not disturb the harmony of the human, but rather brings it to its true perfection.

By journeying with Teilhard de Chardin to the center of the universe, the reader will discover how easy it is, once human fears have been set aside, to breathe freely.

THE DIVINE MILIEU

PART THREE

Nemo sibi vivit, aut sibi moritus . . . Sive vivimus, sive morimur, Christi sumus.

No man lives or dies to himself. But whether through our life or through our death we belong to Christ.

T he first two parts of this Essay are simply an analysis and verification of the above words of St. Paul. We have considered, in turn, the sphere of passivity, diminishment and death in our lives. All around us, to right and left, in front and behind, above and below, we have considered, in turn, the sphere of activity, development and life, and the sphere of passivity, diminishment and death in our lives. All around us, to right and left, in front and behind, above and below, we have only had to go a little beyond the frontier of sensible appearances in order to see the divine welling up and showing through. But it is not only close to us, in front of us, that the divine Presence has revealed itself. It has sprung up so universally, and we find ourselves so surrounded and transfixed by it, that there is no room left to fall down and adore it, even within ourselves.

By means of all created things, without exception, the divine assails us, penetrates us and moulds us. We imagined it as distant and inaccessible, whereas in fact we live steeped in its burning layers. *In eo vivimus.* As Jacob said, awakening from his dream, the world, this palpable world, to which we brought the boredom and callousness reserved for profane places, is in truth a holy place, and we did not know it. *Venite, adoremus.*

Let us withdraw to the higher and more spiritual ether which bathes us in living light. And let us take joy in making an inventory of its attributes and recognising their nature, before examining in a general way the means by which we can open ourselves ever more to its penetration.

1. THE ATTRIBUTES OF THE DIVINE MILIEU

The essential marvel of the divine milieu is the ease with which it assembles and harmonises within itself qualities which appear to us to be contradictory.

As vast as the world and much more formidable than the most immense energies of the universe, it nevertheless possesses in a supreme degree the concentration and the specific qualities which are the charm and warmth of human persons.

Vast and innumerable as the dazzling surge of creatures that are sustained and sur-animated by its ocean, it nevertheless retains the concrete transcendence that allows it to bring back the elements of the world, without the least confusion, within its triumphant and personal unity.

Incomparably near and tangible—for it presses in upon us through all the forces of the universe—it nevertheless eludes our grasp so constantly that we can never seize it here below except by raising ourselves, uplifted on its waves, to the extreme limit of our efforts: present in, and drawing at the inaccessible depth of, each creature, it withdraws always further, bearing us along with it towards the common centre of all consummation.

Through it, the touch of matter is a purification, and chastity flowers as the sublimation of love.

In it, development culminates in renunciation; attachment to things separates us from everything disintegrating in them. Death becomes a resurrection.

Now, if we try to discover the source of so many astonishingly coupled perfections, we shall find they all spring from the same 'fontal' property which we can express thus: God reveals Himself everywhere, beneath our groping efforts, *as a universal milieu*, only because he is *the ultimate point* upon which all realities converge. Each element of the world, whatever it may be, only subsists, *hic et nunc*, in the manner of a cone whose generatrices meet in God who draws them together—(meeting at the term of their individual perfection and at the term of the general perfection of the world which contains them). It follows that all created things, every one of them, cannot be looked at, in their nature and action, without the same reality being found in their innermost being—like sunlight in the fragments of a broken mirror—one beneath its multiplicity, unattainable beneath its proximity, and spiritual beneath its materiality. No object can influence us by its essence without our being touched by the radiance of the focus of the universe. Our minds are incapable of grasping a reality, our hearts and hands of seizing the essentially desirable in it, without our being compelled *by the very structure of things* to go back to the first source of its perfections. This focus, this source, are thus everywhere. It is *precisely because* he is so infinitely profound and punctiform that God is infinitely near, and dispersed everywhere. It is *precisely because* He is the centre that He fills the whole sphere. The omnipresence of the divine is simply the effect of its extreme spirituality and is the exact contrary of the fallacious ubiquity which matter seems to derive from its extreme dissociation and dispersal. In the light of this discovery, we can resume our march through the inexhaustible wonders which the divine milieu has in store for us.

However vast the divine milieu may be, it is in reality a *centre*. It therefore has the properties of a centre, and above all the absolute and final power to unite and consequently to complete) all beings within its breast. In the divine milieu all the elements of the universe *touch each other* by that which is most inward and ultimate in them. There they concentrate, little by little, all that is purest and most attractive in them without loss and without danger of subsequent corruption. There they shed, in their meeting, the mutual exteriority and the incoherences which form the basic pain of human relationships. Let those seek refuge there who are saddened by the separations, the parsimonies and the prodigalities of the world. In the external spheres of the world, man is always torn by the separations which set distance between bodies, which set the impossibility of mutual understanding between souls, which set death between lives. Moreover at every minute he must lament that he cannot pursue and embrace everything within the compass of a few years. Finally, and not without reason, he is incessantly distressed by the crazy indifference or the heart-breaking muteness of a natural milieu in which the greater part of individual endeavour seems wasted or lost, where the blow and the cry seem stifled on the spot, without awakening any echo.

All that is only surface desolation.

But let us leave the surface, and, without leaving the world, plunge into God. There, and from there, in Him and through Him, we shall hold all things and have command of all things. There we shall one day rediscover the essence and brilliance of all the flowers and lights which we were forced to abandon so as to be faithful to life. The things we despaired of reaching and influencing are all there, all reunited by the most vulnerable, receptive and enriching point in their substance. In this place the least of our desires and efforts is harvested and tended and can at any moment cause the marrow of the universe to vibrate.

Let us establish ourselves in the divine milieu. There we shall find ourselves where the soul is most deep and where matter is most dense. There we shall discover, with the confluence of all beauties, the ultra-vital, the ultra-sensitive, the ultra-active point of the universe. And, at the same time, we shall feel the *plenitude* of our powers of action and adoration effortlessly ordered within our deepest selves.

But the fact that all the external springs of the world should be co-ordinated and harmonised at that privileged point is not the only marvel. By a complementary marvel, the man who abandons himself to the divine milieu feels his inward powers clearly directed and vastly expanded by it with a sureness which enables him to avoid, like child's play, the reefs on which mystical ardour has so often foundered.

In the first place, the sojourner in the divine milieu is not a pantheist. At first sight, perhaps, the depths of the divine which St. Paul reveals to us may seem to resemble the fascinating domains unfolded before our eyes by monistic philosophies or religions. In fact they are very different, far more reassuring to our minds, far more comforting to our hearts. Pantheism seduces us by its vistas of perfect universal union. But ultimately, if it were true, it would give us only fusion and unconsciousness; for, at the end of the evolution it claims to reveal, the elements of the world vanish in the God they create or by which they are absorbed. Our God, on the contrary, pushes to its furthest possible limit the differentiation among the creatures He concentrates within Himself. At the peak of their adherence to Him, the elect also discover in Him the consummation of their individual fulfilment. Christianity alone therefore saves, with the rights of thought, the essential aspiration of all mysticism: *to be united* (that is, to become the other) *while remaining oneself*. More attractive than any world-Gods, whose eternal seduction it embraces, transcends, and purifies—*in omnibus omnia Deus (En pasi panta Theor)*—our divine milieu is at the antipodes of false pantheism. The Christian can plunge himself into it wholeheartedly without the risk of finding himself one day a monist.

Nor is there any reason to fear that in abandoning himself to those deep waters, he will lose his foothold in revelation and in life, and become either unrealistic in the object of his cult or else chimerical in the substance of his work. The Christian lost within the divine layers will not find his mind subject to the forbidden distortions that go to make the 'modernist' or the 'illuminati.'

To the Christian's sensitised vision, it is true, the Creator and, more specifically, the Redeemer (as we shall see) have steeped themselves in all things and penetrated all things to such a degree that, as Blessed Angela of Foligno said, 'the world is full of God.' But this aggrandisement is only valuable in his eyes in so far as the light, in which everything seems to him bathed, radiates from *an historical centre* and is transmitted along *a traditional and solidly defined axis*. The immense enchantment of the divine milieu owes all its value in the long run to the human-divine contact which was revealed at the Epiphany of Jesus. If you suppress the historical reality of Christ, the divine omnipresence which intoxicates us becomes, like all the other dreams of metaphysics, uncertain, vague, conventional—lacking the decisive experimental verification by which to impose itself on our minds, and without the moral directives to assimilate our lives into it. Thenceforward, however dazzling the expansions which we shall try in a moment to discern in the resurrected Christ, their beauty and their stuff of reality will always remain inseparable from the tangible and verifiable truth of the Gospel event. The mystical Christ, the universal Christ of St. Paul, has neither meaning nor value in our eyes except as an expansion of the Christ who was born of Mary and who died on the Cross.

The former essentially draws His fundamental quality of unde-niability and concreteness from the latter. However far we may be drawn into the divine spaces opened up to us by Christian mysticism, we never depart from the Jesus of the Gospels. On the contrary, we feel a growing need to enfold ourselves ever more firmly within His human truth. We are not, therefore, modernist in the condemned sense of the word. Nor shall we end up among the visionaries and the 'illuminati.'

The real error of the visionaries is to *confuse* the different *planes* of the world, and consequently to mix up their activities. In the view of the visionary, the divine presence illuminates not only the heart of things, but tends to invade their surface and hence to do away with their exacting but salutary reality. The gradual maturing of immediate causes, the complex network of material determinisms, the infinite susceptibilities of the universal order, no longer count. Through this veil without seam and these delicate threads, divine action is imagined as appear-ing naked and without order. And then the falsely miraculous comes to disconcert and obstruct the human effort.

As we have already abundantly shown, the effect produced upon human activity, by the true transformation of the world in Jesus Christ, is utterly different. At the heart of the divine milieu, as the Church reveals it, things are transfigured, but from within. They bathe inwardly in light, but, in this incan-descence, they retain—this is not strong enough, they exalt—all that is most specific in their attributes. *We can only lose our-selves in God by prolonging the most individual characteristics of beings far beyond themselves:* that is the fundamental rule by which we can always distinguish the true mystic from his counterfeits. The heart of God is boundless, *multae mansiones*. And yet in all that immensity there is only one possible place for each one of us at any given moment, the one we are led to by unflagging fidelity to the natural and supernatural duties of life. At this point, which we can reach at the right moment only if we exert the maximum effort on every plane, God will reveal Himself in all His plenitude. Except at this point, the divine milieu, although it may still enfold us, exists only incompletely, or not at all, *for us*. Thus its great waters do not call us to defeat but to perpetual struggle to breast their floods. Their energy awaits, and provokes, our energy. Just as on certain days the sea lights up only as the ship's prow or the swimmer cleaves its surface, so the world is lit up with God only when reacting to our impetus. When God desires ultimately to subject and unite the Christian to Him, either by ecstasy or by death, it is as though He bears him away stiffened by love and by obedience in the full extent of his effort.

It might thenceforward look as though the believer in the divine milieu were falling back into the errors of a pagan naturalism in reaction against the excesses of quietism and illuminism. With his faith in the heavenly value of human endeavour, by his expectation of a new awakening of the faculties of adoration dormant in the world, by his respect for the spiritual powers still latent in matter, the Christian may often bear a striking resemblance to the worshippers of the earth.

But here again, as in the case of pantheism, the resemblance is only external and *such as is so often found in opposite things*.

The pagan loves the earth in order to enjoy it and confine himself within it; the Christian in order to make it purer and draw from it the strength to escape from it.

The pagan seeks to espouse sensible things so as to extract delight from them; *he adheres to the world*. The Christian multiplies his contacts with the world only so as to harness, or submit to, the energies which he will take back, or which will take him, to Heaven. *He pre-adheres to God*.

The pagan holds that man divinises himself by closing in upon himself; the final act of human evolution is when the individual, or the totality, constitutes itself within itself. The Christian sees his divinisation only in the assimilation by an 'Other' of his achievement: the culmination of life, in his eyes, is death in union.

To the pagan, universal reality exists only in so far as it is projected on to the plane of the tangible: it is immediate and multiple. The Christian makes use of exactly the same elements: but he prolongs them along their common axis, which links them to God: and, by the same token, the universe is thus unified for him, although it is only attainable at the final centre of its consummation.

To sum up, one may say that, in relation to all the main historical forms assumed by the human religious spirit, Christian mysticism extracts *all* that is sweetest and strongest circulating in all the human mysticisms, though without absorbing their evil or suspect elements. It shows an astonishing equilibrium between the active and the passive, between possession of the world and its renunciation, between a taste for things and an indifference to them. But there is really no reason why we should be astonished by this shifting harmony, for is it not the natural and spontaneous reaction of the soul to the stimulus of a milieu which is exactly, by nature and grace, the one in which that soul is made to live and develop itself? Just as, at the centre of the divine milieu, all the sounds of created being are fused, without being confused, in a single note which dominates and sustains them (that seraphic note, no doubt, which bewitched St. Francis), so all the powers of the soul begin to resound in response to its call; and these multiple tones, in their turn, compose themselves into a single, ineffably simple vibration in which all the spiritual nuances—of love and of the intellect, of zeal and of tranquillity, of fullness and of ecstasy, of passion and of indifference, of assimilation and of surrender, of rest and of motion—are born and pass and shine forth, according to the times and the circumstances, like the countless possibilities of an inward attitude, inexpressible and unique.

And if any words could translate that permanent and lucid intoxication better than others, perhaps they would be 'passionate indifference.'

To have access to the divine milieu is to have found the One Thing needful: *Him who burns* by setting fire to everything that we would love badly or not enough; *Him who calms* by eclipsing with His blaze everything that we would love too much; *Him who consoles* by gathering up everything that has been snatched from our love or has never been given to it. To reach those priceless layers is to experience, with equal truth, that one has need of everything, and that one has need of nothing. Everything is needed because the world will never be large enough to provide our taste for action with the means of grasping God, or our thirst for undergoing with the possibility of being invaded by Him. And yet nothing is needed; for as the only reality which can satisfy us lies beyond the transparencies in which it is mirrored, everything that fades away and dies between us and it will only serve to give reality back to us with greater purity. Everything means both everything and nothing to me; everything is God to me and everything is dust to me: that is what man can say with equal truth, in accord with how the divine ray falls.

'Which is the greater blessing,' someone once asked, 'to have the sublime unity of God to centre and save the universe? or to have the concrete immensity of the universe by which to undergo and touch God?'

We shall not seek to escape this joyful uncertainty. But now that we are familiar with the attributes of the divine milieu, we shall turn our attention to the thing itself which appeared to us in the depth of each being, like a radiant countenance, like a fascinating abyss. We can now say 'Lord, who art Thou?'

2. THE NATURE OF THE DIVINE MILIEU.
THE UNIVERSAL CHRIST AND THE GREAT COMMUNION

We can say as a first approximation that the milieu whose rich and mobile homogeneity has revealed itself all around us as a condition and a consequence of the most Christian attitudes (such as right intention and resignation) is formed by the divine omnipresence. The immensity of God is the essential attribute which allows us to seize Him everywhere, within us and around us.

This answer begins to satisfy our minds in that it circum-scribes the problem. However, it does not give to the power *in qua vivimus et sumus* the sharp lines with which we should wish to trace the features of the one thing needful. Under what form, proper to our creation and adapted to our universe, does the divine immensity manifest itself to, and become relevant to, mankind? We feel it charged with that sanctifying grace which the Catholic faith causes to circulate everywhere as the true sap of the world; which, in its attributes, is very like that charity (*Manete in dilectione mea*) which will one day, the Scriptures tell us, be the only stable principle of natures and powers; which, too, is fundamentally similar to the wonderful and sub-stantial divine will, whose marrow is everywhere present and constitutes the true food of our lives, *omne delectamentum in se habentem*. What is, when all is said and done, the concrete link which binds all these universal entities together and confers on them a final power of gaining hold of us?

The essence of Christianity consists in asking oneself that question, and in answering: 'The Word Incarnate, Our Lord Jesus Christ.'

Let us examine step by step how we can justify to ourselves this prodigious identification of the Son of Man and the divine milieu.

A first step, unquestionably, is to see the divine omnipresence in which we find ourselves plunged as *an omnipresence of action*. God enfolds us and penetrates us by creating and preserving us.

Now let us go a little further. Under what form, and with what end in view, has the Creator given us, and still preserves in us, the gift of participated being? Under the form of an essential aspiration towards Him—and with a view to the unhoped-for cleaving which is to make us one and the same complex thing with Him. The action by which God maintains us in the field of His presence is *a unitive transformation*.

Let us go further still. What is the supreme and complex reality for which the divine operation moulds us? It is revealed to us by St. Paul and St. John. It is the quantitative repletion and the qualitative consummation of all things: it is the mysterious Pleroma, in which the substantial *One* and the created *many* fuse without confusion in a *whole* which, without adding anything essential to God, will nevertheless be a sort of triumph and generalisation of being.

At last we are nearing our goal. What is the active centre, the living link, the organising soul of the Pleroma? St. Paul, again, proclaims it with all his resounding voice: it is He in whom everything is reunited, and in whom all things are consummated—through whom the whole created edifice receives its consistency—Christ dead and risen *qui replet omnia, in quo omnia constant*.

And now let us link the first and last terms of this long series of identities. We shall then see with a wave of joy that *the divine omnipresence* translates itself within our universe by the network of the organising forces of the total Christ. God exerts pressure, in us and upon us—through the intermediary of all the powers of heaven, earth and hell—only in the act of forming and consummating Christ who saves and suranimates the world. And since, in the course of this operation, Christ Himself does not act as a dead or passive point of convergence, but as a centre of radiation for the energies which lead the universe back to God through His humanity, the layers of divine action finally come to us impregnated with His organic energies.

The divine milieu henceforward assumes for us the savour and the specific features which we desire. In it we recognise an omnipresence which acts upon us by assimilating us in it, *in unitate corporis Christi*. As a consequence of the Incarnation, the divine immensity has transformed itself for us into *the omnipresence of christification*. All the good that I can do *opus et operatio* is physically gathered in, by something of itself, into the reality of the consummated Christ. Everything I endure, with faith and love, by way of diminishment or death, makes me a little more closely an integral part of His mystical body. Quite specifically it is *Christ whom we make or whom we undergo in all things*. Not only *diligentibus omnia convertuntur in bonum* but, more clearly still, *convertuntur in Deum* and, quite explicitly, *convertuntur in Christum*.

In spite of the strength of St. Paul's expressions (formulated, it should be remembered, for the *ordinary run* of the first Christians) some readers may feel that we have been led to strain, in too realist a direction, the meaning of 'Mystical Body'—or at least that we have allowed ourselves to seek esoteric perspectives in it. But if we look a little more closely, we shall see that we have simply taken another path in order to rejoin the great highway opened up in the Church by the onrush of the cult of the Holy Eucharist.

When the priest says the words *Hoc est Corpus meum*, his words fall directly on to the bread and directly transform it into the individual reality of Christ. But the great sacramental operation does not cease at that local and momentary event. Even children are taught that, throughout the life of each man and the life of the Church and the history of the world, there is only one Mass and one Communion. Christ died once in agony.

Peter and Paul receive communion on such and such a day at a particular hour. But these different acts are only the diversely central points in which the continuity of a unique act is split up and fixed, in space and time, for our experience. In fact, from the beginning of the Messianic preparation, up till the Parousia, passing through the historic manifestation of Jesus and the phases of growth of His Church, a single event has been developing in the world: the Incarnation, realised, in each individual, through the Eucharist.

All the communions of a life-time are one communion.

All the communions of all men now living are one communion.

All the communions of all men, present, past and future, are one communion.

Have we ever sufficiently considered the physical immensity of man, and his extraordinary relations with the universe, in order to realise in our minds the formidable implications of this elementary truth?

Let us conjure up in our minds, as best we can, the vast multitudes of men in every epoch and in every land. According to the catechism we believe that this fearful anonymous throng is, by right, subject to the physical and overmastering contact of Him whose appanage it is to be able *omnia sibi subicere* (by right, and to a certain extent in fact; for who can tell where the diffusion of Christ, with the influence of grace, stops, as it spreads outward from the faithful at the heart of the human family?). Yes, the human layer of the earth is wholly and continuously under the organising influx of the Incarnate Christ. This we all believe, as one of the most certain points of our faith.

Now how does the human world itself appear within the structure of the universe? We have already spoken of this (pp. 27 ff), and the more one thinks of it the more one is struck by the obviousness and importance of the following conclusions: it appears as a zone of continuous spiritual transformation, where all inferior realities and forces without exception are sublimated into sensations, feelings, ideas and the powers of knowledge and love. Around the earth, the centre of our field of vision, the souls of men form, in some manner, the incandescent surface of matter plunged in God. From the dynamic and biological point of view it is quite as impossible to draw a line below it, as to draw a line between a plant and the environment that sustains it. If, then, the Eucharist is a sovereign influence upon our human natures, then its energy necessarily extends, owing to the effects of continuity, into the less luminous regions that sustain us; *descendit ad inferos*, one might say. At every moment the Eucharistic Christ controls—from the point of view of the organisation of the Pleroma (which is the only true point of view from which the world can be understood)—the whole movement of the universe: the Christ *per quem omnia, Domine, semper creas, vivificas et praestas nobis.*

The control of which we are speaking is, at the minimum, a final refinement, a final purification, a final harnessing, of all the elements which can be used in the construction of the New Earth. But how can we avoid going further and believing that the sacramental action of Christ, *precisely because it sanctifies matter*, extends its influence beyond the pure supernatural, over all that makes up the internal and external ambiance of the faithful, that is to say that it sets its mark in everything which we call 'our Providence'?

If this is the case, then we find ourselves (by simply having followed the 'extensions' of the Eucharist) plunged once again precisely into our divine milieu. Christ—for whom and in whom we are formed, each with his own individuality and his own vocation—Christ reveals Himself in each reality around us, and shines like an ultimate determinant, like a centre, one might almost say like a universal element. As our humanity assimilates the material world, and as the Host assimilates our humanity, the eucharistic transformation goes beyond and completes the transubstantiation of the bread on the altar. Step by step it irresistibly invades the universe. It is the fire that sweeps over the heath; the stroke that vibrates through the bronze. In a secondary and generalised sense, but in a true sense, the sacramental Species are formed by the totality of the world, and the duration of the creation is the time needed for its consecration. *In Christo vivimus, movemur et sumus.*

Grant, O God, that when I draw near to the altar to communicate, I may henceforth discern the infinite perspectives.

339

hidden beneath the smallness and the nearness of the Host in which You are concealed. I have already accustomed myself to seeing, beneath the stillness of that piece of bread, a devouring power which, in the words of the greatest Doctors of Your Church, far from being consumed by me, consumes me. Give me the strength to rise above the remaining illusions which tend to make me think of Your touch as circumscribed and momentary.

I am beginning to understand: under the sacramental Species it is primarily through the 'accidents' of matter that You touch me, but, as a consequence, it is also through the whole universe in proportion as this ebbs and flows over me under Your primary influence. In a true sense the arms and the heart which You open to me are nothing less than all the united powers of the world which, penetrated and permeated to their depths by Your will, Your tastes and Your temperament, converge upon my being to form it, nourish it and bear it along towards the centre of Your fire. In the Host it is my life that You are offering me, O Jesus.

What can I do to gather up and answer that universal and enveloping embrace? Quomodo comprehendam ut comprehensus sum? To the total offer that is made me, I can only answer by a total acceptance. I shall therefore react to the eucharistic contact with the entire effort of my life—of my life of today and of my life of tomorrow, of my personal life and of my life as linked to all other lives. Periodically, the sacred Species may perhaps fade away in me. But each time they will leave me a little more deeply engulfed in the layers of Your omnipresence: living and dying, I shall never at any moment cease to move forward in You. Thus the precept implicit in Your Church, that we must communicate everywhere and always, is justified with extraordinary force and precision. The Eucharist must invade my life. My life must become, as a result of the sacrament, an unlimited and endless contact with You—that life which seemed, a few moments ago, like a Baptism with You in the waters of the world, now reveals itself to me as communion with You through the world. It is the sacrament of life. The sacrament of my life—of my life received, of my life lived, of my life surrendered . . .

Pierre Teilhard de Chardin

Because You ascended into heaven after having descended into hell, You have so filled the universe in every direction, Jesus, that henceforth it is blessedly impossible for us to escape You. Quo ibo a spiritu tuo, et quo a facie tua fugiam. *Now I know that for certain. Neither life, whose advance increases Your hold upon me; nor death, which throws me into Your hands; nor the good or evil spiritual powers which are Your living instruments; nor the energies of matter into which You have plunged; nor the irreversible stream of duration, whose rhythm and flow You control without appeal; nor the unfathomable abysses of space which are the measure of Your greatness,* neque mors, neque vita, neque angeli, neque principatus, neque potestates, neque virtutes, neque instantia, neque futura, neque fortitudo, neque altitudo, neque profundum, neque ulla creatura—*none of these things will be able to separate me from Your substantial love, because they are all only the veil, the 'species,' under which You take hold of me in order that I may take hold of You.*

Once again, Lord, I ask which is the most precious of these two beatitudes: that all things for me should be a contact with You? or that You should be so 'universal' that I can undergo You and grasp You in every creature?

Sometimes people think that they can increase Your attraction in my eyes by stressing almost exclusively the charm and goodness of Your human life in the past. But truly, O Lord, if I wanted to cherish only a man, then I would surely turn to those whom You have given me in the allurement of their present flowering. Are there not, with our mothers, brothers, friends and sisters, enough irresistibly lovable people around us? Why should we turn to Judaea two thousand years ago? No, what I cry out for, like every being, with my whole life and all my earthly passion, is something very different from an equal to cherish: it is a God to adore.

To adore . . . That means to lose oneself in the unfathomable, to plunge into the inexhaustible, to find peace in the incorruptible, to be absorbed in defined immensity, to offer oneself, and to give of one's deepest to that whose depth has no end. Whom, then, can we adore?

The more man becomes man, the more will he become prey to a need, a need that is always more explicit, more subtle and more magnificent, the need to adore.

Disperse, O Jesus, the clouds with Your lightning! Show Yourself to us as the Mighty, the Radiant, the Risen! Com to us once again as the Pantocrator who filled the solitude of the cupolas in the ancient basilicas! Nothing less than this Parousia is needed to counter-balance and dominate in our hearts the glory of the world that is coming into view. And so that we should triumph over the world with You, come to us clothed in the glory of the world.

3. THE GROWTH OF THE DIVINE MILIEU

The Kingdom of God is within us. When Christ appears in the clouds He will simply be manifesting a metamorphosis that has been slowly accomplished under His influence in the heart of the mass of mankind. In order to hasten His coming, let us therefore concentrate upon a better understanding of the process by which the Holy Presence is born and grows within us. In order to foster its progress more intelligently let us observe the birth and growth of the divine milieu, first in ourselves and then in the world that begins with us.

A. The coming of the divine milieu. The taste for being and the diaphany of God

A breeze passes in the night. When did it spring up? Whence does it come? Whither is it going? No man knows. No one can compel the spirit, the gaze or the light of God to descend upon him.

On some given day a man suddenly becomes conscious that he is alive to a particular perception of the divine spread everywhere about him. Question him. When did this state begin for him? He cannot tell. All he knows is that a new spirit has crossed his life.

'It began with a particular and unique resonance which swelled each harmony, with a diffused radiance which haloed each beauty . . . All the elements of psychological life were in turn affected; sensations, feelings, thoughts. Day by day they became more fragrant, more coloured, more intense by means of an indefinable thing—the same thing. Then the vague note, and fragrance, and light began to define themselves. And then, contrary to all expectation and all probability, I began to feel what was ineffably common to all things. The unity communicated itself to me by giving me the gift of grasping it. I had in fact acquired a new sense, *the sense of a new quality* or *of a new dimension*. Deeper still: a transformation had taken place for me *in the very perception of being*. Thenceforward being had become, in some way, tangible and savorous to me; and as it came to dominate all the forms which it assumed, being itself began to draw me and to intoxicate me.'

That is what any man might say, more or less explicitly, who has gone any distance in the development of his capacity for self-analysis. Outwardly he could well be a pagan. And should he happen to be a Christian, he would admit that this inward reversal seemed to him to have occurred within the profane and 'natural' parts of his soul.

But we must not allow ourselves to be deceived by appearances. We must not let ourselves be disconcerted by the patent errors into which many mystics have fallen in their attempts to place and even to name the universal Smile. As with all power (and the richer, the more so) the sense of the All comes to birth inchoate and troubled. It often happens that, like children opening their eyes for the first time, men do not accurately place the reality which they sense behind things. Their gropings often meet with nothing but a metaphysical phantom or a crude idol. But images and reflections have never proved anything against the reality of objects and of the light. The false trails of pantheism bear witness to our immense need for some revealing word to come from the mouth of Him who is. With that reservation, it remains true that, physiologically, the so-called 'natural' taste for being is, in each life, the first dawn of the divine illumination—the first tremor perceived of the world animated by the Incarnation. The sense (*which is not necessarily the feeling*) of the omnipresence of God prolongs, sur-creates and supernaturalises the identical physiological energy which, in a mutilated or misdirected form, produces the various styles of pantheism.

Once we realise that the *divine milieu discloses itself to us as a modification of the deep being of things*, it is at once possible to make two important observations touching the manner in which its perception is introduced and preserved within our human horizons.

In the first place, the manifestation of the divine no more modifies the apparent order of things than the eucharistic consecration modifies the sacred Species to our eyes. Since the psychological event consists, at first, solely in the appearance of an *inward tension* or *deep brilliance*, the relations between creatures remains exactly the same. They are merely accentuated in meaning. Like those translucent materials which a light within them can illuminate as a whole, the world appears to the Christian mystic bathed in an inward light which intensifies its relief, its structure and its depth. This light is not the superficial glimmer which can be realised in coarse enjoyment. Nor is it the violent flash which destroys objects and blinds our eyes. It is the calm and powerful radiance engendered by the synthesis of all the elements of the world in Jesus. The more fulfilled, according to their nature, are the beings in whom it comes to play, the closer and more sensible this radiance appears; and the more sensible it becomes, the more the objects which it bathes become distinct in contour and remote in substance. If we may slightly alter a hallowed expression, we could say that the great mystery of Christianity is not exactly the appearance, but the transparence, of God in the universe. Yes, Lord, not only the ray that strikes the surface, but the ray that penetrates, not only Your Epiphany, Jesus, but *Your diaphany*.

Nothing is more consistent or more fleeting—more fused with things or at the same time more separable from them—than a ray of light. If the divine milieu reveals itself to us as an incandescence of the inward layers of being, who is to guarantee us the persistence of this vision? No one other than the Ray of light itself. The diaphany . . . No power in the world can prevent us from savouring its joys because it happens at a level deeper than any power; and no power in the world—for the same reason—can compel it to appear.

That is the second point, the consideration of which should be used as the basis for all our further reflections on the progress of life in God.

Pierre Teilhard de Chardin

The perception of the divine omnipresence is essentially a seeing, a taste, that is to say a sort of intuition bearing upon certain superior qualities in things. It cannot, therefore, be attained directly by any process of reasoning, nor by any human artifice. It is a gift, like life itself, of which it is undoubtedly the supreme experimental perfection. And so we are brought back again to the centre of ourselves, to the edge of that mysterious source to which we descended (at the beginning of Part Two and watched it as it welled up. To experience the attraction of God, to be sensible of the beauty, the consistency and the final unity of being, is the highest and at the same time the most complete of our 'passivities of growth.' God tends, by the logic of His creative effort, to make Himself sought and perceived by us: *Posuit homines . . . si forte attrectent eum.* His prevenient grace is therefore always on the alert to excite our first look and our first prayer. But in the end the initiative, the awakening, always come from Him, and whatever the further developments of our mystical faculties, no progress is achieved in this domain except as the new response to a new gift. *Nemo venit ad me, nisi Pater traxerit eum.*

We are thus led to posit intense and continual prayer at the origin of our invasion by the divine milieu, the prayer which begs for the fundamental gift: *Domine, fac ut videam.* Lord, we know and feel that You are everywhere around us; but it seems that there is a veil before our eyes. *Illumina vultum tuum super nos*—let the light of Your countenance shine upon us in its universality. *Sit splendor Domini nostri super nos*—may Your deep brilliance light up the innermost parts of the massive obscurities in which we move. And, to that end, send us Your spirit, *Spiritus principalis*, whose flaming action alone can operate the birth and achievement of the great metamorphosis which sums up all inward perfection and towards which Your creation yearns: *Emitte Spiritum tuum, et creabunter, et RENOVABIS FACIEM TERRAE.*

Adrian L. van Kaam
1920-

Contemporary efforts in psychology to understand the dynamics of the human personality can make a significant contribution to the spiritual life of the members of the Christian community. While allowing for the exception, it is difficult to perceive how a spiritual life can be healthy and mature if the human personality in which it is grounded and of which it is a manifestation is not.

The theme of the religious personality has become an area of concern and interest for several Catholic authors in recent years. Father Adrian van Kaam, from whose book Religion and Personality the following selection has been taken, is one such author. His background in psychology has enabled him to explore the human structures which underlie religion as it relates to the person. Influences on his approach and style include contemporary philosophers such as Gabriel Marcel and Paul Ricoeur as well as psychologists such as Carl Rogers, Abraham Maslow and Rollo May. Father van Kaam is a native of Holland. For several years now he has been in the Department of Psychology at Duquesne University, Pittsburgh, Pennsylvania.

Part I of Religion and Personality treats the structure of the religious personality. Working from the model of the person as a historical being, van Kaam develops the thesis that man's presence to the world, to other people and to God is always in a state of flux. The human is challenged, as the time being, to grow in self-understanding. Mere adoption of attitudes and life-styles that already exist in a society is not sufficient, though it is all too common. Part 2, "Perfection of the Religious Personality" discusses the will, emotion, relationship to life, to others and to values. Van Kaam concludes that the true personality is totally unique and irreplaceable, and finds its highest mode of existence in commitment to the divine.

The question of the development of the religious personality is taken up in Part 3. The concept of will is explored from several angles. Religious will is "first, my personal openness—in the light of Revelation and under the impulse of grace—to reality as it reveals itself to me as a sanctified member of the Body of Christ. It is, second, my subsequent option and execution of behavior which incorporates all relevant meanings, sacred and profane, of my situation." Various phases of religious development are also discussed. The final part of the book considers deviations of the religious personality. It includes discussions of fixations in the different phases of religious development as well as neurotic tendencies that may appear in the daily effort to reach religious perfection.

A Christian in the present world who wants to respond seriously to the call to religious perfection assumes the responsibility to understand the dynamics of the human person as thoroughly as possible. Knowledge of the findings of the better schools of contemporary psychology is not only an aid but a necessity. Happily authors such as Adrian van Kaam have made available, in a terminology readily accessible to the layman, extremely rich insights on human structure. Properly used, they can contribute to the Christian's growth in holiness.

RELIGION AND PERSONALITY

CHAPTER 3

DEVELOPMENT OF THE RELIGIOUS PERSONALITY

F rom what we have said concerning religion and personality, it has become increasingly clear that the center of existence is the freedom of man. The only ground in which personality can grow is freedom. Unlike man, animals do not have a personality. No one speaks seriously of the personality of an elephant, a flea, or a canary, for where there is no freedom, there is no possibility to decide on a unique project of existence and to realize that project in life. In this last statement we may distinguish two movements of existence. One is to commit oneself wholeheartedly to a project. The other is the execution or the realization of that project. The two are not the same, and the first does not necessarily imply the successful fulfillment of the second. A person can be truly committed to an ideal and still be unable to make this ideal a reality in his daily life. For example, he may decide to develop a life of prayer, but it may require many years before he overcomes the obstacles which make it difficult for him to maintain the recollection necessary for a prayerful existence. In other words, he can really will something and decide for it in freedom while he is at the same time unable to do it in reality. This distinction, to which we shall return later, implies already that willing or not willing is not so simple an issue as we may have thought. Indeed, a misunderstanding of freedom, will, and decision may lead to serious complications in our religious life.

Imagine, for example, that the person who is not yet able to realize in daily life his sincere will to be a man of prayer has the mistaken notion that his failure proves that he really does not will this good, that he is a man of ill will and evil mind. In such a case, he may become discouraged even to the point of desperation. He may imagine that he is not growing in the love of God because he does not immediately succeed in the implementation of his good will in daily behavior, and as a result he may feel at odds with God. In reality, however, his sincere will and his repeated attempts to develop a life of prayer cause him to grow daily in divine love, perhaps even more so than if he had been successful, because his lack of observable results compels him to reaffirm over and over again his commitment to God, his love for God, his trust in God.

When we consider the many ways in which religious persons may misunderstand the nature and the task of the will in their religious growth, we realize that they usually err in one of two extremes which we may call *willfulness* and *will-lessness*. First we shall discuss these two one-sided exaggerations. Then we shall consider the true nature and function of the will in our existence. To distinguish the wholesome conception of our willing from the mistaken notions mentioned above, we shall call the former *existential will.*

Willfulness

Willfulness emerges in man when he loses the experience of his unity. He separates his will, as it were, from other elements of his personality, such as his past history, his inclinations and passions, his imagination, his anxiety, and the power of his habits and customs. For example, a person who has never seriously studied in his life may decide to become a scholar. He foolishly thinks that if he only wills it, he can do it. So he closes himself up in his room with a stack of books and forces himself at once to study eight hours a day. After one week of this sudden change of life he may experience a breakdown. Why? Because his will is not an isolated ruler which need not take into account the other aspects of his life. In this case, the will must defer to the fact that a person who has never studied before has developed a set of physical, psychological, and emotional attitudes, customs, and habits that cannot be broken at once. They can only be changed gradually.

The will has, as it were, to sit down and start a conversation with all the other aspects, both inside and outside, which are involved in this change. If the will does not do so, it runs headlong into trouble. Of course, this is metaphorical language.

In reality, my will is not an isolated thing in me, or a little person in me, which can sit down and have a conversation with other little persons. We may state the matter more explicitly: I-as-willing must take into account all the aspects which are involved in the change which I wish to make in my life. I-as-willing should not set myself apart from I-as-feeling, I-as-thinking, I-as-imagining, I-as-remembering, I-as-participant-in-my-social-milieu, I-as-passionate, I-as-weak-and-sinful, and I-as-looking-toward-the-future.

For example, if I enter a postulancy or novitiate, I enter not only as a person willing to be a religious, but as a feeling, remembering, and thinking person who is willing to become a religious. In other words, I cannot cast aside all my past feelings, emotions, memories, and inclinations when I pass the threshold of postulancy or novitiate. As a beginner in the religious life, I am not reduced to a mere willing person; I am a willing person who carries with him his past. Therefore, I cannot will something as if I had no life history, interest, or feeling which I may have to overcome. To deny this would be foolish, for I would deny the reality which I am. I would be outside of my reality, and therefore I would build on unreality.

Suppose I decide that, as a future religious, I shall not be emotionally overinvolved with my family. This is a worthwhile orientation of my new existence, a necessary beginning of a life that will gradually, in the current of many years, become a life for God alone. However, this decision cannot be implemented all at once. Why? Because the willing person which I am, in this case the person who is willing to detach himself from his family, is the same person who is still bound very closely to his family by tender feelings, living memories, and shared customs which made him part of the family until the moment of his entrnce into postulancy or novitiate. He is the whole me, the real me. I cannot deny any part of him. Whether I like it or not, I shall be overwhelmed at times by my memories. In spite of the fact that I desire to live for the Lord alone, I may at times weep quietly and alone because I miss my family so much. I cannot force these feelings from me. I should not even try to do so.

On the other hand, I should not deliberately foster them or overindulge in them. They should be an occasion for the renewal of my decision to belong to my Lord alone. I should realize that I am still very much attached to my family, but that I am also ready to grow gradually in detachment if the Lord permits me to do so. I may also discover in time what type of thought and imagination is apt to distract me from my new life and immerse me in my past existence at home. I may likewise become aware that certain occasions are conducive to my dreaming of the past. For example, I may discover that when I am not seriously occupied with my daily tasks or do not really participate in recreation, I succumb more easily to thought of the past which I idealize as a little paradise of pleasant company. After a long time, I may even realize for the first time in my life how people are inclined to enhance the attractive features of a past situation and to forget about the unpleasant aspects, such as quarrels, disorder, and lack of religious refinement.

It is clear from this example that the interaction of the willing me with all the aspects of my existence leads to a real growth in wisdom, makes me aware of all kinds of possibilities in myself which I never thought of. In this way I learn more from my own experience than I could ever learn from a textbook or a lecture. I become really at home with myself; I learn how to deal with myself. And because all these aspects are part of me and are precisely the same in no one else, nobody else can really teach me how to solve my problem. There are no easy and fast solutions for the problems of human growth, no solutions that can be handed to me like a medical prescription by a kind superior, and which I can execute at once. Even if such a prescription were possible, I should lose rather than gain from it, for it would rob me of the precious experience of growing insight in the midst of painful crosses.

In the case cited above, what would happen if I refused to recognize my ties to my family which were still overwhelmingly strong? These feelings would not indeed be absent. I would willfully repress the awareness of what I am; I would refuse to take into account all the aspects of my own reality. In short, I would willfully behave as if I did not have such feelings, and my life would be untrue and artificial. Moreover, I would use a tremendous amount of energy to fight off the awareness of my true self. I would have to cut off increasingly all thoughts, feelings, and perceptions which would bring back to my awareness what I refuse to recognize as being me.

When I repress my true feelings, I am not only artificial but I also become rigid, tense, and strained. My life becomes a lie; my make-believe detachment and perfection become a shining paper palace over a dormant volcano. All the feelings, passions, and memories which I refuse to recognize and to take into account are building up within the dormant volcano which I am. I become exhausted from crushing them, and at an unexpected moment later in life the volcano which I am erupts; the paper palace of my willful artificial perfection disappears in fire and smoke. This is true not only of my feelings toward home but also of all my other feelings, passions, and emotions. It is true of my sexual feelings, my envy, my jealousy, my aversion for silence and for certain types of work, my impulsive hostility toward certain persons, and my desire on a beautiful day to break away and have a wonderful time with my old friends.

Thus, I may be said to be willful when I refuse to take into account all the aspects of my life. When I do so, I try to mold my life magically. I behave like an absolute king who regards neither past nor future nor "irrational" feelings, drives, and passions. I attempt to manipulate myself into religious perfection. I deal with myself not as with a sensitive, vulnerable person but as with an inert piece of rock from which I try to fashion with heavy hammer blows the image of the perfect religious person. Such a highhanded approach to sanctity leaves me oblivious of the unconscious anxiety, bodily drives, resentments, hostile inclinations, and secret ambitions which poison my saintly motives, because the stone which I am sculpturing is not inert, without past and passion, without egocentric resistance to the chisel of the sculptor. My nature is a lively existence that moves and grows under the changes that are imposed on its surface. Imagine the amazement of a sculptor who would discover that within his statue of a madonna, a totally different image had developed, for instance, that of a devil.

How disconcerted he would be if suddenly the subtle, refined, and beautiful lines of his madonna would fall apart, and the grinning face of a demon would appear to tell him, "While you were thinking that the center of this stone was inert and lifeless so that you would have to occupy yourself only with changing the surface, I have had the chance to grow wildly inside." This represents what happens to me when I try to mold and manipulate my life as a *thing* with the chisel or hammer of will power.

Superficially speaking, I may seem successful because I alter rapidly and effectively the surface of my existence, the exterior layer that covers my personality, the thin shell of my soul. However, I do not interact with the deeper layers of my existence. My life becomes regular and religious at the surface. In reality, it is a life of pious self-deceit. I can maintain it only by compulsion, for my spontaneous inner life is cut off from this peripheral religious existence. The willful me is thus closed, cumbersome, tyrannical, and compulsive. I isolate myself increasingly from my own source of vitality and spontaneity. Soon my religious existence is marked by an obstinate, stubborn, frozen mentality. My life suggests withered, dead leaves in the fall. It is as if I nailed the green wood of my life into a straight and heavy coffin. My religious existence gives people the sensation of death, of tombstones and cemeteries. Thus, "religion" often comes to be considered incompatible with the vigorous joy of living.

Moreover, when I am strained, willful, and noisily busy about my holiness, I am unable to listen to either the egocentric rumblings within me or the silent voice of grace in the core of my being. I lose my sensitivity to this voice. Nor can I listen quietly to the subtle message of the situation in which I live. My willfulness chains me to only one thing, my idealized self-image of religious perfection which I must maintain against the disturbing demands inside and outside my being. Gradually the unique aspects of my life situation, of my inner moods, and of the subtle intimations of grace are unable to communicate themselves to me at all. I have cut off all bridges between my willful striving for a perfect religious surface and the living reality of nature, grace, and my life situation. Because I no longer listen to the voice of the changing situation, I fail to recognize its uniqueness and the new response which I should create to the ever new challenge of my life history. Therefore, I must invent a pious code of stilted, identical reactions which I have readily available for every situation that may arise. I become a will-power Christian. Instead of being bound to the appeal of God in the unique reality which comes to meet me, I become addicted to my blueprint of perfect external behavior, uninspired, rigid, and precise. I assume a compulsive instead of a dialectic attitude toward my existence. Compulsive comment replaces respectful dialogue. I become a religious engineer who manipulates all objectivated "things" in my life and situation as if they were parts of an electronic computer. I become a would-be holy man. I am so busy engineering my devotional existence that no awareness remains for the sacred dimension of reality, the veiled presence of the Lord as it reveals itself through the relaxed openness of faith.

As a will-power Christian I may even develop a split or schizoid religious existence in which an isolated "higher and holier" self represses, compels, and manipulates all my human behavior without regard for reality. If such a sickness spreads among Christians, it may even give rise to a disembodied, suspended style of Christianity which is foreign to contemporary life by its refusal to be present to it. The willful Christian who is out of tune with the contemporary situation makes it impossible for Christ to incarnate Himself through him in humanity.

Another complication makes the situation more dangerous. Out of touch with myself and with reality, I, the will-power Christian, construct an idealized image not only of myself but of other people and the world. After disregarding my own reality and forcing upon myself an image of religious perfection like a rigid, wooden mask that distorts my own human face, I now feel compelled to do the same to others. My inability to listen to what others really are and to what their situation really is leads me to distort reality and to force it into the same superficial religious mold as my own life. I am tempted to overpower and willfully transform reality in others. At the moment that I as the willful Christian yield to this temptation, Christ dies in my behavior; there is born instead a fanatical,

355

self-righteous style of faith which averts people from the good tidings that the believer claims to represent.

We may now summarize how willfulness may be discerned. When I am willful I become, first of all, closed to reality as it reveals itself to my fresh and naive perception. Instead, I develop a code of stilted perceptions of God, other people, and myself. As a result, I am unable to respond creatively to the real meaning of my situation. Instead of responding, I react blindly in a stereotyped manner. These stereotyped reactions are not real responses to the situation. They merely conform to my standardized code of perception which discloses reality not as it really is but as I should like it to be according to my willful blueprint of life and reality.

Will-lessness

The willful Christian has developed a self-image of perfect control. Basically he does not admit his weaknesses and limitations. He lives in the illusion that he can do anything if he only wills hard enough. The tragic result is that he fails to understand the deepest meaning of Christianity: the need for redemption as expressed in Scripture, dogma, and liturgy. Revelation does not stress the vain building of a perfect personality but the need for grace. It speaks little of the will power of man, but much of his weakness and sinfulness which permeates his life and even his religious motivation. The peace promised to the faithful man is rooted in the awareness of his redemption, not of his perfection. The faithful man knows that his Redeemer lives.

Therefore, I should be aware of the limitations of my will. I should not think that I can willfully build my religious existence without interaction with grace, nature, and life situations. I should not imagine that my will is all-powerful and can direct my life in splendid isolation. On the other hand, while admitting the influence of other aspects of my life, I should not exaggerate these either. I should not declare, for example, that I am so weak and limited that I can do virtually nothing, that my passions and the influence of my past are stronger than I am. Nor should I claim that grace should do all for me because I am too weak and evil to cooperate with grace in my significant way. In both cases I fall from my imaginary absolute will power to an equally imaginary lack of will. I fall from will-fulness into will-lessness.

This extreme, too, is harmful to health and holiness. I now experience myself as driven either by society or by my bodily chemistry and unconscious inclinations on which I drift like a raft in a stormy sea. Such an attitude undermines my vital acceptance of initiative, guilt, and responsibility. As a result of will-lessness, my life loses spirit and inspiration; my religious existence becomes a robot Christian unable to take a personal stand in regard to my own existence. Thus I lose my ability for individual decision and for a truly personal encounter with the Lord.

When I stress too much the weakness and limitation of my will, I may develop the tendency to search for events in my life history which I can blame for my sin, failure, and imperfection. I do this to unburden myself of anxiety and guilt feelings with which I must live when I accept personal responsibility. When I believe that I am merely a puppet moved by the strings of unknown influences from my past, I escape from the experience of personal responsibility, guilt, and anxiety. I may be pleased to be without personal responsibility, like a tiny toy carried by the stream of my surroundings, for I may be unwilling to face the conflict and dialogue which will emerge when I commit myself freely to my life situation.

From the first moment of my life, my freedom is never my full possession. I must maintain it continually, and I shall always remain in danger of losing it to my impulses or to the impersonal crowd. My will is never an absolute sovereign who passes disdainfully by his bowing subjects. My will is rather a constitutional monarch who requires a diplomatic dialogue with the representatives of his unruly population in order to maintain his reign. When I am will-less and unfree, my life is defined by public opinion, social acclaim, my own impulses and passions. I love the ability to respond freely to present and past influences which I have internalized. I do not respond; I react.

When I personally appraise and evaluate a situation and discover the features that are true of this situation and no other, I may be said to be responding. Then I create from my own richness and wisdom the behavior which is most effective for me in this unique situation. When I merely react, on the other hand, I do not think personally and deeply. I do not distance myself from the situation. I do not create an interval between the stimulus and the behavior elicited by this stimulus. I act at once in an impulsive, thoughtless manner. Such a reaction is usually determined by stereotyped customs of the past or by the ways of the impersonal crowd.

For example, someone makes a cutting remark which upsets me. If I really *respond* to this remark, I am not impulsive. I attempt to calm myself, to distance myself from the first impact of the insult. I weigh the aspects of the situation. What made the person so angry with me? Perhaps he was tired, disappointed, had a bad day. Maybe I irritated him. Perhaps I was unwillingly overbearing. Would it really be wise to answer him impulsively, or would it be better to let the matter pass? Maybe I should wait and speak to him later when he feels less irritated. As a result of all these questions, I gain insight into this special person and situation. Finally, out of the richness of my thought, feelings, and past experience, I may grow to a wise response. When I *react*, however, I do not distance myself from the situation. I do not calm my agitation. Before I think, "I let him have it." One cutting remark elicits another, so that soon we insult and humiliate each other deeply. Later I am embarrassed over my unreasonable reaction.

If I am will-less and at the mercy of my impulses, I should not lose heart. No matter how weak I am, there is always a possibility in me of taking some inner stand which will transmute my mere reaction into a response. Every time I do so, my responsibility or ability to respond will expand itself and grow in strength. To be sure, I may find myself in a situation which seems for the moment unchangeable. For example, I may be so overwhelmed by jealousy that it is almost impossible for me to hide this from the other. However, this does not mean that all my freedom is gone. I can always take some stand, at least in the depth of my existence. This stand may be insignificant; it may have no immediate impact on my behavior or feelings, but it will still make a difference in my life. Simply the fact that I do not want to be jealous, even though I feel devoured by envy, already implies my taking a stand in respect to this emotion. At this moment, I already begin a dialogue between my freedom and my mood. This free decision, without having immediate effect on my envy, is nevertheless growth in holiness, magnificent commitment to God, a fresh beginning in spiritual life.

Indeed, such growth in inner holiness is sometimes more genuine, honest, and radical because it is not easily poisoned by the heady wine of successful behavior which makes me look well in the eyes of those around me. This may well be the reason why the Lord allowed certain irritating characteristics to remain in His saints. For example, St. Ignatius of Loyola was petulant and unpleasant shortly before the end of his life when a brother disturbed his nap in the afternoon. We all know saintly persons who, in spite of their best efforts, cannot overcome certain humiliating imperfections. Perhaps this impossibility is God's greatest gift to them and protects their humility. In the meantime, they grow inwardly to saintliness because they must take a stand again and again, a stand in which they reaffirm their deep inner rejection of the bad behavior which they cannot outwardly control.

We may now summarize what will-lessness means in our lives. When I am will-less, I am subservient in an impersonal way to my own impulses or to the opinions of others. I refuse to be personally open to all the meanings of reality which will reveal themselves to me only if I distance myself from my situation. This subservience leads to behavior that is either impulsive or in blind conformity to the opinions of others. The will-less person does not take into account the various meanings of his situation.

Will, Sin, Neurosis, and Organic Illness

We have seen that the will is always able to take a stand even if the situation is physically or psychologically unchangeable for the moment. This is also true on the boundary situations of sin and neurosis. When I am the victim of a habitual sin or of a neurosis, then my freedom and responsibility are diminished. However, I should not underestimate the responsiblity which remains to me in spite of the fact that I cannot at once escape my neurotic or sinful reactions. It is the acceptance of this last shred of responsibility which can save me when I am moved by grace.

If I desire to survive spiritually, there is only one way, namely, not to identify myself with my sinful or neurotic habit, but to assume some attitude against it whenever and to the degree that I am still able to do so. It is necessary for me to maintain some areas of freedom of thought and activity, however insignificant and seemingly ineffective, against the onslaught of passion, habit, and neurosis. I must hold on to this last possibility of "not totally consenting interiorly" to that which seems to draw me in without the possibility of resistance. This preservation of a conviction of freedom, even if it does not help me to transcend totally the symptoms of neurosis and sin, will at least preserve my awareness of a last vestige of that human dignity which extends as far as freedom does. Without this awareness, everything seems lost. It is in this last outpost and refuge of my disturbed existence that grace may move me to turn to God in a dialogue between humble contrition and infinite mercy. *The Power and the Glory*, a novel by Graham Greene which reports the dialogue between the weak will of a priest and his Lord, is representative of such a boundary situation which tomorrow may be mine.

Perhaps I cannot change immediately the overwhelming impact of compulsion or passion. However, I can become aware that I am the one who suffers this weakness, that I, deep down, do not consent to it unconditionally. Then I have already overcome in part my sinful situation. My willingness to face my habitual sin and neurosis is already an act of freedom. To some extent it liberates me from despair. It is this last shred of will that counts, even though it does not lead immediately to ultimate victory.

Unenlightened pity for myself or others may incline me to deny guilt or responsibility in order to relieve anxiety. To be sure, I should strive to be free from *neurotic* anxiety which blocks my awareness of reality. But I should not willfully diminish my spontaneous experience of *normal* anxiety which emerges in every human being when faced with responsibility for his life and actions. If I do so, I may have to pay for this relief with the false conviction that I am essentially a moral cripple without the possibility of taking a human stand in the area of my affliction. In this case, instead of having a neurotic or sinful habit, I become this habit. I immerse myself in it. I identify with it, just as a sick animal is one with its illness and unable to assume an attitude toward it.

Moreover, my repression of normal guilt and anxiety will lead to neurotic guilt and anxiety. To accept free will means to accept responsibility and to bear it. I should not renounce my last shred of potential freedom. On the contrary, I should make it the center of renewal. I should accept, face, and explore my unconscious drives, passions, past sins, and the influence of the sensual civilization which I have unwittingly internalized.

My awareness of sinfulness will keep alive the awareness of my need for redemption. When I unveil the base realities in my life, I orient myself as a willing, searching Christian. I am already engaged in the assumption of a religious stand, in some exercise of freedom, in some acceptance of responsibility. I am already breaking the bond of impulse, passion, and past experience by going beyond it in conscious and courageous exploration. My growing awareness of these deterministic influences in my existence will liberate me increasingly from their dominance.

Today we find an increasing number of psychologists and psychiatrists who realize the primacy of the spiritual or, as they prefer to call it, the primacy of the existential over the organismic, the instinctual, and the environmental. When one attends the meetings of Alcoholics Anonymous or of Recovery Incorporated, one becomes aware how this appreciation of man's existential resiliency has been implemented in certain modes of group therapy. The members of these groups humbly admit the presence of dark impulses. At the same time they recount the ways in which they were able to transcend them, and thus encourage one another to cope spiritually with psychological negativity. Many of these people impress one by a peace and serenity which seem the more tangible because they are maintained in the face of tremendous odds.

It is true that my behavior is conditioned, but I can influence the kind of conditioning by the meaning which I freely impose on my tendencies and my environment. For example, when I perceive my father, teacher, boss, or superior as an authoritarian guardian who watches my movements in order to inhibit my growth and spontaneity, my behavior will be conditioned by that perception. In the presence of my superior, I shall behave as an anxious and subdued, or as a rebellious and aggressive, person. On the other hand, when I perceive my superior not only as a person with authority but also as a human being who is able to understand me to some degree, my behavior will be conditioned to this image. I shall be more at ease, relaxed, and spontaneous in his company. An interesting result is that, in the latter case, I shall be less and less able to speak of conditioning my behavior in the strict sense. As we have seen, the more relaxed, spontaneous, and open I am, the more I grow to unique responses which are newly created, at least in part, by this free spontaneity.

Similarly, when I suffer from sinful or neurotic habits, I bear a degree of responsibility for the meanings which I uncover in these predispositions. For example, I can freely decide that my bad habit means that I cannot do anything about it. In this case, I surrender; my behavior will be conditioned by the deterministic meaning which I have imposed on my sin or neurosis is a challenge, an occasion for growth in humility and self-understanding, a repeated opportunity for reaffirmation of my basic commitment to God. In this case, my behavior will develop in the light of this freely chosen meaning. It may be that I shall never be rid of my sin or neurosis, but my repeated stand may help me to grow to the summit of holiness, to profound understanding of the human predicament as dramatized in my constant struggle, and to merciful and tender love for fellow men who suffer as I do from sin and neurosis.

As we have seen, I can always find a free inner orientation in situations which I cannot immediately change. Is this also true of organic illness? A striking example can be found in the life of the Venerable Francis Libermann. He was a convert from Judaism who revitalized the educational Society of the Holy Ghost Fathers and expanded its originally exclusive dedication to higher education so that the congregation would consist not only of professors but also of members dedicated to elementary and secondary education and to the care of souls in parishes and in missionary countries. The Venerable Libermann suffered

from epilepsy, which postponed his ordination to the priesthood for ten years. He experienced such strong tendencies
toward suicide that in self-protection he had to remove all
sharp objects from his room. Many experts have written on
epilepsy and its physiological and psychological manifestations.
When we compare their descriptions with the accounts of
Libermann's behavior as given by the witnesses to his attacks,
we are aware of a strong difference between the serene response
of Libermann and the reactions described by neurologists.

Traditional psychology and psychiatry are pervaded by
social and biological determinism. They underestimate the
distinction between a patient's spontaneous inclinations, which
are linked with his physio-psychological disturbance, and the
stand which his deepest self may assume when he faces, accepts,
and explores his inclinations. In principle, the ultimate attitudes
of an epileptic can be molded more by what his propensities
mean to him than by the predispositions themselves. We see in
Libermann a spontaneous inclination to suicidal depression,
isolation, and feelings of inferiority. But his will, the core of his
suffering existence, transcended inclinations which he was unable to dismiss. When the option of the spirit transcends the
inclinations which are linked with a serious illness, then the
situation becomes a stepping stone to greater maturity, deeper
spirituality and, in the case of a truly religious man, genuine
sanctity. The illness becomes a blessed illness, a sacred appeal to
live more authentically; the continuous pull of depression compels the patient to renew his spiritual option against the seduction of despair. It makes it impossible for him, moreover, to
succumb to a shallow existence, problemless, impeccable, and
monotonous as a carefully arranged cemetery. He has to choose
between a degenerating and an heroic existence. It is actually
difficult for him to be a decent, mediocre man. A similar
situation may arise in the case of other disturbances, such as
invincible homosexual tendencies, alcoholism, and nymphoma-
nia. Every new fundamental option of such a person in the face
of spiritual and moral destruction reinforces and strengthens
his spiritual stand. The quality and degree of this transcendence
is dependent on the depth of his motivation. Father Libermann's
motivation had a dimension of supernatural depth, inspired as

it was by grace. Therefore, he reached an extraordinary degree of serene transcendence of the negative tendencies aroused by his illness.

Existential and Religious Will

I can thus take some stand even in the situations of sin, neurosis, or organic affliction. I can do so because my will has an existential or dialectical nature. My will is not, as we have seen, the absolute ruler imagined by the will-power Christian. Nor am I the will-less product of my past, my impulses, passions, or environment. My will is my ability to respond to reality as it reveals itself to me in a situation, even when I am not able to change this reality in all its factual aspects. My ability to respond is transformed and nourished by grace. This transformation enables me to respond freely to God and to His will as They manifest Themselves in my life situation. What the Lord allows in a given situation escapes my manipulation. My life situation is a challenge, an invitation, an appeal which comes to meet me in its uniqueness. It demands my personal response. It is not of my making; rather, it makes me while I respond faithfully to its manifestations. Therefore, I-as-religiously-willing am fundamentally "openness" and "affirmation." If I am truly religious, I am open to the presence of the divine. At the same time, my life becomes increasingly an affirmation of the divine will and presence. My religious will becomes unconditional commitment and surrender to His mysterious design. In other words, I-as-religious-will am a fundamental readiness to face and affirm God's presence as it reveals itself in my daily situation.

The manifold reality which God allows to be in and around me manifests itself to me daily if I am open to its message. To be willing is to be open, whereas unwillingness is the refusal to listen to the message of reality. At every moment I can open or close myself to the intimations of God's will. When I am open I am receptive with my whole being, not only with my logical mind but also with my intuition, not only with my eyes and ears but also with my emotional sensitivity, not only with my imagination but also with my memory, for my past experience enlightens me concerning the situation of the moment.

I-as-willing am thus openness to all revelation of reality that Providence allows in my situation. This willing openness is the permanent source of the manifold moods, feelings, memories, imaginations, and perceptions which particularize, as it were, my fundamental openness. They are special modifications of my primordial openness to my situation. For example, if I decide to grow to a truly religious existence, I become increasingly a willing openness for all manifestations of the presence of God in the reality which surrounds me. This willingness to experience the Lord in my life leads to a special openness to all my modalities of existence. When I walk in the country, I see with a new eye the beauty of trees and flowers. I see and hear with eyes and ears like those of St. Francis, whose willing openness to God gave him a fresh perception of the sun, the moon, the stars, and even the graceful animals playing in forest and stream. Moreover, my emotional modality of existence shares in this transformation. When I hear a poem or a sermon which is a moving expression of God's love, I may experience deep joy or awe; my willing openness inclines my emotions to experience God also on this level of my existence. When I must speak of God, my willing openness prompts my memory to recall the tangible marks of His presence in my past. Thus my openness guides me to recollect past knowledge and experience to meet my present need.

This is not all. The willing openness which pervades my existence grows toward a firm decision which is a response of my whole being to that which reveals itself to my openness. For example, I may be willing openness for what God wants me to do in my life, whether it be marriage, the unmarried state in the world, the priesthood, brotherhood, or sisterhood. This willing openness makes my memory stand out toward my past in order to detect any sign of God's plan for my life. At the same time, it enhances my sensitivity and intellectual perspicacity for any manifestation of God's will in regard to my vocation. As a result, I develop probing thoughts, spontaneous feelings, perceptions, and inclinations which all in their own way tell me something of what God seems to want for me as a life vocation. I gather together, in the core of my being, all of the experience yielded by all my modalities of existence. In this inner recollection, I grow increasingly to a final decision. I come to see what my life should be according to God's will. Finally, I bring together all my insights within a prudent project of existence which is in harmony with God's design and revelation.

Thus I reject none of my existential modalities nor the knowledge which they give me. I do not repress nor deny their voice. I do not say to myself that this attraction or that aversion should not be taken seriously, or that I should not consider this memory of the past. On the contrary, all my feelings, all my relevant memories, all my imaginations obtain a fair hearing in the core of my existence, even if they seem initially contradictory. I do not manipulate or repress my emotionality; I discipline it. I should not understand "discipline" in the compulsive, forceful, and rationalistic sense of the punishment of a prison. Rather, I should understand it in the etymological sense of the word, referring to "disciple": My will as openness inclines all my modalities of existence to the divine presence in all things. It makes them disciples of the sacred dimension of reality. Thus, in the example given above, the recollection of past knowledge and inspiration leads to a seeing again, a hearing again, a remembering again, a feeling again, a thinking again until I, as a complete existence, become clear about what reality is telling me concerning the will of God for my life. His presence and will are veiled by daily appearances and unveiled by the eyes of faith.

When I am a will-power Christian, I subdue reality in myself and in my surroundings instead of listening in openness to divine inspiration. I do not look at what is. I have eyes only for my little blueprint of life, my willful plan of self-coercion. This will to power is out of tune with the voice of the Lord. His voice is heard, not by the powerful, but by the meek and humble of heart who possess the earth. Possessing the earth means that they are able to discover and to use earthly possibilities wisely and effectively without violating their sacred dimensions. He who tries to break reality will be broken. Such a breakdown sometimes leads to neurosis or psychosis. When my religious will is authentic, I grow increasingly toward wise and harmonious projects of existence which are in tune with the will of the Lord.

Even this is not the whole story. Authentic will leads not only to the full openness of my existence and to the decision for a project of existence; it also leads to the concrete embodiment of such a project in my daily life. This embodiment makes it necessary for me to be open to the concrete situation in which I hope to realize my decision. But this time my openness is an alertness to the practical aspects of the situation. Now it is not so much a question of making up my mind about what I should be in life, but of prudently and effectively realizing my ideal to some degree at this moment. How can I do something about it in my special environment? What would be a workable long-range plan?

As soon as I decide on a project of existence, I am faced with a never-ending series of theoretical and practical questions. These demand practical proposals which embody my theoretical existential decision. They also demand the execution of these proposals, which will require support from the will. Sometimes I am tired. At other moments I feel aversion to getting down to the task at hand. The over-all readiness of my existential will now translates itself into the thrust necessary to bring me over the hump of inner resistance or childish desire. We may call this action the functional aspect of the will. In all its concrete forms, it is secondary in nature; it is a derivative of my authentic existential will; it is a practical consequence of my primary openness. If I were totally closed in the core of my being toward a certain task or enterprise, I would not even think of theoretical plans and practical ways of executing them. All forms of theoretical and practical knowledge which help me to realize my existential project *presuppose* in me a more fundamental, willing openness. It is willing openness which permits me to see, both theoretically and practically, what I should do in my unique life situation.

The same may be said about my active execution of my plans in concrete behavior. In fact, I should seriously question my will and orientation if I almost never have theoretical or practical ideas about those things which I claim to do willingly. I should doubt my willingness even more if I frequently find it impossible to overcome the small resistance which everyone experiences in getting down to work. Another sign that there may be something ambiguous about my basic decision is the sudden appearance of nearly insurmountable resistance when I am faced with my special duty. In such cases, it is not very helpful to attack the immediate difficulty or to apply brute force to drive myself mercilessly to those tasks for which I experience a mounting aversion. It is better to explore what I really will in the depths of my existence. Perhaps I do not will what I claim to will; what I disclaim as my desire may well be a deep, unconscious but dynamic drive in my life.

For example, a young Christian intellectual may feel that his deepest willingness is to further Christianity by a splendid intellectual performance, by a life dedicated to scholarship, by the countless hours of silent and humble service at his desk. Moreover, he may hope to inspire his fellow Christian intellectuals to the same appreciation of the cultural mission of the Church. However, when he looks carefully at what he is really doing, he discovers a surprising discrepancy between his actions and his ideals. He is content as long as he can talk about his projects, especially before large audiences and admiring students. He is satisfied as long as he can hurl passionate diatribes at those Christians who supposedly do not share the scholarly devotion of the few chosen ones like himself. All goes well as he excitedly pens letters to the editor. He feels on top of the world when his picture appears in the newspapers over his daring statements to the PTA group of his parish. However, he notices one curious thing. As soon as he attempts to put all his high-sounding assertions into action, he fails miserably. He talks splendidly about the scholarly dedication of the modern Christian, but he is unable to spend many hours behind his desk daily, as scholarly non-Christians do. He declares to his adulating audience that the Christian intellectual should be present in the arena of modern thought with his own contribution. But his contribution does not amount to one publication a year. He clamors that Christian education should be reformed, should be brought up to standard. But his lectures are thin, unscholarly, directed more toward gaining adulation from excitable adolescents than instilling in them the discipline of true learning. He is enthusiastic about reforms in the liturgy, but he neglects the literature of his own field of study. He admits to himself that he experiences insurmountable resistance when he is faced with hours of intensive study behind his desk, with the solid preparation of a well-organized, original lecture for his class, with the struggle with the latest ideas in his field of competence.

Such a man may well ask himself, "Is my deepest will really to contribute to the intellectual growth of Christianity? Or is my deepest will to have my picture in the papers, to be adulated by the immature, to be the man about town, to make a name for myself, to be something very special in my own eyes and in the eyes of others?" He may discover that the latter is the drive which motivates him and which tempts him to use the propaganda for Christian scholarship as a springboard for his own aggrandizement. He may now be able, perhaps for the first time in his life, to grow to authenticity, to destroy the lie of his life, to become a sincere person not only on the conscious but also on the unconscious level of his existence. He should not be distressed by his self-discovery, which is a gift of grace, because now he has the opportunity to become a real Christian in deed, not merely in word.

To sum up, when I am a religious person my willing openness for the manifestation of God's presence in all situations is the permanent source and foundation of all my actions, judgments, and decisions and of all my theoretical and practical knowledge.

My religious will, finally, is my primordial decision and readiness to respond to the hidden voice of the Lord, to disclose the sacred dimension of reality, and to let the presence of the divine in all-that-is reveal itself. As a religious man I sanctify the universe, not by conquering it, but by guarding its sacred dimension, for reality can reveal itself to me in many ways. For example, when I look out of my window at the trees in the park, their reality can disclose itself to me in a variety of dimensions. When I look with the eyes of a carpenter, I see the trees as solid material for boards and planks which I may use in the construction of furniture and buildings. Again, I may view the same trees as a biologist. Then they reveal themselves to me as belonging to special classes of plants. This is a dimension of reality quite different from the practical dimension of the carpenter. When I am hungry, I may see the red apples on the trees in the tasty and edible dimension of their reality. In other words, the particular dimension of reality which exists in my world of thought and perception depends on the stand which I take. If no one in the world took the practical stand of the carpenter, the dimension of trees as material for building would disappear in our shared world of meaning. Even if I myself am not interested in trees as a source of usable wood, I am still reminded of this dimension by the carpenters in my society. In this sense, carpenters are the guardians of a practical dimension of trees in the universe of meaning which is my culture.

Similarly, this principle can be applied to religious existence. When a deeply religious man looks at trees in the park, he experiences the presence of the Creator in His creation, the expression of divine beauty in the splendor of green leaves and lacy boughs. He communicates this experience to others in his society, and in this sense, he is the guardian of the sacred dimension of reality. The saint is not the willful ethical superman, but the humble shepherd of the sacred. As the shepherd peacefully tends his flock and does not allow any sheep to stray, so the saintly man carefully cultivates his lively perception of divine presence in all people, things, and events in the world. He does not allow the vision of the divine to perish among mankind. Even if all those around him are attracted by only the profane appearance of reality, the saint remains the lonely shepherd of the sacred dimension of the world. He will not permit it to perish in the cold hearts of men. As long as there is one religoius existence in the world, there will be at least one human being who safeguards the sacred in our world of meaning.

Although I am not a saint, I should realize that the chief meaning for mankind of my religious existence is the same as that of the saint. Therefore, as a religious person I should be present according to my talents in the realms of nature, art, science, and culture. If the religious person refuses to be present, who will rescue the sacred dimension of these realities? What shepherd will tenderly tend the flock of the divine aspects of every realm of human endeavor? As a truly religious existence, I am not primarily a man of many devotions, but the faithful guardian of the religious meaning of the world. The openness of my religious will, transformed and nourished by grace, enlightened by Revelation, gives rise constantly to the sacred dimension of reality and preserves its mysterious, tenuous presence in every situation.

We may now summarize what existential will and religious will really are. My existential will is, first of all, my personal openness to reality as it reveals itself to me. It is, second, my subsequent personal option and execution of behavior which integrates all relevant meanings of my situation. My religious will is, first, my personal openness—in the light of Revelation and under the impulse of grace—to reality as it reveals itself to me as a sanctified member of the Body of Christ. It is, second, my subsequent option and execution of behavior which incorporates all relevant meanings, sacred and profane, of my situation.

Development of Authentic Religious Will

If I desire to maintain and foster my religious existence, it is of primary importance to preserve my religious will, to promote its authenticity, to prevent its decline. First of all, in the relationship between will and "lived" reality, I should never replace dialogue by denial. My "lived" reality is all that I am at any moment: my good intentions, my noble feelings, but also my hostile impulses, sensual urges, and vain ambitions. I, as willing, should not deny the presence of all these modes of existence. Instead of denying them, I, as willing, should interact with them. I should never replace this dialogue by denial in the relationship between me-as-willing and me-as-lived reality.

The will-power Christian abuses his will in the negation of irrational wishes instead of facing them in the light of Revelation. Often I am not humble enough to admit the presence of base inclinations which would deflate my self-esteem. I can maintain such a denial of my "bad" impulses only by a negation of my spontaneous awareness of them. To prevent my becoming spontaneously aware of my desires, I have to curb my spontaneity more and more. This attitude may lead to a virtual extinction of my spontaneity. As a result, I live increasingly in an emotional vacuum. Unfortunately, this death of my sensitivity will also impoverish my possibility of full religious experience, for religious experience is not simply a question of acrobatics of my logical intelligence.

When I increasingly repress my spontaneity, I may sooner or later sense that something is missing in my life. Because of my repression, I cannot define what is missing, but I vaguely suspect that others possess it. As a result, I may resent their naturalness, their relaxed and spontaneous manner. I experience an obscure feeling of irritation with people who seem to exist exuberantly and "dangerously," without fear of doom and damnation. However, my self-image of achieved perfection does not allow me to admit to myself that I have this feeling of irritation. I repress my resentment and envy instead of exploring the message of these emotions in my life. If I investigate what evokes these feelings in me, I may perhaps discover that I cannot bear to see others freely enjoy what I have mutilated in my own life. This is not all. When I deny such feelings instead of facing them and working them through, they do not disappear. They come to the fore in other ways which seem more pious and apostolic and are therefore acceptable to me because they do not conflict with my self-image of religious perfection. My irritation with those who have not killed in themselves the joy of life and the beauty of spontaneity masquerades as aggressive "apostolate," "fraternal correction," "moral censorship," and "holy concern for unholy brethren."

It is clear that such hidden inclinations may spoil my pious enterprise. My repressed hostility may sabotage my apostolic motives, thus transforming my zealous apostolate into something fanatic and distasteful without my realizing it on the level of awareness. I may become a master of indictment and denunciation of fellow Christians who think and speak spontaneously and blaze new trails for Christianity. If my sickness develops, I may become a one-man inquisition; not being permitted to torture my fellow Christians on the rack, I slash them with my tongue and with my small-minded, but well-meant, insinuations. This is the tragedy of my repressed hostility, that I am unaware of it on the conscious level of my existence where I really feel like a holy defender of the Faith. This role is in keeping with the self-image of religious righteousness that I have built up by the repression of the awareness of what my real feelings are.

Spontaneity radiates richness, warmth, and charm in Christian existence and keeps it vigorous and creative. My will, therefore, should not negate spontaneous inclinations but should give them direction. The dried-up, compulsive Christian is the conceited do-gooder with only will and no spontaneity. On the other hand, the person with mere spontaneity is irresponsible, playful, and childish. As an adult he may abuse religion, as a kind of playboy Christian, for his own impulsive ends; or he may become a robot Christian moved by any wind which blows in the collectivity of people to which he blindly belongs without coming into his own personality.

If my religious existence is authentic, my will and my spontaneity are welded harmoniously. Together they lead to my prudent option of the best suitable project of action for me. Then my option ripens in the light of grace and Revelation while I listen respectfully to the spontaneous rise of inclinations which reveal the richness of possibilities in me and my situation. I do not deny nor exclude my spontaneity; I incorporate and transcend it. My wholesome growth in religious existence means that I integrate my spontaneity, will, and decision in the light of grace and Revelation.

This religious harmony is possible in me only when I am aware of my spontaneous inclinations, no matter how mean or exalted, childish or mature, hostile or loving, envious or altruistic, greedy or generous. I may feel anxiety and shame when I admit to myself my immaturity, my smugness, my jealousy and hate, for such feelings belie the elated image of my religious perfection. It is this image which has led me to repress the awareness of such demeaning inclinations in myself. The practice of a deep and genuine examination of conscience will help me to maintain this honest self-awareness which is the foundation and beginning of all growth in the spiritual life. I may need a spiritual director who is able and willing to assist me in unmasking my deceit and pretension. In the case of neurosis, psychotherapy may be necessary to remove cataracts which blur my vision. This *becoming aware* is central in the beginning of my religious life. Later I may be focused on living union with the divine presence. But even then a marginal attention to what deep down I "am inclined to be" should remain a permanent precaution against decline in religious authenticity.

It is crucial for my growth that I relate the initial awareness of my spontaneity with the awareness of myself as a responsible person. I must admit that my inclinations are my own. I have to face them and answer for them. I should not look on my inclinations as if I were an outsider, safe and withdrawn. I cannot take a vantage point outside myself from which I manipulate like an engineer all that transpires in my life. I must "own" my spontaneous experiences which reveal my reality, my situation, my world. I should experience deeply that my situation reveals itself in my feelings and inclinations as an appeal of possibilities to be realized in action.

I can respond to this appeal in a variety of ways, but I should not deny any awareness which announces itself in my lived experience. The authentic will chooses to be open to reality as it reveals itself. As soon as I open up to what is, reality reveals itself in ever-increasing detail; each particular revelation implies a challenge to respond to it in an authentic way, once I experience this aspect of reality as mine. I am the one who has these inclinations. They are appeals to me, invitations to options and actions of mine. They reveal to me a world of attractive possibilities which I can realize or not realize, totally or only partially realize. I am the person who must bind some of these inclinations to a consciously assumed project of life, while omitting others which would distort the harmony of my project.

It is my spirit which enables me to transcend my immediate situation, to assume a distance from impulse and inclination and from the attractive aspects of the world which they reveal to me. As a human spirit, I can distance myself and ponder in terms of the possible. This taking of distance is a necessary condition for the possibility of my will to assume weight in my life; hence, the necessity for asceticism, recollection, and inner moderation which, among other things, keep my ability to distance myself flexible and available at moments of confusion, crisis, and temptation.

This detachment enables me to ponder which inclinations I should foster and which ones I should pass by, without repressing my humble consciousness that it is I who have these inclinations. Then grace will enable me to decide on a religious project, which is not a denial of all inclination, but an incorporation of spontaneity on the higher level of consciousness in the light of grace and revelation. In other words, the good will of the religious person cannot blindly act on his propensities but can only live with them in a dialectical relationship. To give an example: the experience of my inclination toward an attractive person on the level of spontaneity may bring delight and the longing to continue or renew the experience; but the realization that I am the person who is experiencing this excitement and desire makes me aware of the implications which the willing affirmation, continuation, or renewal of this experience may have for my life, my relationship with God, with my marriage partner, my children, my vocation. The prudish refusal of willful peity to admit that it is I who experience this delight and longing may lead to a risky relation under false pretense of utility or concern. This bad faith veils the real inclination which is driving me on. Repressed from awareness, the excitement grows coarsely like a hidden, unchecked cancer which may overwhelm my existence. Finally it may be detected, when perhaps only traumatic surgery may be able to save the integrity of two self-deceived people and the happiness of others linked with their existence.

My option as a Christian should be a religiously responsible option. Religious responsibility involves, first, responding to my situation in the light of the Revelation of my religion; second, responding to God's unique revelation in my unique situation as it manifests itself to me in my daily life. Thus, my response to what I experience as God's personal revelation to me in my unique situation should always be in conformity with the Revelation which God has given to all mankind in and through Christ and His Church. Both responses presuppose that I see reality with the eyes of faith. It is faith which makes visible to me the dimension of the sacred. This vision of faith is a gift which cannot be forced, but which will be bestowed on me when I am ready for its intimation. The constant practice of asceticism, recollection, and inner moderation leads to an attitude of silent readiness in which the vision of faith may appeal to my existential will. Finally, in this light of faith I shall respond wisely to all the aspects of my situation. In this religiously responsible attitude, my will transcends the immediacy of impulse and inclination.

But, again, I can transcend only what I own in awareness. Therefore, it remains important, even for the deepest religious decision, that it be preceded by a dialogue with spontaneity. As a result of this dialogue, I may have to decide to do what is precisely the opposite of some of my most intense desires, while affirming other inclinations which can be ratified by my project of religious existence. Again, a serene and moderate practice of mortification will keep me ready and capable, with the grace of God, to follow up my decisions in so far as they are always necessarily opposed to some part of myself which is neither denied nor realized. In any case, I shall not bury that spontaneity which I cannot promote in my project of existence. Otherwise, I may be sabotaged by unconscious propensities which corrupt the behavior necessary to carry out my project. Neither shall I fall into the opposite extreme and willfully excite and foster the awareness of propensities which I cannot realize without distorting the harmony of my religious mode of being. Willful excitation as well as willful repression of inclinations which are irrelevant to my authentic religious project injure the peace and wholeness of my existence.

Although I should quietly examine my impulses lest they betray the consistency of my religious being-in-the-world, I must also accept the fact that I can never assess exhaustively all my inclinations under all possible aspects. Therefore, I can never be sure that my religious option or project has attained optimal purity and perfection. My humble suspicion of the taint of selfish impulse keeps alive in me the need for redemption. I shall humbly accept that my motives are not fully transparent to me because I am not a pure spirit, but a fallen human being in need of purification. I shall be satisfied with a peaceful pondering of my intentions within the limits of reason and possibility. The rest I shall leave to God in surrender. A disregard for the limits of my capacity of self-awareness will betray itself in tenseness, anxiety, compulsion, scrupulosity, and an over-all loss of serenity of heart and mind. These are symptoms of a willful purification of motive and inclination, which is a stubborn attempt of the will to act on the limits of self-awareness instead of relating to these limits dialectically. It is the refusal of my will to admit my essential imperfection, to acknowledge that I cannot plumb the depths of my sinfulness and deceit, that I cannot save myself but need redemption.

The discovery that I cannot willfully force optimal purification may hurt my pride. I may fall from willfulness into the void of will-lessness, thus refusing to be satisfied with the relative purification that I may attain with God's grace. It is this all-or-nothing attitude which defeats the possibility of a truly existential or dialectical will, and which leads to the fallacy of absolute will-power or of will-lessness. The necessary condition for the possibility of existential will is humility. Humility is the recognition of my essential limitation which implies the necessity of dialogue. When grace liberates my will from absolutism, laxity, and determinism, I may be faithful to the existential nature of my will. Then I may grow humbly and serenely to the limited perfection which Providence intended for me from all eternity. Then, I may increasingly discover God's project for me and realize it humbly in my option and action.

René Voillaume
1905-

What is it about the human that makes conversion possible? How can a life of dissipation, laziness, religious insensitivity give way to total dedication of God? Why, in spite of the distance of centuries, does the call of Nazareth continue to haunt mankind, to transform lives radically, to drive humans to do the incredible?

The few personalities known throughout Christian history for their capacity to live out the extremes of human emptiness and divine fullness are real mysteries. Knowledge of their lives makes one look on in uneasy admiration, wondering what they were all about and whether they really can be imitated.

René Voillaume's little book, Seeds of the Desert: Like Jesus at Nazareth, *is about one of these rare persons, Charles de Foucauld. In it, Voillaume writes of the man whose life became the foundation and model for the Little Brothers and Little Sisters of Jesus.*

Charles de Foucauld was born into a French aristocratic family in 1858. Christian ideals meant little to him and he easily found himself at home in a life dedicated to pleasure. After completing the St. Cyr Military Academy program, he wandered aimlessly through the social world of Paris. Looking for something unusual to do, he undertook in 1880, a voyage into the heart of Morocco which was at that time closed to Europeans.

He travelled disguised as a Moroccan Jew. The published results of his journey amazed Europe and made him famous overnight.

The years of dissipation, the military formation, the discipline of the journey to Morocco worked—each in a different manner—to create a restlessness in the heart of Charles de Foucauld. He spent some time in serious reading and in conversation with a spiritual guide. Suddenly he knew what to do. Nazareth was calling. "The moment I realized that God existed, I knew I could not do otherwise than to live for him alone." First, several years as a Trappist in France and Syria; then two years as a poor man in Nazareth; finally, the Sahara. He settled in Tamanrasset, in the Hoggar region and lived among the Touareg tribes, some of the poorest people in the world. Here he lived a life of silent service until he was murdered in 1916.

His life and death would have been forgotten had they not given birth to the fraternities of the Little Brothers and the Little Sisters of Jesus. These two groups have brought the message of Charles de Foucauld to fruition. It is their ideal to imitate the poor workman living in obscurity in Nazareth. They seek to share the lot of the poor workers, regardless of consequences, and to be a living presence of Christ among them. Their spirituality is anchored, not in the quiet setting of a monastery, but in the noise of the working class which includes the fatigue, the anxiety and the insecurity of the poor man's world.

Much like Charles de Foucauld, these Little Brothers and Little Sisters lead paradoxical lives. They seek to shoulder human suffering at its worst yet dwell in peace, joy, gentleness. Theirs is a vocation for the unusual person, though their basic insight is that total sanctity is attainable in the everyday life of the Christian. The contemporary world, with its emphasis on efficiency, gain, production, status, power, and the like, will find these people incomprehensible and will tend to judge their lives a waste. Herein lies their very purpose—actually to exist the way they do, which serves to throw into question everything that the twentieth century values and, in the face of justifications and explanations, to point in silence toward Nazareth. Whether theirs is a significant role in contemporary Christianity depends on Christianity's capacity to take itself seriously.

SEEDS OF THE DESERT

"NAZARETH" AS A FORM OF THE RELIGIOUS LIFE

T he originality of Father de Foucauld's life may tend to hide for some the true nature of his vocation. He always said himself that it was to imitate the life of Jesus at Nazareth, but even if we did not know this, it would, I think, be clear to anyone really familiar with his history. For, from the day of his conversion to the time of his death, this ideal stands out as the focus of all his aspirations, the point towards which his every act and his every step were directed. I believe it will be equally clear that it was part of his vocation to make imitation of the mystery of Nazareth a veritable form of the religious life.

At first sight, there would seem to be nothing particularly new or original about this latter ambition. A whole current of authentic religious life has long been feeding upon the "spirituality of Nazareth." But one senses unmistakably—through the example of his life still more than through his writings, and despite the fact of his having lived out his life alone—that the religious ideal brought us by the "brother of the Touaregs" is something really new, though—and perhaps partly because—it was not to fructify until after his death.

The objection has been made to us more than once that a spirituality too closely centered upon the life at Nazareth would inevitably be narrow and incomplete. "Nazareth," they have said was after all only one phase in Jesus' life and, long as it may have lasted, simply a period of preparation for His mission or a period of silent waiting until the moment fixed by the Father should come for Him to begin the work of the redemption. Why then, confine oneself to this single aspect of Christ's example?

If certain insufficiently enlightened souls have sometimes failed to avoid the risks connected with devotion of a kind in which the mystery of Jesus is not included in its entirety, one can hardly put the blame for this on Father de Foucauld. To be certain of this, one only needs to read his meditations on the Gospel, on the one hand, and, on the other, to observe how he was little by little configured to Christ in the depths of his soul—not to the Workman of Nazareth alone, but to His errant life in search of the most lost of the lost sheep as well and, above all, to His agony on the Cross. It nevertheless remains that the mystery of the poor workman living in obscurity at Nazareth exercised a determining influence on Father de Foucauld's choice of the *status* he was to have, as well as on his plans for the religious congregation which he started thinking about at the very beginning. The inspiration he drew from "Nazareth" resulted in a *new outward form* for that life, his *spirituality* meanwhile taking its sustenance from the whole mystery of Jesus as he came upon its different aspects in the Gospel.

There are two particular features which seem to me to have been intrinsic to Brother Charles's manner of picturing the ideal religious life, two features which were to stand out little by little from the countless aspirations crowding into his soul, and which, little as he may have realized their full importance at the beginning, nevertheless contained the germ of a veritable renewal of the religious life.

The first of these made its appearance when he was still "Frère Alberic" at the Trappist Monastery at Akbes and went one day to pay a visit to a family of very poor working people in the neighboring village. The shock he received on seeing how these people lived by comparison with life at the monastery, simple and hard as this was, he recorded thus on his return: "Oh, the difference between these buildings of ours and that poor working man's house! It makes me long for Nazareth." From then on, "Nazareth" was to embody his ideal for the religious life, and this was to comprise the hard toil, the low scale of living, the meager housing and the insecurity of a family of workers.

But the question may be asked whether, in one's desire thus to attain religious perfection in the status in which the majority of mankind lives, one is not confusing somewhat the religious status and the normal situation of any Christian pursuing holiness in the world. The nature of Christian perfection is the same for all who have been baptized, whether laymen or religious, and the religious life is definable simply as a particular body of means to that end. Father de Foucauld himself emphasized that the ideal model for a layman to follow was the mystery of Nazareth. Yet it was the life at Nazareth and no other that he felt himself impelled to choose as a religious.

The second original feature of Brother Charles's ideal was to accentuate still further this unprecedented approach to the religious status. It would doubtless have been possible to restrict imitation of the life at Nazareth to a framework (withdrawal from society, enclosure, silence, etc.) which would have left it a traditional monastic cast, and Brother Charles indeed tried to see things that way for some time. But the inner pressure of his vocation was too strong; he was soon to abandon all idea of separations and live in direct contact with the people around him, a contact, moreover, made constantly closer by his growing charity and the need he therefore felt of expressing it more and more with the familiarity of simple, fraternal friendship. This gift of self, this constant availability were, then, the fruits of love and a great desire to bring these people the living presence of Christ. Nor should one hesitate to recognize here the apostolic spirit in the broadest sense of the term, provided one has fully grasped not only the particular nature of this kind of apostolate, but also that of the means it involved to the exclusion of all others. Merely being present was one of these, but there were also, as I say, the brotherly friendship, the gift of self, the intimate conversations, the testimony of the way he lived—in a word, whatever love could counsel a man of poverty in order to make his Lord known and loved by those around him.

Again, the objection has been made that if observances are done away with, or practically so, and more particularly still, if there is not at least some minimal separation from the outside world, there can be little use talking about any real religious life, as what would be left would merely be tantamount to the life of Christian laymen in the world. Two different problems are thus raised: first, whether minimal separation and observances are really essential factors in the religious life as such, and, secondly, whether the religious state is superior to that of the layman or not.

Surely, it is one of the most important achievements of contemporary Christianity to have awakened consciousness of the fact that sanctity, total sanctity, is attainable in everyday life. Due to the rapid changes in general conditions which began towards the beginning of the century and the tragic upheavals which ensued, the great majority of people living the ordinary life of the world suddenly found themselves faced with an almost relentlessly hard and precarious existence, and this has been a challenge to Christians to get beyond themselves—often not without a certain heroism. At the same time, the Church was confronted in certain countries with the problem of winning back the de-Christianized masses of the people and, with many of the laity belonging to Catholic Action movements, this has helped to develop an active charity and an understanding of social facts and of the necessity of providing fraternal assistance, which the difficulties encountered in the daily struggle have only made the deeper.

On the other hand, a fairly large number of religious communities have remained unaffected by these conditions, as if sheltered from the changes going on outside—though quite involuntarily on their part. Very few religious in the monasteries and convents have been called upon to lead anything like a hard, let alone a heroic, life; rather have they been preserved from the harshness of life today by the very rhythm of their existence. It would be difficult to admit that this has been privilege, from the standpoint of the life of the Gospel.

Comparisons of this kind have had some share in the falling-off in respect for the religious status. The rapid evolution of people's minds today ought to have been met with a certain adaptation of religious observances and means to perfection to the new needs. This adaptation has not taken place as it should have, and it would seem as if the very slow change occurring in certain sides of the religious life had been considerably outdistanced by changes in the modern world.

Thus various deficiencies, which are sometimes real and sometimes only apparent, are partially responsible for the severity with which people today often regard the cloister; they do not, however, by any means justify all their statements, for these often spring from mistaken or inadequate ideas as regards our relationships with God.

There are two particular sides of the religious life which are especially badly understood nowadays: the *necessity of discipline and asceticism* not having as their direct aim or immediate purpose a tangible improvement in human values or observable results in the sphere of the apostolate, and the *value of consecrating one's life to God alone* outside any charitable activity or service to others.

At the root of this lack of comprehension, there is a reaction against the Jansenist, or, if you prefer, Puritan conception of man: people have difficulty in admitting original sin and the flaws and injuries with which it has left human nature. Original sin is hardly ever mentioned any more, and the idea of asceticism is only acceptable when presented for what it can do for people by augmenting their capacities. The significance of penitence and mortification is thus no longer perceptible; certain sacrifices that go with the vows of poverty and obedience are no longer understandable, and celibacy consecrated by vows no longer excites the same respect.

In addition, consciousness of the urgency of making society over on new bases and of winning back to Christ a world gone pagan to the marrow of its bones, has caused the greater part of Christian thinking to crystallize around productive social activities and efficiency of effort in human charity. An enrichment has indubitably thus been brought about, but it has had its unhappy counterpart in an impoverishment of *feeling for the sacred.* The intrinsic value of *separating oneself off* for the sake of God is contested; likewise, sometimes, the very legitimacy of an existence consecrated so completely to God as to entail withdrawing from all human activity. The tendency is to judge the spiritual value of an action by what that action is capable of producing in the way of results in social activity and service to one's neighbor. This is an error, and this error explains why people no longer properly appreciate the religious value of the vow consecrating men and women to God.

We must therefore assert—in line with the position unvaryingly held by the Church since the first centuries—that there is no question but that consecration to God by the three vows is superior to the ordinary Christian status. In making this assertion, we automatically make likewise the assertion, not only of the legitimacy, but of the superiority *per se* of the *essential* separations—which must, first of all, be inner and spiritual—involved in the observance of the vows, in particular that of chastity. As for the question whether separation, even when reduced to a minimum, is compatible with the kind of life, in intimate contact with people and with everything it entails in the way of instability, uncertainty of the morrow, daily cares and daily toil, which Father de Foucauld dreamed of from the time he left the Trappist monastery, I think we may answer in the affirmative.

The essential factor in the religious status, the thing which defines and distinguishes it as such, is the *spiritual reality* of the promise one makes to God, with the public acceptance of the Church, to live in a state of chastity, poverty, and obedience. Separations are, of course, entailed here; they can, however, be obtained under the most varied and different circumstances. A second factor, which, though secondary and non-essential in itself, may well be indispensable to some, is met with in the current conception of the religious status, and consists in a body of arrangements—enclosure, regulated silence, various forms of physical separations, and prescriptions concerning the organization of the community life—looking to the observance of the three vows in practice. These are but means as regards the actual practising of the evangelical counsels. It is consequently possible to conceive of a true religious life making use of these different means to a lesser degree, provided it offers a sure road to perfection in charity through the practice of poverty, chastity, and obedience. Such a road has been opened up for us by Father de Foucauld. It lies in sharing the lot of the workers and the other poor, with all the consequences involved, and being a living presence of Christ among them.

Here, then, is a new type of religious life, where less attention is paid to sheltering oneself off from risks with separations, or to being helped by observances superimposed upon one's daily occupations, than to ordering one's entire life into a single movement of charity for Christ and men, and learning to make use of the very difficulties attendant upon such a life as so many means to self-dispossession and the very concrete realization of one's profession of the three vows.

Those who are inclined to question the viability of this kind of religious life need only consult the pontifical documents in which Pope Pius XII gives solemn recognition to the form of life offered by the Secular Institutes as a canonical state of perfection and, in so doing, asserts in a manner which leaves no room for doubt, that the perfection of the evangelical counsels can be reached by a path which, at first sight, may seem opposed to the one hitherto followed by religious Congregations. By emphasizing that which is essential to the state of perfection with such fresh clarity and precision, these documents far exceed by their importance their immediate object, and open up the way for a renewal of the conception of the religious life itself.

"To lead at all times and in all places a life of true perfection, to embrace such a life in cases where the canonical religious life would be either impossible or insufficiently adapted, to re-Christianize families, professions and civilian society with intensity through immediate and daily contact with a life fully and completely consecrated to one's sanctification. . ." (Apostolic Constitution, Provida Mater Ecclesia).

"Nothing must be retrenched from the complete profession of Christian perfection, solidly based upon the evangelical counsels and truly religious as regards its substance, but that perfection must be achieved and professed in the world; it must consequently be adapted to secular life in all things which are licit and compatible with the obligations and works of that perfection.

"The entire life of the members of the Secular Institutes, dedicated to God for the practice of perfection, must be converted into an apostleship. . . . This apostleship of the Secular Institutes must be exercised not only in the world, but likewise by the means of the world, so to speak, and consequently in professions, activities, forms, and in places and under circumstances corresponding to this secular condition" (Motu Proprio, *Primo feliciter*).

Slightly transposed, these lines would be a perfect definition of Father de Foucauld's spirituality in its most essential features. The two ideas which I stressed above are both here: first, the will to practise the three vows in an ordinary life, working at almost any kind of work; then the need to be 'saviors' with Jesus. This latter is the very reason for our Fraternities being buried away, as it were, in the heart of mankind; and it is likewise the thing that justifies the choice of such a vocation despite its risks. When one stops to recall how Father de Foucauld's mind and heart were tortured over men's salvation—"For the spreading of the Gospel, I am ready to go to the ends of the Earth and I am likewise ready to live till the Day of Judgment"—that this was what made him push farther and farther into the desert so as to reach the most forsaken of the native tribes, what made him spend so many hours not only in adoration, before the Host, of the world's Savior but studying the language and holding innumerable apparently useless conversations; that this was why he gave himself in such disinterested, and often quite fruitless, friendship—when one realizes all this one can but admit that his life could not be better described than by saying that it was "entirely converted into an apostleship." It was because his life itself was thus "entirely converted" that there was no need for him to have recourse to other means—those, I mean, which are usually associated with the commonly accepted idea of the apostolate.

You Little Brothers must therefore seek the perfection of love not only in contact with men, but with such contact as a means to it, or, to use the words of the pontifical document again, "not only in the world, but . . . by the means of the world."

Here is what takes the place of observances with us. If, in your lives of hard work, there were too frequent exercises or other moments of escape (though a harmonious use must, of course, be made of these with the appropriate rhythm), you would not succeed in consecrating the whole of them to God so well as you will by making the most of all the opportunities for abnegation, and meeting all the demands of charity, which your days will bring you almost at every turn. Your insecurity in your poor men's lodgings will help you to learn the joy of detachment from things material; the proletarian unsteadiness of your work, the fatigue of your everyday goings and comings and your travels will help you to learn to carry through with your renunciation of your restlessness and your self-interest. Your falls, experience of your weakness will not stop you, either; for, over and beyond it all, you will learn to seek the Lord's mercy, the source of the divine life. Finding yourselves, as you often will, unable to keep any time for yourselves, because people poorer than you will be taking possession of your very existence, will help to lead you to the inner peace of perfect poverty. You must nevertheless constantly have the same desire as Jesus to go apart by night and pray, and you must grasp every chance of satisfying that desire.

If a road like this has been formally recognized as a way to perfection for the Secular Institutes without the life in common, must this not be still more the case with us who possess the additional advantage of the strength of our Fraternity life? If, again, the Church recognizes the possibility of people leading a life of poverty, chastity and obedience in the world, whatever their profession and whatever their status, this can but obtain even more in the particularly humble, particularly poor kind of life voluntarily chosen by the Little Brothers.

An objection sometimes made with regard to our vocation is that the material conditions under which the industrial worker has to work preclude any genuine religious life. But how is it that so simple a thing as adopting a skill or a trade because one wishes to be like the innumerable wage-earners in the world today; how is it, I say, that such a gesture, which has been made out of sheer love by so many saints through the centuries since our Lord Himself lived as a manual worker, raises such questions that the idea of integrating work with the religious life has become almost inconceivable outside the very limited framework of the closed, and often very special, economy of a monastery? Has the life of the modern workman then become such as to be incapable of supplying a basis on which to build an authentic religious life?

If this had to be admitted, it would be something tragically serious; for the mass of people condemned to the servitude of the conditions under which the worker often lives is growing every day, and the opposition, the painful, the unacceptable opposition reigning in so many different countries between the people and the Church of Jesus would then become an accepted fact.

If religious, impelled by the call of Jesus and sustained by everything the training and framework of the religious life can bring them, can find no means of striving towards the perfection of love in toiling like the workers, what will be the case with the workers themselves? And there are hundreds of millions of men in these circumstances!

Not one among us can entertain any doubt on the point. Nor is there any separating, in our line of vison, Jesus working at Nazareth and the immense mass of workers plodding under the weight of a daily drudgery too often made inhuman by other men's wills or some blind machine. We firmly believe that we can share their lot with all the love in us, and that we can carry them Jesus through our lives; we also trust that it will be made possible for them to attach themselves, through the Fraternities, to the Church. If we are to achieve this purpose, we must in all ways remain men of the Church, yet make ourselves true brothers to the workers both in heart and in lot.

Among the obstacles which would supposedly prevent us from making a life entirely consecrated to God out of a worker's life, are the *fatigue* involved, as ill disposing the mind for prayer, and the *limited time* left for prayer by the schedule of working hours. This is the kind of objection most often put forward by religious of the contemplative Orders, and I quite understand their point of view, because the trend of their religious life is all in the direction of separation, solitude and silence. Their souls are thus properly predisposed for contemplative prayer and made receptive to the particular action of the gifts of the Holy Spirit which is meant to go with that *form of prayer*. This latter is more especially a peaceful contemplation of the divine beauty and truth under the light of love. It does not therefore cover the whole ground of prayer; nor does it appear to be the kind of prayer which Jesus wishes from the Little Brothers, at least not as a rule. The kind of prayer to which we are specially committed by the character of our life is what I might call "redemptive prayer" and this, different as it may be in form from that of the cloistered religious, is nevertheless true and authentic prayer. Not only does it not take place with us within the same framework, it must be exercised under conditions which would seem to be the exact opposite to theirs. In other words, it more than often has to be offered in the fatigue and the pain and the difficulties of a life of poverty, which can also be a very busy one.

This self-injection of ours in suffering humankind is indicative enough of the way our prayer should come, and there should be no question of any mixing of forms in this respect. For the Carthusian or the Trappist, it is a duty to make their prayer a thing apart so it may be pure contemplation; the Little Brother, on the other hand, must carefully avoid acquiring the habit of separating his prayer from the share of human anguish which he bears within him. Rather must he take into his soul the prayer of mankind harnessed to its daily drudgery. Let it therefore be no surprise to you, Little Brothers, to find that your prayer, more often than not, must take the form of a painful straining, or an empty wait in darkness, or a thirst stretching up towards the Savior to be quenched, with an awareness of your insufficiencey and weakness at times so acute as to be an affliction to you. I do not believe that your vocation admits normally of your being given any form of prayer that you could stop and rest in. Your lot is bound up—and you have also willed it so—with the lot of your fellow men moving painfully towards the light. By exercising prayer of pure faith, you can secure for them that minimum of faith which they must needs have in order to turn their lives in God's direction; by the effort of hope by which your hearts at certain moments will be heavily lifted up to Jesus, you can succor those who despair; by a love which will be more of an unsated hunger to find Jesus or to possess Him more—by that cast of love which is more desire than repose in possession—you can obtain for mankind, bent towards the earth, that they shall desire, even though confusedly, Him who is all Love.

This is how the Holy Spirit will work in your hearts, and it is well that you should know what direction He will lead you in, so that you may avoid hampering His action and, at the same time, be more at ease in this kind of prayer. Here, as always, Jesus Himself is the model; and His more especial call to us is to live over the prayer that welled up in Him when, already tired from journeying on the hot, dusty roads, He would be so pressed by the crowd of the poor and the sick, so jostled and harried by them all with their beseechings, that He would even be unable to find time to eat—it is this prayer He wishes us to share with

Him, the kind that brought to His lips those words recorded by St. Mark, "I am moved with pity for the multitude; it is three days now since they have been in attendance upon me, and they have nothing to eat" (Mark 8:2); the kind that made Him take "pity on them, since they were like sheep that have no shepherd" (Mark 6:34); the kind that made Him cry out, ". . . and now my soul is distressed. What am I to say? I will say, Father, save me from undergoing this hour of trial . . ." (John 12:27).

It will likewise be the oppressed, blood-drawing prayer at Gethsemani, when Jesus, in agony, offered Himself to the Father with the piercing vision of men's misery before His eyes—that misery which you will elbow every day; which nothing should make you forget. It will also be the prayer that still kept burning, like the small, wavering flame of a night-lamp hidden under the thick, heavy, smothering mantle of His suffering body, as He dragged Himself over the stones with the crushing weight of the Cross on His back, and as He writhed in the last struggle upon it. Prayer in the peace and repose of contemplation was far away indeed (though it might, of course, have been otherwise, had it been otherwise willed) when Jesus came to the great act of His life, to the act that was to be the great proof of His love, to the act that saved the world.

What good reason could there be *for not consecrating a religious life more especially to allowing Jesus to live such prayer over again in us?* If we were to attempt to introduce into our life as Little Brothers a type of prayer like that of the Carthusian or the solitary, we should quickly become divided against ourselves; we should have wagered against the impossible. We have left behind, once for all, the conditions requisite to solitary contemplation, and this for love of our fellow men; nor has Jesus ever demanded that all who wish to follow Him should employ that form of prayer. What He has insistently urged, on the other hand, is perseverance up to continual prayer. The action of the Holy Spirit is quite many-sided enough to be able to give birth to, and then establish, in us a way of praying which will be both continual and pressing—the kind, I mean, that Jesus bids one to when He says one must pray "at all times," which is also the kind we promised to assume to the full extent of our generosity when we became Little Brothers. The Little Brothers' prayer, in other words, is to be no different in nature from that which Jesus asks of *all men*, all sinners; and we must seek to make ourselves perfect in it.

It is not Jesus' custom to mock the poor and the humble; anything He requires of us is always *possible* with His help. To help carry to the perfection of love the prayer of the publican, of the woman taken in adultery, of all the sick and the maimed and the blind that besieged Jesus day and night—such is the grace we must open our hearts to. Then our prayer will come straight from our lives and not from outside them. It is there, too, that it will find its nourishment, because we shall have learned to see all things *in faith*, with the eyes of the Lord Himself.

But while our participation in the toil and suffering of the world is our starting-point for a life entirely offered up in prayer, we should never be unmindful of the fact that our prayer must likewise be *adoration*, and adoration on behalf of the many. Our continual contact with people might well tend to make us forgetful of this. Regular exposition of the Blessed Sacrament, bringing one back as it does into the presence of Jesus sacrificed to the Father for all mankind; our night adoration, our days of monthly retreat, and the existence of the Adoration Fraternities will, however, keep us reminded of this other side of our vocation, and therefore of all our prayer must be; otherwise, we should be running the risk of forgetting that it is Jesus' desert to be loved and worshipped for Himself, to have time "wasted" on Him for His own sake, even while there are people weeping and suffering in the world.

This loss-of-time-for-love's-sake guise under which the pure act of prayer will sometimes come to us is also a means of verifying the quality of our faith in the divine transcendence and so purifying our relationships with others. In an atmosphere of materialism, where efficiency is fast becoming an absolute criterion of a man's worth, people will seldom understand this side of our lives, that seemingly "serves no good purpose" and "does nobody any good." There is a hidden source of temptation for us here, a temptation which, in the end, might lead to the weaking of our faith in the mystery of God without realizing it sufficiently.

Some of you may wonder whether our night adoration or our solitary retreats may not prove conducive to prayer like that of the cloistered religious. My answer would be this. Jesus is, of course, free to do as He likes, and can therefore pour contemplation into our souls in torrents, if He will. Yet it would hardly seem to me, even in that event, that our way of contemplating the mystery of God would ever be quite the same as that of the solitary contemplative. Our minds would very likely be too unaccustomed to abandoning themselves to that form of prayer, and our bodies too heavy with fatigue. The important thing for us is to let the Spirit of Jesus have His way, with all the generosity in us. It is Jesus' own silent adoration of the Father that must come into us through the Holy Eucharist. And since we shall not be able to leave behind the weight of other souls with their misery, our prayer will be more like what occurred with Jesus when, worn with fatigue, He would go up into a mountain to pray in secret, carrying with Him (how, indeed, could the Redeemer have done otherwise?) the whole load of the moral and physical sufferings He had seen displayed before Him in the course of the day.

Perhaps we shall thus reach a purer kind of adoration. Adoration is admiration of the supreme mystery of the Divinity, hidden in eternity. Jesus has shown us that that mystery is all one of love and mercy, for it was expressed in its entirety in the divine acts of the incarnation and the redemption. Adoration that comes from a heart completely open to its neighbor is therefore the truest and purest kind of adoration. It is none too easy to say exactly what I mean here and I must leave it to you to grasp it. But you may be sure that it all consists, whatever your prayer may be like at any time, in connecting it up with the Heart of Jesus and, when you have done all you can yourselves, opening up your emptiness to Him and letting Him fill it with His own prayer. The trouble, of course, is that we are so loath to admit our emptiness. We always want to have *something that is ours* to give. But perfection, even where prayer is concerned, lies in being able to accept one's indigence.

CHAPTER 5

"SAVIORS WITH JESUS"

When people inquire about our Fraternities I always find it awkward to answer clearly once they get on to the "What-kind-of-a-life-is-it?" and "What-are-your-activities?" and "What-sort-of-a-schedule-do-you-follow?" plane with their queries. This is all beside the question. I feel quite incapable of expressing the whole of our ideal in any formula; quite apart from the fact that, at first sight, our life appears in certain respects to be complex and inconsistent. For the Little Brother must be at one and the same time a worker and a man of prayer—a man of silence, who must also be alive and attentive to the cares and concerns of his brothers and his friends; a completely detached contemplative, but with a certain freedom of movement and a certain freedom in the use of things. These apparent contradictions must resolve themselves in the simplicity of the inner principle of our life. This, then, is the thing to be defined; the rest is only part of its consequences.

"I cannot conceive of love that feels no constraining need of resembling, of becoming like You, and especially sharing all the hurts and pains, all the difficulties, all the hardships of life. . . . I judge no one, Lord; the others are also your servants, and my brothers, and I must love them. . . . But it is impossible for me myself to understand how one can love You and not seek to resemble You, and not feel the need of sharing every cross." The call we have heard is this same call; and so it is that we have been led to choose Father de Foucauld as our guide. Loving our Lord, we wish to share His labor and His sufferings. Loving men, our brothers, we wish to share the life of the poor, of those who suffer, simply out of love. That is why we find, in actually carrying out our ideal, that we have equal need for prayer and detachment and for working with men in their weariness and their poverty.

We encounter difficulties, risks and conflicts in the undertaking. It could not be otherwise. So it behooves us to have a firm grasp upon the initial attitude which constantly underlie this kind of life. This attitude can be summed up by saying that, out of love for Christ, we must desire to share Christ's suffering. To be more precise, I mean the suffering of Christ *the Savior*; for all our suffering, and even that which comes from sharing other people's afflictions, thus becomes a continuation in us of Jesus' Passion. This orientation is something fundamental and, unless we possess it, I do not believe any one of us can either really understand the meaning of our life as Little Brothers or bear the weight of it.

"Jesus" means "God who saves," and the name is so dear to us—as it was to Father de Foucauld—for this reason. It expresses the whole of the reason for Christ's existence. He was indeed all "savior," nothing but "savior," through the Cross. We also have no other reason for our life as Little Brothers. But it is not written in the nature of our beings that we are to be saviors as it was with Jesus. This, moreover, is why it is so hard for us. Yet this vocation for sharing the redemptive suffering is something so essential that, if we were to recoil from giving ourselves up to it completely, our life would cease to be truthful.

So we must entertain no illusions as to what God will ask of us all though our lives. To this end, we can do no better than listen more attentively than we are ordinarily inclined to do to what Jesus replies to those who say that they wish sincerely to follow Him: "You do not know what it is you ask. Have you strength to drink of the cup I am to drink of, to be baptized with the baptism I am to be baptized with? They said to him, We have. And Jesus told them, You shall indeed drink of the cup I am to drink of . . ." (Mark 10:38). It is really their share in the sufferings with which He was to save the world, that Jesus promises His friends, and therefore His Little Brothers. Hence the thing for us to do is to grasp what Jesus demands here with all our faith and as concretely as we can, and then, fully aware of what we are doing, answer with unreserved, whole-hearted, resolute and confident assent.

Obviously, you are not expected to start out fully prepared and knowing to perfection how to take suffering. No one can know this until he has been taught by our Lord Himself, sometimes through the experience of an entire lifetime. Nor are you expected to say whether you are certain of being capable of it. We must simply have clearly understood the meaning of the Cross in our life, and have generously and gladly consented to let Jesus take us into His work with Him. We must be ready, in our souls, to accept suffering and to learn to comprehend its significance and to come little by little to love it.

The first temptation to come may be discouragement. Our daily experience has already shown us how weak we are before the slightest suffering. We are downcast over the slightest failure, held back by the slightest fatigue, sickened of praying by the slightest inner obstacle, wounded by the slightest lack of consideration. We likewise realize that these insufficiencies recur every day, and we ask ourselves how we can ever really succeed in sharing Jesus' Cross.

Considered from this angle, our problem would seem to be insoluble, and it is; and you must be thoroughly convinced that it is. Both the painful experience of your personal weakness and the things that happen to you every day will, moreover, see to it that this conviction is properly instilled into you. But if you *want* to love, you can come to desire with all your hearts that Jesus, through His love, shall make you capable of sharing His redemptive suffering. A true desire and a deep desire must come first; then you must tell Jesus so indefatigably, with the boldness of the sons of Zebedee and St. Peter. Then you must be humble enough, simple enough to abandon yourselves to Jesus with utter confidence and assurance that, by keeping yourselves united with Him, you will become capable, first, of enduring, and then of loving, the Cross. Lastly, you must go to work with all your will and cooperate with God in His action in your lives.

In all this—as always in the spiritual life—you must be simple, true, and straightforward. Place yourselves well under the light of honest truth. The object is not to picture yourselves as any braver or stronger than you are in face of physical or moral suffering. Neither is it to make yourselves think you **desire** heavier crosses or more difficult tests than you are actually capable of bearing. No more is it to imagine yourselves incapable of a braver effort than any you have so far made. It is mostly a matter of *willing* to start and making a very definite and joyful effort in any way accessible to you.

I say you must make a joyful effort. There are two reasons for this. First, God does not like one to give forlornly. You must give out of love for Jesus; and where there is real love of Jesus, there must be joy. Secondly, you must guard against taking your little difficulties and daily sufferings too seriously. I keep harping on these, because they are the very fabric of our lives. If we can succeed in turning into live crosses these things of every day which, though small in themselves, can become so heavy through constant repetition, we shall know how to embrace the bigger ones. Furthermore, we may sometimes be kept waiting a long while for the bigger crosses. Our courage might then turn out to be more imaginary than real, and our love, of a quality little different.

In order to avoid self-indulgent reversions, your offering in immolation should be made with your eyes fixed on Jesus' Cross and not your own. By getting away from yourselves, you will lighten your own sufferings (partly by forgetting them) and you can then really offer them up with greater freedom. For, you must always remember, it is not the suffering or the trouble itself that has the redemptive virtue, but the attitude of oblation in it, the love it arouses and the degree to which it is united with the Passion of Christ. The natural flow of our life as Little Brothers is for our inclusion, with all our personal sufferings, in the great current of Jesus' Passion and the passion of the world. This is the direction for us to look in.

"The Passion of Jesus," "the Cross of Jesus"—these are no doubt words which have lost much of their meaning, words which have become worn with use. We must rediscover the reality behind them in all its concreteness. Penetrating behind the sober wording of the Gospel, we must become alive to the horrible, brutally mathematical sufferings which Jesus endured to the ultimate depths of both body and soul. Against the humiliations, the insults, the contempt, the monstrous physical and mental pain, and the anguish and the agony suffered by Him whom we claim to love—the Son of God!—we must place our all too miserable little trials and difficulties. Between the Cross on which Jesus hung bleeding and our day of today, our lives at this moment, there is a living bond, an actual connection; and it is this that we must become more especially conscious of. Upon each moment in our days, there is some of Jesus' blood. It is there as an unassailable proof of love and a pledge of strength.

Then there is the mystery of all the suffering in the world, all the distress of mankind, which you will find more and more disconcerting. It must be viewed in the perspective of the Cross. But, first of all, be well aware of its existence; do not let yourselves turn aside. Be aware of it tangibly, concretely. You have plenty of opportunity to do so; it is all around you. Of this whole great passion of the world you must grasp the mystery and the meaning.

What weight can your days have against it? you may ask. Your personal suffering, you may be certain, amounts indeed to very little; it nevertheless becomes all-powerful if it serves as a bond between the Cross of Christ and this great—and often just formless and featureless—mass of human affliction. Insofar as the spirit of self-immolation in you is pure and full of courage and love, it causes a bit of the divine life to penetrate into this immense distress, plants the Cross of Jesus there; and thus, through you, with your help, it acquires a meaning: it becomes more a part of Jesus' Passion continuing in His Mystical Body.

So, do not cut yourselves off from what brings suffering to others, but never let yourselves be crushed by suffering. Be particularly careful to avoid the delusion that it is enough if you sympathize with your feelings. True communion in the suffering of Christ, and in that of our fellow men, is of another sort. Contradictory as this may seem, it should not breed depression or sadness but, on the contrary, the strength and peace which union with Christ always brings when it is real. No, no excessive emotion before suffering, whether it be yours or someone else's; no mere sensitivity, above all; that sort of feeling simply empties the soul of its strength, and prevents the real kind of love.

Nor must you yield to bitterness before the unbearable sight of other people's suffering, or its seeming unfairness, or when you see them rebel against it. Keep your souls in peace and gentleness. More especially still, do not allow your own sufferings, whatever their cause and however unwarranted you may think them, to arouse bitterness or resentment in you. You must be absolutely frank and loyal with yourselves on this point, and keep a perfectly open mind. Bitterness almost always comes from wounded self-esteem or from pride insufficiently subdued. Let us not be too quick either to lay responsibility for this kind of feeling at other people's doors or to accuse circumstances. Peace, together with the gentleness we must also have with ourselves, returns with humility and the spirit of childhood.

The true spirit of self-immolation presupposes that we behave towards suffering—again, both our own and that of others—as Jesus Himself behaved towards suffering. What is expected of us here is a *compassion,* a communion in the work of redemption, which is understandable only within the plans of God; and Christ alone—Christ as both God and man—can show us how to comprehend it and how to carry it as we must.

Only insofar as we allow Christ crucified really to live His own sentiments over again in us shall we be "saviors with Him." Such is the whole mystery of the Sacred Heart. To grasp the role which suffering plays in redemption, one must have an infinite sense of the mercy of God the Father, of His holiness and His justice, coupled with knowledge of the heart of man, and of his misery, and a strong and tender love for men. This can be found altogether only in the mind and heart of the Son of Man. We can obtain it, through prayer, if we desire it ardently enough, ask for it often enough, and make ourselves little enough to receive it. By displaying courage in bearing our trials and sharing those of others, we shall be beginning our apprenticeship for what God will little by little put in our hearts. Our prayer and our daily actions will thus come to meet in a single reality: our life with Jesus—Jesus crucified, Jesus suffering in His Mystical Body. Without such prayer, the spirit of self-immolation cannot descend into us, and we should merely be aping it out of presumption. Without the testing of our courage, our prayer would be liable to become illusory. It requires all this together to be able to participate in Jesus' work of redemption on the Cross.

I hope I have now made clear how absolutely fundamental it is for you to achieve this disposition to live in a *state* of self-immolation, and also how important it is that this disposition be healthy, truthful and sincere, and well-rooted in faith in Christ. Actually, it is subjacent to your prayer, to your work, and to the thousand and one things that happen to or around you every day. Turning all to use, it can transfigure all and cause all to fructify for the good of those we are called to love. Nothing in our days is then useless, nothing is without its meaning, and there are no more failures; or rather, failures, when they come, bear fruit. Remember that, from the human point of view, Christ's passion was a failure; so too were the life of Charles de Foucauld and the kind of death he met at Tamanrasset. Our own failures and limitations need not be excluded from a like transfiguration by love, provided they finish off in a hymn of humility and self-abandonment. It will take many a day to establish ourselves in this state of immolation, but the important thing is to begin working towards it at once.

Offering oneself thus to suffering out of love, which, as I have suggested, becomes little by little an habitual disposition when one combines one's efforts with the action of the Holy Spirit, is but a development of the quality of a victim stamped upon one's soul with baptism. We all know that one exercises this quality liturgically if one offers oneself really with Christ at the Mass. There is therefore no need for me to emphasize here the primary importance of the Eucharistic Sacrifice in our life as "saviors with Jesus."

The Mass does, however, enable us to accede to the maximum of this communion with Christ crucified and offering Himself, this communion of which our own life of self-immolation must become a day-long continuation. It is the Eucharistic Sacrifice itself—now no longer something exterior to us, for we are then actually integrated into it—that thus fructifies through us.

Living thus in the spirit of sacrifice for others, we shall also be making effective in our lives the mysterious bonds by which we are united to other men in the Mystical Body. The solidarity on the human plane which is affirming itself more and more today in the world of the workers, as also in connection with the organization of society, has a hidden but infinitely more real and fertile side to it: the solidarity of all men in Christ; and this we must really live. By putting ourselves in the midst of people with this spirit of complete spiritual solidarity and self-immolation and reparation, we shall therefore be giving our life as Little Brothers not only its proper outward appearance, but also its true meaning. Workers with the workers, Arabs with the Arabs, Colored with the Colored, Easterners with the Easterners, Westerners with the Westerners—this we are, or shall be, by a profound gift of self; and our "belonging" will express itself through our unreserved desire for the same destiny and the common suffering. So you can easily see how incomplete, how purely exterior our gift would remain in the end, unless it were carried to the point of spiritual substitution before God. *You must, then, actually succeed in offering yourselves for a ransom for your brother men.* There will be no imagination or vain desire about this. In the measure of your communion in the Passion, you will find a great reality embracing your entire lives—provided only that you have truly delivered yourselves up to Christ crucified, with no thought for yourselves.

May what I have now said help you to see better how you will be giving unity to your lives by establishing your souls in this state of self-immolation, how your lives will become one long single action turned in the direction of God, a single every-moment oblation. This is what makes the life of the Little Brother a true contemplative life, though a contemplative life with its own "coloring" to it, due to this particular spirit of reparation and redemption.

Karl Rahner
1904-

The task of the theologian in the twentieth century is a difficult and challenging one. His quest for the meaning of Christian reality must express fidelity to a tradition that has been developing for almost two thousand years. At the same time he must be equally faithful to the contemporary world of which he is child, to its knowledge explosion in the natural and behavioral sciences, to its many revolutions, to its philosophies. Today's theologian, while sustaining fidelity to both the traditional and the contemporary, must further have the capacity to communicate with the ordinary Christian.

Father Karl Rahner is all of this. He is known and respected throughout the professional theological world for the richness and originality of his insight, for his serious, reflective scholarship, and for his capacity to blend the foundational truths of Christianity with contemporary ideas and terminologies.

Everyday Faith is a collection of Father Rahner's conferences, articles, letters and lectures. The topics are arranged around the liturgical year. Our particular selections present his insights on Advent, Christmas and Easter, and on the theme of love. Several interesting elements in Father Rahner's thought, as contained in these selections, are worth observing.

Christianity is steeped in matter. In fact, properly understood, it is the most radical materialism. This is its glory, and its *confusion. By Incarnation God pours Himself totally into matter, becomes flesh. This is too human a way of salvation for many people and becomes a scandal, a stumbling block. But for anyone who is willing to be human, it is grace and truth. Neither the death of Christ nor His resurrection is a departure from the earth. Rather, by death Christ goes to the very center of matter, there to remain forever; by resurrection He transforms matter, assumes it unto Himself forever. Thus the Christian in no way flees from matter. On the contrary, he loves and rejoices in the earth.*

Christianity is optimistic about the human. "It must be worthwhile being a human being, if God was not satisfied to be in Himself but also willed in addition to be one of these human beings, and if that was not too dangerous or too trivial for him." There is no need to call for a superman. The human, as conceived by God, suffices. There is no room for bitterness or disillusion concerning the human, nor for wanting to be less than the brother of the eternal Word of the Father who became flesh.

Christianity is founded on love. The first commandment, love of God, is basic, simple, strange. It demands the gift of self, to which most will say no. Too often it is replaced by fear of God, which is much easier. But, without love of God, Christianity cannot be. Our knowledge and love of God are proportionate to our knowledge and love of the human. Love of neighbor is the fundamental act of human moral reality. Yet, to what degree is it possible in a predominantly secularized world?

Christianity is highly conditional. That is, all the grounding mysteries of Christianity are contingent upon the human for realization. Only if the human accepts the silent reality of God's presence; only if the human has the courage to be along, to bear with itself, to trust; only if the human is willing to be thoroughly human; only if the human will love unreservedly, unconditionally—can the great joy and glory that is Christianity be realized.

Father Rahner provides a firm theological structure for Christian spirituality. The reader will discover that his insights make the liturgical feasts more relevant to the everyday world and show how, through the ordinary events of life, one can grow into full Christian holiness.

EVERYDAY FAITH

THE YEAR OF THE LORD

ADVENT

The Stumbling-Block of the History of Redemption

Luke 3:1—6

The scandalous thing about Christianity, Christ himself and his Church will always be that they are historical. Precisely in the fifteenth year of the Emperor Tiberius, people think, precisely in Judaea and Galilee, precisely under the petty princes of those days, under a certain Pilate and under Annas and Caiaphas! Why did the salvation of all men not begin at the very beginning of all? Why not everywhere and always? Is the God of eternity, to whom all the world belongs, not equidistant from every place and time?

And yet it was then and there that the word of the Lord went forth to John and the decisive phase of the sacred history of redemption began. And so things have remained. People have to be baptized precisely with water, and nothing else will do. They have to have the word of forgiveness of sins spoken to them by a human mouth precisely on a Saturday afternoon in a wooden box—called a confessional—and not merely want to hear God's quiet voice in the voice of their own hearts. And the beauty of God's nature is not in fact the Church in which men find the body which once suffered on the Cross for us under Pontius Pilate. The words in the catechism and not the ideas in the empyrean of metaphysics are the truths by which people can live and die.

God himself can find man everywhere, where man inculpably and with a clear conscience cannot advance. And God in his mercy will do so liberally, without our having to arrange for it. But that does not prove that we can prescribe to him where we will be pleased to allow ourselves to be found by him. He can follow all ways; we, his creatures, only those which he has prescribed for us.

Now he *has* marked out certain definite ways of salvation for us. It is not the case that all our ways lead to God. He has marked out definite paths for us so that we may know and acknowledge that salvation is *his* grace, his free, gratuitous grace and not a right of our own, something he owes us. So that we may realize and acknowledge that he is not at our disposal but that we have to stand at his, that he is God and we his creatures. He has marked out definite ways of salvation for us because he himself—grace beyond all measure!—willed to walk them, because he himself willed to become a human being, caught like us in space and time and history from which in truth no human mind can extricate itself in this world. He himself was born under the Emperor Augustus, precisely in Nazareth from which no good can come, suffered under Pontius Pilate, imprisoned in the here and now, in the not-then and not-there of a real human being. Dear grace of a God who loves man. We do not need to seek God in his kingdom of infinity where after all we would hopelessly lose our way as though in a trackless void.

In fact Christianity is so human and so historical that it is too human for many people, who think that the true religion must be inhuman, i.e., not of the senses, non-historical. But the Word was made flesh. The word of the Lord went forth to John in the fifteenth year of the Emperor Tiberius. And so it has remained. Christianity is an historical and a very concrete and sturdy religion, a stumbling-block to the proud, who really—at least in religious matters—do not wish to be human beings, but it is grace and truth for those who with humble hearts are willing to be human beings in space and time even when they are adoring the God of eternity and infinity.

CHRISTMAS

The Answer of Silence

Letter to a friend

Christmas? One says the word almost with despair, for can one really explain to anyone nowadays what it means to cele-

brate Christmas? It is obvious that the feast is not merely the
Christmas tree, presents, family gatherings, and other emotionally appealing customs which are themselves only kept up with
a certain scepticism. But what more is it? Let me attempt to
give you something like a recipe.

The great experiences of life are of course one's destiny,
a gift of God and of his grace, but they nevertheless mostly
only fall to the lot of those who are prepared to receive them.
Otherwise the star rises above a man's life but he is blind to it.
For the sublime hours of wisdom, art and love, a man must
prepare himself wholly with soul and body. So it is with the
great days on which we celebrate our redemption. Do not leave
them to chance; do not drift into them listlessly in an everyday
frame of mind. Prepare yourself; determine to prepare yourself—that is the first thing.

Another thing. Have the courage to be alone. Only when
you have really achieved that, when you have done it in a
Christian way, can you hope to present a Christmas heart, that
is, a gentle, patient, courageous, delicately affectionate heart,
to those whom you are striving to love. That gift is the real
Christmas-tree gift, otherwise all other presents are merely
futile expense which can be indulged in at any time. First of
all, then, persevere for a while on your own. Perhaps you can
find a room where you can be on your own. Or you may know
a quiet path or a lonely church.

Then do not talk to yourself the way you do with others,
the people we argue and quarrel with even when they are not
there. Wait, listen, without expecting any unusual experience.
Do not pour yourself out in accusation, do no indulge yourself.
Allow yourself to meet yourself in silence. Perhaps then you
will have a terrible feeling. Perhaps you will realize how remote
all the people are whom you are dealing with every day and to
whom you are supposed to be bound by ties of love. Perhaps
you will perceive nothing but a sinister feeling of emptiness
and deadness.

Bear with yourself. You will discover how everything that
emerges in such silence is surrounded by an indefinable distance, permeated as it were by something that resembles a void.
Do not yet call it God! It is only what points to God and, by

its namelessness and limitlessness, intimates to us that God is something other than one more thing added to those we usually have to deal with. It makes us aware of God's presence, if we are still and do not flee in terror from the mystery which is present and prevails in the silence—do not flee even to the Christmas-tree or to the more tangible religious concepts which can kill religion.

But that is only the beginning, only the preparation of a Christmas celebration for you. If you persevere in this way and, by keeping silence, allow God to speak, this silence which cries out is strangely ambiguous. It is both fear of death and the promise of the infinity which is close to you in benediction. And these are too close together and too similar for us to be able of ourselves to interpret this infinity which is remote and yet close. But precisely in this strangeness and mystery we learn to understand ourselves rightly and to accept the dear familiarity of this strange mystery. And that is precisely the message of Christmas: that in reality God is close to you, just where you are, if you are open to this infinity. For then God's remoteness is at the same time his unfathomable presence, pervading all things.

He is there with tender affection. He says: Do not be afraid. He is within, in the prison. Trust to this close presence, it is not emptiness. Cast off, and you will find. Relinquish and you are rich. For in your interior experience you are no longer dependent on what is tangible and solid, what by affirming itself isolates itself, what can be held fast. You have not merely things of that kind, for infinity has become presence. *That* is how you must interpret your interior experience and in that way know it as the high festival of the divine descent of eternity into time, of infinity into the finite, of God's marriage with his creature. Such a festival takes place in you—the theologians aridly call it "grace": it takes place in you when you are still and wait and—believing, hoping and loving—interpret correctly, that is, in the light of Christmas, what it is you experience.

It is only this experience of the heart which brings proper understanding of the message of the Christmas faith: God has become man. Of course, we repeat that so easily. We think of the incarnation as though it were a sort of disguising of God, so that fundamentally God remains purely and simply God and we do not rightly know whether he is really here where we are. God is man—that does not mean he has ceased to be God in the measureless plenitude of his glory. Nor does it mean that what is human about him is something which does not really concern him and is only something assumed accessorily which says nothing really about him but only something about us. "God is man" really says something about God.

God's human nature must not be equated with God's divinity in total identity of kind nor yet simply be juxtaposed with God as a reality which perpetually relapses into its own mere identity. We must not link it with him merely verbally by an empty "and". If God shows this human nature of his, it always comes to us in such a way that *he himself* is there. Because we only juxtapose divinity and humanity in the incarnate Word of the Father, instead of understanding that they both spring from the one self-same ground, we are constantly in danger of missing each time the point where the blessed mystery of Christmas finds the place in our self-transcending human reality at which it fits into our life and our history as our salvation.

Do not forget that, as faith testifies, Jesus is true man, that is, one like you and me; a finite, free human being obediently accepting the unfathomable mystery of his being; one who must answer and does answer, who is questioned and hears the question, the question which is infinite and to which answer is only given in the ultimate act of the heart which surrenders itself lovingly and obediently to the infinite mystery, in an act in which acceptance takes place in virtue of the very reality which is accepted. That was the case also for him whose beginning you are going to celebrate. Because he accepted as a human being, you too can dare to do what he did: quietly and with faith to say "Father" to incomprehensibility, to accept it, not as deadly remoteness and consuming judgment on our wretchedness, but as measureless, merciful presence. For he is both God and man: giver, gift and reception, call and answer in one.

It would be good, then, if we were to call on the experience of our heart, in order to form some faint conception of what is meant by the incarnation of the eternal God. It would be well if this were to be done in that silence in which alone we are present to ourselves in self-awareness. Such silence, correctly understood in faith in the Christmas message, is an experience of what is infinite in man's reality, an experience of man's being which tells us something which is only so because God himself became man. We would experience ourselves differently if God had not been born man.

If we accept the silent tremendous reality which surrounds us like remote distance, yet close and overwhelming, if we accept it as saving presence and a tender unreserved love; if we have the courage to understand ourselves in a way which can only be done in grace and faith—whether this is realized or not— then we have had the Christmas experience of grace in faith. It is very simple but it is the peace which is promised in their goodwill to the men of God's good pleasure.

The Great Joy

Let us keep Christmas, a festival of faith and of love for the Word who became flesh, a festival also of love for one another because man can love man since God himself became man. Let us worship God because he loved man and his poor flesh so much that he placed it imperishably for all eternity in the very midst of the blazing flame of his Godhead. Incomprehensible God, adventurer of love! We had thought that man, pitiable as he is, could only be a primitive, unsuccessful trial-model for the superman who has still to come; it is hard for us to bear with ourselves—and especially with others—just as we are. Not unreasonably, for man is difficult to endure, for he is a continual failure and falls from one extreme to another.

And yet, as the Church sings in its noblest hymn, he did not disdain the Virgin's womb. He himself came into his creation, into humanity. If it were not for this fact of facts, would we have the courage to believe that God was successful with his work? He himself has entered into all the narrow limits of man which it would seem could only exist at an infinite distance from him: his mother's body, a small defeated native country under foreign occupation, a desperate state of the age, a narrow-minded milieu, unsuccessful politics, a body marked out for death, the prison of incomprehension, the monotony of the working day, of complete failure, the dark night of abandonment by God and of death. He spared himself nothing. The narrow confines, however, into which God himself has entered, must have an issue. It must be worthwhile being a human being, if God was not satisfied to be in himself but also willed in addition to be one of these human beings, and if that was not too dangerous or too trivial for him. Mankind is not a herd, but a sacred family, if God himself is a member of it as a brother. The tragedy of its history must after all have a blessed outcome, if God does not just observe this hardly divine comedy unmoved from the throne of his infinity but takes part in it himself, as seriously as all the rest of us, who have to do so whether we want to or not.

The so-called "genuine reality" both of the embittered and disillusioned and of the superficial "bon vivant" is reduced to a mere semblance which only unbelieving fools take in deadly earnest or with greedy seriousness, now that God himself has become the true reality behind and in the midst of this appearance. Eternity is already in the heart of time, life is at the centre of death, truth is stronger than lies, love more powerful than hatred, the wickedness of man already irrevocably conquered by God's grace. Christianity is indeed an optimism about man such as only God could conceive. It is not surprising that it seems so unlikely to us. There is no need for the superman if God himself became man. Mere humanism is long since obsolete if in the Son of the Father and of the Virgin man is to become God, as the Fathers say, if man is infinitely more than man. Man can be exacting; in fact, properly understood, he can never be demanding enough in regard to God; there is only one thing which he may not do: will to be less than the brother of the eternal Word of the Father who became flesh.

Up, then, and let us be kind at least on this day and this holy night. Perhaps we shall then see that it is not really so difficult, and then we shall also contrive to be so in the New Year too. Let us be kind! We have no right to demand a better world if we do not begin the improvement ourselves in our own heart. Let us be kind today! After all we do not have to be malicious and bitter and defend ourselves greedily and anxiously against others. God has come. No one can take him from us and he is everything. He is our brother. So it is right to bear in our own heart our brother's love of humanity and his kindness, to be gentle and forgiving, hopeful, serene and cheerful, unsuspicious and loyal. God himself has tried this and has told us that it works. His experience is more decisive and credible than ours: we can be better than we think. More can be made of us than we suspect. If Christ is formed in us, we can never form too high a conception of ourselves. We are more than we can imagine.

So let us sing with the gaiety of a heart which is set free for God's eternal youth. The darkness has become bright. God himself has prepared a festival for himself which did not exist before in his heaven: he has become man. Heaven and earth ring out in God's silent, holy night which is lighter than the gloomy day of men: Glory to God, peace to man in whom God was so well-pleased. Let us fall on our knees and joyfully read the Gospel: At that time a decree went forth from the Emperor Augustus . . .

EASTER

Beginning of Glory

If someone had already lit the fuse for a tremendous explosion, but was still waiting for the explosion which will follow with dreadful certainty, they certainly would not say that the lighting of the fuse was an event of the past. The beginning of an event which is still in course of development but is moving inexorably and irresistibly towards its culmination, is not past but is a kind of present, and already contains its future; it is a movement which continues by comprising past and present in a present real unity. These concepts must be clear if we are to attempt to say something meaningful about the Lord's resurrection.

Easter is not the celebration of a past event. The alleluia is not for what was; Easter proclaims a beginning which has already decided the remotest future. The resurrection means that the beginning of glory has already started. And what began in that way is in process of fulfilment. Does it take long? It lasts thousands of years because at least that short space of time is needed for an incalculable plenitude of reality and history to force itself through the brief death-agony of a gigantic transformation (which we call natural history and world history) to its glorious fulfilment. Everything is in movement. Nothing has an abiding place h'ere. We are gradually finding out, at least in outline, that nature has its own orientated history, that nature is in movement, that it develops and unfolds in time and by an incomprehensible self-transcendence behind which there stands the creative power of God, attains ever higher levels of reality. We are gradually realizing that human history has its purposeful course and is not merely the eternal return of the identical ("there is nothing new under the sun"), that the nations are summoned in a certain sequence and have each their definite historical mission; that history in its totality has its pattern and an irreversible direction.

But what is the goal of this whole movement in nature, history and spirit? Is everything advancing towards a collapse, to meaninglessness and nothingness? Are we only going to lose our way? Is what happens ultimately only the demonstration of the emptiness and hollowness of all things, which are unmasked in the course of the history of nature and the world? Are all the comedies and tragedies of this history mere play-acting which can only deludedly be taken seriously while they are still going on and are not yet played out?

How far has this history already advanced? Has its meaning already emerged in this game of limitless scope? Has the ultimate, all-decisive keyword already been spoken which gave all that came earlier its meaning, and already clearly contains the outcome of the whole drama?

We Christians say that this whole history of nature and mankind has a meaning, a blessed and transfigured, all-embracing meaning, no longer mixed with meaninglessness and darkness, a meaning which is infinite reality and unity comprising all possibilities and glory in one. And when we invoke the absolute meaning in this way, we call it God. God as he is in himself is the goal of all history. He himself is at hand. All the streams of change in us flow towards him; they are not lost in the bottomless void of nothingness and meaninglessness. But when we say this, when we declare infinity to be the meaning of the finite, eternity the meaning of time and God himself (by grace) to be the purpose of his creature, we are not speaking simply of a distant, not yet wholly realized ideal, which we hope vaguely may be realized one day but which for the moment and for an incalculable time is still a distant future existing only in thought.

No, we say Easter, resurrection. That means, it has already begun, the definitive future has already started. The transfiguration of the world is no ideal, no postulate, but a reality. The history of nature with all its developments and self-transcendence has already—though for the moment only in its first exemplar—reached its unsurpassable culmination: material reality which, wholly transfigured, is for eternity the glorious body of God. The most tremendous and definitive self-transcendence of the material world (through the grace-given power of God alone of course) has already taken place. It has leapt beyond itself into the infinity of God's spirituality and, in this upward flight into God's immeasurable flame, it has not been consumed but has survived, definitively transfigured.

If we thought about it correctly, we Christians would really have to say that we, not the others, are the most radical materialists, for we say that God's pure and substantial self-utterance (the divine Word of God) has a true body for all eternity. The history of humanity, so we say when we celebrate Easter, has already reached its goal in a representative or, rather, in *the* representative of this whole history (in him and through him for the others). And this has happened where not simply spirit and glorified soul, but the one human being in his totality who acted and suffered this history of his, attained perfect fulfilment, where everything abides, nothing is lost and everything is disclosed as meaningful and glorious. This end which is the beginning of the fulfilment of all things, has arrived and has manifested itself to humanity still advancing through history just as the front of a procession which has reached the goal calls back with cries of triumph to those still marching: We are there, we have found the goal and it is what we hoped it would be.

The place at which such a beginning of the end and completion has appeared is called Jesus of Nazareth, crucified and risen. Because his tomb is empty, because he who was dead has shown himself to be living in the unity of his whole concrete humanity, we know that everything has already really begun to be well. Almost everything is still on the way. But on the way to a goal which is not a utopian ideal but an already existent reality.

Man likes to give half answers. He likes to escape to where he does not have to make a clear decision. That is understandable. We are travellers and consequently in a condition in which everything, meaning and meaninglessness, death and life, is still mixed together, half finished, incomplete. But it cannot remain so. It is moving on. And the end cannot be other than clear and plain. Consequently reality compels us, whether we wish or not, to give a plain answer in our own lives. And so the question is put to us: Death or life? Meaning or meaninglessness? Ideals which are nebulously inconclusive or real facts? If by faith and action we plainly decide for meaning and life as facts, and consider life and death as mere *ideals* to be inadequate, if we affirm life and meaning as a fact, not half-heartedly but whole-heartedly in endless magnitude and scope, then whether we know it or not we have said Easter. And we Christians know this. We know that the reality of Easter is not simply the essence hidden in the depth of our life but is the truth and reality of our faith called by its name and explicitly professed. And so we comprise the whole history of nature and of mankind in a celebration which in rite contains the actual reality celebrated, and we make the ultimate statement about it: I believe in the resurrection of the body (flesh) and life everlasting. I believe that the beginning of the glory of all things has already come upon us, that we, apparently so lost, wandering and seeking far away, are already encompassed by infinite blessedness. For the end has already begun. And it is glory.

A Faith that Loves the Earth

It is difficult in well-worn human words to do justice to the joy of Easter. Not simply because all the mysteries of the

Gospel have difficulty in penetrating the narrow limits of our being and because it is even more difficult for our language to contain them. The message of Easter is the most human news brought by Christianity. That is why we have most difficulty in understanding it. It is most difficult to be, do and believe what is truest, closest and easiest. For we men of today live by the tacitly assumed and therefore to us all the more self-evident prejudice that what is religious is purely a matter of the innermost heart and the highest point of the mind, something which we have to do for ourselves alone and which therefore has the difficulty and unreality of the thoughts and moods of the heart. But Easter says that God has done something. God himself. And his action has not merely lightly touched the heart of some human being here and there, so that it trembles at the inexpressible and nameless. God has raised his Son from the dead. God has called the flesh to life. He has conquered death. He has done something and triumphed where it is not at all a question merely of interior sensibility but where, despite all our praise of the mind, we are most really ourselves, in the reality of the earth, far from all that is purely thought and feeling, where we learn what we are—mortal children of the earth.

We are children of this earth. Birth and death, body and earth, bread and wine—such is our life. The earth is our home. Certainly, for all this to be so and to be splendid, mind has to be mingled with it like a secret essence, the delicate, sensitive, perceptive mind which gazes into the infinite, and the soul which makes everything living and light. But mind and soul have to be *there*, where we are, on the earth and in the body. They have to be there as the eternal radiance of earthly things, not like a pilgrim who, not understood and himself an alien, wanders once like a ghost across the world's stage in a brief episode. We are too much the children of this earth to want to emigrate from it for ever one day. And even if heaven has to bestow itself for earth to be endurable, it has itself to come down and stand over this abiding earth as a light of blessedness and itself break forth as radiance from the dark bosom of the earth.

Karl Rahner

We belong here. We cannot become unfaithful to the earth, not out of autocratic self-will, which would not suit the sons of serious, humble mother-earth, but because we must be what we are. But we suffer from a secret and mortal sorrow which lodges in the very centre of our earthly nature. The earth, our great mother, is itself in distress. It groans under its transitoriness. Its most joyful festivities suddenly resemble the beginning of funeral rites and when we hear its laughter we tremble in case in a moment tears will be mingled with it. The earth bears children who die, who are too weak to live for ever and who have too much mind to be able entirely to renounce eternal joy. Unlike the beasts of the earth, they see the end before it is there and they are not compassionately spared conscious experience of that end. The earth bears children whose hearts know no limits, and what the earth gives them is too beautiful for them to despise and too poor to enrich them, the insatiable. And because the earth is the scene of this unhappy discord between the great promise which haunts them and the meagre gift which does not satisfy them, the earth becomes a fertile source of its children's guilt, for they try to tear more from the earth than it can rightly give. It can complain that it itself became so inharmonious through the primordial sin of the first man on earth, whom we call Adam. But that does not alter the fact that the earth is now an unhappy mother, too living and too beautiful to be able to send its children away even to conquer a new home of eternal life in another world, and too poor to give them as fulfilment what it has contributed to give them as longing. And because the earth is always both life and death, it mostly brings neither, and the sad mixture of life and death, exultation and lament, creative action and monotonous servitude is what we call our everyday life. And so we are here on the earth, our home, and yet it is not enough. The adventure of emigrating from what is earthly won't do, not out of cowardice but out of a fidelity imposed on us by our own nature.

What are we to do? Listen to the message of the resurrection of the Lord. Has Christ the Lord risen from the dead or not? We believe in his resurrection and so we confess: he died, descended into the realm of the dead and rose again the third day. But what does that mean, and why is it a blessing for the children of the earth?

The Son of the Father has died, he who is the Son of man. He who is at once the eternal plenitude of the godhead, self-sufficient, limitless and blessed as Word of the Father before all ages *and* the child of this earth as son of his blessed mother. He who is both the son of God's plenitude and the child of earth's need, has died. But the fact that he died does not mean (as in a really un-Christian way we "spirituals" short-sightedly think) that his spirit and soul, the vessel of his eternal godhead have freed themselves from the world and the earth, and as it were fled into the immensity of God's glory beyond the world because the body which bound them to the earth was shattered in death and because the murderous earth showed that the child of eternal light could find no home in its darkness. We say "died" and immediately add "descended into the realm of the dead and rose again". And this gives the "died" quite a different sense from the world-forsaking sense which we are tempted to attribute to death. Jesus himself said that he would descend into the heart of the earth (Mt 12:40), that is, into the heart of all earthly things where everything is linked into one and where in the midst of that unity death and futility sit. In death he descended there. By a holy ruse of eternal life he allowed himself to be overcome by death, allowed death to swallow him into the innermost centre of the world so that, having descended to the primordial forces and the radical unity of the world, he might establish his divine life in it for ever. Because he died, he belongs in very truth to this earth. For although the man—the soul, as we say—enters in death into direct relation to God, it is only when the body of a man is laid in the earth that he enters into definitive unity with that mysterious single basis in which all spatiotemporal things are linked and in which they have as it were the root of their life. The Lord descended into death into this lowest and deepest of all the visible creation. He is there now, and not futility and death. In death he became the heart of the earthly world, divine heart in the very heart and centre of the world where this, prior even to its unfolding in space and time, sinks its roots into God's omnipotence. It was from this one heart of all earthly things in which fulfilled unity and nothingness could no longer be distinguished and from which their whole destiny derived, that he rose. And he did not rise in order finally to depart from hence, not so that the travail of death which gave birth to him anew might transfer him to the life and light of God and he would leave behind him the dark bosom of the earth empty and without hope. For he rose again in his *body*. That means he has already begun to transform this world into himself. He has accepted the world for ever. He has been born again as a child of the earth, but of the transfigured, liberated earth, the earth which in him is eternally confirmed and eternally redeemed from death and futility. He rose, not to show that he was leaving the tomb of the earth once and for all, but in order to demonstrate that precisely that tomb of the dead—the body and the earth—has finally changed into the glorious, immeasurable house of the living God and of the God-filled soul of the Son. He did not go forth from the dwelling-place of earth by rising from the dead. For he still possesses, of course, definitively and transfigured, his body, which is a piece of the earth, a piece which still belongs to it as a part of its reality and its destiny. He rose again to reveal that through his death the life of freedom and beatitude remains established for ever within the narrow limits and sorrow of the earth, in the depth of its heart.

What we call his resurrection and unthinkingly regard as his own personal destiny, is simply, on the surface of reality as a whole, the first symptom in experience of the fact that behind so-called experience (which we take so seriously) everything has already become different in the true and decisive depth of all things. His resurrection is like the first eruption of a volcano which shows that in the interior of the world God's fire is already burning, and this will bring everything to blessed ardour in his light. He has risen to show that that has already begun. Already from the heart of the world into which he descended in death, the new forces of a transfigured earth are at work. Already in the innermost centre of all reality, futility, sin and death are vanquished and all that is needed is the short space of time which we call history *post Christum natum*, until everywhere and not only in the body of Jesus what has really already begun will be manifest. Because he did not begin to save and transfigure the world with the superficial symptoms but started with its innermost root, we creatures of the surface think that nothing has happened. Because the waters of suffering and guilt are still flowing where *we* are standing, we think the deep sources from which they spring have not yet dried up. Because wickedness is still inscribing its runes on the face of the earth, we conclude that in the deepest heart of reality love is extinct. But all that is merely appearance, the appearance which we take to be the reality of life.

He has risen because in death he conquered and redeemed for ever the innermost centre of all earthly reality. And having risen, he has held fast to it. And so he has remained. When we confess him as having ascended to God's heaven, that is only another expression for the fact that he withdraws from us for a while the tangible manifestation of his glorified humanity and above all that there is no longer any abyss between God and the world. Christ is already in the midst of all the poor things of this earth, which we cannot leave because it is our mother. He is in the wordless expectation of all creatures which without knowing it, wait to share in the glorification of his body. He is in the history of the earth, the blind course of which in all victories and all breakdowns is moving with uncanny precision towards his day, the day on which his glory, transforming all things, will break forth from its own depths. He is in all tears and in all death as hidden rejoicing and as the life which triumphs by appearing to die. He is in the beggar to whom we give, as the secret wealth which accrues to the donor. He is in the pitiful defeats of his servants, as the victory which is God's alone. He is in our powerlessness as the power which can allow itself to seem weak, because it is unconquerable. He is even in the midst of sin as the mercy of eternal love patient and willing to the end. He is there as the most secret law and the innermost essence of all things which still triumphs and prevails even when all order and structure seems to be disintegrating. He is with us like the light of day and the air which we do not notice, like the hidden law of a movement which we do not grasp, because the part which we ourselves experience is too short for us to discern the formula of the movement. But he is there, the heart of this earthly world and the secret seal of its eternal validity.

Consequently we children of this earth may love it, must love it. Even where it is fearful and afflicts us with its distress and mortal destiny. For since he has entered into it for ever by his death and resurrection, its misery is merely temporary and simply a test of our faith in its innermost mystery, which is the risen Christ. That this is the secret meaning of its distress is not our experience. Indeed it is not. It is our faith. The blessed faith which defies all experience. The faith which can love the earth because it is the "body" of the risen Christ or is becoming it. We therefore do not need to leave it. For God's life dwells in it. If we seek the God of infinity (and how could we fail to?) *and* the familiar earth as it is and as it is to become, in order to be our eternal home in freedom, then one way leads to both. For in the Lord's resurrection God has shown that he has taken the earth to himself for ever. *Caro cardo salutis*, said one of the ancient Fathers of the Church with an untranslatable play on words: the flesh is the hinge of salvation. The reality beyond all the distress of sin and death is not up yonder; it has come down and dwells in the innermost reality of our flesh. The sublimest religious sentiment of flight from the world would not bring the God of our life and of the salvation of this earth down from the remoteness of his eternity and would not reach him in that other world of his. But he has come to us himself. He has transformed what we are and what despite everything we still tend to regard as the gloomy earthly residue of our spiritual nature: the flesh. Since then mother earth has only borne children who are transformed. For his resurrection is the beginning of the resurrection of all flesh.

One thing is needed, it is true, for his action, which we can never undo, to become the benediction of our human reality. He must break open the tomb of our hearts. He must rise from the centre of our being also, where he is present as power and as promise. There he is still in movement. There it is still Holy Saturday until the last day which will be the universal Easter of the cosmos. And that resurrection takes place under the freedom of our faith. Even so it is *his* deed. But an action of his which takes place as our own, as an action of loving belief which takes us up into the tremendous movement of all earthly reality towards its own glory, which has begun in Christ's resurrection.

LOVE OF GOD AND THE NEIGHBOUR
The First Commandment
Matthew 23:34—40

A lot is said and written nowadays about love of one's neighbour. By pagans who have salvaged it from Christianity, for it is not an inheritance of their own. By Christians, for even if very little is practised, at least it has to be talked about. This is very right and proper. For it has to be preached and we have to be admonished, threatened, warned. There cannot be too much talk about love of the neighbour, provided of course that talk is not a mere pretext for doing nothing. But we must not forget all the same what we read in today's gospel: the *first* commandment is love of God. Love for *him* with all our heart, with all our soul and with all our mind. A "decent life" is no substitute for this love, nor is love of the neighbour, philanthropy or social justice. All these things are also necessary. But they are not love of God. And this is required of us—that great, living and heartfelt love which is so much the first and unique commandment, that we have to forget we are fulfilling a precept by it, and love not because it is commanded but simply because God is God.

This strange commandment does not demand a particular measurable performance, so that if we had achieved this we should have fulfilled our obligation. Love demands our very heart, what is innermost and ultimate in us, ourselves. But we will give anything away rather than ourselves; everything can be measured and filled except the heart. And this has to give itself to God for ever and without limit. Do we love God like that? Do we love him as someone who loves, who is near and faithful, who asks for our love by offering us his own heart and his own eternal love? Or is God for us only the name of a supreme world rule, thought of in an extremely impersonal way, which one respects, with which one may come into conflict, which one really only wishes to avoid by fulfilling the commandments? To fear God is almost easier than truly to love him. But precisely this love is an obligation laid on us, so much so that without this love all fear of God—would we at least had it!—would be of no avail to us. For damnation is ultimately only the despairing incapacity to love God.

Our heart is so inert and tired. It is worn out with everyday things. And God is so far away. So it seems to us, the spiritually blind and lame. Consequently our heart feels it cannot love. When love is preached to it, it remains dumb, unmoved, stubborn, and even "good will" seems incapable of commanding the heart to love. No, of ourselves we have not got the love which the first commandment speaks. Only he who demands it of us can give it to us. And so we will at least seek this love from him. We will pray for this love. If the first commandment is love of God, the first of prayers is to ask for this love. We must pray for this love. For God himself must pour out this love in our hearts by his Holy Spirit. He must give the life, light and strength of this love. He must himself love himself in us and through us in his Holy Spirit, for our love to be worthy of him.

Humble alarm at our lovelessness in regard to God is the God-effected beginning of our love. Prayer for love of God, a prayer which protests against our heart's secret and unavowed aversion from God, is our beginning of love of God and we can always make this by his grace, which is always offered to us. We have often recited in Church the formula by which the three theological virtues are "revived" (as the phrase goes). But it is to be hoped that we have also already prayed from the depth of our heart for the love which only God himself can give, although he has commanded it of us in that commandment which always remains the first. God hears such a prayer. For he has promised it to us in his most truthful word. For our part we should believe him rather than our own heart. If it prays for love, it loves, even if the poor heart feels little more than sorrow at still having fulfilled so little the first of all commandments.

The New, Single Precept of Love

We shall be concerned here with the unity of love of the neighbour and love of God. Are they simply two things side by side, linked in some way by God's commandment, so that God is in fact loved, as he wills to be, if his commandment to love the neighbour is also respected and carried out as far as possible? Or are the two things more closely connected? It might of course, be thought that God has commanded all kinds of things and that he regards as it were the fulfilment of these various precepts as a touchstone and concrete effect of what in the last resort is his sole will, namely, that man should love him, the eternal God, from his innermost centre, with his whole heart and strength. But fundamentally that is not so. The love of God and the neighbour form a much greater unity than they appear to have in the common view of them. We shall submit this to a little reflection.

In addition to the fundamental gravity of the theme, special importance also attaches to it, I think, from the situation at the present time. It is a fact, and as Christians we should be deceiving ourselves if we tried to ignore it, that people today have considerable difficulties in the question of God. The world seems to have become as it were opaque and solid. The relation to God, the living, eternal God transcending the world, is no longer as easy as in times when people to some extent had the impression, perhaps ultimately without any real right, that the mysterious rule of God can be directly grasped everywhere in his world.

People today live in a secularized world. In the present context we need not consider how far this situation has a positive significance despite its danger. Now why and to what extent and within what limits the henceforth secularized world is an element in the destiny of the Christian which was to be expected and can be regarded in a positive light as an opportunity for a genuine relation to God and for genuine Christian life. At all events, in the concrete the present situation is such (if I may briefly summarize what is in question here) that only where, and to the extent that, a man has a genuine, loving and really heartfelt relationship with his fellow-men, does he find God and can he convince other men that this reality which we call God exists. All merely theoretical talk on the subject, all worship even, everything explicitly religious would no longer appear credible to people today unless it were based on, comprised in and attested by genuine love, and that means love between human beings. People today have an almost radical need, I should say, to demythologize everything, to tear down all facades, abolish all taboos, and to ask what is left if we drop all pronouncements and demolish all ideologies. There really only remains one thing then, that we can only live if we love one another, if this love is genuine. Perhaps the actual human being of today does not achieve this love, but he knows he is under an obligation to do so. On the whole he will be ready to acknowledge this obligation, this love, even today as what is genuine, enduring, and not simply ideological, as something which is not merely a topic for pious or sublime speeches at meetings but as something that is a necessity of life like business and food. If we Christians did not know that this love which survives all demythologizing and abolition of taboos, in reality comprises the whole of Christianity, though hidden as in a seed which has to develop and come to blossom, I do not think that in our present situation we should be equipped really to understand our Christianity. We could not bear witness to it even today as the sustaining power which perpetually revives to new life. That is the up-to-date reason why it is meaningful, I think, to say something about the unity of love of God and the neighbour.

This theme is already found, of course, in scripture. There it is said that there are two commandments of which the second, Jesus Christ says, is like the first. One commandment of love of God and the neighbour. Paul says that this love is the bond of perfection; he is speaking of love of the neighbour when he says that anyone who has it has fulfilled the Law as such. And he says that this love is the genuine, better way. At the same time he warns us that this love and external outward help, though they belong together, are not the same. For if I were to give away all I have to the poor and delivered my body to be burned, but had not charity, I should be nothing. He does not mean that some feeling or interior disposition is everything. For that interior disposition has to find expression in the activity of life, in the real practice of love, otherwise it is all empty talk and for all our feelings we should be nothing but sounding brass and tinkling cymbal. And yet we see what very radical significance Paul attributes to the innermost nature of this love of the neighbour, when he says that it is the fulfilment of the Law, the bond of perfection.

All this, however, is far from self-evident and a matter of course. If I may so express it, though this would certainly be paradoxical and exaggerated, it almost looks as though Paul were not thinking of God at all, but were actually working out an atheistic ethics of Christianity.

How is the Law fulfilled if I have loved my neighbour? How is this love not merely a part, but the bond of perfection? How is it that on this love the whole of the Law and the prophets depends?—the Lord says this. For in that case surely the love of the neighbour would itself have to contain everything else, including precisely what is everything, what is ultimate and decisive: that God must be loved. If for the moment we leave John out of account, scripture does not actually tell us how it is that there are not merely two commandments, similar to one another, perhaps equally important and linked in some way, but that one is contained in the other. We might perhaps understand quite well that we only love God if we also love our neighbour. But with Paul it is clearly the case that if we love our neighbour we already love God.

How is that possible? John in his first letter perhaps takes us a little farther by asking how we can love the God whom we do not see if we do not love the brother whom we do see. Of course it may be said that that is a simple and obvious argument which really amounts to nothing more than: If you do not love the neighbour whom you have concretely and practically there in your life, how little you will succeed in loving the invisible God who is so remote from your immediate circle. But clearly John means even more, for in the fourth chapter of the First Letter of John we find the remarkable statement that God abides in us. And clearly this also contributes to make it possible that we already love God if we really love our neighbour with absolutely genuine personal commitment. And so this thesis—to express it in theoretical, pedagogical terms—amounts to this: love of God and love of the neighbour are mutually inclusive; when man acts with real unselfishness, commits himself absolutely, with real renunciation of his freedom in relation to the other human partner, and thus really performs what is meant by love of the neighbour, he already loves God. And this is so even if he does not explicitly know this, or tell himself it is so, even if he would not make God as such in explicit concepts a motive for love of his neighbour. The thesis means that by really loving his neighbour, man as it were falls or penetrates into the ultimate realities of created reality and, even if he does not explicitly say so, is really mysteriously concerned in this love with the God of his eternal, supernatural salvation. How is it possible to maintain such a thesis?

In the first place we may refer to scholastic theology. This speaks of three theological virtues, that is, three modes of human activity in which, supported by the Holy Spirit, by the Spirit of God in the depths of his own heart, man is concerned no longer simply with the realities of the world but directly with God. Three fundamental modes of man's ultimate orientation towards the God of eternal life himself in his own glory and independence of the world, so that we all become really and directly the partners of God himself. Faith, hope and love are the fundamental acts of man, in which he has dealings with God, the triune God of eternal life. And these three alone, as Paul says, remain.

Now theology says that by this divine fundamental power of charity, in which faith and hope are already comprised and integrated, the neighbour also can and must be loved. If we as Christians really love our neighbour in a way conducive to salvation, we are not merely fulfilling one or other of God's commandments which we fulfil with his help. There actually takes place that ultimate, and really the only, eternal occurrence in our life, in which man truly comes directly to God himself.

When we love our neighbour in supernatural love of God, there takes place, and strictly speaking nowhere else, salvation, justification, divine life, eternity. There is no doubt in Catholic theology that there is such a divine virtue in which man finds his neighbour in the ultimate depth of his own being. And once again, it is not merely a question of the fact that because one loves God one regards the rest of his creatures with a certain goodwill and avoids transgressing the precepts of the beloved God in regard to these other human creatures. In genuine supernatural love of the neighbour, love of God is accomplished by the power of God himself.

Now it might be thought that by saying this in accordance with Catholic theology, we have already reached the point aimed at. Yet that is not quite the case. Of course, when someone loves his neighbour's very self with the consciousness of faith and from the motive of divine love of God himself it is clear from what has been said that *caritas*, the divine virtue of love of God, is accomplished. Catholic theology has been in agreement on this for centuries as a matter of course, and expounds it more or less as we have just briefly indicated. I should like, however, to try to carry the radical character of this thesis somewhat further.

I should like to say that where man really abandons himself and loves his neighbour with absolute selflessness, he has already come to the silent, inexpressible mystery of God and that such an act is already based on that divine self-communication which we call grace and which gives the act of which it is the ground its saving meaning and importance for eternity.

We may raise the question from quite a different angle. We meet many people who are not professedly Christians and do not even wish to be. Let us assume that such a person were really to love with ultimate radical selflessness his neighbour, the brother whom he sees. Then what has actually happened? Only a very good deed worthy of recognition but to which ultimately the most important thing is lacking? Or is there already present there an ultimate relation to God which ought indeed to develop and as it were receive its name, which still has to be measured and named in its ultimate, inexpressible but real dimensions in relation to God, but which is nevertheless already there? This is precisely what I mean when I say that the love of God, charity, is always and everywhere present in that ultimate, genuine, radical love of the neighbour in which a man really engages himself and the ultimate strength of his being and gives himself. Not, of course, because the natural structure of such an act necessarily entails this, but because we live under the universal saving will of God. We live in a world which always and everywhere is directed by the secret grace of God towards the eternal life of God, always and everywhere where a man does not expressly shut himself off by really culpable unbelief from this innermost supernatural, grace-given dynamism of the world.

Now an act of love of the neighbour is not simply one moral action among others, but basically it is the fundamental act of human moral reality, of man himself. Cognition is immanent presence to self, and freedom is ultimately free, personal, deliberately final and definitive disposition over oneself.

Both of these, however, can only take place in loving communication with a personal partner. For man, as a spiritual, personal subject, the world is primarily the human world around him. We do not simply live in an environment in which every imaginable kind of thing exists. That world has an inner structure deriving from the human subject and from the reality which man encounters. Ultimately it is a communication by love with another human person. The whole world of things with which we have to deal, even in economic life, society etc., is fundamentally only the material, the condition and the consequence of loving communication with other persons. Man disposes over himself in radical freedom productive of eternal consequences, and this self-disposal in the last resort is simply either the loving openness in regard to the human partner or a final self-closing in egoism, which throws man into the damning, deadly isolation of the lost. This fundamental act is of course only possible because man is dynamically oriented towards the absolute of reality, that is, because in fact in a non-explicit, unanalysed way he has to do with God. For we do not begin to have something to do with God only when we explicitly invoke him or when we expressly name and profess this mystery towards which we are always moving and which alone bestows the possibility of spiritual freedom and love. Always and everywhere in the activity of cognition and most certainly in that of love, we have to do with God in an implicit way. And if a human being in the fundamental act which actualizes his human reality, adopts an attitude of love towards his fellow-men, then this fundamental act of his life, through the universal divinizing saving will of God which is everywhere at work even outside the Church, is supported by God's Holy Spirit and his grace and at least implicitly and tacitly but really, is at the same time an act of charity, of the love of God.

In a more precise description of what love of the neighbour means, we should of course have to show how in reality it always approaches the mystery of God even if it does not expressly wish or intend to. If we are silent, if we forgive, if without reward we give ourselves wholeheartedly and are detached from ourselves, we are reaching out into a limitlessness which exceeds any assignable bounds and which is nameless. We are reaching out towards the holy mystery which pervades and is the ground of our life. We are dealing with God. And something of this kind happens necessarily and always in the act of loving freedom of real, radical personal communication with one's neighbour. Consequently in the present order of God's saving will, this is always based on God's grace; it is charity.

Whenever a human being in real personal freedom opens his heart to his neighbour, he has already by that very fact done more than simply loved that neighbour, because all that was already encompassed by the grace of God. He has loved his neighbour and in his neighbour he has already loved God. Because he cannot meet his neighbour with love except through the fact that the dynamism of his spiritual freedom supported by the grace of God is already itself always a dynamism towards the unutterable holy mystery which we call God.

This does not mean that love between human beings just as it is usually found is equated with the Christian's explicit love in faith and hope. All we are saying is that genuine love of God is already exercised in it. But this must of course become conscious. It must be such that the goal towards which this love always tends is expressly invoked, named, known, honoured in explicit faith, explicit hope and explicit love. The human love which in its innermost nature is already by God's grace a love of God, must also become explicit love for God who is named, explicitly invoked, religiously sought. This inner dynamism of development is implanted in all love by the grace of God. It has the duty to develop into the explicit specifically Christian character of divine charity. Conversely, it is true for the same reason that this explicit love of God, of the God who is named, although he is not seen, is already intrinsically present in the love of the brother whom we do see. Now it is a fact that there are many people who are redeemed, justified and sanctified by God's grace, although they do not know this. It is also the case that what we as Christians believe, hope and thankfully proclaim of ourselves, is something which is present as an offer in all human beings through God's supernatural, free, unmerited grace. In fact of course, it can also be present as accepted even though many think they are not Christians and not believers. In the depth of their being they can nevertheless be so, and particularly if they really succeed wholeheartedly and with utter unselfishness in loving the brother whom they see. Whether they do this, we of course do not know. We actually do not know it about ourselves either. We of course endeavour in our activity and our lives to love God and our neighbour and both in one. God's judgment alone will decide whether we really summon up this ultimate strength by the efficacious grace of God or whether all that we do is ultimately merely a specious facade behind which a profound, unacknowledged egoism prevails. But we have begun to endeavour to love God in deed and truth, by trying to love the neighbour. All that we experience thereby, disappointment, toil, fret, is fundamentally only the way in which we try to contrive to turn from ourselves to the person of our neighbour and to God.

That is difficult. It is the ultimate reality and the hardest task of our lives. We can be deceived about it time and time again. But if we have turned in love from self to our neighbour, we have come to God, not by our strength but by God's grace. God who, as John says, had loved us so that we might love our neighbour, has truly laid hold of us, has torn us as it were from self and has given us what in conjunction constitutes our eternity, a personal union with others in which we are also united to God.

It is possible to view the same thing once again from an entirely different angle.

Jesus says to us, "As you did it to one of the least of these my brethren, you did it to me". How often we have heard this statement and used it in pious, edifying talk. But suppose we ask ourselves how Jesus could really say that. Is it not really just a juridical fiction: I give you credit for it, as though you had done to me personally what you have done to the least of these other human beings? No, this saying of Jesus is not a legal fiction, a moral make-believe, a kind of compensation. It is truly the case that we meet the incarnate Word of God in the other human being, because God himself really is in this other. If we love him, if we do not as it were culpable impede the dynamism of this love and fundamentally turn it back towards ourselves, then there occurs precisely the divine descent into the flesh of man, so that God is in the place where we are and gazes at us in a human being. This divine descent continues through us and it then happens that we, because God loves us, love our neighbour and have already loved God by the very fact of loving our neighbour. For, of course, we cannot achieve this love at all except of the basis of that divine love for us which in fact made itself our brother. The Christological side, if I may so call it, of our brotherly love would have to be taken really seriously and really realized in life. Where the other human being confronts me, there Christ really is, asking me whether I will love him, the incarnate Word of God, and if I say Yes, he replies that he is in the least of his brethren.

One theological aspect may be added in clarification. If we are to take the Christianity of the Incarnation seriously, it will still be the case in eternity that the incarnate Word of God in his humanity is eternally for us the mediator, the gate, bridge, God's actual concrete form, when we see him face to face. Jesus's humanity is not a barrier between us and the immediate presence of the God of grace. Nor is it something which served to mediate only in time, then to be abolished as it were. We shall always be dealing with the God who himself became man. To all eternity there is no theology that is not anthropology.

Is it not the case that we Christians have perhaps still not sufficiently understood our faith, that the various dogmatic affirmations of our faith, though we profess and accept them, nevertheless lie much too far apart, that we have the impression of living in an endlessly complicated world of propositions, dogmas and precepts? In reality, however, the truth is that God is man—and consequently love of God is love of man and vice versa.

Karl Rahner

The only condition is that we allow the innermost specific movement of this human love to come to its ultimate radical goal and essential fulfilment. Then where this happens, everything is already present—the whole of Christianity, for there is ultimately only one commandment, just as for the Christian there is only one God, he who in the eternal Word became flesh and dwelt among us and who remains not only yesterday and today, but for ever.

Ultimately we know nothing of God if we know nothing of man, of him whom God himself assumed as his own reality and in whom also the ultimate mystery, the ultimate depth of all humanity is comprised. We can ultimately only express the deepest thing about ourselves if we say that we are the reality which God could and has made most entirely his own. Only if we say that, if as it were we spring from anthropology into theology, have we understood what we ourselves are. And consequently we have only understood ourselves in the activity of our life (and that is the only way we understand ourselves) if we are people who love, if we are human beings who in unselfish love have found other human beings and not, of course, merely here and there in some festive hour, but in the brutal, grey, everyday course of our life. There we find God. And we may certainly say that all prayer, worship, law and institutions of the Church are only secondary means for us to do one thing: to love God and the neighbour. And we cannot love God unless we love him in our neighbour. Where we do that we have already fulfilled the Law, thrown the bond of perfection round our whole life, taken the better way which Paul has shown us. Only if we understand that there is a real ultimate unity between love of God and love of the neighbour do we really understand what Christianity is and what a divinely simple thing it is after all. What is divinely simple has, of course, to be expounded, and our whole catechism with all that it contains is the true and genuine exposition, the articulation, the verbal expression of what at bottom we have already grasped if we love our neighbour.

I finally return to what I tried to suggest at the beginning. How as witnesses to the truth and love of God are we to con-

433

vince people that what we profess in faith actually exists? God seems remote. But there is one thing we can do, love unselfishly and try to tell men that when they do this they have already begun to love God. We can repeatedly exemplify and demonstrate to them the one possible convincing starting-point for the whole of Christianity: love of the neighbour. If we do that we have done what our life must do and we have borne the first and last fundamental testimony to Christianity. We will still have to say very much more about Christianity in the pulpit and in teaching etc. But if this whole message does not begin with the profession by action and life that we are determined to love our neighbour unselfishly, all we say remains unintelligible. The very first key-word capable of convincing anyone today is missing. If we wish to become messengers of God and his love we must quite simply do one thing: love our neighbour, in our life, in care for him, in patience, forgiveness, toleration. Then we have not only begun to practise authentic Christianity, but we already have it whole and entire in germ and kernel. Out of that it can develop in us and bear witness to God's love in Christ Jesus for us, so that men may believe that God exists because they have experienced his love in the love which those who are his bear towards their fellow-men.

Catherine
de Hueck Doherty
1900-

When the better elements of the Eastern and Western Christian traditions fuse together, the result is a most unusual human being. Catherine de Hueck Doherty is such a fusion; her person and mission give witness to the dynamic love on which Christianity is grounded.

Catherine Kolyschkine was born in Russia in 1900. She belonged to a fairly wealthy family and grew up in the atmosphere of the Eastern Christian tradition. At age 15 she married Baron Boris de Hueck. In 1917, the young couple was caught up in the horror of the Russian revolution. They eventually escaped Russia, travelled to England and then moved on, by 1920, to Canada. They now had an infant son. Life in their new homeland was difficult. The Baron's health was broken. Catherine supported the family. She worked as a waitress, a maid, a sales clerk. Her break came when she joined a lecture bureau. She rose rapidly in the organization and suddenly life, from the material and financial point of view, was more than comfortable.

Strangely, the evangelical call to poverty haunted her. In 1931, she sold what she had and went to live, as a witness to the poverty of Christ, in the slums of Toronto. Her husband had died. Catherine's magnetism drew people to her. A Friendship House came into existence. Misunderstandings forced its closing. She moved on to the slums of New York's Harlem to work in an interracial apostolate. More people came. Another Friendship House. Then Chicago, Washington and other cities. In 1943, she married Eddie Doherty. Together, in 1947, they established Madonna House in Combermere, Ontario. The community that has grown up there lives a life of silence, prayer and Christian service.

Social structures can sometimes make it difficult to believe that the everyday layperson can both thirst for and be capable of sanctity. Perhaps that is why Catherine's life mission was not readily understood and welcomed in the dioceses she visited. For she moved about society in no official capacity—simply as a Christian deeply sensitive to the sufferings of her brothers and sisters. The expansion of perspective that accompanied the Second Vatican Council has made it possible to comprehend such persons more easily, to take them more seriously, and to listen to their message. Poustinia is Catherine's way of bringing her Russian Christian traditions into the western world that became her home. Poustinia is the Russian word for desert and carries the overtone of a life of solitude and calm, even in the midst of turmoil. It is written for the city dweller, subway rider, housewife, the men and women of contemporary America. At its foundation, the message surpasses terms such as east and west. It is a call to mankind to dwell in silence and solitude while never leaving the modern city; a challenge to stand still in the face of twentieth century pace of life; an invitation to love with the love of Christ.

This is a message that sounds distant and strange to our contemporary competitive society. One could set it aside as quaint or overly naive were it not for the fact that Catherine's life history declares it to be not only realistic but, for the Christian, absolutely essential. She lives what she writes. And in doing so, gently challenges anyone who would call himself Christian to face his situation honestly and courageously.

Poustinia is a significant contribution to the spiritual literature rising up from the world of the everyday Christian. Its simplicity will quickly capture the reader and inevitably its basic insights, either as nourishment or as question, will work their way into his existence.

POUSTINIA

Dan Herr, publisher of the *Critic*, once said, "Retreats are out . . . deserts are in!" Perhaps I am being presumptuous in thinking that his gentle little arrow was partially directed at me. For I haven't noticed too many other people on the North American continent writing about deserts or going to them.

For the last few years I have been talking and writing a great deal about silence, solitude, and deserts, and I will continue to write about them because I think they are vitally important to our growing, changing, technological, urban civilization. It is obvious that humanity is facing many problems, will have to face many more, and that these problems are deeply disturbing the souls of all men. It is just as certain that we cannot, must not, reject the new, strange, adventuresome, frightening world that is opening before us . . . that is already with us. Especially we Christians cannot do this because Christ has inserted himself into this world and we are his people, his body, and so we belong as he does to this world of IBM machines, to this world of cybernetics, that daily bring vaster problems before our minds, hearts and souls. For science moves faster and faster, so much faster than the men of today—or even the men of tomorrow—are able to apprehend, comprehend or assimilate.

Science continues to destroy, in its own relentless fashion, what might be called false myths, superstitions, and accretions that surround not only the Christian religion but even God himself, accretions which cling to the Church's robes. In one sense, science is doing a good job, and we should welcome its findings, always, however, appraising such findings in the light of the true revelation of the risen Christ.

This appraisal is so necessary especially in the age in which we live. So many people are going to seek Christ in so many places. He predicted as much: "Or, if people should tell you, 'Look he's out in the desert!'—don't go there; or if they say, 'Look, he is hiding here!'—don't believe it" (Matt 24:26). The Fathers of the Church, the bishops, have been given graces by the Holy Spirit to make true appraisals. We must be watchful here.

Many "top secret" and as yet unpublicized findings of science have the power of making a robot out of man. It can, we are told, even change man himself genetically, or brainwash him into submission. At the same time, the world of science, together with the spiritual renewal, invite men (the center of creation) to an *experience* of a "liberty of the children of God" seldom known before.

Now, man can truly have an encounter with reality and rise to the very source—to the Origin that has no origin. For the mystery of men in the midst of the world, nature, technology, and urbanization is intrinsically a *Divine Mystery*. But it is still on the *cross* that God reveals himself to this scientific, technological civilization of ours. As usual, he is close and distant. As usual, he reveals himself through what is not himself, so that even modern man can recognize the fullness of truth—the image of God manifested in the world and its temporality.

But it is to be understood that this Mystery, first of all, is not found in the world as such. It is found and seized upon in the hearts of the men who seek him, without denying his existence. It is because man is fundamentally spirit—open to the absolute of the Divine—that he is always dissatisfied, in one manner or another, with all created reality. Nature is not divine. It is only a sign of God, a cry toward God.

It seems strange to say, but what can help modern man find the answers to his own mystery and the mystery of him in whose image he is created, is *silence, solitude—in a word, the desert*. Modern man needs these things more than the hermits of old.

If we are to witness to Christ in today's marketplaces, where there are constant demands on our whole person, we need silence. If we are to be always available, not only physically, but by empathy, sympathy, friendship, understanding and boundless *caritas*, we need silence. To be able to give joyous, unflagging hospitality, not only of house and food, but of mind, heart, body and soul, we need silence.

True silence is the search of man for God.

True silence is a suspension bridge that a soul in love with God builds to cross the dark, frightening gullies of its own mind, the strange chasms of temptation, the depthless precipices of its own fears that impede its way to God.

True silence is the speech of lovers. For only love knows its beauty, completeness, and utter joy. True silence is a garden enclosed, where alone the soul can meet its God. It is a sealed fountain that he alone can unseal to slacken the soul's infinite thirst for him.

True silence is a key to the immense and flaming heart of God. It is the beginning of a divine courtship that will end only in the immense, creative, fruitful, loving silence of final union with the Beloved.

Yes, such silence is holy, a prayer beyond all prayers, leading to the final prayer of constant presence of God, to the heights of contemplation, when the soul, finally at peace, lives by the will of him whom she loves totally, utterly, and completely.

This silence, then, will break forth in a charity that overflows in the service of the neighbor without counting the cost. It will witness to Christ anywhere, always. Availability will become delightsome and easy, for in each person the soul will see the face of her Love. Hospitality will be deep and real, for a silent heart is a loving heart, and a loving heart is a hospice to the world.

This silence is not the exclusive prerogative of monasteries or convents. This simple, prayerful silence is everybody's silence— or if it isn't, it should be. It belongs to every Christian who loves God, to every Jew who has heard in his heart the echoes of God's voice in his prophets, to everyone whose soul has risen in search of truth, in search of God. For where noise is—inward noise and confusion—there God is not!

Deserts, silence, solitudes are not *necessarily places but states of mind and heart*. These deserts can be found in the midst of the city, and in the every day of our lives. We need only to look for them and realize our tremendous need for them. They will be small solitudes, little deserts, tiny pools of silence, but the experience they will bring, if we are disposed to enter them, may be as exultant and as holy as all the deserts of the world, even the one God himself entered. For it is God who makes solitude, deserts, and silences holy.

Consider the solitude of walking from the subway train or bus to your home in the evening, when the streets are quieter and there are few passersby. Consider the solitude that greets you when you enter your room to change your office or working clothes to more comfortable, homey ones. Consider the solitude of a housewife, alone in her kitchen, sitting down for a cup of coffee before beginning the work of the day. Think of the solitudes afforded by such humble tasks as housecleaning, ironing, sewing.

One of the first steps toward solitude is a departure. Were you to depart to a real desert, you might take a plane, train or car to get there. But we're blind to the "little departures" that fill our days. These "little solitudes" are often right behind a door which we can open, or in a little corner where we can stop to look at a tree that somehow survived the snow and dust of a city street. There is the solitude of a car in which we return from work, riding bumper to bumper on a crowded highway. This too can be a "point of departure" to a desert, silence, solitude.

But our hearts, minds, and souls must be attuned, desirous, aware of these moments of solitude that God gives us. To be so attuned we must lose our superstition of time. God laughs at time, for if our souls are open to him, available to him, he can invite them, change them, lift them, transform them in *one instant!* He can say to someone driving that car bumper to bumper, "I will lead you into solitude and there I shall speak to your heart" (Hos 2:14).

There is no solitude without silence. True, silence is sometimes the absence of speech—but it is always the act of listening. The mere absence of noise (which is empty of our listening to the voice of God) is not silence. A day filled with noise and voices can be a day of silence, if the noises become for us the echo of the presence of God, if the voices are, for us, messages and solicitations of God. When we speak of ourselves and are filled with ourselves, we leave silence behind. When we repeat the intimate words of God that he has left within us, our silence remains intact.

Silence is truth in charity. It answers him who asks. But it must give only words filled with light. Silence, like everything else, either makes us give ourselves, or it becomes miserliness and avarice, in which we keep ourselves to ourselves. The scripture says that we will have to give an account for every word. Perhaps we may also have to render an account for the words that we have not spoken and should have!

Deserts, silence, solitude. For a soul that realizes the tremendous need of all three, opportunities present themselves in the midst of the congested trappings of all the world's immense cities.

But how, really, can one achieve such solitude? *By standing still!* Stand still, and allow the strange, deadly restlessness of our tragic age to fall away like the worn-out, dusty cloak that it is— a cloak that was once considered beautiful. The restlessness was considered the magic carpet of tomorrow, but now in reality we see it for what it is: a running away from oneself, a turning from that journey inward that all men must undertake to meet God dwelling within the depths of their souls.

Stand still, and look deep into the motivations of life. Are they such that true foundations of sanctity can be built on them? For truly man has been born to be a saint—a lover of Love who died for us! There is but one tragedy: not to be a saint. If these motivations of life are not such that they can be true foundations for sanctity, then the soul must start all over again and find other motivations. It can be done. It must be done. It is never too late to begin again.

Stand still, and lifting your hearts and hands to God, pray that the mighty wind of his Holy Spirit may clear all the cobwebs of fears, selfishness, greed, narrow-heartedness away from the soul: that his tongues of flame may descend to give courage to begin again.

All this standing still can be done in the midst of the outward noise of daily living and the duties of state in life. For it will bring order into the soul, God's order, and God's order will bring tranquillity, his own tranquillity. And it will bring silence.

It will bring the silence of a lover listening with all his being to the heartbeats of his beloved. The silence of a bride, who in her utter joy listens to her heart reechoing every word of the beloved. The silence of a mother, so deep, so inward, that in it she listens with her whole being to the voice of her children playing in a nearby yard, cognizant without effort, of the slightest change in each voice. Hers is a listening silence which takes place while she competently, efficiently and lovingly attends to her daily duties.

This silence will come and take possession also of lover, bride, mother, worker, nurse, apostle, priest, nun—if only the face of their soul, in the midst of their daily occupations, is turned to God.

At first such silences will be few and far between. But if nourished with a life of liturgical prayer, mental prayer, with the sacramental life of the Church, slowly, slowly, like the seedling of a mighty tree, silence will grow and come to dwell in a soul more and more often. Then suddenly, it will come to stay one day.

Then the soul will turn itself to its Beloved. Walking softly on this incandescent path of silence, he will come. His coming— once experienced—will make silence, henceforth, a precious thing. Now it will deepen, and, encompassing the whole man, will make man its own.

Yet, strangely enough, with silence dwelling constantly in the soul—a Mary of Magdala at the feet of Christ—speech will come more easily to people whose souls are completely recol- lected—in that silence—in the Lord. Speech and works too. They will move among men gently, softly, kindly. Love will shine in their every gesture, in their every word. There will always be time to do something more for someone, somewhere.

Nourished by the waters of silence, *caritas* will begin to sing its song of love, making all men and women literally spend themselves for others—at home, abroad, in any and every state of life, on all streets and marketplaces of the world. And lo! Behold. Their strength—even as their youth—will be renewed as an eagle's!

Slowly, imperceptibly, the world roundabout them will change. For the silence within them will become part of God's loving, mighty, creative, fruitful silence. His voice will be heard through them. His face will be seen in theirs! And the light of it will become a light to their neighbor's feet.

Thus silence will bring peace to all. The prayer of silence will be heard in our land far and wide. And the Beloved will once more come to dwell among men, for his vineyard—the world—will be restored to him. Yes, "Be still, and know that I am God" (Ps 46:10).

By the infinite grace of God, men and women of the 70's, having left behind them the "death of God," the question of their "relevance or irrelevance," have now turned their faces to prayer. Perhaps not only their faces, but their minds and hearts and souls as well. The hungry heart of man could not stand the terrible desert that surrounded it. It had to renew its contact with God—it had to begin to pray again.

So, prayer is "in." Families talk about it. Young people discuss it. Contemplative religious argue about it. All religious orders are trying to understand it. Books that teach about prayer in a variety of forms are best-sellers. People pilgrim to find someone who can teach them how to pray. People search for prayer houses, solitude, aloneness where they feel they can really pray. Yes, God's goodness once again reveals itself in this hunger for prayer and in this hunger for communication with him. Once again we realize that "without him we can do nothing."

But there is a danger here similar to the one discussed above. Just as people fail to distinguish between silence and physical solitude, so there is a danger not to distinguish between prayer and solitude. These are two different aspects of the spiritual life. Prayer, of course, is the life of every Christian. Without prayer, without contact with God, this life dies. Solitude, on the other hand, is a special vocation; it is for the few, not the many. Yet, today, so many are thinking of prayer houses and little places of physical solitude. So many priests, sisters, brothers, whose vocation is really an active one, suddenly have decided that they can enter the solitude of a Carthusian monk. In the majority of cases, this is just a daydream, a romantic temptation of the spiritual life. Frankly, it is an escape from the tensions that are holding priests, nuns, families, and youth in a sort of unrelenting grasp these days. *Accept, first, the solitude of your own heart*. Prayer, like silence, is a matter of a journey inward, as are all pilgrimages of the Spirit. I must journey inward to meet the Triune God that dwells within me.

To say all this may seem strange in the first chapter of a book which concerns, as you will soon see, a desert experience. But it is vitally important at the outset to emphasize that there is no need for a log cabin, cottages, huts, in order to lead a life of prayer. Prayer is interior. The hut, the log cabin, the chapel, is the human heart in which we must learn how to pray. Solitude sometimes helps prayer, and for special vocations is the cradle of prayer, and powerful prayer at that. But for the average Christian, prayer doesn't need a geographic spot. Prayer is a contact of love between God and man.

Married people don't need a bedroom to make love. One can make love anyplace, and "making love" does not necessarily mean immediately what people think it means! Making love can mean looking into each other's eyes. It can mean holding hands tightly. It means being aware of each other in the midst of a crowd. So it is with prayer. In the intense stillness of a loving heart all of a person strains toward the beloved, and words— simple, gentle, tender—come forth, audible or inaudible as the case may be.

To confuse prayer with solitude, to say that I must have solitude in which to pray, is a fallacy. It is good to have periodic solitude. Such is the plea of the present book. It is good to gather oneself up, to be awake with the Lord in Gethsemane, to watch not only one hour with him but perhaps more, all along the way of his Incarnation and on to Golgotha, on to the Resurrection, on to the bosom of the Father and the Spirit.

But this "solitude" requires only a small place. It can be a room in a large convent or monastery. It can be a place in the attic or the basement of a family home. It may be a part of a room, separated by curtains. That would be a sufficient temporary solitude for simple recollection and greater peace. The daily noises of the street, of the family, of the staff of convents and monasteries would form a gentle reminder that we never pray alone, and never for ourselves alone.

Prayer is a full-time affair: solitude, unless called to a lifetime of it by God, must always be a temporary thing, lest it ceases to be solitude and becomes an escape. Unfortunately, the two are often mentioned in the same breath, whereas their roles in our lives with the Lord are different. Thanks be to God for the renewed desire to pray! But let us walk softly, and consult wise men, about our desire for solitude. It may be a grave temptation.

CHAPTER II

POUSTINIA AND POUSTINIK

While firmly believing that silence and solitude are above all else attitudes of the mind and heart, I have for a long time now felt that we should be doing something more. Ours is a tragic century when men are faced with tremendous decisions that shake the souls of the strongest. This is also the age of neuroses, of anxiety, of fears, of psychotherapy, tranquilizers, euphoriants—all symbols of man's desire to escape from reality, responsibility and decision-making.

This is the age of idol-worship—status, wealth and power. The idols dominate the landscape like idols of old: they are squatty and fat. The First Commandment once again lies broken in the dust. The clouds of war, dark and foreboding—an incredible war of annihilation and utter destruction—come nearer. Dirge-like symphonies surround us and will not let us be.

What is the answer to all these darknesses that press so heavily on us? What are the answers to all these fears that make darkness at noon? What is the answer to the loneliness of men without God? What is the answer to the hatred of man toward God?

I think I have one answer—*the poustinia* (pronounced "pou" as in "you"). Poustinia stands for prayer, penance, mortification, solitude, silence, offered in the spirit of love, atonement, and reparation to God! The spirit of the prophets of old! Intercession before God for my fellowmen, my brothers in Christ, whom I love so passionately in him and for him. It is not enough to lead a life of dedication and surrender as so many of the religious orders do. Every Christian must do more—with vows or without vows—wherever they are, whoever they may be!

That "more" can be a poustinia, an entry into the desert, a lonely place, a silent place, where one can lift the two arms of prayer and penance to God in atonement, intercession, reparation for one's sins and those of one's brothers. Poustinia is the place where we can go in order to gather courage to speak the words of truth, remembering that truth is God, and that we proclaim the word of God. The poustinia will cleanse us and prepare us to do so, like the burning coal the angel placed on the lips of the prophet.

The word "poustinia" is Russian meaning "desert." It is an ordinary word. If I were a little Russian girl, and a teacher during a geography lesson asked me to name a desert, I might say, "Saharskaya Poustinia"—the Sahara Desert. That's what it really means. It also has another connotation, as so many words have. It also means the desert of the Fathers of the Desert, who in ages past went away from everything and settled there. In the Western sense of the word, it would mean a place to which a hermit goes and, hence, it could be called a hermitage.

The word to the Russian means much more than a geographical place. It means a quiet, lonely place that people wish to enter, to find the God who dwells within them. It also means truly isolated, lonely places to which specially called people would go as hermits, and would seek God in solitude, silence and prayer for the rest of their lives.

However, a poustinia was not necessarily completely away from the haunts of men. Some people had reserved, in their homes, a small room to which they went to pray and meditate, which some might call a poustinia.

Generally speaking, however, a "poustinik" (a person dwelling in a poustinia) meant someone in a secluded spot. A poustinik could be anyone—a peasant, a duke, a member of the middle class, learned or unlearned, or anyone in between. It was considered a definite vocation, a call from God to go into the "desert" to pray to God for one's sins and the sins of the world. Also, to thank him for the joys and the gladness and all his gifts.

I got to be very familiar with one poustinik to whom my mother went for advice. I never knew who he was. We used to go there on foot and return on foot. When we arrive my mother knocked on the door and opened it. There was no latch on the

446

door. The poustinik was always there to welcome anyone who came. Mother bowed to the cross that was prominent against the log wall, and to the icon of Our Lady. Then she would bow to the poustinik and say, "Peace be to this house," and he would say, "May the peace of the Lord be with you." I did the same. Then he would offer us some tea and some bread, whatever he had, and say, "Come and partake of what God in his mercy has sent me." Upon doing so, I went to play outside, and my mother talked to him. Then we went back home.

It is difficult to simply relate this man, and other poustiniks that I came to know through my lifetime, with what is called a "hermit." There was some kind of difference. The poustinik seemed to be more available. There was a gracious hospitality about him, as if he were never disturbed by anyone who came to visit him. On the contrary, his was a "welcome" face. His eyes seemed to sparkle with the joy of receiving a guest. He seemed to be a listening person. A person of few words, but his listening was deep, and there was a feeling that he understood. In him St. Francis' prayer seemed to become incarnate: he consoled, he understood, and he loved—and he didn't demand anything from anyone for himself.

He was available in other ways. If someone from the village was in need (for instance, if a farmer needed his hay in before the rain), he rushed over to the poustinik and asked his help. The poustinik immediately dropped everything and went with the farmer. He was always available.

Usually the poustinik was a man, though there were women poustinikki also. Sometimes they were single people, sometimes they were widows and widowers. Not all of them were educated in the academic sense of the word. Quite often they were just ordinary peasants, but usually they had what we call "letters," that is to say, they could read and write. Amongst the "staretzi"— the old and wise ones—could even be found the nobility. It is said that one of the czars, Alexander I, went into a poustinia. There is a mystery about the many years of his absence, so they say.

Whoever these people were, they were not necessarily old in age. In Russia, the "old one," *staretz* (or *staritza* for a woman) means "wise one." Usually they were people who went into the poustinia around the age of 30 or 35. Others may have been older, in their late 50's or early 60's, who had been married, reared their children, and then felt the attraction of the desert. But the majority of the lay people were around 30 to 40 years old.

There was no big fuss about going into a poustinia. From some village, from some nobleman's house, from some merchant's house—from any part of our society in Russia—a man would arise. (Of course, only God knows *why* he did arise.) He would arise and go into the place (as the Russians say) "where heaven meets earth," departing without any earthly goods, usually dressed in the normal dress of a pilgrim. In summertime, this garb was a simple handwoven shift of linen of the kind that ladies wear these days, only it came down to his or her ankles. It was tied in the middle with an ordinary cord. He took along a linen bag, a loaf of bread, some salt, a gourd of water. Thus he or she departed, after, of course, taking leave of everyone in the household or in the village. Some didn't even do this. They just stole away at dawn or in the dark of the night, leaving a message that they had gone on a pilgrimage and maybe would find a poustinia to pray to God for their sins and the sins of the world, to atone, to fast, to live in poverty, and to enter the great silence of God.

There were other poustinikki, both men and women, who had been monks and nuns of an order. Since Russian orders are contemplative in the Western sense, these people would get permission from their abbots or abbesses to become poustinikki, dwellers of the poustinia and the desert. Since some of the real estate holdings of the monasteries were large, which often included much wild and uncultivated land, it would not be difficult to find a place where they could build themselves a poustinia, or have one built for them if they were women. Also, they might simply be given permission to go and find their desert for themselves. In this case, they would go on a pilgrimage to a holy place, pray there, and get some inspiration as to where to go. Or, they might just simply walk around prayerfully until they found a place. Yet, there were a variety of poustinikki or dwellers of the desert—*startzi* or *stapooha* as we call them in Russia. Women were in the minority; usually they began to dwell in the poustinia in their old age.

My father had a friend, his name was Peter. He was well-born, of the nobility, the eldest son of an old Russian family. He was pretty close to what is called in America a millionaire. He had a lot of gold and silver in the bank, besides having real estate and so forth. One day he came to my father and said, "Theodore, I have been reading the gospels and I have decided, as so many before me, to accept them literally." My father listened. He continued: "I am going to gather my goods, especially my gold and silver. I am leaving my farms, my real estate to my family, but my money in the bank I am changing literally into silver and gold pieces." This he did, and my father accompanied him through the whole transaction.

In those days there were no trucks. There were what we called drays that carried what today trucks carry. They were pulled by two horses. My father said that it was a big dray, perhaps the equivalent of a one- or one-and-a-half-ton truck. It was filled with sacks, and the sacks contained gold and silver. Peter, with my father accompanying him, went to the poor section they call the slums now of Petrograd. There, family by family, house by house, Peter gave away his pieces of gold and silver. When the dray was empty Peter said: "Now, I have in some small measure ransomed the 30 pieces of silver for which God was sold. And now I must go."

So they returned to his house, where on his bed, there was laid out a linen tunic. He took a linen bag, a loaf of bread, and in another little linen bag he took some salt. He also had a gourd of water and a staff. On foot, my father walking with him, he went through the streets of Petrograd. My father accompanied him to the outskirts of the city and into the country roads. The last he saw of him was just a silhouette against the setting sun—a man in a long garment with a staff in his hand. He had no cash in his pockets (he had no pockets), nor in his bag. He had only some bread, water, salt, and a staff. Not even shoes. That was all.

Years later, my father chanced to be in Kiev, which was a large city in the south of Russia. He went to Mass, and as was the custom in those days, all the beggars assembled on the church steps before Mass to beg from the good people who went in. Amongst them was a man with a beard, matted and seemingly uncombed, long hair, and tattered garments. He looked like a fool, a retarded person. His eyes were vacant, no expression on his face, except the one usually associated with retarded people or idiots. But a ray of sun came and fell on his face—and my father recognized his friend Peter! He called out his name and intelligence returned to that face. They embraced. They went to Mass together and then had breakfast. My father asked, "Why have you chosen this vocation of idiot or retarded person?" Peter answered, "I am atoning for the men who have called Christ a fool during his lifetime and during all the centuries thereafter." They kissed each other again, and Peter disappeared. My father never saw him again.

Peter had belonged to the *jurodivia*. These were a group of people who lived with the poor, totally poor themselves, begging their alms at church doors and street corners. They fasted. One might say that they stood side by side with the poustinikki, for these latter too, though living in abject poverty, lived alone, prayed, and listened. But their vocation and their goal was atoning for one thing and one thing only: for men once upon a time having called God a "fool."

Because men continue to call God a fool, the *jurodivia* feel they have a continuous vocation of poverty, atonement and prayer—like the poustinik, yet different from him.

Then there were the pilgrims who constantly crisscrossed Russia carrying their poustinias in their hearts, sleeping under the trees, in haylofts, wherever they were allowed to. They were poor, alms-begging people, praying for the whole world constantly.

These spiritual traditions still go on. For when I was in Rome in 1967 for the International Lay Congress, I had occasion to translate for four Russian theologians. They spoke neither French nor English, so I had to translate back and forth for them.

We became very well acquainted. I asked them: "Are the Russians still pilgrimaging?" They just looked at me and said, "Do you think communism can stop pilgrimaging in Russia?" I felt like falling through the floor! Nevertheless, I asked another ques-

450

tion along the same lines: "And what about the poustinikki?" They answered that the forest were still full of poustinias and poustinikki, and that even the communists were known to go into the forests to look for the poustinikki—and somehow or other remain there! But, they added, these were unconfirmed reports.

Perhaps we (Russians) as a nation have been chosen for this somewhat strange vocation—lest the world forget about the essence of our faith, which is above all to render glory to God. The essence of our faith is to eternally seek to know God better in order to glorify him more and to serve him better in men.

We Russians tend to identify ourselves especially with the poor, and so to be cold, to be homeless, to be pilgrims for those who have no holy restlessness and who don't want to arise and seek God. All this seems quite natural to us. So many of us feel that the rest of men are looking for him where he cannot be easily found—in the comfortable life which is in itself not sinful, but which can become a sort of asphyxiation and isolation from the rest of mankind. Comfort can become an idol too.

So these strange vocations are the vocations of my people and of many other peoples who follow the Eastern spirituality.

PART II

CHAPTER VII

BASIC SPIRITUALITY

For the past few months now I have been getting together almost weekly with the poustinikki here at Madonna House. I have been trying to share, in an informal way, some aspects of the spirituality of the poustinia, and I would like to share some of them with you.

The poustinik lives very closely with the Blessed Trinity: Father, Son, and Holy Spirit. He should witness to the Trinity. When someone comes to the poustinia he should say, "Peace be with you," and the poustinik answers, "May the peace of the Father, the Son, and the Holy Spirit overshadow you." When a poustinik comes to a priest, and especially to his or her spiritual director, the poustinik says, "Bless me, Father, in the name of the Holy Trinity." Constant awareness of the Trinity engenders an ability to consider the Incarnation and thus to incarnate in one's life the Incarnation. The poustinik is plunged in the Trinity. Whenever you say the word "God," your heart must move toward the Trinity.

The Trinity moves, for God is eternally creative, and creation is expressed in movement. God is light, and you come to realize that you are being drawn by the Trinity into the light and into the movement of the Eternal Family. You begin to know with a knowledge that you could never acquire by reading a million books. As you touch the Trinity you realize that God is love—and you know this with a knowledge that no one can take from you.

One enters the poustinia with an absolute simplicity, the simplicity of a little child, and there are no gimmicks of any kind. There is no, what you call, protocol. There is no horarium. There are none of these things. The poustinia is timeless. You must come to understand that you came from eternity and you will return to eternity. Especially those who live in the poustinia permanently, they live in timelessness. He who lives in timelessness lives in eternity, and he who lives in eternity is in touch with God, because that's what eternity is all about.

So you enter into the poustinia with a simple heart, knowing that you come from eternity, that from all eternity you were in the mind of God, and that you are *in it now*. With this simplicity comes a tremendous peace, a peace which shatters the division between life and death. The great fear of death gradually disappears, and that is the ultimate of simplicity, the simplicity of a child.

A child approaches death with perfect joy. I remember a child of about four or five years who was brought to view the body of his grandmother. He sort of waltzed up to the coffin, kissed his grandmother, patted her on the head, and said, "Oh, you're so cold. Don't worry, soon you'll be very, very warm. Everything is going to be warm." Somebody asked him (this was in Russia) why he said such a thing. "Oh," he said, "my mother told me that Grandma was going to Jesus. It's very cold on the way but warm when you get there." Now that's the simplicity of a child.

Catherine de Hueck Doherty

The poustinik should have a gentle attitude toward himself, toward other people, and toward all of God's creation. In other words, the attitude of the poustinik is a cosmic tenderness, a tenderness toward all God's creatures. But that tenderness and gentleness begin with oneself, a proper love of oneself. Gentleness leads to a good kind of order—order in the poustinia, order around it, a caring for the trees, the plants. The poustinik is possessed by a gentleness ·in loving himself, creation, and all others in the way God loves everything. God said that everything he made was very good, and the poustinik has a gentle care for this goodness.

You should always remember that the goal of the poustinia is to interiorize it. You must not think that the poustinia is the only place where you can be a poustinik. The Eastern tradition talks about "monasticism interiorized," which means that everyone is to live the life of the Trinity wherever they might be. Monasticism, in this sense, is for everyone.

My father was a layman. He lived as an ordinary man all his life. He enjoyed a good meal. But he also fasted a lot and prayed a great deal. He interiorized monasticism and fed his family with the scriptures and with the writings from the Fathers of the Desert. In like manner, the poustinia is a matter of the heart, and is for everyone.

Russia, as you know, is a very large country, and we like to roam around a great deal. And so we roam all over Russia with our pilgrimages. But one day you come to realize that all these geographical spaces are not enough, that they do not satisfy one's desire for space. At that point Russians begin the journey inward. This journey is far more beautiful and satisfies far more deeply. The poustinik, you might say, is involved in the great journey inward, exploring the vast spaces of God.

The poustinia is somehow always connected with the notion of pilgrimage. The poustinik is an eternal pilgrim. Now a pilgrim cannot take along too much luggage. You can't take along 40 suitcases if you want to travel. Especially when we are talking of the journey of the poustinik—which is the journey inward, the journey toward the Trinity—we must travel lightly, taking only bread, salt, and water, symbols of our freedom of movement.

We have a saying that there are only three walls of a poustinia. The poustinik lives with one wall absent. At God's pleasure, in less than a second, he can be transported into any part of the world. His horizons are limitless. He begins to understand why he is in the poustinia. He begins to understand that he has been baptized to be the messenger of the Glad Tidings, and that his service is for the whole world and not only for his little village or apostolate.

Christ says to him: "Here is the way of the Cross. We are going to retrace all my footsteps, not in Palestine but in the whole world." One day the wall will fall down completely, and the poustinik will understand that his vocation is to "arise and go" while standing still! This is the mystery of the poustinia. He goes into the farthest reaches of the cosmos, standing still. That is his pilgrimage.

What is it to go into the cosmos? It's to be a messenger of God, following the one who sent him. The poustinik moves into the bloody footsteps of Christ and then he sees all around him the real tragedy of mankind. It is lack of faith in God. The daily cross of the poustinik will be to see this lack of faith, and especially among Christians. Every night he will return from his pilgrimage during which he stood so still, and on his back will be the cross of the day. Its special pain will be lack of faith, hope, and then love. He will go forth from his poustinia day in and day out, or maybe it will be next month or next year. He waits on God's good pleasure. Sooner or later, however, the wall will fall down again, and his pilgrimage will begin—the strange pilgrimage of the poustinik that takes place while he is standing still.

The poustinik strives for the greatest poverty. There is a delightful little story about poverty from the Fathers. One of the monks named Serapion sold his book of the gospels and gave the money to those who were hungry. He said: "I have sold the book which told me to sell all that I had and give it to the poor."

I see Christ in poverty. He is most comfortable in poor places. He likes uncomfortable chairs; he likes to sleep on the floor. A good question to ask yourselves is whether he would be comfortable or not in your poustinias!

This doesn't mean that you shouldn't have comfort. That's not the most important point. It's more a matter of being totally detached from it. God is happy in simplicity and in poverty, especially poverty of spirit. A goal to strive for is when "the need to have becomes the need *not* to have." It is an interiorization of poverty that desires with a passionate desire to get rid of everything. Sometimes this is not possible. But the desire is possible. We speak of the desire of baptism. There is also a "baptism of poverty," a passionate desire to be totally detached when total exterior poverty is not possible.

One of the hardest things to be detached from is our daily routine and life-style. Poustinikki, like everyone else, can become very attached to their horarium or daily schedule. Like everyone else, he has to have a horarium, times for getting up, cleaning, work, tending to his garden—or whatever else he has to do. He has hours for prayer, and so on. But when you live alone it is so easy to attach yourself to your horarium, to what you are doing or have planned. It's easy to go around and say, "I'm busy for God," implying, "Don't bother me." No, the poustinik is one person who drops everything at the slightest knock at the door. This knock stands for all kinds of things. It may be a person knocking; it might also be God knocking. You must not forget that you went there for God and that God might knock at your door and enter just like anybody else. At that moment you must drop everything. You must be available especially for God.

How do you know if it is the Lord knocking? You don't. In the beginning there is lots of emotionalism, especially among women. It is difficult to sort out our own interruptions from those of the Lord. Let us say I am working at something. Suddenly, everything stops. I feel suddenly drawn to just stop. It's a very dangerous moment, exceedingly dangerous. The devil can draw you, and God can draw you. The Russian poustinik falls flat on his face and begins to pray. He is afraid of who might be drawing him, and where. But something happens within him that makes him feel that this is God. Now he just sits on the floor, on a chair, or wherever he is, and he is completely quiet. He listens in total silence. If it is Christ walking in, it is because he has something to say. Yes, when Christ comes in, he has something to say.

How does Christ speak? How did God speak to the prophets? Loud and clear, or was it more like a breeze that passed through their minds? It is possible for God to speak to us through our thoughts. The Russian poustinik will write them down and eventually ask his spiritual director about them. He has no faith in himself. This is one detachment that you have to have—total detachment from anything that might come to you through seemingly mystical phenomena. You have no faith in it until it is checked out by your spiritual director. Be very careful about such things, as you can enter into a tremendous amount of confusion and interior noise this way.

People often ask if they may study in the poustinia. What do they mean by the word "study"? Study God? Impossible. His chief study should be to ask the Lord, "Please teach me about yourself." He does this so that he may bring to the community the pure word of God.

But I know what question is being asked. They are asking about study "*academia*-style." Let me put it this way. I could see a poustinik studying after he has come to a point—and it's a strange point. It will need a bit of an explanation because it is part of the journey inward.

It's as if you were walking through a wide desert where there are only a few little water holes scattered here and there. You are staggering from thirst. You always have just enough water to survive. But now you begin to feel the weight of the desert, for the desert is God. You feel a terrible heaviness and you feel more thirsty. You want the consolation of God, an emotional gimmick of some sort, you want help. You haven't reached the stage yet where you want God himself. God will give us little holes of water along the way, but he loves us too much to give us any other artificial supports.

The water is faith. As you move from hole to hole the water becomes fresher and you have the feeling that you can really move now. Now faith begins to grow in you. You begin to understand that faith is not of the understanding, but is a gift of God. Your throat becomes unparched. The water in each hole now is neither bitter nor salty, but fresh. Now you can stand up, whereas before you were practically crawling from hole to hole. You can walk straight toward the next hole because faith has increased in you by the grace of the Holy Spirit, through the gift of the Father. Now you walk like a man or a woman walks—straight.

The last hole is the biggest yet. You have enough to assuage your thirst, and you know that somewhere, someplace, you are going to be covered and inundated by faith. It will burst in on you like a sudden revelation and you will realize that you are a baptized, that is, a saved Christian.

That's when you suddenly arrive at a beautiful river. You come to the edge of it and know that you can drink from it until you die. Now faith has taken hold of you and nothing, nothing, nothing can separate you from the river. You realize that through your journey you have fallen in love with God, and that it was really his face you saw in each water hole. The water holes were God's gift of faith to you, for God alone could quench your thirst. *When the poustinik has arrived at this river of faith, then he can study.* Then he will never be misled by what he studies.

To continue with this image of the desert: The poustinia means desert—is a desert. Why does anyone want to go to a desert? To follow Christ. The desert is the land of detachment. To follow Christ is to deny ourselves. The first kind of detachment in the poustinia is from oneself. I think that the greatest challenge of the poustinia is this detachment from oneself. This is not simply detachment from my "will," as some Western spiritual writers put it, it's detachment from many things. From food, from studies. But even more than all these material things, it's the ability to take out a boat that has no rudder and no oars. It's the ability to drift wherever God wants to lead you. One of the characteristics of a poustinik is this ability to let yourself go wherever God wants to lead you. I may come to a nice little river where I would like to stop and have lunch! Wssssh, a storm comes up! So I don't stop to eat but head into the storm. It's this going with God wherever he wants to take you that is the essence of detachment.

The question arises sometimes whether a poustinik can write. You live in the poustinia for three days, of course you can write, why shouldn't you write? All the things I've been reading to you were written by the great poustinikki, from the czars down to the paupers.

If someone asks if he can come to see you, don't ask why. Simply say, "I'd be delighted to be of any help to you that I can." (Stress the word "help"!)

If such a person comes in and sits down, it may become apparent very soon that he has only come out of curiosity. You are not in the poustinia to satisfy curiosity seekers. If they are simply asking questions like "Where do you come from? How long have you been here?"—cut them off gently but firmly. Try to get them to pray with you. This is what I call the "courtesy of the poustinia." It is your duty to make the other person aware that the place you are in is holy. Your approach in such a situation will be a mixture of courtesy, gentleness, tenderness— while using a scalpel! People should not come to you simply for a cup of tea and a little gossip.

Perhaps this would be a good place to discuss the poustinia as a dwelling. First and foremost, a poustinik is not a solitary. In the English language, the word solitary means "alone." In the Russian language *it means to be with everybody*. A solitary person, for a Russian, is a hospice, an inn, for every person. It is not simply a question of "loving humanity." In some sense, one wall of the poustinia is entirely open, and the poustinik is *in* Bangladesh, or India, or Northern Ireland. Every Father of the Eastern Church has practiced this kind of hospitality.

Hospitality has to be total. It is not enough to share your bread or your tea or your coffee with whoever comes to visit, though this is the first kind of hospitality offered. Thus when a person comes in, the first thing you offer is food. We live by food. Without food we cannot exist. God comes to us as food. Almost in the same act of opening the door, the poustinik asks, "Have you eaten? Can I share something with you?" In Russia we would say, "May I offer you what God in his mercy has sent me?"

I remember once pilgrimaging with my mother. We came to a household. All the family had were a large loaf of black bread and some yogurt. There was hardly enough food for the family, but when we came in they cut it so we could have a share. Even if there's nothing to give, we can still offer a cup of water.

So hospitality is first and foremost of this practical kind. The ideal to strive for, however, is hospitality of the heart. It is the serene acceptance of any and all interruptions by visitors whom you may not even know personally. Some visitors you should especially accept because they can teach you something. It is very important to have a serenity about hospitality, a sort of peace that radiates much like the offering of food creates a feeling of fellowship. Actual food is, however, only the first step. Christ said that man cannot live by bread alone. The poustinik should practice this by also offering himself.

What does a Russian mean by offering himself? It means a kenosis, an emptying of myself in order to be filled with the other. We in the East consider every person to be Christ, in an exaggerated sort of way. This point is well exemplified in a little story found in the book, *What Men Live By*.

It concerns a man who was told, through prayer, that Christ was going to visit him on a certain day. He went about his business as usual; he was a shoemaker. His first customer was a prostitute, the second a mother with a sick child, the third was an alcoholic. He hurried around, trying to be hospitable to all these people. When evening came he was rather disappointed. It was time to lock up—and Christ still hadn't come. He was very unhappy. Suddenly he heard a voice, "But I had come, in the person of each of the people to whom you offered hospitality today." Thus must the poustinik see Christ in each person who comes to him.

Thus the poustinik must be completely available to everyone. He is available to God during the days he is in the poustinia, as well as being available to the community. It is so easy for the poustinik to say, "I am entitled to three days in my poustinia where I can have a life of my own. Then I'll give four days of service to the community." No, he may be called upon at any time to help his brother. He is completely indifferent to his prayer being interrupted, to being called hither and yon. He is indifferent because he is absorbed in the prayer of the presence of God (which is the Jesus Prayer for the Russian). So, as far as he is concerned, he is walking out of the poustinia and remaining in it—if you know what I mean. He is eternally in a poustinia. That is the very essence of the poustinia. Men went into the poustinia to learn the prayer of the presence of God. When you have this presence of God in your heart, you have a poustinia in your heart, and then you are a light to the world.

In order to be available, the poustinik must be *flexible*. Flexibility flows from the fact that he is beginning to live in eternity and in the *freedom of Christ*. He is unperturbed about himself and about what is happening to him. He adapts easily. He never stands on ceremony. All this flows from his freedom. He realizes that a totality of dependence on God and totality of surrender to him is true freedom. It is an entirely different freedom from the kind that men usually speak about. It is a freedom of total subjection to God. It is a freedom of the silent heart which is constantly moved by the thought of God and his desires. It is the freedom of a person who sees in every face God's face. It's the freedom of a person who cannot be angered because his idea of himself is such that he considers any insult a compliment.

A poustinik is known by his fruits. One of the fruits of the poustinia is a defenselessness which flows from his freedom. If someone walks over you with hobnailed boots on, you kiss his feet and say, "Thank you very much for treating me like this, for I am a sinner." The poustinik is like a rubber ball. The worse you treat him the harder he bounces back! You just can't keep him down. One of the poustinik's great contributions to the community is a real example of defenselessness, of forgiveness.

A poustinik is a living forgiveness. You cannot hurt him. He is tempered like steel, refined like silver seven times. In the poustinia something happens. The poustinik becomes supple through hardness and hard through being supple.

The poustinia is a place for resting in the Lord. The Lord says to us, "Go into the inward journey of your heart, and I shall be your rest." You are not cognizant of any kind of mystical resting on the bosom of God. It's just plain, plumb rest. We Russians used to talk about this in New York. We had a very rough time when we first came. We were overworked and underpaid. We used to discuss among ourselves how we survived. We came to the conclusion that we survived because we really believed that God was our rest. When I asked a friend of mine, "How do we survive?" this is exactly what she said: "Oh, we have Christ for a pillow." The poustinik comes to experience this kind of resting in the arms of the Lord.

The final result of all these attitudes is peace. The sign by which you know a good poustinik is peace. Whether he knows it or not, he exudes an intense peace. He is so peaceful that just being next to him has a settling effect. There are very few people in the world with whom you feel at peace. There are very few people who encompass you with peace as with a mantle. The poustinik is supposed to be not only a peace-maker, but a peace-giver.

CHAPTER X

LIBERATION IN CHRIST

"God said, 'Let us make man in our own image, in the likeness of ourselves, and let him be master of the fish, of the sea, the birds of the air, the cattle, all the wild beasts, and all the reptiles that crawl upon the earth.' God created man in the image of himself, in the image of God he created him, male and female he created them."

While I was in the poustinia of the Little Sisters of Charles de Foucauld in Montreal the words that came to me out of the poustinia were simple and yet complex—freedom and liberation. Since then I have thought a lot about them, because I didn't have time to set them down as I usually do here at Madonna House. The poustinia at the Little Sisters is a bit different from here. So I kept the words in my heart and let them cling to me, trying to discover what they meant. It came to me that God had created all the earth and then he wanted to create man. "Let us make man in our own image and likeness." What is the image and likeness of God but love and freedom? By creating man he endowed him with a free will because God is free and he created man in his own image.

I'm not a theologian. I'm just a person who tries to listen to the words of God and meditate on them. It struck me that God wanted someone like himself to "talk things over with," as the scriptures say. Why did God give us freedom? Because he

461

wanted to be freely loved. He loved us deeply because he created us. The act of creation is an act of love. But we know that God extended his act of love further than creation. He sent his Son to become a holocaust for us. The suffering servant of Yahweh was a bridge, a restorer, for at some point we misused our freedom. So the love of God extended into great depths and so did his gift to us, the gift of free will and freedom. I, as a Christian, must choose and should choose and will choose that which God wants me to choose freely, namely his will.

It struck me, as I meditated on this freedom God gave us, that it was unlimited in the sense that we had the power to say "no" to God as well as "yes." For a long time I pondered over these words, no and yes. The more I pondered, the more I was awed that I did have this fantastic freedom of saying yes and no to God. Because I had this power, I was God's heir, I was the sister of Christ, since I had been baptized into his death and resurrected life. Somehow, even before I was his child, I had it, because I was created in his image and likeness.

I looked at my hands, though my hands had nothing really to do with this whole thing. But I looked at my hands because hands are used to hold, and somehow my hands held freedom. I looked long and hard and meditated in the depths of the night on what my hands held. I knew also what sin was. Sin was really the turning of my back on God, the definite "no" to his love, the surrender to someone else who was not God. Sin was a chaining of my freedom even though I was free to say this no. When I said no something happened *to me* and *because of* me. But I was still free to say no.

On the other hand, if I said yes, as I was free to do, something else happened. I walked into a sort of sunrise. My pilgrimage toward the Absolute became suffused with light instead of darkness (as it did with the "no"). This freedom of mine when I said yes became a song that I sang with God. There is a song today which goes, "I am the Lord of the dance." I felt like singing, "I am the Lord of the song." When I say yes and use my freedom to really be free, I become one with the whole song of creation.

The more I meditated on freedom the more things I discovered. First I discovered that I *was* free. This was the foundation of my meditation. No one was pushing me, no one was telling me what to do. I presume that I am a Christian who understands her religion and who has taken part in the sacraments and has lived the life of the Church. (For I am speaking now of Christians.) So as a Christian I meditated on this gift of freedom. God is here, and I can love him or not. I can be hot, cold, or tepid toward him.

I am free to choose, to act, and for this freedom I rejoice and thank God, even though I know the terrific responsibility of it, the total insecurity of it also. For *I* have to decide—that is so very important. True, I can have advisors, spiritual directors, books, but ultimately, in the great reality of my relation to God and men, I alone must make the decision when the time comes. That is freedom.

So God gives us freedom. I meditate a little deeper. In fact, the meditation ceases and a sort of quiet enters my soul, heart, and mind. In that quiet, that silence, that beautiful silence of God who allows me to enter into it and become silent myself, my horizon expands and I see a fantastically immense horizon of unsurpassed beauty. It lies alongside a desert. On one side is the desert of the power of Satan whose one desire is to bind my will to do his will. On the other side there is the Lord, the Trinity. The Holy Spirit, the Crimson Dove, the God of love, hovers over me like an immense and flaming bird. Perhaps it's not a bird at all. Perhaps it's a fire that I mistake for a bird. Quietly, in total and utter stillness, Christ stands there beside me somewhere, but leading to the Father as he usually does.

The more I behold this freedom of mine, poised between these two choices, the more tired I get. Everything suddenly becomes very clear, very simple, and that kind of simplicity is intensely tiring to us human beings. For the vision is clear. There is the burning desert, and there is the other side of the desert which appears so restful. I am somewhere in between. I must decide to go either to the right, into the will of the Father, or to the left, into my own will and into the desert of Satan. Yes, I am tired because the sight is so clear. I see confusion and demonic powers calling me to do my will contrary to the will of God.

Then, suddenly, all these thoughts leave my mind and I simply realize that God has given me the freedom of choice and a free will, and that he has sent his Son to show me how to do his will. That is what his Son came down to do—to do the will of the Father freely, without compulsion, at the request, as it were, of his Father. I was like that too, like Jesus. I had a free will, and I was not being compelled.

Now my mind begins to clear and my meditation becomes simple. Yes, I am the sister of Jesus Christ. Yes, I have come to do the will of the Father. Yes, that is what I am going to do. I have made the decision. I know that my *fiat* will have to be repeated again and again, but I am ready, with the grace of God, to do so.

At this moment a strange, indescribable sensation comes over me. Because in accepting the will of the Father I surrender all things to him—father, mother, brothers, sisters, relatives, the life that I lead—in short, everything. Once I have decided to put my will into the immense sea of Christ's will, I seem to come to a moment of nonexistence, and there are no ways in which I can put it into words. It is as if by total surrender of my will I also surrender my body, my mind, my senses, everything that is me, and I am as if I were not.

Suddenly I come out of this nonexistence and I look at myself. I realize that I have been changed in the twinkling of an eye. Now indeed I am free. I am not worried about anything anymore. I am like a bird soaring in the air and all things are mine because all things are God's and I am his too. Now I am unbound. I repeat, I am unbound. I am free like the air. I possess everything and God possesses me. Now my free will blends with his and a strange fire enters my soul. Now I understand that a will freely given to God becomes transformed by a joyous and fantastic zeal in the service of God and his Church. Now indeed I step easily and simply into the steps of him who calls himself "the Lord of the dance," and I sing to him and with him whose music is given to the world only as an echo, for all music is an echo of God's music. Now I suddenly understand that by using my free will freely I entered God. The reason for using free will is love, and the gift of love was given to me in the gift of faith. Now in love and in faith I sing of hope.

It is all so very simple, my dear ones. I bring you the words that I heard without hearing, the sights that I saw without seeing; I bring you the results of man's right choice: the gift of liberation. Now I am free. I am liberated. Alleluia! Alleluia! Alleluia! For I have surrendered, and while I surrendered, all my bonds have been cut. Behold, I am free. In union with the will of God I soar, I dance, I sing. But above all, day in and day out, I do his will. Alleluia! Alleluia!

The poustinia, then, is the place of freedom, the freedom which *I* am very conscious of exercising. It's *I* who decided to go into the poustinia. It's a way of freely declaring that I love God and a way of showing it. I say to him: "Now look. Very freely, without any coercion, I'm going a little further than other people. I don't know what it's all about yet, but I know it's a place that will bring me closer to you. Because I am falling in love with you, I want to come closer to you of my own free will." If you stay in the poustinia, there will be a *liberation*.

What's the difference between freedom and liberation? Liberation comes from Christ. It's the freedom that God gives you because you have freely accepted him—it's a gift of God. It's a fantastic thing. It has made you free. When *I* choose to go to the poustinia, to fast, to pray, to be faithful to the Roman Catholic Church and to God—when *I* choose to do those things —that's freedom. But liberation comes from God.

He says to us, "Now that you have really tried, I'll give myself to you to a degree and in a way that you have never suspected possible." He liberates you from the things that "bugged" you. It's very funny. Not that the things that bugged you cease to bug you. They still are there to bug you, but you don't care about them anymore. You have been liberated by this gift of God. You have reached the apex of that freedom which you can give God, then suddenly, he gives you his liberation. People may still annoy me, but somehow they do not affect me. I have been liberated by God. It's as if I were traveling through the cosmos of the Lord all by myself. It's as if everything that now comes across my path has a reason in God's plan for being there. It's as if the gift of discernment has become a sixth sense. Life used to be heavy and difficult. Now it is light and natural.

The gift of wisdom is also part of this liberation. Discernment and wisdom—the gifts which relate especially to people—coalesce and make me free from all the things that try to pull me down. At no time does the poustinik think that he has achieved this by himself, or that there is any way of achieving it by himself except by the constant, free, following of Christ.

When a poustinik enters a poustinia he really faces himself. Much of the gospel is concerned with this facing of oneself. Christ said that it is what comes out of a man that defiles him. We are not able to face what is inside us. The poustinik is the free man. He enters there of his own free will, to face himself. Many things, but especially the devil, will conspire to force you to leave the poustinia—to block this confrontation with yourself.

Perhaps I can put it this way: When you enter the poustinia you enter the orbit of God. You hold on to his coat. A thousand hands try to pull his coat out of your hands. You are free to give in to the temptation, to flee from the poustinia, or to resist.

It's because of this freedom that a poustinik has no rules. There is nothing to guide yourself by except what is within. This is where discernment comes in. Among the variety of things that people want you to do, you have to discern from your heart what to do. Your life ought to be a life of service to the community. There is only one thing you do *not* do: satisfy your own ego.

The essence of the poustinia is freedom, total freedom of action, directed by your love of God and God's love for you. Should you do this, should you do that? Consult your heart! Put your head into your heart, get down on your knees, prostrate yourself or whatever you do, and find the answer from God. Most of the duties will be obvious. But precisely because you have this freedom, the poustinik should be the most obedient of all. When something is really necessary (in the apostolate), he should be the one who runs to the task with the greatest joy.

The poustinik has no security because he depends entirely on God. God tends to turn our lives upside down every three minutes. The poustinik must have the freedom to break any routine he might have at a moment's notice.

The same freedom is present in relation to Christ. Christ is present in the poustinia. You came to encounter him there. He draws us with his ointments and with his beautiful aromas. Sometimes this attraction in the poustinia is so powerful that you can almost touch it. But along with this positive attraction, there is always an opposite attraction. So I have to exercise my free will again, my freedom, to move toward Christ or away from him every second of the day in the poustinia. The poustinia is present to give eternally new dimensions to these attractions of Christ.

Darkness also comes into the poustinia. Up until now I may have walked in the light, or in the twilight. It wasn't so bad. I could distinguish things for myself. (Remember that I am always talking about the eyes and ears of the heart.) Suddenly I'm confronted with what St. John of the Cross calls darkness. I must make a decision whether or not I am going to freely enter that darkness. Here is where the poustinik usually stops facing the darkness. I stand there and must take my first step freely into that night.

This is the time of the spiritual director, because it's a time when we are tempted to run away. This is the time for all sorts of rationalization. This is the time when I am tempted to process everything through my head instead of through my heart. Many forces will marshal themselves to prevent you from entering that darkness. The role of the spiritual director is important here because the territory ahead is unknown and uncharted.

Then, by the grace of God (the gift of liberation), and by your own free will (freedom), without being forced in any way, you enter into the darkness. What do I mean "by your own free will"? I mean that there is no inner fear. There is no fear that God is displeased with you. Freedom here joins with faith and knows that God is never displeased with you. Jesus has changed all that.

Or, the temptation may work in the opposite way. "I am here in the poustinia and I am supposed to be here. If I don't enter into this night, then I will displease God." Confusion is always from the devil. This last thought doesn't seem to limit your freedom, but it does nonetheless. The Evil One is already lassoing you. You've got to be very careful here. Never move on *any* idea of guilt or any kind of rationality at all. Freedom means freedom.

So you enter that dark night. You brace yourself. This is the moment when you really and literally fold the wings of your intellect, but totally. Now you have to go through a painful process, painful even for an Eastern person who may be more used to it than you. There is an emptying of the mind as you enter this dark night. One must walk without any mind. In a sense, we could say that only fools (which in some English translations means mad people, (in-sane, "without minds") walk into and open themselves deliberately to this night.

There is a strange emptiness toward which one moves. It doesn't happen in a day. I realize that part of the effort is mine. I seem to latch onto a little bit of something. I don't know what it is. It helps me to fold the wings of my intellect and empty a little bit more of myself. St. John of the Cross says, "I jumped into the abyss and caught my prey." The poustinik jumps into the abyss and may not necessarily catch his prey. But he still must jump into that emptiness. Frankly, it's one of the most painful things. It's not painful to quiet your thoughts and all those other preliminary things. That's relatively easy. It's when this emptiness takes hold of you, or you allow it to take hold of you (I don't know which); then for a moment or two you seem to cease to exist.

Sartre talks much about moving toward nothingness. But Sartre really *has* nothing. There is nothing behind his nothingness. It's just despair. It's the end. Christianity moves into this "nothingness" and finds God. There comes a moment in this movement toward nothingness which seems to be a moment of nonexistence. It appears idiotic, positively idiotic to say such a thing. But it's true. It's a moment in which you are nonexistent as far as being a person is concerned. Everything has disappeared. You are not even cognizant that "you are." You are only cognizant of darkness. Whether you are in depths or heights is unimportant; you are not even cognizant of that. But there is a moment of nonexistence out of which you come. And when you come out, prayer begins.

This moment of nonexistence is short, exceedingly short. It hits you and is gone. But after that, prayer begins. Now it's a very strange prayer. It's a prayer that is no prayer, because it takes place in an *interiorized passivity*. It has no connection with what you are doing—walking, sleeping, whatever. In you now there is a tremendous change. Prayer now begins to make sense because you don't pray; God prays in you. This is where true liberation enters. Up till now, freedom has been operating. You've submitted yourself to God of your own free will. Now he takes over, and that's where true liberation begins.

All these struggles bring us back again, as it were, to the Trinity, to whom we must bring ourselves by the scruff of our necks. We know there is a great reluctance to go to the Trinity. Why? Because we know that our surrender is not total. There are moments in our lives, especially in the poustinia, when God reminds us of the hidden corners in our souls and minds that we haven't surrendered to him. This, I think, is what I mean by picking yourself up by the scruff of your neck and bringing yourself to the Trinity. It is so that the luminosity of the Trinity may enter like a beam into our soul and get every corner clean, for the luminosity of the Trinity burns, sears deeply.

I am speaking for myself, but I think this applies to every poustinik. I cannot totally desire to bring myself to be thus scorched. Even though I know that the scorching will be done with great love, I don't feel that I want to be scorched. This struggle will repeat itself constantly in the poustinia. God is gentle. He doesn't let us see all the corners of our hearts in one minute.

When I have brought myself to the Trinity and allowed myself to be scorched by his luminosity, I will be able to listen to God. This is a very heavy thing. I find it heavy. What it really means is that God now says to me, "Put your roots deep into wisdom. This is the moment. I give you the gift of wisdom because the gift is mine but I want it to be given to others. I have ceased to call you my servant. I call you my friend and heir. You are the brother or sister of my Son. So now put your roots deep into wisdom."

Somehow you agree to this, because you have to *agree* to everything. God wants a free lover, a lover who loves freely. He will not push you to do one little thing unless you agree to every bit of it. So the roots go in. Now you begin to *listen* to God. The spirit of discernment comes into you. You begin to understand what God wants, what men want, what you want—the whole shebang!—but mostly what God wants.

Sure, there are moments when you don't want to have these gifts. But they come to you and you accept them because you love God.